Reconstructing Ashkenaz

STANFORD SERIES IN JEWISH HISTORY AND CULTURE

EDITED BY *Aron Rodrigue and Steven J. Zipperstein*

Reconstructing Ashkenaz

The Human Face of
Franco-German Jewry, 1000–1250

David Malkiel

STANFORD UNIVERSITY PRESS

STANFORD, CALIFORNIA

Stanford University Press
Stanford, California

© 2009 by the Board of Trustees of the Leland Stanford Junior
University. All rights reserved.

Publication assistance for this book was provided by the Taube
Center for Jewish Studies of Stanford University.

Printed in the United States of America on acid-free, archival-
quality paper

Library of Congress Cataloging-in-Publication Data

Malkiel, David Joshua.
  Reconstructing Ashkenaz : the human face of Franco-German
Jewry, 1000–1250 / David Malkiel.
    p. cm. — (Stanford series in Jewish history and culture)
  Includes bibliographical references and index.
  ISBN 978-0-8047-5950-2 (cloth : alk. paper)
  1. Judaism—Relations—Christianity. 2. Christianity and other
religions—Judaism. 3. Crusades. 4. Ashkenazim—Europe,
Western—History—To 1500. 5. Sephardim—History. I. Title.
II. Series.
  BM535.M327 2009
  943'.0004924—dc22

                                     2008018645

Typeset by Bruce Lundquist in 10.5/14 Galliard.

To My Wife

Contents

Preface

Ashkenaz appears in a genealogy of the descendants of Noah after the Flood: He was great-grandson to Noah, grandson to Japheth, son to Gomer, and brother to Riphath and Togarmah (Gen. 10:3). The biblical text sums up the list of progeny by explaining that "from these the nations branched out over the earth after the Flood" (Gen. 10:32), leaving postbiblical readers to match Noah's heirs to contemporary nations. For Jews living in medieval Europe, Ashkenaz referred to Germany, although the only rabbinic source from late antiquity to correlate the biblical list with current nations associates Germany with either Togarmah or Magog, Gomer's brother, rather than with Ashkenaz.

The accepted term for France in the Middle Ages is Zarephath (Obad. 1:20), but in this study, as in most modern usage, Ashkenaz refers to France also. This makes historical sense, given the unification of these lands under Carolingian rule and especially given the close cultural ties between the Jews of these two centers. The terminological and ethnic distinction between France and Germany faded following the eastward migration of large numbers of central European Jews in the late Middle Ages; this migration created the enormous diaspora of eastern Europe, the cradle of roughly half of modern Jewry (the Jews of medieval England and Provence are historically linked to those of France, but they are largely irrelevant to this study and will scarcely be mentioned).

The genetic and cultural link between the Jews of eastern Europe and medieval Franco-Germany explains the prominence of the latter in the heritage and identity of modern Jewry, not only in Europe but also in today's leading demographic and cultural Jewish centers—Israel and the United States. Important facets of the cultural heritage and self-image of millions of Jews can be traced back to the Jews of medieval Ashkenaz, and they continue to resonate.

Hence we come to the chronological focus of this book, the first quarter of the second millennium CE, the formative period of Ashkenazic Jewry and its heyday. Jewish communities began springing up along the Rhine in the early decades of the tenth century, and a century of intellectual growth culminated in Rashi, or Solomon of Troyes (1040–1105), whose commentaries on the Bible and Babylonian Talmud have been the foundation of Jewish education everywhere from that day to this. The Talmud has dictated the law and lifestyle of the Jewish people for the last thousand years, and even young students move fairly quickly from Rashi's Talmud commentary to Tosafot, the glosses penned by twelfth- and thirteenth-century French scholars. The study of Rashi and Tosafot became, and remains, the staple of the traditional curriculum.

The years 1000–1250 also saw the emergence of a second feature of the Ashkenazic legacy that continues to shape Jewish identity. In 1096, during the First Crusade, as thousands upon thousands of crusaders moved across Europe en route to the Holy Land, large numbers of Jews were killed in communities along the Rhine. What precisely happened continues to be debated by historians, but there is no doubt that among the victims were those who slaughtered their family members and themselves. Thus was born the reputation of Ashkenazic Jewry for *Kiddush ha-Shem*, the sanctification of the Name (of God), the forfeit of life for faith. This legacy is commemorated in the synagogue on Sabbath mornings, in the following prayer:

> May the merciful Father who dwells on high, in his infinite mercy, remember those saintly, upright and blameless souls, the holy communities who offered their lives for the sanctification of the divine name. . . . They were swifter than eagles, braver than lions, in doing the will of their Master and the desire of their Rock. May our God remember them favorably among the righteous of the world; may he avenge the blood of his servants which has been shed.

The memory of the martyrdom of 1096 grips Jews more powerfully than ever in light of the Holocaust and of the lives laid down on behalf of the state of Israel. To the modern Jew, Ashkenazic martyrdom represents the never-ending struggle for Jewish survival, its awful cost in lives and suffering, and the heroic refusal to accept defeat, of the spirit if not the body.

The strength of the religious commitment implicit in the martyrdom of German Jewry is also partly responsible for this society's characterization as saintly, as absolutely faithful to Jewish law and subject to rabbinic authority. In this respect the Jews of medieval Ashkenaz might anachronistically be portrayed as the forerunners of today's ultra-Orthodox communities in B'nai Brak or Williamsburg; allegedly the rabbis held sway over the community, and observance of the law among the rank and file was punctilious and unswerving.

These characteristics mesh with, or perhaps dictate, the prevalent image of Jewish-Christian relations in the Franco-German communities of the Middle Ages. Although the livelihood of these Jews depended on their relations with Christian clients, accounts of medieval Ashkenaz in modern historiography generally present an image of mutual, unremitting hostility. The Christian side is seen as exerting constant conversionary pressure, which of course the Jews resist, and when, all too often, Christian animosity and persecution results in violence, the Jews bravely face death or expulsion rather than heed the call to convert.

This book revisits these themes in the hope of fashioning a more human image of Ashkenazic Jewry. Although it has been important for modern Jews to view the Middle Ages as an age of faith, in contrast to the secular culture of the modern world, the resultant dichotomy is an oversimplification. The conditions of medieval life were of course very different from those of the modern era; nonetheless I argue that medieval Ashkenaz was not a community of saints and martyrs but simply of people, with both the heroism and the foibles found in other eras and locales. Lowering Ashkenazic Jewry from its pedestal complicates the picture of the Middle Ages as an era of a purer religious life, and by implication it may grant strength to contemporary Jews as they face their own challenges to religious fidelity, for although one can admire saints and martyrs, it is difficult to identify with them.

"Image," the introductory chapter, sets the stage for the ensuing discussion by examining the portrayal of Ashkenazic Jewry in premodern and modern historiography. In this overview I do not include

the Hebrew narratives of the First Crusade, which are treated later at
length, but rather focus on the image presented in other medieval and
early modern works, such as Solomon ibn Verga's *Shevet Yehudah*. I
then move to the writings of the first modern scholars of Jewish history, such as Heinrich Graetz, and from there to the leading historians
of the twentieth century, especially Yitzhak Baer, Jacob Katz, and Salo
Baron. In the chapter I explore the contribution of each age to the development of the memory of Ashkenaz, highlighting cultural forces that
underpinned the perspective of thinkers in each period.

Chapters 2, 3, and 4 are about the First Crusade, which has dominated the historical memory of medieval Ashkenaz. The catastrophe
of the First Crusade was of such enormity that scholars were forced to
confront the question of its antecedents and possible adumbrations.
Consequently, sketches of Jewish-Christian relations in Europe from
840 (after the Carolingians) to 1096 tend to present litanies of persecution, which combine to give an impression of "clouds on the horizons,"
portents of the devastating storm. In "Adumbrations" (Chapter 2) I
study these events, which are mainly eleventh-century incidents, to
show that the portents thesis does not hold water. This issue resonates deeply today, as Jews wrestle with a similar problem vis-à-vis the
Holocaust. However, the historiographical importance of this revision is that it establishes a less fraught, more normal image of Jewish-
Christian relations in place of one that recognizes only alienation and
confrontation.

Studies of the First Crusade have uniformly portrayed the assailants
as presenting the Jews with the choice of baptism or death. This element of choice has been responsible in large measure for the creation of
an image of Ashkenazic Jewry as saintly. In "Martyrdom" (Chapter 3) I
maintain that the element of choice is largely absent from the primary
sources. Those in Latin provide few details, and thus the emphasis is
on the Hebrew narratives. According to these documents, the Jews expected slaughter, with no option of conversion, and this is also what
reportedly occurred. The Jews anticipated that their children might be
baptized, rather than killed, but we read that this expectation was mistaken, for the murderers spared no one.

There are, however, two exceptional scenarios, in which some Jews
were offered a choice: (1) those who met their attackers after hundreds

of fellow Jews were already killed and the crusaders' bloodlust satiated; and (2) when small groups of Jews and Christians, who were often acquainted, encountered each other in secluded locations, rather than in a mass, public context. Yet these two scenarios are the exception to the rule of death without a choice, which renders the mass suicides less heroic and therefore more human and in some sense more comprehensible.

Martyrdom, particularly mass suicide, is the focus of the twelfth-century Hebrew narratives of the First Crusade persecutions, which extol the lofty ideal of *Kiddush ha-Shem*. In "Survival" (Chapter 4) I illuminate an aspect of the narratives that has attracted little scholarly notice, namely, expressions of ambivalence about the martyrdom option or its outright rejection. I present evidence of unheroic conduct and of the separation of family members during the chaotic conflict. This is followed by a discussion of the importance of social pressure in the situations described in the Hebrew sources. I then devote a section to the conduct of young people in particular, whose behavior is singled out by the narrators. All these expressions of ambivalence present an image of Ashkenazic society that is heterogeneous and hence both credible and human.

The prevailing image of apostasy in medieval Ashkenaz posits that apostasy was rare; that the few apostates were almost all forcibly baptized, rather than true converts to Christianity; that the few, coerced, apostates were steadfast in their observance of the commandments and reverted to Judaism at the earliest opportunity; that in the eyes of his family and community, an apostate ceased to exist; and that ideological apostasy was more significant than venal apostasy. In "Apostates" (Chapter 5) I argue that coerced apostates did not necessarily outnumber voluntary ones and that the distinction was generally unimportant to medieval rabbis. Furthermore, even coerced apostates did not always revert, or did not necessarily do so promptly, and there was also the phenomenon of serial reversion, movement back and forth across the religious divide. And although there were those who apostatized because they became convinced of the truth of Christianity, there were also those whose apostasy was venal. These apostates hurdled the Jewish-Christian divide with ease, as if they did not consider it terribly significant. In brief, in this chapter I use apostates to challenge the image of the absolute fidelity of medieval Ashkenazic Jewry.

The Jews of Ashkenaz are generally portrayed as the halakhic society par excellence, utterly subservient to Jewish law and rabbinical authority, but in "Deviance" (Chapter 6) I offer abundant evidence to the contrary from a broad range of ritual behaviors. Women appear in many rabbinic sources as blithely contravening the law of the Talmud and, what is more, as refusing to respond to the efforts of rabbis to correct their behavior. This pattern is also found among men, who are depicted as equally intractable. The tosafists, leading rabbis of twelfth-century France and Germany, posited that nonhalakhic behavior must be based on some sort of halakhic rationale, which they labored to supply, but in "Deviance" I argue that nonhalakhic behavior should be accepted for what it is. Contrary to the prevailing image, the Jews of medieval Franco-Germany violated talmudic law and rabbinic dictate when they saw fit to do so, and the rabbis were painfully aware of the limits of their own authority.

The image of a pristine Ashkenazic society presents these Jews as culturally autonomous, as dwelling entirely within the four ells of their own tradition and lifestyle and conducting contact with gentiles almost exclusively within an economic context. In "Christians" (Chapter 7) I survey a number of realms in which the Jews of medieval Ashkenaz are seen to have been well integrated into the majority culture, both socially and culturally. The Jews of France and Germany, rather than leading a ghetto existence, were an integral—if marginal—component of European society, adopting and adapting Christian ideas and values into the fabric of their own civilization.

The large-scale collapse of Spanish Jewry in the wake of the 1391 riots and the missionary pressure of the early fifteenth century typically forms the backdrop to characterizations of Ashkenazic Jewry as faithful unto death to their religious identity and to the dictates of Jewish law. The regnant interpretation, championed above all by Yitzhak Baer, assigns responsibility for the Spanish breakdown to the sizable class of Jewish courtiers, affluent and well-connected Jewish government officials. Ostensibly, the education of the elite in "Greek wisdom," namely philosophy and science, eroded their religious conviction. This factor combined with a natural reluctance to surrender positions of power, prestige, and comfort, to drive the courtiers to the baptismal font when the crisis arrived. Because these aristocrats were also leaders of the Jew-

ish community, their treachery demoralized the rank and file and resulted in mass apostasy.

In "Sepharad" (Chapter 8) I question the explanatory power of the
courtiers' Greek wisdom and hedonism and then challenge the basic
Ashkenaz-Sepharad dichotomy. Broadly, the upshot of this discussion
is that the gap between the Spanish and Franco-German communities
is narrower than it has appeared. Both societies exhibit nonhalakhic
behavior and apostasy, as well as martyrdom, and both engaged their
Christian neighbors intensively in many areas of daily life. At the same
time, there were real and important differences in the social and cultural
characteristics of the Spanish and Franco-German communities, which
limit the feasibility and utility of comparative analysis. When the nexus
between Spanish deviance and Ashkenazic fidelity is sundered, a nuanced image of medieval Ashkenazic Jewry can finally take shape, one
with scope for martyrs and apostates, piety and deviance, commitment
to tradition and cultural integration.

Responsibility for the reconstruction of medieval Ashkenazic culture
presented in the ensuing pages is my own. Nevertheless, that reconstruction did not spring from my mind *ex nihilo*, but rather built on
the scholarship of many colleagues over the past few decades, whose
achievements I gratefully acknowledge. A glance at the notes to this
book will make apparent my debt to David Berger, Robert Chazan, Jeremy Cohen, Avraham Grossman, Ephraim Kanarfogel, Ivan Marcus,
Haym Soloveitchik, Kenneth Stow, Israel Ta-Shma, and Israel Yuval.
Many of these esteemed colleagues offered much needed encouragement in the early stages of my involvement in this particular arena of
scholarly discourse, for which I am also deeply appreciative.

I would also like to thank my colleagues in the Department of Jewish History at Bar-Ilan University for their support and encouragement,
particularly Gershon Bacon, Elisheva Baumgarten, Shmuel Feiner,
Elliott S. Horowitz, Kimmy Kaplan, Moises Orfali, Moshe Rosman,
Adi Shremer, and Ariel Toaff. I gratefully acknowledge the contribution of my friend Moshe Benovitz, who suggested the title. Thanks are
also due to those who read and commented on individual chapters or
the entire manuscript and particularly to my long-time colleague and
friend, Abraham Gross of Ben-Gurion University. I am also thankful to

the highly skilled and conscientious staff of Stanford University Press, including Norris Pope and Carolyn Brown, and copyeditor Mimi Braverman. I gratefully acknowledge the Taube Center for Jewish Studies at Stanford University for its grant in aid of publication.

I dedicate this book to my wife, Brenda, with thanks for all the gifts she has given me, and especially for her ability to read texts sensitively, a talent she has demonstrated throughout our married life.

Reconstructing Ashkenaz

One Image

Was it for you, oh giants of the Talmud, that he toiled? He was
forced to create a book that would provide refuge from the Greek
philosophers, to afford some distance from Aristotle and Galen.
Have you heard their words? Have you gone astray after their
proofs? Not for you, my masters.

Moses ben Nahman, letter to northern France

These words were penned in 1232 by Moses Nahmanides, doyen of
Aragonese Jewry, in an effort to dissuade the leading rabbis of north-
ern France from supporting a campaign against the teachings of
Moses Maimonides. Maimonides should not be condemned, reasons
Nahmanides, because his purpose was noble: He sought to provide
the Jews of Arab lands with a theology compatible with the Greco-
Arabic science and philosophy in which they were steeped, but one
that would also safeguard them from the heresies of the ancient Greeks.
Nahmanides explains to his northern addressees that they cannot possibly appreciate the challenge facing Maimonides because they were
never exposed to philosophy and its perils.

Nahmanides' passage is among the earliest recorded testimonies by
an outsider about the nature of Jewish culture in Ashkenaz, or Franco-
Germany, in the Middle Ages, which is the subject of this book.[1] In
referring to the northern rabbis as giants of the Talmud, Nahmanides
spotlights the centrality of the Talmud in the culture of Franco-German
Jewry, and more important for his purpose, he emphasizes the Ashkenazic Jews' innocence of Greco-Arabic philosophical thought and its
pernicious theological impact.

The comparison between Spain and Ashkenaz has been a common
theme in the historiography of medieval Jewry, although intellectual horizons is only one issue concerning what differentiates the two cultures.
And just as the comparative exercise served Nahmanides in the raging   1
Maimonidean controversy, so too has it served a variety of agendas in
modern Jewish historiography. Surveying the range of portrayals of medieval Ashkenaz offered by latter-day historians is the goal of this first chapter, which sets the stage for the reexamination of the prevailing image.

Medieval and Early Modern Perspectives

Modern Jewish historiography begins in nineteenth-century Germany, in the wake of the Haskalah, or Jewish Enlightenment, and these early historians certainly had a great deal to say about the Jews of medieval Ashkenaz for reasons particular to their own historical context. But as the Nahmanides quote illustrates, characterizations appear before the modern era in various genres, and for the most part these early discussions were known to modern historians and provided grist for their mills. Our story begins, therefore, in the Middle Ages.

Medieval Jewish writers rarely left accounts of historical events involving medieval Jews or Jewish communities. The most popular genre of writing about the past is the so-called chain of tradition, which lists scores of rabbis in chronological order, from master to disciple, to convince the reader of the integrity of the Oral Law. Although these texts usually focus on late antiquity, they sometimes continue into the Middle Ages, naming the heads of the Babylonian academies. Abraham ibn Daud's *Book of Tradition*, written in twelfth-century Toledo, falls within this genre and was highly influential. At the end of his particular chain, which concentrates on the Jews of Andalusia, Ibn Daud turns his gaze on those of northern Europe: "We have heard that in France there are great scholars and geonim, and that each and every one of them is a rabbi who inherits the Torah appropriately, [that is,] with the intention of passing it on." Ibn Daud names a few scholars from Narbonne, which was relatively nearby, and then adds the name of the greatest of the French tosafists or glossators, Jacob of Ramerupt, who is generally known as Rabbenu Tam.[2] Clearly the Jews of France had acquired a reputation for excellence in rabbinic scholarship, word of which had reached the Iberian peninsula. This was also the impression of Benjamin of Tudela, who visited the Jewish communities of southern France in the twelfth century as he began his journey to the East. In his well-known itinerary, Benjamin expresses great respect for their institutions of rabbinic scholarship, singling out the academy of Rabad, that is, Abraham ben David of Posquières, the leading talmudist of southern France.[3]

At around the same time, Moses Maimonides notes a distinction between the halakhic expertise of rabbis living in the Christian domain and those of the Islamic realm. He observes that the scholars of "France" (i.e., the lands of the Franks) and of the lands of the uncircumcised generally (i.e., Christendom), are not expert at the laws of jurisprudence (*dinin*) "because they do not use them extensively, since the uncircumcized do not allow them to judge, as the Ishmaelites do. Thus, when a case comes before them, they go on and on, and do not know it [the law] until they search the Talmud thoroughly, as we do today regarding the laws of sacrifices, for we do not deal with them."[4] True or not, this is an astute suggestion about the significance of the political-religious context for the course of halakhic scholarship in Europe.

In contrast to the halakhic expertise of the Franco-German scholars, Jews from the Islamic realm noted their ignorance of other disciplines. Sephardic Jews saw their Ashkenazic brethren as deficient in Hebrew language and literature, in which realms the Sephardic Jews had made great strides under the influence of Arabic linguistics and literature.[5] For instance, Joseph Kimhi, a Spaniard who settled in Provence in the mid-twelfth century, disparages the contribution of French Jewry—primarily Jacob of Ramerupt—to the linguistic debate about the nature of Hebrew, an issue over which Menahem ben Saruq and Dunash ben Labrat, the master grammarians of tenth-century Spain, had locked horns: "The Jews of France and environs engaged primarily in Talmud, and occasionally in Bible . . . but not in Hebrew usage, and thus they did not gain mastery thereof."[6] A bit later, Judah Alharizi, who pioneered Hebrew *maqamah* (rhymed-prose tales interspersed with metered verse), terms the poetry of French Jewry "not worth hearing . . . hard as iron . . . their rhymes are full of errors, they strain for innovation but are incomprehensible without explication."[7] He sums up, "When the sages of France and of Greece set their hearts on the Torah and claimed its domain, all knowledge and wisdom they won for themselves—but abandoned song's kingdom to Spain."[8]

The Jews of Germany and France were weak in Hebrew linguistics because they knew no Arabic, the language used by the Andalusian giants even when discussing Hebrew language. This curricular handicap also denied them access to the scientific achievements of the Islamic world, including those of its Jewish thinkers. In reply to a letter from Samuel ibn Tibbon, a Spaniard living in southern France who was then preparing a Hebrew translation of Maimonides' *Guide of the Perplexed*, Maimonides expresses astonishment at his interlocutor's erudition: "How could it be in the nature of one born among the mumblers to chase after the sciences . . . ? This can only be 'like a root out of arid land' [Isa. 53:2]."[9] Maimonides' amazement and his reference to Christendom as the land of the mumblers, an arid land, barren of scientific knowledge, fleshes out the curricular aspect of the prevailing image of northern European Jewry in the Sephardic and Oriental world.

The translation of numerous scientific works from Arabic to Hebrew, beginning in the twelfth century, is eloquent testimony to the deficiency of European Jewry in the arts and sciences. Abraham ibn Ezra, a twelfth-century scholar who left Spain and spent several years in Latin Europe, wrote new works in several fields, including Hebrew language, for the edification of the European audience, on account of their ignorance of Arabic and thus of scientific knowledge.[10] In a poem bemoaning his own ill fortune, Ibn Ezra writes, "In Edom [Christendom] there is no glory for any scholar who dwells in the land of the son of Qedar [Islam], and they hoot at us; whereas if there were to come a Greek grasshopper, whom they esteem, and he were to ride anyone's back, he would be deemed one of the giants!"[11] Ibn Ezra's feeling that he commanded little respect among the Jews of Latin Europe, who were intellectually oriented toward Byzantine rather than Arab culture, sits well with other medieval Sephardic scholars' statements regarding the nonphilosophical character of European-Jewish cultural creativity.

The scientific mind-set of the Jews living in Qedar stimulated efforts to offer allegorical, rationalistic interpretations of biblical and aggadic passages, particularly of texts conveying an anthropomorphic conception of God. Although this exegetical tendency appeared briefly in twelfth-century France, ultimately it did not displace the traditional literalist interpretation of the images and texts that exercised the Andalusians so vigorously. Thus a Maimunist writes that the Jews of France (i.e., northern Europe) "appear to know the blessed Creator only when they eat boiled beef dipped in vinegar and garlic, in the dip known in their language as *salsa*: the fumes of the vinegar and garlic ascend to their brain, and then they think that these enable them to perceive the blessed Creator at any time." Here we have a satirical characterization of northern European Jewry as believing that God can be visualized, which is a fundamentally anthropomorphic notion. This writer also portrays the Europeans' conception of God as radically immanent; they allegedly believe that God is close to them when they pray and when they study Talmud and other texts, as well as when they speak freely about him, as they often do.[12] The anthropomorphic and immanent conception of God imputed to Ashkenazic Jewry in this text differs significantly from that of the Jews of Islam, whose theology was framed by their rationalist *paidaea*.[13]

Further testimony to the nonphilosophical image of Ashkenazic Jewry is found in the Bible commentary of Zerahiah ben She'altiel Hen of Barcelona, who lived in thirteenth-century Rome. Zerahiah records a conversation with a student who was unable to grasp the esoteric meaning of a verse in Ecclesiastes (10:1) and then notes that he realized that the student "was a disciple of the Ashkenazim." Zerahiah may have meant that the student was literally an Ashkenazic Jew, and hence that he was untrained in allegorical interpretation, or else perhaps that the student merely preferred literalist exegesis, for which the northern Europeans had gained renown.[14]

Beginning in the twelfth century, the Jews of medieval Ashkenaz left abundant evidence about how they evaluated their own culture. Self-evaluations are supremely important, although they pose different methodological problems than do the impressions of outsiders. The Ashkenazic sources require sensitive and thorough treatment, and I therefore discuss them at length in later chapters. The next cluster of non-Ashkenazic texts about Ashkenazic Jewry dates from the sixteenth century, when a series of Sephardic writers wrote litanies of persecution, shifting our attention from intellectual to political activity.[15] Gedalya ibn Yahya's *Shalshelet ha-Qabbalah* ("Chain of Tradition") devotes a section to the chain-of-tradition genre as well, but most of the other histories of this period do not. These litanies include tales from Ashkenaz and offer a variety of approaches to the behavior and fate of various Jewish ethnic groups under adverse circumstances.

The most famous and influential of these works is Solomon ibn Verga's *Shevet Yehudah* ("Staff of Judah"), first published in Adrianople in 1553 and frequently thereafter. *Shevet Yehudah* contains different types of narrative materials, and our particular concern is with the tales of persecution, in which typically the Jews must either convert to Christianity or choose between death and expulsion. There are dozens of such stories, involving the Jews of many lands, including Ashkenaz, which in Ibn Verga's work refers specifically to Germany, as Ibn Verga also offers stories about France and Provence.

Ibn Verga has relatively little to say about Ashkenaz, and he explains that this is partly because these Jews have recorded their own legacy and partly because they are simply too distant for him to know much about them. "Those of Ashkenaz and their leaders wrote a scroll about their troubles, and made a great big book about their matters in those lands, and because they were already written, I have not seen fit to write them here, especially when the truth of the matters did not reach us, for we are far away."[16] All the same, Ibn Verga offers three Ashkenaz tales, and they are quite revealing. He writes that in 1300 the Jews of Ashkenaz were accused of poisoning the rivers, and the king ordered them converted or killed. There were "decrees," that is, persecution, "throughout the lands of Ashkenaz and Provence," and "everywhere the Ashkenazim sanctified the name of the great God and his Torah and did not exchange their honor," namely apostatize.[17] The text does not spell out how the Jews of Provence behaved on this trying occasion, and this silence might be interpreted to mean that they exhibited lesser fortitude.

A second tale also has an Ashkenazic community facing the choice of conversion or death, this time with a three-day waiting period in which to make their decision. At the end of the waiting period, we read, because salvation did not miraculously materialize, "they all agreed to die."[18] However, Ibn Verga records that this time "the young men of the community decided to avenge themselves on their persecutors before dying for the sanctification of the [divine] name," and so they stabbed all the townsmen, and their wives set the town ablaze (at their husbands' instruction), and thus the Jews perished with the Christians in the fire.[19] This account adds the element of active resistance to the victims' willingness to suffer martyrdom, indicating that passivity was not part of Ibn Verga's image of Ashkenazic Jewry.

Ibn Verga also reports another case in which German Jews were given three days to convert or die. These Jews agreed among themselves "to slaughter each other, rather than [die] at the hands of the gentiles, and that whoever is not sufficiently brave would beg the beadle to kill him. And so it was."[20] Here, too, the Jews of Ashkenaz do not suffer martyrdom passively—they slaughter each other and themselves, a behavior famously associated with the First Crusade, an episode to be discussed at length in later chapters.

The historicity of these stories is not our concern. Unfortunately, most of Ibn Verga's sources have not been identified, and therefore it is impossible to identify any subtle changes he might have introduced and thereby obtain a better grasp of how he understood the tales. In any case, what matters most is the stories' inclusion in *Shevet Yehudah*, which indicates that they reflect Ibn Verga's image of Ashkenazic Jewry.

Ibn Verga's Ashkenaz tales mark German Jewry as steadfast in the face of persecution. Ibn Verga also narrates the martyrological acts of Jews from other lands. In the Spanish persecution of 1391, we read that "many were killed in sanctification of the name of God," although Ibn Verga admits that most Jews apostatized.[21] There is also a story of self-slaughter from France: Ibn Verga reports that in 179, namely 1219,[22] the Jews of Anjou, Poitiers, and Bretagne faced forced conversion and that more than 3,000 were martyred "and many slaughtered themselves," and that more than 500 apostatized. Elsewhere in France, Ibn Verga writes, "all the Jews sanctified the [divine] name, and were burned with their children."[23] The Jews of France and Germany are not the only ones to prefer martyrdom to apostasy in *Shevet Yehudah*; in a persecution in Greece, says Ibn Verga, "all the Romaniote Jews, big and small, sanctified the name [of God]."[24]

Nevertheless, it appears that Ibn Verga thought that the Jews of Ashkenaz had a more marked martyrological propensity than did their coreligionists from other lands. In a broad statement about the reduction in the number of Jews worldwide, he observed that, whereas one in a thousand remain of those who settled in Spain, among Franco-German Jewry "many sanctified the [divine] name, were killed in the thousands, and only one in five thousand of the original settlers remain."[25] The reference to martyrdom in this sentence leaves no room for the suggestion that Ibn Verga attributed the greater decimation of French and German Jewry to apostasy; in his mind, martyrdom was especially prevalent in northern Europe, and the Jews were persecuted more severely there than in Spain.[26]

Ibn Verga's view of the medieval persecution of European Jewry differs markedly from that of Samuel Usque, a Portuguese ex-Marrano, whose *Consolation for the Tribulations of Israel* serves up a broad assortment of Jewish suffering, including libels of various sorts and their fatal consequences. In an effort to convince the Marranos of Portugal to return to Judaism, Usque argues that the Jews' suffering represents divine retribution for their shortcomings, and he often tags the tales of woe with particular transgressions. Usque's "explanation" of a tragic, violent episode is never the Jews' failure to recognize Jesus, and thus he implicitly justifies the rejection of Christianity while also assuring his reader that divine redemption is as certain as divine punishment.

Usque's pattern of recording both punishment and sin sheds light on his perception of Jewish life in northern Europe. Unlike Ibn Verga, Usque conflates France and Germany. Usque's narrative highlights the economic success of the Jews and the tension supposedly created by the economic gap between them and their Christian neighbors, and in this he also differs from Ibn Verga. For Germany, he records, "In Torti, a province of Germany, where my children were thriving in number and riches, I saw envy breed such a hatred in the populace that they sought any means to plunder and destroy them."[27] Usque sometimes adds that the Jews' usury habitually engendered gentile hatred, as in the following: "Because the Christians in France hated the Jewish usurers, the poor Israelite people living in Paris were charged with having killed a Christian youth in order to celebrate the Passover with his blood."[28] Yet Usque does not differentiate between European countries; the pattern of crisis and response is basically the same in Germany, France, Spain, and elsewhere. Nor does Usque depict the Jews of Franco-Germany as more steadfast or pious than their Iberian confreres, and in his account they do not appear as martyrs in greater numbers or percentages.

Joseph ha-Kohen's *Emek ha-Bakha* ("Vale of Tears") also fails to distinguish between ethnic groups. This sits well with the fact that, although ha-Kohen carefully records the incident that sparked a particular anti-Jewish act, he does not search for root causes. There is, however, an exception: "The Jews of Paris and environs grew in number, wealth and property, and took slaves and maidservants, the daughters of alien gods [Mal. 2:11], whereupon the French envied them greatly" and accused them of desecrating Christian chalices.[29] As in Usque's *Consolation for the Tribulations of Israel*, this passage highlights the envy aroused among the gentile population by Jewish prosperity, but here the reference to the verse from Malachi discloses that the Jews' misfortunes were the product of their own sexual malfeasance.

How widespread this social ill was among the Jews of northern Europe cannot be determined, but the vice of sexual relations with "the daughters of alien gods" is documented in a penitential manual by Eleʿazar of Worms, a leading thirteenth-century pietist, who records the corporeal mortification to be self-inflicted as penance for transgressions of various sorts, including sexual malfeasance.[30] However, the issue of sex with the daughters of alien gods is not particular to Ashkenaz, for it occupied a prominent position in the image of Iberian Jewry and consequently in the perception of Spanish-Jewish history. In the thirteenth century, it is the subject of homiletical exhortation by Moses of Coucy and Moses Nahmanides, and it appears in Zoharic literature as well.[31] In 1281 the Toledo community enacted a set of penitential measures, including a ban on Jewish-Christian sexual activity.[32] This proscription crops up again in a penitential text by Judah ben Asher of Toledo in the mid-fourteenth century.[33] Abraham Zacut, whose history, *Sefer Yuhasin* (Book of Lineage), antedates the other sixteenth-century historical works mentioned, suggests that this vice was responsible for the Spanish riots of 1391.[34] Joseph ha-Kohen's use of the phrase from Malachi may therefore reflect the particularly Sephardic resonance of this socioreligious issue rather than—or more than—the sexual mores of Parisian Jews.

The sixteenth century also marked a new, large-scale social and cultural encounter between Iberian and Ashkenazic Jewry, as immigrants from these regions relocated in Italy and the Ottoman empire and established multiethnic Jewish communities. Conflict was inevitable, and its literary expressions include generalizations about the qualities of the ethnic rivals, chiefly the Ashkenazic and Sephardic blocs. One of the themes of this discourse was the northern Europeans' tendency to adopt stringent positions on halakhic issues.[35] This reputation is attributable, at least in part, to the historical development of Franco-German halakhah, which was less wedded to the institutional chain of tradition than its counterpart in the Islamic realm and hence more easily disposed to break new ground.[36]

Stringency in Jewish law has always been equated with piety, and thus the Sephardic communities were perceived by some as more worldly and less pious than the French and Germans. David Messer Leon, an Italian Jew living in sixteenth-century Albania, contrasts the spiritual purity of the northern Europeans to the Sephardim, "most of whose great men and authors were always with the kings and lords of the gentiles, in their courts."[37] The courtly culture of Spain was a time-honored target of homiletical criticism, long before the Expulsion, and Messer Leon's comment reflects the symmetric link between Sephardic worldliness and halakhic laxity on the one hand and Ashkenazic insularity and scrupulous observance on the other.

The Ashkenazic image did not change perceptibly during the seventeenth and eighteenth centuries, although the large-scale destruction during the so-called Chmielnicki massacres in eastern Europe in the mid-seventeenth century reinforced the impression that the Jews of northern Europe suffered greatly and frequently from religious persecution and violence. This feature was already laden with the connotations that Ashkenazic Jewry was faithful unto death, that Jewish-Christian relations in northern Europe were tense and polarized, and hence also that the society and culture of this ethnic bloc were insular and parochial. The obverse of this caricature was a society in which Jews were acculturated, relations with gentiles were cordial, and Jewish culture included the arts and sciences. This was also obviously a caricature, the caricature of Sepharad. The *paidaea* of Jewish culture and the nature of Jew-gentile interaction were the core issues of premodern Jewish life, which is why they are the subtext of medieval and early modern Jewish historiography, dictating the image of both Ashkenazic and Sephardic Jewry. As we will see, the same issues exercised the first modern historians, despite the enormous difference in historical context between the ages.

Haskalah and *Wissenschaft des Judentums*

In the late eighteenth and early nineteenth century, the Maskilim, or proponents of Haskalah (Jewish Enlightenment), urged their contemporaries to acquire a general education and attain proficiency in the vernacular and emphasized the novelty of their enterprise by contrasting their ethos and their achievements in these areas with those of their benighted ancestors. These writers characterized the premodern period as a Dark Age, and as a rule they affixed this label to the entire period separating their age from late antiquity. For example, Saul Ascher, in *Leviathan*, identified the beginnings of decline in the Second Temple period, and Solomon Maimon and Lazarus Ben-David posited a similar chronological scheme.[38] David Friedländer argued that the decision to record the Oral Law drove the Jews to pay excessive attention to halakhah and messianism rather than to science, signaling a decline in the quality of Jewish creative thought.[39] Enlightenment writing also associated the culture of premodern Europe with mysticism and magic, which were antithetical to the rationalistic ideal and hence dismissed as superstition. Beshtian Hasidism, with which the Maskilim associate these vices, was often the implied target of this veiled but pointed criticism.[40]

More common in Maskilic writing is the distinction between the ignorant and parochial Ashkenazic Jew and his educated and cultivated Iberian cousin. The record of Andalusian involvement and achievement in the humanities, philosophy, and science and the conspicuous absence of such activity among the Jews of northern Europe for most of the Middle Ages invited the invidious comparison between the two blocs. The Maskilim associated their own society with that of medieval Ashkenaz, which they perceived as backward and introverted, and as the obverse of Sephardic culture, which they praised and with which they identified. Solomon Maimon, a child of traditional Lithuania who became a Berlin intellectual, heaped praise on the enlightened state of Andalusian Jewry and bemoaned the state of medieval France, which he said was characterized by "unparalleled political upheaval, ignorance and vulgarity."[41]

The ethnic slant of the Maskilim is mostly expressed by the silence in which they gloss over, in their historical writings, the record of intellectual achievement in medieval France and Germany. This is particularly striking in the series of biographical essays published in *Ha-Me'assef*, the Maskilic periodical first published in Königsburg in 1784. In the preface to the first issue, the Hebrew Language Society announces that the journal will offer a column on "the Greats of Israel," including scholars in Torah and in science (*ḥokhmah*) as well as laymen who aided Israel financially and politically.[42] The list of biographical subjects includes Spanish-Jewish figures, who are portrayed as broadly educated, rationalistic thinkers. Naturally, Maimonides is the model and hero of this kind of historical narrative, and other subjects, from other lands and later centuries, include Isaac Abarbanel, Azariah de' Rossi, Joseph Solomon Delmedigo, and Menasseh ben Israel, as well as lesser known figures, among them Isaac Orobio de Castro, Moses Raphael D'Aguilar, and Jacob Judah Leon. Not one biography was devoted to a personage from medieval France or Germany.[43] Similarly, *Ha-Me'assef* published an article on the Spanish Expulsion, but none about the fate of northern European Jewry.

The biographical essay on Delmedigo illustrates the didactic, Maskilic purpose of this type of writing. The statement that Delmedigo's father was a great talmudist and a great scholar in philosophy in Padua is followed by the following footnote:

> Remembering this, my heart is saddened within me when I see many of our people's teachers heaping scorn on every branch of wisdom and science; and they do not even understand the language of the people among whom they live, and nevertheless they do not hesitate to heap scorn on those who seek after it in order to confound them, saying that they have acted against God and despised his Torah. Look at the family of great, godfearing individuals, who taught Torah but also chose to walk in the path of wisdom and clung to science. Would that they would take this to heart, and it would serve for the greater dignity and fame of the pride of Israel.[44]

The writers of these biographical articles cast the medieval past in terms of their own struggle for enlightenment. Thus Shimon Baraz, author of the Maimonides essay, depicts the Maimonidean controversy as a struggle between the forces of reason and ignorance.[45] Solomon Maimon also sees in the medieval conflict a reflection of the divide between Spain, which he considers enlightened, and France, which he equates with ignorance and rigid orthodoxy.[46]

But the emphasis on Sephardic figures did not just reflect internal, curricular considerations. Tsemah Tsamriyon writes, "As usual, in *Hameassef* the criterion of 'what will they [the gentiles] say' carried a certain amount of weight. . . . Thus it comes as no surprise that Rashi . . . and his like, who were only active in the Jewish realm and who were of no interest to the gentiles, did not merit biographical treatment in *Hameassef*."[47] From this perspective it would seem that Andalusian talmudists, such as Joseph ibn Migash, would have been no more likely to receive biographical treatment than Rashi or Rabbenu Tam.

The lofty praise for Sephardic culture and corresponding criticism of and disdain for Ashkenaz is also evident in the writings of Enlightenment thinkers from Galicia, such as Joseph Perl and Solomon Rapoport. Rapoport also wrote biographical essays, which appeared in the Maskilic periodical *Bikurei ha-'Itim*, and again his subjects are all from either the Islamic realm or the Mediterranean basin. Rapoport praises medieval thinkers for their ability to blend Judaic and general culture; those praised include Saadia Gaon, Abraham ibn Ezra, Maimonides, and Ovadiah Sforno, but no native of France or Germany.[48] Similarly, Zvi Hirsch Chajes applies the term *scholars* to Sherira Gaon, Maimonides, Abraham Zacut, Azariah de' Rossi, and Hayyim Joseph David Azulay, although he also lists in this category Moses Isserles, David Gans, and Yehiel Heilperin, who hailed from Ashkenazic lands.[49] The proponents of Haskalah in Prague exhibit the same historical bias. In their contributions to *Sulamith*, the Maskilic periodical first printed in Dessau in 1806, Ignaz Jeitteles and Markus Fischer express interest in the Middle Ages but never in Ashkenaz.[50]

The biographical efforts of the Enlightenment writers represent the beginning of a new Jewish interest in Jewish history, notwithstanding the blatantly tendentious character of these writings. The image of medieval Ashkenaz was an important theme in the early works of modern Jewish historiography and began appearing in print in the first half of the nineteenth century. Although perspectives on the image of medieval Ashkenaz have continually evolved from the nineteenth century to the present, there is a literary continuity in the treatment of our theme from that day to this.

For the writing of history, nineteenth-century historians had at their disposal a few medieval historiographical texts, especially *Yosiphon*, the chain-of-tradition literature, and the sixteenth-century historiographical corpus. However, the early historians also made use of non-Jewish writings, prominent among which was the first comprehensive history of the Jews, by the Huguenot divine, Jacques Basnage, which the Maskil Solomon Maimon began translating into Hebrew.[51] Basnage views all of Jewish history as "but a continual series of calamities" (*une enchainure de maux*)[52] and devotes a great deal of space to the historical record of religious persecution. He maintains that in their campaign against the Jews, the secular authorities used legislation as well as violence, and he debunks both the blood and host libels.[53] Basnage proceeds to discuss the anti-Jewish legislation of the medieval Church, which he depicts as inhumane. Subsequently, Basnage describes in detail the expulsions from France and England as well as the persecution of the Jews of Germany and Hungary.

This history echoes the sixteenth-century litanies of persecution, such as Joseph ha-Kohen's *Emek ha-Bakha*, but with the significant difference that the writer is Christian. Basnage intended his severe critique of the manhandling of medieval Jewry as a polemic against the Catholic Church rather than as an expression of philosemitic compassion, for he associated Protestantism with tolerance and Catholicism with persecution. Thus, also, Basnage has little patience for talmudic literature and thought; he deems the Sages ignorant, and he dismisses their ideas as corrupt distortions of the Bible and their customs as superstition. Sympathetic to their medieval plight, Basnage admits that his purpose is to bring about the Jews' conversion.

A less noted feature of Basnage's history, of particular interest here, is his balanced treatment of the creative efforts of medieval rabbis. Abraham ibn Ezra, Maimonides, and David Kimhi are among the thinkers Basnage surveys, but he expresses no preference for Sephardic scholars and is equally interested in Rashi and Rabbenu Tam. Similarly, although he lists Alharizi as an example of the Jews' poets and Abraham Bar Hiyya as a Jewish astronomer, side by side with them appear "the celebrated professors" Isaac of Dampierre and his student, Judah Sir Leon of Paris.[54] After describing the travails of German Jewry in the high Middle Ages, Basnage notes that despite persecution, the Jews not only remained in Germany but also continued to produce "illustrious and wise" scholars, including Barukh of Worms, Ele'azar of Worms ("one of the great kabbalists of his age"), Isaac of Vienna, his disciple Meir of Rothenburg, and his student Asher ben Yehiel ("who surpassed his teacher").[55] Basnage says nothing about Ashkenazic Jewry's ignorance of the sciences and does not spotlight either their superiority or inferiority to the Jews of the Iberian peninsula, singling them out neither for their piety nor for their martyrdom.

Basnage's *Histoire et la réligion des Juifs* served as an important source for the early efforts of modern Jewish historians. The leap into the age of modern Jewish historiography was taken by Isaac Marcus Jost, whose *History of the Jews from the Time of the Maccabees to the Present*, published in Berlin (in German) in the 1820s, represents not only a return to the writing of Jewish history but also the expression of the new notion that the study of history is a valuable tool for charting the course of the individual and the collective. Jost was one of the young intellectuals who founded the Society for Culture and Science of Judaism (Verein für Cultur und Wissenschaft der Juden) in Berlin in 1819. These thinkers and this organization maintained that the scholarly study of history could provide direction for the future development of Judaism.[56]

Jost's history of medieval Jewry has been characterized as a history of "suffering and scholars" (*Leidens- und Gelehrentesgeschichte*),[57] and this is a particularly apt assessment of his perception of Jewish history in northern Europe. Yet it requires refinement, for within the Middle Ages Jost saw distinctions and development rather than a monochromatic, homogeneous whole. Specifically, he describes the political and economic status of the Jews under the Carolingians in positive terms, writing not only that "the Jews were then no longer the most unfortunate of peoples"[58] but also that "commercial prosperity, which benefitted both the Jews and the State, caused people to ignore the obstacles placed by religion on social intercourse, and Christians and Jews lived in friendship with one another."[59] The downturn, in Jost's presentation, came in the next phase of Ashkenazic history, after 1000 CE, when "in spite of outer appearances, [the Jews] were the most unfortunate of people,"[60] and it lasted until 1320.[61]

The caveat that the Jews did not appear to suffer probably refers to their affluence. Jost echoes the sixteenth-century theme of the deleterious impact of Jewish prosperity, particularly money lending. Unlike Usque and the others, who hold that money stimulated gentile jealousy, Jost stresses the harm that money and business did to the Jewish soul. He describes the Ashkenazic Jew as utterly devoted to the accumulation of lucre: "The Jew as moneylender was concerned only with making money, squeezing the poor terribly, and mercilessly driving them into hardship."[62] Jost deplores the Jewish community's failure to act against the unscrupulous conduct of business, which he contrasts with its intervention in other types of sinful behavior.

Jost offers a psychological explanation for the importance that money attained in the Ashkenazic scale of values. He suggests that "for the Jews, money became a pathetic antidote for ignominy and neglect."[63] This idea, and the theme of Jewish greed generally, both familiar from Shakespeare's *Merchant of Venice*, is part of the Pauline portrait of the Jew as carnal rather than spiritual and has its roots in the New Testament condemnation of the Pharisees. Jost is therefore internalizing a Christian anti-Jewish stereotype and integrating it into his image of medieval Ashkenazic Jewry.

The foil for Ashkenaz is, once again, Spain, and Jost portrays the Spaniards as totally divorced from the financial industry, owing to their more worldly and scientific upbringing.[64] In northern Europe, he explains, the Jews did not engage in agriculture and artisanry, and it was left for them to choose between the pursuit of science or commerce. They opted for commerce because in their geocultural sphere "theology was predominant," and as a result Ashkenaz produced no scientists, jurists, or doctors.[65]

The theme of Jewish economic activity thus links up with the Ashkenazic Jews' reputation for ignorance: "While the Spanish Jews educated themselves in the higher sciences . . . those over here [in Germany] stuck to theology, to its allies jurisprudence and polemic, soon to the elevation of perspicacity and insight, also the kabbalah, and they seldom chose one of the medical sciences."[66] Jost returns to this theme in his exposition on Rashi, who, we are told, "knew nothing about nature, geography, world history, mathematics, languages, but everything about the earlier sources of Jewish study: Bible, Talmud and other, later, works."[67] Jost characterizes Rashi's work as naïve and unoriginal with respect to the nature of reality: "He arrived at no substantial perception of things, [but rather] devoted himself entirely to perceiving the sense of the thoughts of his predecessors."[68] This approach, he believes, became the intellectual posture of Rashi's students and of northern European Jewry in general. It is obviously one that Jost considered inferior to the Spanish pursuit of substantive knowledge, which requires the acquisition of scientific training.

The French method of Talmud study pioneered by Rashi comes under fire for another reason as well. Jost describes the tosafist project of completing and homogenizing Rashi's Talmud commentary and maintains that the keen dialectic of these scholars sparked an insatiable passion for intellectual combat: "They [the tosafists] imprinted as a character trait on these same Jews the search for conflict over anything which is not absolutely established as holy."[69] Ultimately, we read, French Jews abandoned all other intellectual pursuits and earthly values and became estranged from their non-Jewish neighbors, except for the conduct of usurious transactions.[70] As a result of the focus on Talmud, Rashi's commentary, and the tosafist glosses and as a result of the taste for disputatious reasoning, the Jews of northern Europe lost sight of the actual knowledge preserved in the Talmud in various disciplines.[71] Here, again, Ashkenazic Jewry is held inferior to that of the Iberian peninsula, where the goal was knowledge, not perspicacity. According to Jost, this taste for cleverness and subtleties also manifested itself in the poetry of the two lands. The liturgical poetry of Spain embodies the goal of clarity and plain language, but that of France and Germany strives for obscure references and allusions to biblical and postbiblical formulations.[72]

Jost also holds the northern European mode of thought responsible for the growth of kabbalah, which he thinks was transplanted to Europe during the Crusades. According to Jost, kabbalah could not have flourished in Spain because of its incompatibility with Aristotelian philosophy. However, the Jews of Ashkenaz, on account of their curriculum and intellectual tastes, were receptive to the new superstition, with its magical formulas and wonder working, all rooted in the world of aggadah, or legend.[73]

Ignorance, persecution, insularity, mysticism—these are the qualities that Jost identifies in the medieval Ashkenazic Jew, as opposed to
the Sephardic Jew, whose broad education and economic diversity enabled him to engage the surrounding society and culture with pride and
honor.[74] Jost returns to this dichotomy in his discussion of the early
modern era, as he contrasts the mediocrity and stagnation of the Ashkenazic leadership with the education and dignity of the Sephardim, who,
he points out, were the first enlightened Jews.[75] Plainly, Jost shot his
arrow before painting his bull's eye; his portrayal of Jewish culture in
medieval Ashkenaz mirrors his antipathy for the "rabbinism" (his term)
of his own day, with its casuistry and superstition, as well as the provin-
cialism, insularity, and alienation of the northern European Jew. By the
same token, his sympathy for Spain reflects qualities he deems desirable
for the nineteenth-century Jew, particularly the ability to conduct oneself among the gentiles with dignity, by virtue of one's sophistication
and worldliness.

Another member of the Verein was Heinrich Heine, who, although
a poet rather than a historian, supplies a clear image of medieval Ashkenazic Jewry in *Der Rabbi von Bacherach*, a novella he completed by
1825.[76] Heine recapitulates the story of the persecutions suffered by the
Jews of the Rhineland town of Bacherach in the Middle Ages.

> The Great Persecution of the Jews began with the Crusades and
> raged most grimly about the middle of the fourteenth century, at the
> end of the Great Plague which, like any other public disaster, was
> blamed on the Jews. . . . Another accusation, which even before that
> time, and throughout the Middle Ages until the beginning of the
> past century, cost them much blood and anguish, was the absurd tale,
> repeated *ad nauseam* in chronicle and legend, that the Jews would
> steal the consecrated wafer, stabbing it with knives until the blood
> ran from it, and that they would slay Christian children at their feast
> of the Passover, in order to use their blood for their nocturnal rite.
> The Jews—sufficiently hated for their faith, their wealth, and their
> ledgers—were on this holiday entirely in the hands of their enemies.[77]

In this passage the Ashkenazic Jew's relationship with the non-Jewish
world is characterized by persecution and violence. Like Usque and
Joseph ha-Kohen, Heine attributes medieval hatred of Jews not only to

religious differences but also to the Jews' wealth, and especially to their money lending, represented here by the reference to their ledgers.

The inner world of the medieval German Jew is characterized in Heine's tale by a piety and a severity that is contrasted with the more libertarian and libertine culture of Sepharad. The narrator relates that Rabbi Abraham, the main protagonist, had spent seven years in Spain, which occasioned gossip about his orthodoxy.

> At the mention of Spain the sly ones used to smile in a knowing way; probably because of a dark rumor that while Rabbi Abraham had studied the holy law zealously enough at the Academy of Toledo, he had also copied Christian customs and absorbed ways of free thinking, like the Spanish Jews who at that time had attained to an extraordinary height of culture. In their hearts, though, those gossips hardly believed their own insinuations. For the Rabbi's life, after his return from Spain, had been extremely pure, pious and earnest; he observed the most trivial rites with painful conscientiousness, fasted each Monday and Thursday, abstained from meat and wine except on the Sabbath and other holidays, and spent his days in study and prayer.[78]

Jewish culture in Spain appears here as subject to Christian influence and therefore, by implication, as diluted, and it is also seen as freethinking and cultured. In contrast, the German Jew is seen as ascetic and as single-mindedly devoted to the service of God. The passage also characterizes Ashkenazic Jewry as punctilious in its halakhic observance, perhaps even excessively so, and once again a contrast with Spain is implied.

Heine expands on the theme of Spanish Jewry later in the tale, when Rabbi Abraham encounters none other than Don Isaac Abarbanel. Abarbanel could not look less like an Ashkenazic Jew, for his dress is flashy, complete with spurs and sword. Indeed, Heine's Abarbanel is an apostate, the inevitable and gloomy consequence, we infer, of his Sephardic mind-set and lifestyle.[79] The narrator does in fact allude repeatedly to the less than austere mores of the Iberian nobleman. For instance, Abarbanel describes in colorful and mellifluous prose the physical charms of the proprietress of a Jewish food establishment, whose bosom, we read, "rivals the sweetest pineapple for tenderness and color."[80]

Abarbanel's rhetorical gift in the Bacherach tale represents the high regard in which Heine held the great poets of Muslim Spain, whom he treats lavishly and enthusiastically in his poem *Jehuda ben Halevy*. There Heine recounts Halevi's upbringing, including his training in religious studies, and unlike Jost, he does not condemn the Talmud and its study as irrational, superstitious, or trivial. On the contrary, Heine terms halakhah "that great fencing school, where the best dialectic athletes of Babylon and Pumpeditha fought out their tournaments."[81] His portrayal of aggadah is equally sympathetic, and clearly Heine resented the rejection of Talmud study by the seemingly progressive thinkers of his day.[82]

Heine's poem also extols the poetry of Abraham ibn Ezra, Moses ibn Ezra, and Solomon ibn Gabirol, as well as the *maqamah* tales of Judah Alharizi.[83] How much of the corpus of these poets Heine read, or was able to read, is unclear, but plainly he admired these figures and identified with them. The poets of France or Germany go unmentioned, and plainly when Heine thought of Hebrew poetry, he did not think of them. Poetry embodies aesthetic sensibility in general, and thus the cultural implications of Heine's point of view are rather broad.

Heine's view of medieval Jewish culture is more balanced and nuanced than that of Jost. He expresses awareness that Iberian Jewry was known not only for its education and worldliness but also for its lack of religious zeal, its acculturation, and ultimately its apostasy, none of which are depicted as praiseworthy. Conversely, Rabbi Abraham's pietism and fastidious observance are not condemned as parochial.

Like Heine, Leopold Zunz, the Verein's preeminent scholar, largely rejected the binary conception of medieval Ashkenaz and Sepharad articulated by the Maskilim and by his colleague Jost. Initially Zunz interested himself in the achievements of medieval Spain. He was awarded the doctorate in 1821 for a study on the Spanish philosopher Shem Tov Falaquera and his *Sefer ha-Maʿalot*. The following year Zunz published an essay on Sephardic place names in Hebrew literature, which begins with praise for Sephardic literature: "Compared to the cultural desert in Germany and Poland, it was simply an oasis. There Jews achieved a cultural level they had not known since the loss of political independence and which often left Christian Europe far behind."[84] This adulation reflects the Enlightenment bias accepted by most members of the Verein. Zunz goes on to comment that the refugees from the Spanish Expulsion achieved great things in their new communities, which apparently refers to Menasseh ben Israel and other figures surveyed in the *Ha-Me'assef* biographies. This statement echoes the sense that nineteenth-century historians deemed the Sephardic Jews of their own day worthy of emulation.[85]

Zunz's second essay in the Verein's periodical, which appeared in 1823, breaks with convention and urges a radical change of direction, toward a more positive evaluation of the culture of medieval Ashkenaz. The essay is a biography of Rashi, and Zunz's immediate purpose is to replace the prevailing image of Rashi as "bereft of spirit and laden with nonsense"[86] with serious study of Rashi's achievements. But the very existence of the Rashi article is a critique of Maskilic scholarship, which found no place for Ashkenazic figures in its biographical enterprise.

The Rashi essay exudes a new enthusiasm for the culture of Franco-Germany.

> At the beginning of the eleventh century, Gershom b. Judah, Ma'or ha-Golah, announces the dawning of a new day. . . . Amid this active period . . . I will show you, dear reader, the flowering of the literature of French Jewry in the form of a man who may be called the representative of that century, a man . . . who deepened what Gershom, his predecessor, had founded, and was known by all as Rashi Parshandata.[87]

Zunz reconstructs Rashi's library, citing all the works mentioned by him, from the Bible to his teachers; the list contains eighty works and occupies thirty pages. This section also includes short discussions of some of these earlier writers, their first such scholarly attention. Zunz goes on to list neglected areas of Rashi study.

Zunz does not replace the benighted Rashi with an Enlightenment Rashi. He dismisses the image of Rashi as "a tolerant man, who knew Persian, Arabic, Latin, Greek and German; who was active in astronomy and medicine, who had a thorough knowledge of kabbalah and grammar."[88] This portrait of an ecumenical and worldly intellectual is wrong, Zunz explains, because it ignores the intolerant environment of northern Europe: "One must not forget that he lived, with his brethren, under conditions of persecution, and witnessed the First Crusade. . . .

It can also be proved that he sympathized with the forced converts and was the theological and political adversary of his gentile contemporaries."[89] Thus, Zunz maintains, Rashi's attitude toward non-Jews was nothing like the liberal model exalted by Enlightenment thinkers.

Zunz's treatment of Rashi is pathbreaking not only because it is so positive but also because it is unapologetic about the particularistic nature of Rashi's oeuvre and indeed of Ashkenazic learning in general. Zunz senses that his contemporaries feel distaste for anything that is exclusively Jewish and not clearly in step with the march of European culture. Zunz sees the scholarship and creativity of medieval Ashkenaz as a world unto itself, and in his day this was not the fashion; Sephardic culture, with its Hellenic components, was considered more universalistic and hence more highly esteemed.[90]

The return to Ashkenaz espoused by Zunz also expresses a paradigm shift in one's attitude toward the past. The Verein's members and other Jewish intellectuals of the day agreed that Judaism was in need of revitalization, but Zunz rejected the strategy of Jost and others, who pushed for change by trumpeting the weaknesses of the premodern era. Rather than condemn the past, Zunz strove to appreciate its legacy. As a historian, he opted for empathy over criticism, and this enabled him to discern achievement where his predecessors saw darkness and degeneration.[91]

Zunz sounded the call for the study of medieval Ashkenaz again some twenty years later, in *Zur Geschichte und Literatur*, which appeared in 1845. For one thing, he writes, Christian scholars would be more likely to view the history and culture of northern European Jewry positively if Jewish scholars did so. On the intellectual plane, Zunz asserts that proper scholarship must be complete and impartial, which would hardly describe the current state of Ashkenaz research. In an argument that is both scholarly and political, Zunz holds that an honest and full picture of the past is essential for an accurate understanding of the current condition of European Jewry: "The complex problem of the fate of the Jews may derive a solution, if only in part, from this science [of Judaism]."[92]

Charting virgin territory, Zunz abandoned Sephardic studies and devoted his research to the life of the synagogue, particularly liturgical poetry and midrash, realms that were perceived as particularistic and that, in fact, were the platform for the creativity of medieval Ashkenaz.[93] This phase of Zunz's career began with the appearance, in 1832, of his history of Jewish sermons. In the section on the Middle Ages, Zunz presents the conventional image of northern European Jewry as introverted and persecuted. He explains that in medieval France and Germany the development of the sermon was hampered by the tendency to expend time and energy on the study of halakhah to the exclusion of other intellectual and spiritual pursuits. He adds that the preacher's tongue and the listeners' ears were also stopped by fear, that is, by the frequent incidents of persecution and violence, which "destroyed every institution that began to flower in France and Germany."[94] In Spain, on the other hand, the Jews cultivated philosophy, grammar, and especially poetry, and their liturgical poetry was correspondingly more aesthetic and uplifting than the obscure compositions of northern Europe.[95]

This portrayal of medieval Ashkenazic Jewry as spiritually stunted by persecution receives panoramic treatment in Zunz's book on medieval liturgical poetry (*Die Synagogale Poesie des Mittelalters*), printed in 1855. The book's second chapter, titled *Leiden* ("Suffering"), chronicles the persecution of the Jews in the Middle Ages, in the lachrymose tradition of Joseph ha-Kohen and others. Zunz characterizes the Middle Ages as "the period of barbarism, that is, of the united sway of physical force, ignorance, and priestcraft."[96] He cites a few instances of persecution in Islamic lands and their echoes in the liturgical compositions of the Spanish poets. Yet the travails of medieval France and Germany dominate the narrative, and Zunz lavishes attention on grisly tales of torture and martyrdom dating from the Crusades to the sixteenth century, interspersing liturgical poems on these events and themes. Zunz explains that his survey renders the liturgical poetry of the Middle Ages more comprehensible, for it "explains the motives of wrath and exasperation, it lays open the source of tears, it reveals sorrows and wounds. We feel the sufferings, we hear the imprecations, we share the hopes."[97]

Zunz's decision to concentrate on liturgical poetry was not a purely scholarly one, for this was the heyday of the Reform movement, which saw the excision of this kind of poetry as a seminal element of liturgical reform.[98] In his youth Zunz had served as preacher in the Beer Temple in Berlin, but he became disillusioned with the Reform movement and distanced himself from it. His work on liturgical poetry and especially on that of northern Europe represents a rejection of the Reformers' efforts to reconfigure the Jewish service in the image of the Protestant one. Zunz's honest appraisal of Ashkenazic liturgical poetry awakened in him a sense of ethnic pride, which ran counter to the prevailing trend among the intellectual and spiritual leaders of German-Jewish society.

More representative of the dismissal of medieval Ashkenazic culture, and of liturgical poetry in particular, is the view of Leopold Dukes that this poetry is "ungrammatical, unedifying and artless." Dukes attributes these characteristics to the narrow curriculum to which Franco-German Jewry was exposed in the Middle Ages. In contrast, Dukes explains, the Jews of al-Andalus composed poetry on universal themes because they thirsted for knowledge and appreciated language.[99]

This bias draws fire from Samuel David Luzzatto (Shadal) of Padua, who had little sympathy for liturgical reform. Like Zunz, Luzzatto concedes that the Spaniards' rhetorical devices are more aesthetically pleasing, but nonetheless he contends that the poets of Ashkenaz were greater because they evoked a greater emotional response in their audience. Luzzatto also prefers the northerners for their use of powerful imagery, drawn from the storehouse of popular folklore, to maximal effect. Then Luzzatto argues, based on literary convention, that the convoluted and obtuse language of Ashkenazic liturgical poetry is its virtue rather than its Achilles' heel, and he cites the superiority of Dante to Tasso as an analogous case. In sum, writes Luzzatto, all the defects usually attributed to the liturgical poetry of Ashkenaz stem from the literary qualities that rightfully merit praise.[100]

Luzzatto also wages his campaign against the hegemony of Spanish poetry in his correspondence with Michael Sachs, who was preparing a book on the Hebrew poetry of medieval Spain.[101] In an 1842 letter, Luzzatto offers to send Sachs some poems from France, Germany, and Italy that he prefers to the Sephardic ones, notwithstanding their lack of meter and rhyme, because they are older and more original and display greater emotional force.[102] Luzzatto's offer fell on deaf ears, and in a later letter Luzzatto takes issue with Sachs's assumption that only Ashkenazic poets wrote *"nationale Lieder."* As proof to the contrary, Luzzatto cites the following line from a poem by Ibn Gabirol: "Overturn, like Sodom, the land of Edom, in which I am the footstool under their feet," and asks Sachs, "Have you ever heard something like this from one of the greatest of lunatics in Ashkenaz and Poland?"[103] Luzzatto's rejection of the stigmatization of Franco-German poetry as nationalistic—that is, particularistic—in contrast to the supposed universalism of Andalusian verse reflects his Zunz-like reversal of the scorn for the culture of medieval Ashkenaz voiced by intellectuals identified in those days with the Reform movement and the Science of Judaism (*Wissenschaft des Judentums*).

Luzzatto's view of liturgical poetry is emblematic of his larger struggle to disentangle Judaism from European culture, which he terms "Atticismus." Luzzatto decries the perversion of authentic Judaism by the introduction of foreign, Hellenic elements, such as in the work of Ibn Ezra and Maimonides, and he sees Rashi and Halevi, especially the latter, as authentically Jewish.[104] Luzzatto's crusade against Atticismus takes the revisionist approach to Ashkenazic culture one step further than Zunz, for the Italian scholar sought not only to remove a distorted, tendentious perception but also to instill in scholars an appreciation of a Judaism he viewed as pristine. This was a new value, quite different from that espoused by proponents of Haskalah and *Wissenschaft des Judentums*, who sought a form of Judaism that would be most compatible with European sensibilities.[105]

In the 1840s the campaign for Jewish toleration and emancipation suffered severe setbacks, beginning with the Damascus blood libel and culminating in the failure of the revolutions of 1848. Reform leaders such as Samuel Holdheim urged ever more radical measures, designed to yield a more universalistic brand of Judaism, which would hopefully stem the erosion of Jewish emancipation and spur the acceptance of Jews by the Christian majority. Other thinkers, however, resisted the Reformers' efforts to jettison messianism, dietary laws, the Talmud, and other components that the Reformers had branded irrational. One direction this resistance took was the insistence, by Zacharias Frankel, Zunz, Michael Sachs, and others, on an objective appreciation of premodern Judaism, including its particularistic elements.[106]

These developments form the backdrop to the historiographical labors of Heinrich Graetz, whose survey of Jewish history, which began appearing in 1853, became far more influential than that of Jost. Graetz identified with the more conservative, traditionalist, branch of *Wissenschaft* scholars, and his attitude toward Jewish history reflects his rejection of the views of assimilationists and radical Reformers. Instead of viewing the Jews as a community of believers, Graetz sees them as a nation, even after the Temple's destruction, and in support of this claim he points to their continued cultivation of the Hebrew language and literary canon. Moreover, Graetz affirms that despite their wide-ranging geographic dispersion, the Jews are a single nation.[107] Both of these positions are antithetical to the assimilationist ideal popular in the first half of the nineteenth century.

Graetz also differs from his *Wissenschaft* predecessors, especially Jost, in his attitude toward his subject. Jost had assumed an objective, critical stance toward the Jews of earlier centuries, issuing blame as well as praise, but Graetz identifies with them passionately, reveling in their achievements, empathizing with their suffering, and excoriating their enemies, and he writes with great pathos in order to forge a bond between reader and subject. This, for instance, explains his use of the historiographical convention that persecution was a leitmotif of medieval Jewish history; he does so neither to excuse the Jews for character flaws, as contemporary apologists did, nor to justify religious reforms.

The portrait of the Middle Ages in Graetz's history differs markedly from that of Jost and other more senior scholars. Graetz maintains that Jewish history and culture must be studied in its entirety, including periods, such as the Middle Ages, that do not appear to accord with contemporary intellectual and cultural trends. Furthermore, he rejects the grim evaluation of the Middle Ages and the correspondingly laudatory view of the modern era, a scheme he sees as fundamentally Christian.

> [We must] prove that Jewish history reveals no Middle Ages in the pejorative sense of the word, that, in fact, the apparent state of death of Jewish history in the darkest days of the Middle Ages was merely an assumed disguise to escape from bloodthirsty brutality, or even a healthy, invigorating winter sleep, which fitted Judaism to enter into a daring, universal race against a more fortunate, younger opponent.[108]

This formulation rejects the Christian view of the Jews as having no history after the Crucifixion except for their (theologically justified) suffering. But Graetz's last sentence is the most striking, for here he hints broadly at his belief in the glorious future of Judaism, the belief that the period of the dispersion would be succeeded by one of national redemption.

Graetz contrasts the Jewish and Christian medieval experiences. Whereas in Christian history the Middle Ages was a period of "intellectual stupor, brutishness, and religious madness," for the Jews it was one of "intellectual greatness, ethical idealism, and religious purity."[109] More specifically, Graetz maintains that the Jews spent the seventeen hundred years from the Destruction to Mendelssohn formulating their doctrine and striving for a higher level of self-understanding.[110] As a child of the Science of Judaism, Graetz sees this process in rationalistic terms, and thus he spotlights the achievements of Philo and the medieval Jewish philosophers, culminating in the colossal Maimonidean corpus.[111]

The course of Jewish history, in Graetz's scheme, is therefore Hegelian, with the Jews moving from exile to self-consciousness (in the Middle Ages) and ultimately to redemption.[112] But within this overall image of the Middle Ages Graetz draws distinctions between smaller chronological units and between geocultural spheres. In keeping with his insistence on the unity of the Jewish people, Graetz attempts to present a single, integrated Jewish history. Unity does not mean homogeneity, however, and Graetz paints a vivid picture of French and German Jewry in the Middle Ages, in which these two centers display different complexions, although both differ radically from the Jews of Spain.

Graetz describes the Jews of Ashkenaz as having been uneducated and ignorant until Charlemagne brought Qalonymos of Lucca to Mainz.[113] They remained so in the eleventh century, when, in Graetz's view, the character of this diaspora crystallized. The Jews of Franco-Germany, he writes, were as morally upright, cultured, and educated as their Christian neighbors, but not more so, and they lacked the spiritual greatness, intellectual horizons, and generous spirit of Spanish Jewry. Talmud was their only intellectual pursuit, and hence their liturgical poetry was clumsy, obscure, and lacking in poetic flair. After Rashi, the French outshone the Spaniards in Torah scholarship, but

Spain continued to reign supreme in other fields of Jewish and general studies, as well as in poetry and belles lettres.[114]

Apart from ignorance, Graetz sees eleventh-century German Jewry as characterized by naïveté and fear of God. In a characterization reminiscent of Heine's Rabbi Abraham, Graetz depicts the Ashkenazic disposition as gloomy and as typified by the pious penitent who engages inordinately in prayer and fasting. Following the First Crusade massacres and subsequent acts of violence and persecution, asceticism and pietism became the norm, and Graetz describes Ashkenazic Jewry as "cloaked in a spirit of sadness and walking in darkness all day long. . . . Their appearance and manner expressed sorrow and subservience, and a cloud of sadness and mourning on their faces."[115] Countering this inclination to pietism, asceticism, and melancholy was Talmud study, which alone protected the Jews from superstition and intellectual darkness and from a monastic withdrawal from worldly existence.

The Jews of twelfth-century France, on the other hand, were "free in body and spirit," prosperous, and politically secure and thus free to devote time and energy to Talmud study.[116] The tosafist method offered a spirit of research, keen dialectic, and an atmosphere of unhindered criticism, all of which Graetz appreciates, but he notes again that Talmud study stood in lieu of other disciplines. Poetry, in particular, could not develop, because "where logic and analysis reign there is no room for metaphor and beautiful expression."[117] The heyday of French Jewry ended in midcentury; Graetz sees evidence of decline in the new political definition of the Jews as *servi camerae* and portrays cultural creativity and political fortune as deteriorating in tandem.[118]

With the pontificate of Innocent III in the early thirteenth century, European Jewry went into a downward spiral of decline, which proceeded until the Spanish Expulsion.[119] The period was characterized by "shame and humiliation from without, and intellectual impoverishment within."[120] Creative power declined, and both thought and literature were more conventional and less original than before. *Sefer Hasidim*, a thirteenth-century pietist work replete with tales of demons and spirits, is evidence of this deterioration. The literalist (*peshat*) Bible exegesis of northern France disappeared, and Talmud study was all that stood between the Jews and spiritual putrefaction.[121]

The heyday of medieval Jewish culture ends with Maimonides, and the downturn is signaled by the Maimonidean controversy and by the appearance of kabbalah in its wake. Graetz has nothing but praise for Maimonides, and his discussion of the Maimonidean controversy is remarkably even-handed; he concedes that opposition was aroused in part by the excesses of the radical Maimonideans of Provence. The controversy of the 1230s, in his view, gave rise to kabbalah, and although his bias against kabbalah is immediately apparent, he presents it as playing a leading—pernicious—role in Jewish history only after the expulsion from Spain.

In sum, for Graetz the Ashkenazic Middle Ages was a period of creativity in Talmud study but little else. The Jews of France and Germany enjoyed periods of prosperity and security in the tenth and eleventh centuries, but persecution intensified thereafter, and the subsequent decline in their political fortunes was mirrored by intellectual and cultural stagnation. Throughout the period the Jews of Spain outshone those of France and Germany in both literature (especially poetry) and the sciences, although the latter excelled in Talmud study. As a whole, Graetz saw the Middle Ages as a more fruitful era than the centuries that followed, which were characterized by one-sided rabbinism (Jost's term), moral decline, and ignorance, which fostered the spread of mysticism and superstition.

Looking back on the historiography of the nineteenth and twentieth centuries, we can begin to discern a swing of the pendulum. The struggle for emancipation and the related campaign for enlightenment undergirded the Sephardic bias found in the historical writing of late eighteenth- and early nineteenth-century thinkers, who focused on the economic and intellectual homogeneity and monotony of Ashkenazic Jewry and their resultant backwardness. This attitude also reflects the agenda of the Reformers, who resented the authority of talmudic law and sought to effect changes, especially in the liturgy, including the abolition of liturgical poetry. Zunz called for a new and more positive assessment of medieval Ashkenazic culture, based on intensive scholarly labor. Luzzatto, too, attempted to redress the imbalance between Ashkenazic and Sephardic studies, but out of a more profound reexamination of the subtext of the existing cultural portrait, which glorified what he called Atticismus over authentic Jewish culture. The historiographical watershed of this period was Graetz's monumental survey, which presents Spain as culturally richer than Ashkenaz but portrays the pietism and talmudism of the north in sympathetic terms.

The Swing of the Pendulum

The high regard in which Graetz held the Middle Ages and his empathetic treatment of Ashkenazic as well as Sephardic Jewry differentiate him from his Maskilic and *Wissenschaft* predecessors, as does his fervent belief in the unity of the Jewish people and in their national redemption. In the latter half of the nineteenth century, historians went even further in their reevaluation of the Ashkenazic legacy while affirming their fidelity to the principle of scholarly objectivity and to the methods of scientific research. Abraham Berliner's essay, *On the Inner Life of the German Jews in the Middle Ages*, was the first such endeavor.[122] Meir Wiener, headmaster of a religious school in Hanover, published a digest of primary sources on the history of medieval Ashkenazic Jewry.[123] Otto Stobbe, a legal historian, produced a history of medieval German Jewry that makes intensive use of a range of primary sources, particularly legal documents.[124] The appearance of scholarly works devoted specifically to the history of medieval Ashkenazic Jewry implicitly acknowledges the legitimacy and importance of the subject.[125]

Far more original and wide ranging than these works in its vision of medieval Ashkenaz, and ultimately also more influential, was Moritz Güdemann's *History of the Education and Culture of Western Jewry in Medieval and Modern Times*, which appeared in the 1880s.[126] Güdemann studied with Graetz at the Breslau rabbinical seminary and went on to become Vienna's leading Orthodox rabbi.[127] Like its predecessors, Güdemann's book is a work of social history, and this represents a methodological shift from Graetz's concentration on biography and literary materials.[128] The turn to social history also offers a level playing field, a plane on which the culture of Ashkenaz could be shown to be as important and valuable as the culture of the Iberian peninsula.[129]

The Viennese rabbi also departs from his teacher Graetz's isolationist approach to Jewish history and compares Jewish social mores and intellectual and spiritual trends with those of the surrounding non-Jewish environment. Güdemann views it as axiomatic that two groups of people who live together are bound to affect each other's way of life.[130] Similarly, Güdemann uses non-Jewish sources. For example, the sermons of Christian preachers, such as Berthold of Regensburg, contribute to his analysis of Judah the Pious and his pietist movement.[131] Güdemann does not see cultural cross-fertilization as a threat to Jewish identity, a position that in all likelihood had contemporary significance for him.

Güdemann's history focuses, not on the intellectual and literary elite, but on the average person, and this too was novel. To approach his subject, who by definition left no literary legacy, Güdemann attempts a pioneering study of popular culture, including not only education but also language, dress, and folklore.[132] This is bottom-up history, and its radical implication is that even the lives of the uneducated, or of women and children, are important and merit scholarly attention. The shift in focus also deemphasizes the *Leiden* aspect of medieval Ashkenaz, and the result, perforce, is an image of Jewish-Christian relations far more harmonious than that depicted by Jost or Graetz.[133]

Güdemann's portrait of Franco-German Jewry in the Middle Ages divides into two chronological parts: He depicts the social, political, and cultural of this diaspora first as practically ideal up to the end of the twelfth century and, second, as declining rapidly thereafter on all fronts. The image of the first period is innovative and refreshing, for it does not display the Hispanophilic tendency of *Wissenschaft* historiography. Echoing Nahmanides, Güdemann depicts Sephardic Jewry as a hellenized Judaism, polluted by alien influence. By contrast, Judaism in northern Europe, he claims, was innocent and pristine and thus able to develop along traditional, natural lines. It was also free of internal strife and of friction with the gentile environment.[134] Thus Güdemann presents interaction with non-Jews as corrosive in Spain but not in France and Germany.

Güdemann's image of the later Middle Ages is more conventional and gloomy. This, he writes, was a period of persecution and of a souring of Jewish-Christian relations, which caused the Jews to decline ethically and intellectually. Internally, the Maimonidean controversy also damaged the creative spirit of the northerners, causing them to become excessively pietistic and intolerant.[135] To this period Güdemann attributes lamentable traits observable in the Jews of Europe in his own day: a certain lowliness of spirit, anxiety, a picayune concentration on religious minutiae, and a fascination with mysticism.[136] Like his *Wissenschaft* predecessors, Güdemann apologizes for those shortcomings of the modern Jew targeted in antisemitic literature while critiquing characteristics that strike him as backward.

The generation after Graetz saw the production of two new general surveys of Jewish history, by Simon Dubnow and Ze'ev Ya'avetz. Both writers were peripatetics of eastern European origin and were deeply influenced by Graetz, but they deviated from his methodological and ideological approach and also differed greatly from each other. Dubnow has little new to say about medieval Ashkenaz, but like Güdemann and unlike Graetz, he highlights the importance of the political and sociological planes for achieving a proper understanding of history. More significant for our purposes is Ya'avetz's fourteen-volume history of the Jews, written in the first quarter of the twentieth century. This is not really a scholarly work, for Ya'avetz derives most of his information from Graetz, except for primary sources that originate in rabbinic literature, which he controls. Furthermore, Ya'avetz's magnum opus is largely a history of scholars, in the tradition that Graetz sought to overturn.

The significant shift in Ya'avetz's perspective concerns Jewish culture, which, in his opinion, both Maskilic and *Wissenschaft* historians failed to regard with due respect and appreciation. Ya'avetz resembles Luzzatto in his celebration of the uniqueness of Jewish culture, which he terms "the pure spirit of Israel" and which he believes to be of divine origin.[137] Thus Rashi did not achieve greatness through external sources, "the fruit of the Greek and Arab spirit," as did the Jews of Spain, for this did not reach France; rather, he drew from the Torah and from his own intellectual capabilities and character.[138] Ya'avetz sees *Sefer Hasidim* as the acme of medieval Ashkenazic culture, and he therefore surveys its contents at length. Once again northern Europe compares favorably to the Iberian peninsula: "The heart of the Spanish scholars was inclined after wisdom (*hokhmah*) and study, while the heart of

Franco-German scholars was inclined after ethics and action, like the words of Judah the Hasid."[139]

Given his preference for the culture of Ashkenaz over Sepharad, Ya'avetz was forced to grapple with the Spaniards' reputation for superior poetry. He admits that the Sephardic Jews exhibited superior language skills but praises the liturgical poetry of Franco-Germany as solid, weighty, and powerful and presents it as pure and uncontaminated by foreign elements. Ya'avetz also prefers the content of Ashkenazic poetry. He lauds the modesty of the French and German rabbis, who did not compose love poetry. He also sees Spain's poetic lamentations over the destruction of the Temple and the condition of exile as indications of a false scale of values. The Sephardim feel these tragedies so deeply, he suggests, because it galls them that the gentiles enjoy greater grandeur than they do; the northerners, on the other hand, do not compare themselves to their non-Jewish neighbors and are therefore more joyous on their festivals.[140]

Admiration for the purity of Ashkenazic Judaism is coupled with criticism of "Greek wisdom," particularly in the context of the Maimonidean oeuvre and controversy. Ya'avetz labors to present Maimonides in a positive light but views his philosophy as alien—or even contradictory—to authentic Judaism. Conceding his inability to synthesize the Maimonides of the *Guide* with that of the *Mishneh Torah*, Ya'avetz decides to deal only with the latter, which he regards as true to "the method of Torah,"[141] a method he also associates with the thought of Saadia Gaon and Judah Halevi.[142] Apart from his survey of the Maimonidean controversy, Ya'avetz offers a chapter-length critique of Graetz's treatment of the subject. He argues forcefully that the rationalists, rather than the traditionalists, were the first to excommunicate their enemies and that they did so because they were filled with pride and with hatred for those who refused to follow their path. It was the rationalist camp, says Ya'avetz, and not the traditionalists who attempted to quash freedom of thought.[143]

Ya'avetz also expresses antipathy for Greek wisdom in his portrayal of kabbalah, which he sees as a reaction to the corruption of philosophy. Kabbalah, he observes, lent the commandments a sense of majesty and infused the performer with religious energy, which was a welcome response to the loss of enthusiasm among the Jews of Spain. For Ya'avetz, kabbalah compares favorably with philosophy from a number of other perspectives as well. Whereas the Greeks devalued the individual, kabbalah restored the image of the individual to greatness. Philosophy focuses on the universe, but kabbalah ascribes central importance to the Jewish people. Unlike philosophy, kabbalah attaches significance to terrestrial existence. Philosophy sees the world as mechanical and eternal, lacking direction and purpose, but kabbalah portrays a dynamic humanity that rises ever higher spiritually.[144]

Ya'avetz's corrective to the *Wissenschaft* assessment of Ashkenazic culture, and specifically to Graetz, can be traced to his religious orthodoxy. This is probably also true for Güdemann, the leading rabbi of Vienna, although Güdemann made a number of important methodological contributions, whereas Ya'avetz's position is merely a throwback to critiques of Hispano-Jewish culture voiced by early modern writers. In any case, the pendulum had swung decisively toward a more favorable view of the cultural legacy of Franco-German Jewry, which was now pegged as authentic and pristine in contrast to the polluted faith of the Sephardim.

The historiography of the first half of the twentieth-century is marked by the pervasive influence of Jewish nationalism, although this ideal had already touched the lives and thinking of the historians I have already discussed. Graetz, as we have seen, expressed nationalist sentiments and the hope of redemption, and Herzl courted Güdemann's support for his own political vision, albeit without success. Nationalist sentiment impelled Ya'avetz to leave Poland for Palestine, where he wrote the first two volumes of his history before circumstances forced him to relocate. The next cadre of historians, however, were completely caught up in the Zionist enterprise, if only because they lived in Mandatory Palestine. Foremost among these scholars was Yitzhak (Fritz) Baer (1888–1980), whose interpretation of medieval Jewish history dominated the field until his death.[145]

Baer came to Jerusalem from Berlin in 1930 to join the Institute of Jewish Studies. He had already published the first volume of his *Die Juden im christlichen Spanien*, a massive collection of archival documents.[146] But Baer believed that the Jewish past must be studied in an integrated fashion; historians need to analyze both archival and literary sources so as to arrive at a unified view of social and intellectual history.[147] Baer's summa, his Hebrew study of Jewish history in Christian Spain, concretizes his novel methodology.[148]

The belief in an integrated, unified view of Jewish history is of a piece with Baer's conviction that Jewish culture has a core, a fundamental spirit or life force that is ever present and expresses itself throughout Jewish history. According to Baer, Jewish life has a basic coherence and unity, which is manifest in both the social and spiritual spheres and in all ages and locales. Baer writes, "In every episode of Jewish history one can recognize . . . the signs of that same special, immanent, principle and consistency which exists throughout the history of our people."[149] This doctrinal tenet of the unity of the Jewish people and its culture is the central expression of Baer's nationalism.[150]

In keeping with this crucial principle, Baer insists that the basic dynamic of Jewish history is immanent and organic. In his formulation, "Jewish history, from its earliest beginnings to our own day, constitutes an organic unit. Each successive stage in its development reveals more fully the nature of the unique force guiding it."[151] Thus Baer maintains that, although the Jews adopted non-Jewish practices and ideas when they found them useful, Jewish culture always represented the development of concepts and principles derived from their own ancient heritage.[152]

The conception of immanent and organic development sets up a binary view of Jewish history in which historical phenomena are constantly being classified as either Jewish or alien. By definition, Jewish culture is in a better state when it develops autonomously, following its own internal spirit, and it is corrupt and decadent when it strays after "outside influence," cultural input from non-Jewish sources. Baer was constantly probing for outside influence, weighing developments to determine whether they were of authentic or alien origin.[153]

The principle of immanent development implies a fundamental distinction between Jewish and European civilization, and on this point Baer offers an open, if veiled, critique of his *Wissenschaft* predecessors: "Our people's scholars sinned in not understanding the special historical personality of Judaism, since they strove to blur the contrasts between Judaism and the European culture to which Judaism is tied by the links of similarity and by various historical encounters; nonetheless, there are fundamental contrasts between these two forces."[154] The emphasis on the inherent Jewish force echoes Luzzatto's dichotomy between Judaism and Atticismus, and in this respect Baer was indeed Luzzatto's disciple.

Ironically, notwithstanding the particularistic flavor of Baer's Jew-gentile dichotomy, his notions of an immanent life force and organic development resemble ideas expressed by earlier historians from nineteenth-century Germany. Wilhelm von Humboldt wrote that, apart from all sorts of forces that affect the course of history, "there remains a principle which cannot be immediately perceived but which moves and directs the other forces: the ideas which have their existence beyond the material world but which rule and influence history in all its parts."[155] Similarly, Friedrich Karl von Savigny thought that "the spirit which was assumed to be basic to the nation became embodied in its various aspects and institutions: at the basis of everything was the national mind."[156] Also, the Romantics, such as Herder, made heavy use of the analogy to plant life, and they described history as unfolding in a natural, unconscious growth process, which they contrasted with the Enlightenment notion of progress.

Baer's notion of an immanent life force is also Romantic in that it underlies his passionate interest in the Middle Ages and in the history of religion, for Baer's concept of the life force is clearly rooted in religion. Its core is the Jews' conviction that they stand in a unique relationship to God, along with the belief that Jewish life must be governed by the Torah—the Written and Oral Law. Baer posits that this philosophy crystallized during the Second Temple period and remained in place, mutatis mutandis, until the modern period. This is the period defined by Baer as the Middle Ages, the era when religion played a more central role than politics in Jewish life.[157]

In Baer's mind, it was not the priestly aristocracy that embodied the culture that emerged during the Second Temple period but rather the Hasmonean leadership and constituency. Baer is thus a populist. He sees the struggle between the aristocracy and the proletariat as a universal historical dynamic,[158] and in the Jewish case he sides unequivocally with the masses. Baer holds in particularly high regard the pietists of the Hasmonean age, who appear in the sources as ascetic and self-sacrificing, and he places these values at the heart of authentic Judaism.[159]

Equality and simplicity are additional values in Baer's vision of the true Jewish ethos.[160] A concrete example of this is Baer's emphasis on the democratic nature of the Jewish community.[161] Baer also makes lyric reference to the Jews' connection to nature, which he sees as bound up with the religious ideal: "The early chapters of the history book," he writes, tell "of a simple, popular life, far from high civilization, of righteous commandments and laws, nature and longing for nature, the nearness of God and the longing for that nearness."[162] Thus Baer also exalts agriculture as a natural occupation and locates in the thinking of *Hasidei Ashkenaz* the German pietists of the Middle Ages, both the egalitarian and agrarian elements.[163] The antithesis of agriculture is money lending, which Baer condemns as "exilic." His jaundiced view of money lending appears to reflect the medieval and modern Christian criticism of the Jewish character, whereas the agrarian and egalitarian ethos may indicate support for the platform of socialist Zionism.[164]

The obverse of Baer's sympathy for the pious, simple farmer is his disdain and even loathing for the affluent. He portrays the members of this stratum as hedonistic and shallow and views their bourgeois materialism as corrosive of an authentic Jewish ethic. In the Second Temple period this type would correspond to the priestly aristocracy of Jerusalem, whom the Hasmoneans and later the Zealots saw as rivals and enemies, but Baer sees the split between the pious masses and the jaded upper class as a perennial component of Jewish social history.

Alongside this ethical and social conflict, Baer views the Hasmonean revolution as a struggle against Greek rationalism. This, too, in his mind, is a fundamental dynamic in Jewish history, for rationalism surfaces again later in the form of medieval Jewish philosophy and the eighteenth-century Haskalah. As heir to nineteenth-century German Romanticism, Baer condemns rationalism as alien and hails a mythical mind-set as authentically Jewish.

The epic struggle between the ascetic, self-sacrificing, and egalitarian ethos on the one hand and the culture of rationalism and bourgeois hedonism on the other plays out in the Middle Ages in the contrast

Baer constantly draws between the Jews of Spain and those of Franco-Germany. He associates the Sephardim with the Jewish philosophical tradition, epitomized by Maimonides, and the Ashkenazim with the ascetic piety of *Hasidei Ashkenaz*. For Baer, the Ashkenazic Jews are the medieval torchbearers of the Jewish life force, and he expresses his admiration starkly when he refers to them as "the purest embodiment of the people of God."[165]

The critique of rationalism is a leitmotif of Baer's monograph on the Jews of Christian Spain.[166] The book describes the Spanish experience as an episode in the cycle of Judaism's confrontation with Hellenism. Yet it was not all of Spanish Jewry who, in Baer's eyes, betrayed their ancestral faith and identity but specifically the class of affluent courtiers. Because Baer associates spirituality with an ascetic lifestyle, for him it is axiomatic that material comfort compromises religious commitment. The fluidity of social boundaries in Spain, where upper-class Jews associated freely with Christians, was also destructive.[167] These two social forces lead Baer to perceive the Spanish courtier class as doomed, and for him they are paradigmatic of the Sephardic experience.

Yet Baer assigns even greater weight to the impact of general education on the Jews of Iberia, particularly science and philosophy. This, he believes, caused them to succumb to an "Averroistic," that is, relativized, view of religion, which led perforce to their neglect of religious observance. This was also the ineluctable result of the extreme allegorical interpretation of the Oral and Written Law: "One who rejects the literal meaning of laws and legends . . . will ultimately be unwilling to accept the burden of exile, will seek a compromise between the way of Israel and that of the gentiles, and will ultimately betray his religion and his people in time of trial. Here lies the significance of the Maimonidean Controversy."[168]

Baer identifies Judah Halevi and later the kabbalists as the Spanish heirs to the Hasmonean ethos.[169] But these are exceptions; in Baer's scheme, authentic Judaism survived in the Middle Ages—nay, thrived—in Ashkenaz. In keeping with his pattern of binary classification, Baer characterizes Ashkenazic Jewry as the mirror image of Sepharad: learned in Torah but still simple and pietistic. "Living in the lands of the wild barbarians," he writes, the Jews of northern Europe "withdrew into the four ells of halakhah and aggadah and found there substance for their private and historical lives."[170] In other words, European civilization of-fered little to tempt the Jews of Ashkenaz, who were therefore able to develop organically and autonomously in the authentic Jewish spirit.

In a fascinating twist, Baer seems to contradict this view of Ash-kenazic autonomy in his pathbreaking, panoramic article on German pietism, positing that the Jews of Franco-Germany were highly sus-ceptible to outside influence.[171] First he portrays the Jewish commu-nity qua institution as influenced by the development of the medieval European city.[172] He then identifies numerous parallels between Ash-kenazic and Franciscan piety, as well as ideas and cultural practices that are Christian, if not strictly Franciscan.[173] But Baer explains that this receptivity to outside influence does not level the playing field between Ashkenaz and Sepharad, for in northern Europe the influence is Chris-tian rather than philosophical. He posits that Christian ideas could take root in the Judaism of northern Europe, rather than Spain or Italy, be-cause in Spain and Italy the Jews' philosophical education somehow blocked the influence of external stimuli or limited their circulation.[174] We therefore encounter the paradoxical notion that Sephardic Jewry lost its way because of its exposure to the Greco-Arabic philosophical tradition, whereas the Jews of Ashkenaz, despite their receptivity to Christian ideas and institutions, not only remained faithful but embod-ied the authentic life force dating back to the Second Temple period.

Implicit in this characteristic of heavy cultural borrowing is an image of Jewish-Christian relations as easygoing and even friendly, akin to the way Baer usually describes Jew-gentile relations in Spain or Italy. As we have seen, however, this is not the way he normally de-picts Jewish-Christian relations in northern Europe. On the contrary, according to Baer, the quintessence of Ashkenazic culture, and indeed of the Hasmonean ethos, is the martyrological spirit, which he views as the extension or logical outcome of the ascetic lifestyle and as the defin-ing theme of Ashkenazic Jewish history.

The German pietists renewed the martyrological legacy of the Second Temple era and of the post-Destruction period of persecution, and their example was followed by the Jews of France, England and even-tually also of Spain. . . . The degree of commitment [to martyrdom] among the medieval pietists was greater than among all their Jewish predecessors and than among all those who resemble them among other nations and religions. For a few generations and in broad circles, preparation for the hour when they would be called "to ascend to God" and "to stand in the king's palace" was the end all and be all of their existence and their greatest desire.[175]

Baer traces this martyrological spirit back to the eleventh century and forward to the end of the Middle Ages, but its classic expression is the mass martyrdom reportedly suffered by the Jews of the Rhineland during the First Crusade.

This aspect of Ashkenazic history is contrasted throughout Baer's writings with the large-scale apostasy of Spanish Jewry in the 1391 riots and under the heavy conversionary pressure of the early fifteenth century. Baer correlates the degree of persecution suffered by a given diaspora with its level of holiness, and this leads him to glorify the medieval Jews of Franco-Germany over those of the Iberian peninsula. In Spain, Baer maintains, the upper-class Jews lived a worldly existence, educated their children in "Greek wisdom," and ultimately left the fold, whereas the Jews of northern Europe led the simple, pious, and ascetic life exemplified by *Hasidei Ashkenaz* and bared their throats to the slaughter time and again.

It is the Ashkenazic Jews, avers Baer, who brought the Jewish life force to Spain—for example, Moses of Coucy, who conducted a preaching tour of Spain in the early thirteenth century, or Asher ben Yehiel, who emigrated from Germany to Castile half a century later and assumed the mantle of rabbinic leadership in Toledo.[176] This Ashkenazic import made it possible for the spirit of humility and penitence to penetrate Spain, at least among the simple folk, among whose ranks Baer includes the kabbalists. Ultimately, Baer explains, in the dismal last century of Spanish Jewish life, it was this spirit that enabled the lower social stratum to withstand the violence and conversionary pressure, whereas the wealthy and sophisticated aristocrats opted out.[177] Thus Baer portrays the Jews of medieval Ashkenaz as traditional but by no means conservative. "From the outset," he writes, "the Ashkenazim . . . entered our people's historical saga as a great innovating and reformatory force, like their predecessors in the time of the Temple."[178]

For Baer, then, the Jews of medieval Ashkenaz, like the Hasmoneans of yore, were heroes for preserving, in creed and in deed, the ancient, authentic ethos of humility, piety, asceticism, and martyrdom, which constitute the immanent life force of Judaism. This image is uniquely Baer's, and yet it picks up strands woven by both premodern and modern scholars. As we have seen, Abraham ibn Ezra and Nahmanides note the distinction between Sepharad and Ashkenaz in the realm of education, and Ibn Verga singles out the Jews of Ashkenaz for their martyrological spirit. *Wissenschaft* writing also paints Jewish life in medieval Franco-Germany as one of unremitting persecution, and—unlike Baer—sees this as the root of the northerners' ignorance, sterile reasoning, and moral shortcomings. With Graetz and later Güdemann, the emphasis shifts decisively from ignorance to innocence and piety, and in Ya'avetz's history we encounter the "spirit of Israel," which was pietistic and ascetic. Thus Baer's symmetric dichotomy, associating Ashkenaz with piety, asceticism, and martyrdom and Sepharad with hedonism, Greek wisdom, and apostasy, is the elucidation of motifs that run through centuries of meditation on the character of medieval Ashkenaz.

It also marks the vertex of the trajectory in that particular swing of the historiographical pendulum. Criticism of Baer's views was fairly prompt. Isaiah Sonne published a trenchant critique in 1949, following the appearance of Baer's monograph on Christian Spain.[179] Sonne targets Baer's dichotomy between the internally Jewish, popular (*völkisch*), mythical mode of thinking and the rationality that had its origins in Greco-Arabic philosophy. He notes that Baer revised the traditional view by hailing the thirteenth century, when the anti-Maimunist and pietist-ascetic forces took on the philosophical-hedonistic culture of Spain, as a renaissance of the Jewish life force, instead of viewing it as the end of the Golden Age and the commencement of a long era of intellectual and spiritual decline. More to the point in the present context, Sonne remarks that Baer's revision "means the substitution of Germany, the very heart of pietistic religiosity and mystical leanings, for Spain as the center of gravity of the Jewish creative spirit in the Middle Ages."[180]

Baer's glorification of popular religion, Sonne notes, was common in Germany between the two world wars, as was the attribution of primacy to Ashkenazic over Sephardic civilization.[181] Sonne sees Baer's conception as fundamentally flawed, because, he argues, the human mind is both rational and irrational. Hence Baer's concept of the Jewish life force is a misconception, for it recognizes the mythical mind-set as authentically Jewish and stigmatizes the rational one as alien, whereas, Sonne argues, both are not only Jewish but also universal. As an alternative to Baer's approach, Sonne proposes that the historian's task is to situate developments and trends in Jewish creativity and spirituality within the broader context of those appearing in the broader stream of humanity at any given point in time and space.

Baer's neat delineation of the axes of Ashkenazic martyrdom and Sephardic apostasy also comes in for criticism. Sonne makes the argument that the number of forced converts among Rhineland Jewry in 1096 was not insignificant and hence that martyrdom was far from a universal response in that famous case, as Baer's portrait of Ashkenazic culture implies. By the same token, Sonne calls for a more balanced view of the martyrdom of Iberian Jewry. He maintains that the Jews of both Spain and Franco-Germany exhibited both types of responses to persecution and thus that neither is particular to, or typical of, one center or the other. Sonne also questions Baer's conviction that the treachery of Sepharad is to be attributed to the pernicious influence of rationalism.

Another critique of Baer's conception of Jewish history, by Ephraim Shmueli, appeared shortly before Baer's death. Baer is guilty, writes Shmueli, of the "Ashkenazization" of Judaism, because he applies a double standard to the cultures of medieval Spain and Ashkenaz: "He viewed anything that Sephardic Jewry absorbed from *Hasidei Ashkenaz* as fundamental and beautiful, and at the same time everything else was, in his eyes, spiritually flawed vis-à-vis that particular 'unique historical force' that constitutes the essence of Judaism."[182]

The heart of Shmueli's critique is that, in his own view, Judaism is characterized by heterogeneity and by the divisive struggle between competing ways of life and streams of thought, as opposed to Baer's monistic notion of a single, coherent doctrine and lifestyle. Thus, whereas Baer takes Salo Baron to task for failing to identify Judaism's immanent principle, Shmueli applauds Baron's pluralistic approach, with its emphasis on diversity and conflict.[183] Shmueli offers his own pluralistic perspective on medieval Judaism, which identifies three camps: the rabbinic (or Talmudist), the poetic-philosophical, and the mystical. He faults Baer for accepting as fact the rabbis' and mystics' denigration of the poetic-philosophical camp of medieval Spain, without acknowledging that this was a partisan critique.[184] Like Sonne, Shmueli emphasizes that in the period of Spain's travails, apostasy was not only the prerogative of the "Averroists" or poetic-philosophical camp but also of its competitors, and conversely that martyrdom can also be located in both groups.[185]

These criticisms did not resonate. Baer's interpretation of medieval Jewish history held sway until his death, and only in the last generation of historical scholarship has it undergone a gradual but far-reaching reevaluation. The present study picks up strands from Sonne's and Shmueli's critiques, as well as issues raised by historians over the last quarter of a century. Although Baer's notion of the immanent life force of Judaism and his Hasmonean ideal are no longer part of the currency of historical dialogue, residual traces of his interpretation are easily discerned in post-Baer historiography, specifically the heroic image of Ashkenazic Jewry in the Middle Ages. As noted, this image was not Baer's innovation, and thus the revision presented here addresses a much broader historiographical consensus. Nonetheless, Baer's domination of the field and his clear and extreme formulation of the thesis of Ashkenazic heroism make him the pivot and point of departure for our discussion.

Two   Adumbrations

Historians routinely assemble data in an effort to offer a cogent narrative or to explain a puzzling phenomenon. Certain events or figures usually stand out as major landmarks or foci of investigation, and facts deemed of lesser importance play a supporting role, as illustrative or explanatory. The task is often to locate points of contact between the discrete pieces of information to create a coherent chain of links, allowing for smooth, logical movement from one landmark to another. Fitting together the pieces is a creative act, for the sources reflect their own generic contexts rather than the agenda of the modern student of history. The forging of links between landmarks is also the crucial act of historical interpretation, on which the strength and coherence of a presentation depends. The audience critically evaluates the proposed hierarchy of events or phenomena and considers whether "secondary" ones really do support those labeled primary.

This chapter is just such an evaluation. I focus on Jewish-Christian relations in early medieval Ashkenaz. Pictured as a landscape, Carolingian dominion and the First Crusade are familiar and towering signposts, and the territory in between is the lowland, invisible or insignificant. The Carolingian era is a watershed because the reign of Charlemagne saw a noticeable intensification of the Jewish presence in northern Europe. Jews are mentioned in imperial legislation and in Latin chronicles, and they are depicted as cosmopolitan merchants with connections at Charlemagne's court in Aachen. Louis the Pious continued his father's political and economic tradition, granting the Jews liberal conditions of settlement, specifically in the charter issued to the Jews of Lyon in 825. This document offered terms so liberal as to contravene the Catholic doctrine of "witness," which mandated that the Jews be tolerated in a position of subservience and humiliation, so as to testify to their crime of deicide. This arrogant trampling of Church doctrine triggered a literary response, in the form of a series of essays by Agobard, the local archbishop. Agobard's effort was futile, as was the anti-Jewish campaign of Amulo, Agobard's successor to the archbishopric of Lyon.

The period of Carolingian rule was therefore a fruitful one in European Jewish history. Development continued in the tenth and eleventh centuries as Jewish communities sprang up in the Rhineland and new intellectual centers emerged. The next milestone was the destruction wrought upon Rhineland Jewry in 1096 and the simultaneous persecution of Jews in France and eastern Europe.[1] For history books to move from golden age to catastrophe is sensible as well as predictable because—as in journalism—so long as the security and prosperity of European Jewry continued unhindered, there was little to report. Salo Baron put it this way: "It is in the nature of historical records to transmit to posterity the memory of extraordinary events, rather than of the ordinary flow of life. A community which lived in peace for decades may have given the medieval chronicler no motive to mention it, until a sudden outbreak of popular violence, lasting a few days, attracted widespread attention."[2] However, the tranquility of the pre-Crusade period contrasts starkly with the ferocity of the crusader onslaught, and this dissonance begs explanation.

James Parkes saw no particular need to explain the anti-Jewish violence of the First Crusade because he viewed it as consistent with the persecution that dated back to the dawn of the Middle Ages: "The whole Carolingian interlude and its survivals stand as an unexpected interruption of what is otherwise a logical sequence from Theodosius II, to the establishment of the badge and the ghetto, to the accusations of ritual murder, the poisoning of wells, and the profanation of the Host."[3] Parkes saw the liberality of the Carolingian age as the anomaly; for him the First Crusade was part of a continuum that not only harked back to the harsh measures of the early Christian centuries but also anticipated the horrors that awaited the Jews in centuries to come.

A more common strategy has been to look back on the boring landscape and to question whether it was indeed as serene as it appeared.

For many scholars a medley of isolated developments from the death of Louis the Pious in the middle of the ninth century to 1096 presaged the doom that awaited Ashkenazic Jewry. Noting the failure of Amulo to influence Charles the Bald to implement anti-Jewish legislation, Graetz adds that "gradually the poison spread from the clergy to the people and the princes."[4] Baron formulates this approach clearly: "In retrospect the events of 1096 appear as but a culmination of anti-Jewish trends gradually building up among the Western masses over several generations."[5] Similarly, Léon Poliakov writes that the persecution of the early eleventh century "was merely the premonitory sign of that tide of religious enthusiasm that . . . would also give the signal for the great persecutions."[6] Notwithstanding disclaimers about the tentative, speculative nature of conclusions based on source materials that are both meager and heterogeneous, most surveys give the impression that the massacres of the First Crusade were the predictable and inevitable denouement of a century and a half of accelerating hostility to European Jews and Judaism.

In this chapter I probe the soundness of this conclusion by examining both the primary and secondary sources about the incidents that have served as landmarks on the historiographical map. I offer no new data; on the contrary, my point is that the familiar, traditional sources have yet to receive careful scrutiny in the context of the adumbration thesis. Nor do I suggest an alternative to the current consensus, primarily because any such alternative would inevitably exhibit the very methodological weakness identified here: the conflation of sources from diverse places, times, and contexts without sufficient regard for the particular historical context of each.

After Louis the Pious

The historiographical dynamic with which we are concerned portrays a reaction, following the death in 840 of Louis the Pious, against the favorable status that Jews had enjoyed during the reigns of Charlemagne and Louis. Allegedly the clergy, primarily at the episcopal level, were the force behind this reaction. This trend may seem implied by the intensive anti-Jewish lobbying in which the archbishops of Lyon,

Agobard and Amulo, engaged in Louis's day. Alternatively, it may have been simply the continuation of a consistently hostile policy. Throughout the early Middle Ages, church councils generated a steady flow of canons restricting social relations between Jews and Christians, banning sovereigns from placing Jews in positions of authority (political and social) vis-à-vis Christians, and combating Jewish efforts to limit conversion to Christianity. These measures were consistent with Augustine's doctrine of witness, later echoed by Gregory the Great and integrated into the papacy's theological doctrine.

It is difficult to know who read this sort of legislation and what impact, if any, it had on the streets of Europe. In Carolingian Europe, many were illiterate and European politics were so chaotic that no one in a position of authority could publish a document with any confidence that its contents would be honored. This was also true for popes and archbishops, whose decrees were dismissed not only by kings and noblemen but often by lesser Church officials, who commanded respect within the limited radius of their local religious and political domain.

Moreover, attempts to limit Jewish power and Jewish-Christian interaction suggest that the reality was actually the reverse and that even after the Carolingian era Jews exercised substantial political influence and socialized freely with their Christian neighbors. This is uncertain, for documents with virtually identical complaints and remedies were issued periodically, but these documents may have been published by rote and might therefore be useless as indicators of social conditions. Perhaps even the promulgators of these canons did not take them terribly seriously. In brief, to draw conclusions about the *sitz-im-leben* of the edicts of a particular church council would require more knowledge than is usually available about the conditions at the specific time and place of the council.

The immediate focus of these deliberations is the legislation issued by the church council in Meaux and Paris in 846. This body ordered Jewish children removed from their homes and placed in monasteries or in the homes of Christians. The legislation states that no new synagogues may be built and that if any are, they should be handed over to the Church and their builders fined. Jews are barred from holding government positions or any positions of honor and dignity. Jews are forbidden to plead their cases in Christian courts, nor may Christians plead in Jewish courts. Christians who dine with Jews or fraternize with them are to be punished. Jews and Christians are not allowed to marry, and Christians and Jews may not interact in public during the week of Easter. There are also a number of statutes about Jewish slave ownership.[7]

All these canons had been legislated by earlier councils. For example, the prohibition against holding government positions appears in the legislation of the council in Rheims in 624–625,[8] and the rule that Jews may not appear in public during Holy Week was legislated by the council in Orléans in 538 and in Macon in 581.[9] It is therefore difficult to know why they were legislated again at this juncture and what conclusions can be drawn from their current appearance. It is also clear that the common folk, and perhaps even the nobles, did not share the anti-Jewish animus of Agobard, Amulo, or the churchmen of Meaux-Paris. Of particular significance is Charles the Bald's rejection, at the Diet of Epernay in June 846, of the council's anti-Jewish program, specifically canon 73, which mandated the separation of Jewish children from their parents and their upbringing by Christians.[10] It would appear, then, that the Meaux-Paris decrees highlight the happy state of Jewish affairs at this historical juncture. In any case, a century and a half separates the Meaux-Paris council from the First Crusade, which bears no resemblance to the issues raised in the Meaux-Paris decrees, other than the fact that both incidents sought in some fashion to harm the Jews. This generalization is utterly banal, and it is not even completely justified, for the canons are nothing more than reiterations of the remarkably consistent Jewry policy of the Catholic Church.

The exception to this characterization is the clause that calls for the removal of Jewish children from their homes and for their forcible baptism, which stands in contradiction to the doctrine of witness. The anti-Jewish campaign of the Meaux-Paris council appears, therefore, to have been rooted in the radical, violent policies of the seventh-century Visigothic kings and clergy. For example, canon 60 of the fourth Council of Toledo (633) also calls for the separation of Jewish children from their parents and their transfer to monasteries or Christian families.[11] The Visigoths of Spain were proximate to southern France and are thought to have influenced its leading clergy, Agobard and later Amulo. If so, this clause indicates that the Meaux-Paris legislation represents an attempt, presumably by Amulo, to unravel the favorable Jewry policy adopted by Charlemagne and Louis the Pious and to implement the more aggressive line adopted and zealously pursued by the kings of Spain. The context of the Meaux-Paris decrees is therefore narrow and immediate and reflects conditions remote from those that existed in Franco-Germany on the eve of the First Crusade.

A similarly specific historical context characterizes the successful efforts, sometime between 830 and 850, to convert large numbers of Jews, including children. The letter documenting this event does not say that the conversions were the result of coercion; on the contrary, it states that conversionary sermons preached in the synagogue helped facilitate them.[12] Ostensibly, then, this episode is the unusually successful culmination of a campaign by zealous clergy to convert Jews, a perennial goal of the Catholic Church. However, the primary source, a letter from a bishop to Emperor Lothair, actually tells a different tale. It records that some parents from Chalon-sur-Sâone, Mâcon, and Vienne had spirited their children away to Arles, implying that the conversion campaign contained an element of coercion. This policy is perfectly in keeping with what we know of Agobard and Amulo's anti-Jewish agitation, particularly their liberal attitude toward forced conversion.

Just a year or two after the Meaux-Paris council, the Danes conquered Bordeaux and despoiled and burned it. A Latin chronicle states that this happened "because of the treacherous Jews."[13] This incident also has been cited as indicative of a serious downturn in Jewish-Christian relations.[14] The same chronicle records that the Jews of Barcelona handed the city over to the Moors in 852, who destroyed it, with great loss of life.[15] A third accusation in the same text relates that when Charles the Bald fell ill with fever in 877, his Jewish physician Sedechias poisoned him with a medical potion, which killed him after eleven days.[16]

The third accusation, although clearly anti-Jewish, can be situated within the broader context of the popular distrust of medieval physicians, whose cures truly were as likely to kill as to cure.[17] When the victim of a doctor's ministrations was a powerful political figure, the suspicion of foul play was inevitable and need not be included in a scheme of antisemitic activities. There is therefore no need to doubt that Charles the Bald died at the hands of his Jewish physician. This is precisely why it is fascinating that the chronicle of Regino of Prüm reports first that Charles the Bald took ill and died and only then adds the version involving his Jewish physician.

> Rumor has it that a certain Jew, named Sedechias, gave him a deadly potion to drink. He belonged to his household, and was said to have singular experience at the healing of the body. He later became a charlatan, and deluded people with incantations and magical acts. He [Charles] actually died on the day preceding the ninth of October.[18]

Regino expresses mild doubt about the historicity of the Sedechias story. This is remarkable, not only because the truthfulness of anti-Jewish accusations was rarely challenged in the Middle Ages but also because it was unnecessary, for Jewish loyalty to the monarchy could have been salvaged by portraying the incident as an "occupational hazard." In fact, Regino does not say that Sedechias poisoned the king intentionally but rather implies that he was incompetent.

The assertions of Jewish treachery during the invasions have as their common cultural context the perception that in their efforts to repel the Vikings and Saracens, the Franks were waging war on behalf of their faith as well as their land. This identification of the Frankish military force as the army of Christ dates back to the days of Charles Martel and must have seemed entirely realistic in the face of latter-day non-Christian enemy forces. From this point of view, accusations of Jewish treachery during these wars are scarcely surprising, because the Jews, who were traditionally depicted as the enemies of Christ, Christianity, and Christendom, had been the target of this claim for centuries.[19]

This group of three accusations underscores the importance of context for the interpretation of texts. Bernard Bachrach notes that the source of these anti-Jewish reports is the annals of Saint Bertin, which were then being kept by Bishop Prudence of Troyes (835–861) and Archbishop Hincmar of Rheims (861–882).[20] It is impossible to pinpoint which of these figures wrote the entry in question, but its anti-Jewish content suggests that it was Hincmar. Ben-Zion Dinur notes that Prudence of Troyes (whom Dinur thought wrote the text) was a close associate of Louis the Pious, making him an unlikely candidate.[21]

For Hincmar to fabricate such charges, on the other hand, accords with his known penchant for anti-Jewish rhetoric and particularly with his leadership role at the Council of Meaux-Paris.[22] Hincmar's authorship makes it seem possible that the accusations are either fictitious or misrepresentations of the historical record.[23]

It is therefore surprising that Bachrach claims that the stories of the betrayal of Bordeaux and Barcelona may be true, albeit distorted. He hypothesizes that Charles the Bald, who was known to have continued the pro-Jewish policy of his Carolingian forebears, prevailed upon the Jews of Bordeaux to side with the Norsemen in order to enable him to capture the city from William, the ally of his enemy, Peppin. The ploy succeeded, but William fled to Barcelona, and so once again Charles enlisted the aid of his Jewish protégés. This time conquest resulted in William's capture and execution.[24]

Bachrach's suggestion confirms the information presented in the Saint Bertin annals but depicts the Jews as acting in the service of their Carolingian benefactor rather than of the pagan, alien enemy force. It explains why the Jews would act treacherously despite the support they enjoyed from Charles the Bald. Although it remains entirely speculative, it removes this group of stories from the category of events that supposedly foreshadowed the First Crusade massacres, because the stories are not libels at all but the truth. Moreover, the Jews are described as masters of their fate (and of the fate of others, too), whereas in 1096 they were the pathetic victims of an overwhelmingly powerful enemy.

The next supposed harbinger is nearly incomprehensible. Odoranne de Saint-Pierre de Sens reports in his chronicle that Ansegisus, the archbishop of Sens (871–883), expelled the Jews and the nuns "certainly with cause" (certe de causa) and forbade them to return.[25] Baron believes that this incident illustrates that "the hierarchy, often enjoying political power as well, felt free occasionally to depart from the canonical doctrines of basic toleration of Jews."[26] This is no doubt true, yet it does not bring us closer to an understanding of what happened here and why.

Odoranne does not record a precise date, although he supplies the date of Ansegisus's death, 883, which is the terminus ad quem. The dating of the incident, however, is only one of many mysterious aspects. More perplexing and significant is the expulsion of the nuns from the city. What could have motivated the archbishop to expel them? Simon Schwarzfuchs reads the opaque phrase "certe de causa" as an allusion to unseemly behavior; he links the two expulsions and supposes that the Jews were expelled from Sens "for having seen too much of the local nuns, who were expelled at the same time."[27] This suggestion is not only groundless but also far-fetched, for the crime of illicit relations would not seem to justify the punishment of the entire population of both groups. Henri Gross notes that, although no other record exists of the expulsion of the nuns of Sens, in 876 they were evacuated from the city, for fear that a Norman invasion was imminent.[28] This possibility, Gross believes, was also behind the very real expulsion of the Jews, who, he conjectures, fell under suspicion of serving as a fifth column, as in Bordeaux and Barcelona. This suggestion places the expulsion in a relevant and plausible historical context, but the nuns supply the link to the Norman invasion, and it makes no sense for Odoranne to have described their evacuation as an expulsion, particularly because he adds that they were not allowed to return.

Bernhard Blumenkranz wonders whether the report was perhaps an error on Odoranne's part, because the Sens expulsion has no external confirmation.[29] This reason is not compelling, for much of the history of these centuries is known from isolated reports. Nevertheless, to shift attention from the testimony to the witness is a sensible critical move. Odoranne wrote his chronicle sometime in the second quarter of the eleventh century,[30] and the chronological lag per se raises concerns about its credibility.

A curious coincidence also raises doubts about the historicity of the incident. A rabbinic document from eleventh-century France offers evidence that at the very time Odoranne put pen to paper, the Jews of Sens were accused of destroying a Christian statue and were stiffly fined.[31] This may signify that Odoranne was projecting onto an earlier period the accusation hurled against Sens Jewry in his own day. If, indeed, "certe de causa" implies unseemly behavior, the defilement of a sacred symbol would seem to fall under that rubric.

If, nonetheless, Ansegisus really did expel the Jews of Sens, what would Odoranne's point of view on the matter likely have been? Odoranne was a monk at the monastery of Saint-Pierre-le-Vif in Sens, and presumably he would have sought to glorify the archbishops of yesteryear. A possible context for such a tendency may have been the pressure exerted by Robert the Pious in the early eleventh century on Count Eudes II of Blois and Champagne to bring the archbishopric of Sens into the royal domain. After Robert's death in 1031, his heir, Henry I, exerted great efforts to gain control of Sens, including warfare, but he was thwarted by Eudes.[32] Historical sources testifying to the broad authority traditionally exercised by the archbishop over the local Jewish community would provide much needed ammunition for those engaged in the contemporary struggle to retain autonomy from royal authority.

Regardless of the accuracy of Odoranne's report, the relevance of a decree of expulsion to the catastrophe of 1096 is also questionable. An act of expulsion would resemble the massacres of 1096 if it represented a theologically based rejection of the principle of limited toleration, à la Visigothic Spain. Even then the comparison has severe limits, which would have to be articulated. In the case of Sens, however, the alleged expulsion is said to have been some sort of judicial punishment, which seems altogether irrelevant to the persecutions of the First Crusade.

In Baron's narrative, "outbreaks" in Metz in 888 are another station on the road to 1096.[33] This apparently refers to the anti-Jewish indictment read by Guntbert, the primate of Metz, to the Council of Metz in that year and to the canons adopted by the council that forbade Christians to eat and drink with Jews or to receive food and drink from them.[34] This is an excellent example of a recycled canon, for the prohibition against eating with Jews had been proclaimed at seven previous church councils, beginning with the Council of Elvira in 306.[35] Similarly, the prohibition against Jews maintaining in their homes Christian nursemaids, servants (male and female), slaves, and day laborers had already been legislated a number of times, such as by the Council of Orléans in 538.[36] Moreover, as stated, this sort of legislation testifies to the opposite reality rather than to a deterioration in Jewish-Christian relations.

Some of the episodes of persecution that are described as harbingers of 1096 occurred in the German lands; two are reported for the tenth century. The Council of Erfurt (932), convened by Emperor Henry I, referred to a letter that Henry and Archbishop Hildibert of Mainz had received from the Doge of Venice and the local patriarch, telling of a miraculous victory of the Christians in a religious confrontation with the Jews of Jerusalem, which was followed by the conversion of "all the Jews on this side of the sea" (*omnes Judei qui citra mare erant*). The letter reports that after this incident, the Patriarch of Jerusalem successfully appealed to Emperor Romanus Lepicanus to compel the Jews to convert. The doge closes with a similar appeal to Henry to force all the Jews in his realm to accept baptism or depart. However, Henry, who presided over the council, chose to ignore the canon on forced baptism, as Charles the Bald had done in 846.[37] The issue of the legality of forced baptism, or rather its strict definition, was not new and would remain problematic throughout history; it neither signals a deterioration in the Jews' status nor presages approaching doom.[38]

Pressure to forcibly baptize the Jews mounted again in Germany in 938 or 939. According to a papal document, Archbishop Frederick of Mainz asked Pope Leo VII whether he should force the Jews to be baptized or expel them from the city. The pope replied that preaching, rather than force, was the appropriate method for bringing about conversion but that Jews who prove obdurate could certainly be expelled, "for we do not need to have anything to do with the enemies of God" (*quia non debemus cum inimicis dei societatem habere*).[39]

Again the possibility is suggested, this time by Kenneth Stow, that the incident in question simply did not happen: "It is also possible that the texts recounting these conversionary pressures are once again the products of monastic fiction, founded on the difficulties which the Jews in the Byzantine Empire then were facing [under Romanus Lepicanus], and perhaps all growing out of one original literary source."[40] This may be true, but if so, the fabricator could have cast aside diplomatic restraint and had the pope issue a ringing endorsement of the use of force.

If, on the other hand, the story is true, the significant element may be the identities of writer and recipient. Blumenkranz suggests that the exchange of letters expresses the conflict between the archbishop and

Otto the Great regarding the authority of Church and State. Otto had continued the liberal Jewry policy of his Carolingian predecessors, and Archbishop Frederick enlisted papal intervention in an attempt to bolster ecclesiastical independence.[41] The episode reflects the significance that control over the Jews often assumed during periods of intense domestic political competition. Although to both the persecutor of the Jews and their defender the issue of political authority mattered as much as, or more than, Jewry policy, this type of conflict could have disastrous results, as the expulsion of the Jews from England demonstrates. In this respect, the exchange between the archbishop of Mainz and the pope adumbrates the struggles of the thirteenth century rather than the storm that broke in 1096.

Apart from the litany of minor episodes of hostility to Jews and Judaism, scholars highlight the heightened animosity toward Jews that was expressed annually in Latin Europe during the period of Easter. The bishops of Béziers delivered passionate sermons against the Jews, authorizing the audience to attack them and pelt their homes with stones in revenge for the stoning of Jesus. The regulations of the order of St. Vincent of Chalon-sur-Sâone state that this practice was observed in that city as well, on Palm Sunday.[42] Another Easter ritual was the *Colaphus Judaeorum* of Toulouse, in which a local Jew would receive a blow in symbolic punishment for the Crucifixion. Both practices were officially abolished in the twelfth century.

Graetz saw in these customs symptoms of the decline of Carolingian rule and the fragmentation of the Frankish body politic. He writes that for the Jews, the loss of Carolingian support opened the door to their persecution at the hands of local leaders, secular and clerical.[43] James Parkes understood the *colaphus* in much the same way.

> From the standpoint of historical continuity, it is the steady effort to reintroduce the laws and canons of Rome, the introduction of new regulations against the Jews, the stoning of Chalons and Béziers, the buffeting of Toulouse, and not the friendship and free criticism of the Court of Louis which are the significant episodes of the period. By the beginning of the eleventh century the last flicker of the Carolingian freedom expired; and before the middle a new series of outrages heralded the massacres of the First Crusade.[44]

Baron's interpretation is less sweeping. He also cites the Toulouse *cola-phus* and the Béziers violence as indicative of a downturn but notes that they were limited to southern France.[45] I would stress the differences between ecclesiastical legislation and customs that persisted over time. We have seen a number of examples of restrictive canons and the difficulties involved in their interpretation. As a rule, efforts to stigmatize the Jews and curtail their social interaction with Christians highlight the normalcy of Jewish-Christian relations. There are even indications of philo-Judaic sentiments in the early Middle Ages, as Léon Poliakov asserts.

> The very terms of the anti-Jewish propaganda in the ninth century show that at this time there was no trace of a specific, popular anti-Semitism. On the contrary, it seems that Judaism still exerted a definite attraction for the Christian population. In general, one may say that so long as a solidly dogmatized Christianity had not established its complete ascendancy over men's souls, these remained receptive to Jewish propaganda.[46]

The crucial difference between the Eastertide customs and the intolerant canons of church councils was the participation of the masses in the Eastertide customs. Whatever the motivation of the bishop in the pulpit, words led to deeds, and the distance from here to the massacres of 1096 no longer seems an unbridgeable chasm. However, the remarkable feature of the *colaphus* and stoning was that it was an annual event, a ritual of sorts, apart from which life seems to have proceeded peacefully. This paradox was true not only for ninth-century Provence, or for crusader violence, but also for the Middle Ages in general. Cecil Roth puts it this way:

> How a man was treated throughout the year was more important than how he was treated during Easter-tide. . . . The picture of the honoured Jewish merchant who travelled about unmolested throughout the year, but was stoned and buffetted at Easter-tide, may not be logical, but it may nevertheless be true.[47]

Roth stresses the perennial nature of the Easter rituals, and his image of a relatively stable environment suggests that the Jews of Europe could have expected to continue their lives as minority enclaves until the end of time.

992

As the first millennium drew to a close, an incident occurred that is among the most colorful and curious of the period's episodes in Jewish-Christian relations. Unlike the incidents surveyed thus far, the 992 affair is derived from a Hebrew source. It is a fragment of a letter, extant in just one manuscript, recounting the miraculous salvation of the Jewish community of Le Mans from destruction at the hands of a malicious apostate, Sehok ben Esther.[48] This blackguard left his home in Blois and wandered from town to town, supporting himself by presenting himself as a Jew to Jewish communities and receiving alms from them. Eventually his trick became known and his income dwindled. Arriving in Le Mans, Sehok settled in the home of his maternal aunt. After falling into a disagreement with "Levi," a Jewish neighbor, Sehok hired twelve Christian acquaintances from Blois to kill Levi. Levi was mortally wounded but nevertheless identified his assassins. One murderer demanded his fee, but Sehok refused to pay, whereupon the killer took some citizens of Le Mans hostage.

Elders from the Le Mans community rebuked Sehok for his misconduct, and this made him determined to destroy the Jewish community. He formed a human image out of wax, secretly placed it in the synagogue, inside the ark, and then informed the lord of the land (sar ha'aretz) that the Jews were accustomed to piercing this image with a goad[49] three times a year, to (symbolically) destroy him, as their ancestors had killed Jesus. Sehok proposed that the Jews be expelled and their property confiscated and distributed among the lord's servants and subjects. This action would hopefully encourage other sovereigns to act with similar zeal against the people that habitually blaspheme against the lord and his religion. Sehok continued that the Jews similarly defile the image of Christ and daily proclaim imprecations against the lord's name from texts they have composed for that express purpose.

The lord agreed to investigate and to appoint Sehok as his viceroy if his story proved true, or otherwise to execute him, presumably as a punishment for slander. On the following Saturday the synagogue was searched and the image discovered. Accused of treason, those present accused Sehok of plotting against them and undertook to swear to their innocence. Sehok called on the Jews to appoint someone to engage him in a duel, which would determine the fate of the entire community. The lord accepted this suggestion. The Jews demurred, stating that they were unaccustomed to this gentile practice, and offered to pay rather than have their claim and fate tested in this manner. But the lord was adamant and even ordered that the Jews' homes be searched for the texts containing the curses, although none were found. The Jews decided to fast and pray on the following day. Many Christians saw this incident as a sign that the time had come to destroy the Jews, and a certain monk urged the lord to make an end of them and to write to other sovereigns to do the same.

The climax of the story is missing, although the title makes clear that the Jewish community was saved.[50] Robert Chazan writes, "Only two incidents mar the calm of Jewish life in northern France prior to 1096," of which the 992 affair was one. This formulation reflects Chazan's view that the century or so preceding the First Crusade was not replete with ominous occurrences,[51] although Chazan does say that the story reflects "the generally unsettled conditions in late tenth-century France," which he claims were characterized by instability and lawlessness.[52] Other historians, however, including Baron, Schwarzfuchs, and Avraham Grossman, list the 992 affair among the *many* persecutions of this period.[53]

Rarely has this text been subjected to careful scrutiny, and basic questions of historical criticism have yet to be addressed. Abraham Berliner and David Hoffmann published the document in 1878 and noted that their source was a Parma manuscript.[54] Subsequent references to the incident have not gone so far as to identify the manuscript in question, much less describe its basic features. The source is written on parchment, in a neat hand, by an experienced copyist. The writing is an Ashkenazic semicursive script typical of the late thirteenth century.[55] Although there is every reason to suppose that the copyist worked from an earlier text, this remains the only existing evidence of the incident under discussion, and the chronological distance between source and event arouses suspicions as to the story's authenticity.[56]

The apostate's devilish plot seems anachronistic, because of its similarity to the host libel, which appeared in the thirteenth century. The association of Sehok's charge with the host accusation is explicit in the text, when he compares the Jews' crime to the piercing of Jesus. This is the plot's central element, and if it is a later invention, the authenticity of the story is undermined. However, to assume that the text is entirely the product of a later writer's imagination would, I believe, be going too far. As Chazan points out, the omnipotent role of the count in the story, particularly in the judicial realm, accurately reflects the conditions of the late tenth century, the early years of Capetian rule, and is indeed a mark of authenticity. Moreover, notwithstanding the history of the host libel, sympathetic magic was certainly not a thirteenth-century invention, and the incident could have occurred earlier. It seems more likely, therefore, that the incident is not pure invention but that the historical record was colored by patterns of thinking and writing from a later period.[57]

The rhetoric used to describe the sense of crisis is particularly suspect of anachronism. Following the decision to conduct the duel, the narrator has this to say:

> On that day the sighing of the heart of the entire people increased, and the groan of their wailing was very heavy. Their heart melted within them and the city was perplexed. The entire community said: Alas! God has decreed destruction upon the remnant of his people and his patrimony among the gentiles of the land. And now, assemble, every learned person, and pour out your heart to Him in fasting and weeping and lamentation. Perhaps God will have mercy upon the remnant of his patrimony, and not destroy them in his anger among the nations, for the great wrath has emerged from God our Lord [Num. 17.11], on account of our sins. Who knows, maybe God will reconsider and regret his great anger and we shall not be lost [Jonah 3.9], for the God of Israel is merciful, patient, compassionate and regretful of calamity.[58]

The rhetoric of total destruction in this passage strongly resembles that of the Hebrew narratives of the First Crusade. They also speak about the eradication of the "remnant" and have the Jews respond to the sense of impending disaster with fasting, weeping, and lamentation.[59] In the 992 affair, however, the rhetoric appears somewhat exaggerated, not only because the Jews were ultimately spared but also because the lord never comes especially close to sanctioning their annihilation. Therefore, although the writer (and the reader with him) reaches the dizzying heights of salvation by first plunging to the depths of despair, the lachrymose tone seems affected and likely reflects the awful 1096 experience.

The quoted passage alludes to the stories of Korah and of Jonah but most of all to the Purim tale from the Book of Esther, and this is also typical of the First Crusade narratives.[60] The reference to the "perplexed city" is drawn from Esther 3:15, but more important, the dramatis personae appear to be modeled after those of the Esther tale. Sehok is a Haman figure, not only on account of his determination to eradicate the Jewish people but also because he promises to enrich the sovereign's coffers with the Jews' money if they are destroyed. In addition, just as Haman's plot was an outgrowth of his initial clash with Mordechai, an early conflict with Levi triggers Sehok's decision to persecute the entire community. Furthermore, when Sehok exhorts the lord to decree the Jews' ruin, he echoes the argument of Ahasuerus's advisers when he claims that other nations would follow the lord's course of action. And just as in the Purim story, Sehok stands to win appointment as the lord's deputy if he is victorious, but he also risks execution. The story lacks an Esther or a Mordechai, who engineers the Jews' salvation, but the analogy to Purim suggests that Levi may have filled this slot.

The lord also fits the Purim analogy, for he is a perfect Ahasuerus figure: potentially dangerous but for the most part benign and not an antisemite. Why else, one wonders, would he threaten Sehok with death if the accusation proved untrue? Moreover, in light of the narrator's rhetoric of destruction and of the lord's rage when the waxen image is discovered, it comes as something of a surprise when, rather than immediately decree the Jews' destruction, the lord appears to heed their protestations. The lord's unexpected prudence is a setback for Sehok, who attempts to wrest victory from the jaws of defeat by challenging the Jews to a duel, in effect conceding that his attempted manipulation has failed.

The nature of Sehok's accusation also has Purim associations. A number of sources attest that in late antiquity and the Middle Ages Jews interpreted the hanging of Haman as a prefiguration of the Crucifixion and therefore hanged or crucified an image of Haman-Jesus on Purim, to the consternation and wrath of their Christian neighbors.[61] Whether the narrator used the symbolic crucifixion in the service of the Purim theme or vice versa we cannot know.

The late date of the manuscript coupled with the post-1096 rhetoric of destruction and the Purim motif explains the sense that the Le Mans story foreshadows the catastrophe of the First Crusade. The actual plot, historical or not, bears almost no resemblance to the events that took place in the Rhineland. On the other hand, Chazan sees the tale as a harbinger of the political fortunes of French Jewry in later centuries: "It was rulers with unrestricted power over the Jews who were responsible for the persecutions."[62] This was to be the political pattern of medieval France that repeatedly proved so disastrous for French Jewry; it also is utterly unrelated to the First Crusade.

1007–1012

A series of anti-Jewish episodes in the early eleventh century figure most prominently among those that supposedly heralded the downturn in Jewish-Christian relations leading up to the crisis of 1096. Blumenkranz writes, "Two interludes of persecution qualify the generally satisfactory conditions of the Jews of Germany at this period. Coming at the beginning and at the end of the 11th century, they pervade in some measure the whole of this century."[63] Similarly, Chazan comments that "in many ways, the tribulations of 1007 through 1012 presaged the far more serious crisis of 1095–6."[64] Richard Landes sums up the scholarly discussion in the following terms:

> The general literature on anti-Semitism tends to see the Crusades
> as the first major outbreak of widespread violence against European
> Jewry, and these and other incidents from the earlier eleventh century,
> when taken into account at all, are considered the clouds of a gathering storm. Most recently some historians have argued for a still later
> turning point.[65] But the unusually high number of both Christian
> and, even more remarkable, Jewish documents relating to the period
> 1009–1012 suggests a possibly greater significance.[66]

Other assessments are more general. H. H. Ben-Sasson writes that "in the West pressure on the Jews began increasing from several sides."[67]

Similarly, Kenneth Stow views the incidents as indications that "Jews had reason to believe that Christian negativity was becoming more firmly entrenched."[68] These positions convey a sense of a downward spiral, without explicitly invoking 1096. Shmuel Shepkaru concludes his discussion of the 992 and 1007 incidents with the generalization that "both Christian insecurity and Jewish behavior of the early eleventh century herald the violent end of this century."[69]

The stories of 1007–1012 have been the subject of lively debate, about issues so fundamental as whether anything at all occurred, and if so, whether we are faced with one, two, or perhaps even three events. The sources are a Hebrew narrative about a chain of events in Normandy in the years 1007–1011, two Latin chronicles that tell what is basically one story about an incident that took place in Orléans in 1010, a report in a Latin chronicle about an episode in Mainz in 1012, and a few Hebrew liturgical poems from the Rhineland in the early eleventh century.

The Hebrew narrative recounts that in 1007 King Robert II (the Pious) of France, on the advice of his advisers, decided to force the Jews of his realm to convert to Christianity or die. The delegates of the Jews chose death and were martyred. A group of women, possibly the martyrs' wives, drowned themselves, and other Jews fled. The elderly, who were unable to escape, were killed, and a scholar named Seigneur is singled out for having managed to curse Christ and Christianity before he was dispatched.

Like the Le Mans story, this section of the 1007 episode echoes the martyrological rhetoric of the First Crusade narratives. The narrator proudly records the French Jews' decision to cling to their faith, and, as in the Hebrew tales of 1096, the faithful extend their necks for slaughter and provoke their adversaries by cursing Christianity. Also similar is the element of women who commit suicide by drowning.[70] Even their last words could have appeared in a First Crusade narrative: "Let us go to the river and drown ourselves, and let not the name of Heaven be violated by us, for holiness has become the subject of trampling in the streets, and our dear one [the subject of] consumation by fire, and death is better for us than life."[71]

The tightest fit between the 1007 story and the First Crusade narratives appears at the outset. The report of the forced conversion campaign opens with the expression "they plotted craftily" (*heʿerimu sod*), which in the Mainz Anonymous, the shortest and probably the earliest of the Hebrew narratives of the First Crusade massacres in the Rhineland, introduces the story that in Worms gentiles falsely accused the Jews of poisoning the local water supply.[72] The source of this expression is Psalm 83:4, in which the psalmist implores God to be avenged of Israel's enemies, who "plot craftily" against them, saying, "Let us wipe them out as a nation; Israel's name will be mentioned no more" (verse 5). The common thread is the plot to wipe out the Jewish people, which in the Crusade narratives is combined with the prayer for vengeance. The threat of annihilation also explains the use, in the opening passage of the 1007 story, of language from the Book of Esther, as in the tale of 992. In a transparent paraphrase of Haman's counsel to Ahasuerus (Esther 3:8), Robert's advisers tell him, "There is one nation, dispersed among all the nations, which does not listen to us, and whose laws are different from the laws of all nations." Reverting to the chapter in Psalms, they then suggest, "Let us wipe them out and Israel's name will not be mentioned."

Surprisingly, not only are the Jews not wiped out, but also the narrative turns into a tale of salvation. The narrator turns to the heroic activity of Jacob ben Yequtiel of Rouen, who protests that only the pope has the authority to force conversion on the Jews or to harm them. "Richard," the count (*peha*), was in the act of decapitating Jacob when the golden thread that was attached to his sword got tangled in his fingers, causing him to stab his hand. Richard sees this as an omen and decides to allow Jacob to travel to Rome and ask the pope to rescind the evil decree.[73] Jacob asks the pope to issue a decree forbidding anyone to subject a Jew to death, damage, extortion, or forced conversion. The pope agrees, and a legate travels throughout the Frankish realm, circulating the favorable papal decree.

The narrator presents abundant information about Jacob and his family and fills his story with specifics, such as precise amounts of money. This is also reminiscent of the realism of the First Crusade narratives, which express the narrator's desire to relate as vivid a tale as possible, in an apparent effort to convince the reader that his report is historically accurate. Yet in both cases the journalistic elements appear together with components of a clearly mythical nature, such as the miracle tale of the golden thread.

The third and final part of the story is about the origins of Jewish settlement in Flanders. We read that Jacob remains in Rome for four years, until the papal legate completes his mission, and he then returns to his family in Lotharingia. Twelve years later, presumably in 1023, Count Baldwin of Flanders invites Jacob and an entourage of thirty Jews to settle in his land. They agree, but Jacob dies three months later, along the river of Arras, and is buried in Rheims.[74]

The text was published from the same Parma manuscript that contains the 992 tale, meaning that it also was written in a German hand of the late thirteenth century.[75] This accords with the literary features of the Crusade narratives, primarily the rhetoric of Purim, as in the 992 episode. This was noted by Kenneth Stow, who also observed that only from the thirteenth century could "Lotharingia" have been used to describe a region that includes Rouen. In addition, there is no evidence of Jewish settlement in Flanders before the thirteenth century. Also, the Anjou coin mentioned in the story went out of circulation in the early thirteenth century, which is precisely when the Limoges pound was first minted.[76] But Stow's main point is that the central message of the text fits the thirteenth-century context. At that time the Jews of Europe, particularly England and France, felt threatened by the anti-Jewish policies of their monarchs, which threatened the Catholic tradition of limited toleration. Papal policy, although restrictive, was fairly consistent, which is why the writer of the 1007 story prefers papal sovereignty over European Jewry.[77] Stow concludes that the story is a thirteenth-century invention, reflecting the issues and developments of its age.

This interpretation has not been universally embraced. Chazan accepts the story's basic historicity and takes issue with the arguments for a thirteenth-century dating.[78] Avraham Grossman concedes that the anachronisms indicate a thirteenth-century composition but sees no reason to dismiss the story as fictitious.[79] Like the 992 affair, no method has been proposed that would authenticate or controvert the story once and for all.

The resemblance between the literary qualities of the 1007 incident and those of the First Crusade narratives proves superficial and illusory when the tale is viewed in its entirety. The 1096-like rhetoric appears only in the opening section about the persecution and martyrdom. The mythological tone of this section, coupled with the manuscript's post-1096 dating, makes it likely that this part is the product of retrospective projection.[80] Moreover, the story's message is one of salvation, not persecution. The political message of the text, as well as the epilogue about the establishment of a new community in Flanders, expresses an optimism that is at odds with the martyrological tales of the twelfth century. Thus the 1007 tale is anything but a harbinger of the Rhineland pogroms, which were, in any case, quite removed from these events, both geographically and chronologically.

The controversial tale of 1007 is only the first piece of the puzzle. The next component, the two Latin accounts, also exhibits problematic features that cast doubt on the accounts' historicity and raise the question of whether they present a single episode of persecution.

In approximately 1025 Ademar of Chabannes, a monastic chronicler from Limoges and Angoulême in Aquitaine, wrote that in 1010 Alduin, the bishop of Limoges, promulgated a law that offered the Jews of that city the choice of conversion or exile. At the same time he ordered Catholic doctors (*doctores divinos*) to begin discussions with the Jews, to win them over to the Christian faith. Three or four Jews were persuaded, but the rest preferred to relocate.[81]

Alduin's initiative borders on forced conversion, an issue at least as old as Agobard, although he does not pressure the Jews to choose between life and death. A link to more ominous developments appears in a variant, which relates that some Jews slit their own throats (*seipsos ferro jugulaverunt*) to avoid baptism (*nolentes baptismum suscipere*). This detail blatantly contradicts the report that the Jews were offered a choice, and scholars have concluded that it is a later interpolation, possibly written after the First Crusade.[82]

Ademar follows the story of the conversionary campaign with the news that in that very year (1010) the Muslims destroyed the Holy Sepulchre of Jerusalem. He explains that this was caused by the Jews of the West (i.e., Latin Europe), who wrote to the East to announce that Western armies were en route to the Holy Land to fight the Saracens.[83] Ademar then reports that in Rome in 1020, the pope ordered a

Jew executed for having ridiculed a crucifix. He also recounts that "at the same time" a Jew was killed in Toulouse on Easter, when the *colaphus* was administered with extreme force.[84] The stories about Rome and Toulouse teach us little or nothing, for they lack corroboration and are plucked from their contextual environment and are in any case isolated incidents. None of these stories is related to the one about the forced conversion of Limoges. The only link between them is that all relate to Jews, toward whom Ademar, the Cluniac monk, was predictably hostile.

By contrast, Radolphus Glaber, a monk writing in Auxerre in approximately 1036, links the Holy Sepulchre story to the episode of anti-Jewish persecution.[85] Glaber records that in 1009 the "Prince of Babylon" (*principis Babilonis*), that is, the Fatimid Caliph, ordered the Church of the Holy Sepulchre destroyed. This, we read, was the result of a plot by the Jews of Orléans, whom Glaber describes as being not only numerous but also "even more arrogant, envious, and insolent than the rest of their brethren."[86] They bribed Robert, a fugitive serf from Moutiers-Sainte-Marie,[87] "a vagabond masquerading as a pilgrim." Robert proceeded to Cairo with letters in Hebrew, warning the caliph that if he did not destroy the Church of the Holy Sepulchre, the Christians would soon occupy his realm. When Robert returned, he was denounced, interrogated, and put to death. The Jews' role became known and a general persecution ensued.

> Once they knew this all the Christians throughout the whole world decided unanimously[88] to drive the Jews from their lands and cities. They became the objects of universal hatred; they were driven from the cities, some were put to the sword, others were drowned in rivers,[89] and many found other deaths; some even took their own lives in diverse ways.[90]

This wave of violence and expulsion left few Jews "in the Roman world." Bishops forbade Christians to have contact with Jews, and this prohibition spurred some to convert, although they soon returned to Judaism. After five years the Jews returned,[91] and in that same year the Christian mother of the caliph began to rebuild the Holy Sepulchre, which generated an upsurge in pilgrimage.

The main point of similarity between the accounts of Glaber and Ademar is the reference to the conversionary initiative and the resultant, albeit temporary, exodus of the Jews from the area.[92] Both historians narrate the Holy Sepulchre tale, but only Glaber views it as the stimulus for the persecution. This explains why Glaber's story is one of slaughter and suicide, which truly presages the gory martyrological tales of 1096, whereas Ademar, except for his later interpolation, reports a religious confrontation that is nonviolent.

Ademar writes only of Limoges, but Glaber records a worldwide assault, which left few Jews in the Roman world. This appears to be an exaggeration, and Glaber is known to have tampered with the historical record.[93] A good and relevant example of this tendency is the series of four stories Glaber relates immediately before the Holy Sepulchre incident. They focus on Count Raynard II of Sens, who is described as having become so enamored of the wicked ways of the Jews that he demanded to be called King of the Jews. Read in context, it is apparent that Raynard never did any such thing. Glaber paints him as deceitful, merciless, and inhumane—traits associated with Jews—in order to justify the conquest of Sens and the ouster of Raynard by King Robert II.[94] Glaber's penchant for creative reportage suggests that his account of the anti-Jewish violence in 1009 is either totally fictitious or wildly exaggerated. Ademar's tale of conversionary pressure is closer to the truth, but it does not foreshadow the cataclysmic clash of the First Crusade, with its violence and martyrdom.

The persecution related in the first part of the 1007 text bears a vague resemblance to the episode narrated by both Ademar and Glaber, but there are geographic and chronological discrepancies between the tales. Furthermore, the sources name various political leaders and depict them in different ways. In the Hebrew text Robert the Pious instigates the persecution and the pope terminates it, but in the Latin chronicles responsibility for the persecution rests with the bishops.[95] For this reason Chazan rejects the 1007 tale and Glaber's version of 1010 and limits himself to the general observation that the sources depict "an extended period of turmoil in northern-European Jewish life."[96]

Having rejected Glaber's description of martyrdom and suicide as false or greatly overstated and having assessed the narrative of 1007 as a retrospective reflection of the First Crusade experience, all three sources boil down to an episode (or perhaps more than one) of a fleeting campaign of forced conversion, the likes of which had already occurred on various occasions, both in the Latin West and in the Byzantine realm. The only real harbinger here is psychological. Glaber's account may be imagined, but it was definitely written before 1096. Thus his description of the martyrdom and self-immolation of the Jews is not an anachronistic projection but a vision of what enraged Christians might (or ought to) do to Jews. The knowledge that this scenario was played out at the end of the century makes the flesh crawl.

The final component in the cluster of sources for the 1007–1012 period concerns the expulsion of the Jews from Mainz by Emperor Henry II in late 1012, recorded in the Quedlinburg annals.[97] This incident seems to find an echo in a Hebrew liturgical poem by Rabbi Gershom ben Judah of Mainz, which laments—in the typically vague, allusive, and hyperbolic language of such poems—an episode in which the Jews face conversion or expulsion.[98] Baron suggests that the expulsion may have affected the Jews of the entire realm, rather than just of Mainz, for the text merely says that the expulsion took place in Mainz.[99] This ambiguity apparently underlies the comment often found that Henry expelled the Jews of Mainz "among other cities."[100]

The background of the expulsion is unclear. Many scholars, beginning with Graetz, link it with the conversion to Judaism of a cleric named Wecelin, a clerk of Duke Conrad, which so enraged Henry that he ordered a court cleric named Henry to refute Wecelin's anti-Christian polemic.[101] The difficulty with this explanation is that Wecelin converted significantly earlier, in 1005 or 1006.[102]

Other historians, including Baron, view the Mainz episode as a consequence of the Holy Sepulchre incident.[103] In fact, Baron neatly knits these stories to that of the persecution of 1007. He posits that in 1012 Henry did not promulgate an edict of expulsion; he revoked one, perhaps as a result of Jacob ben Yequtiel's mission to Rome.[104] In support of this hypothesis, the various tales all deal with a conversionary campaign and are chronologically proximate. On the other hand, each text invokes its own sovereign and has its own particular accent, including thematic undercurrents and textual and contextual difficulties. Therefore there does not seem to be an adequate basis for assuming that the sources concerning 1007–1012 refer to a single event or to a chain of connected incidents.[105]

How the episode ended is also controversial. Baron believes that Henry revoked the decree and allowed its victims to return to Judaism. This conclusion is based on the presence of Jews in Mainz shortly after the expulsion, as attested by a marriage contract given in Mainz on January 30, 1013, by the same Rabbi Gershom to his wife Bonna, in place of the original document, which had been lost.[106] Blumenkranz, however, proposes that Henry did not expel the Jews but merely issued an ultimatum, forcing them to choose between expulsion and forced conversion. If so, the Jews never actually left Mainz but simply returned to Judaism.[107]

In keeping with his overall philosophy of history, Yitzhak Baer sees the Hebrew poetic sources as the first expressions of "the spirit of religious self-sacrifice that was particular to Ashkenaz."[108] Baron thinks that the tale illustrates "the sovereign's inability to stem the rise of those hostile forces which threatened to submerge German Jewry." This, he claims, prompted later leaders to issue charters of settlement and—I would add—presaged the catastrophe of 1096.[109] However, Baron's assessment rests on the unproven—and I believe unwarranted—assumption that Henry acted against his better judgment, and thus there is no reason to view the episode as an omen.

Other assessments are both more general and more conservative. The liturgical poetry, the 1007 story, and the expulsion of Mainz Jewry in 1012 lead Ben-Sasson to conclude that "in the West pressure on the Jews began increasing from several sides," although he adds that "their value to society was still recognized," as is indicated by the charters of 1084 and 1090.[110] Chazan characterizes the various incidents collectively as an "initial crisis of northern Jewry."[111] Stow doubts one can go even this far, on account of the difficulties involved in the interpretation of the sources.[112] The scope and complexity that these problems, some of which have been aired here, warrant a critical and cautious stance.

The Mainz affair might appear to anticipate the catastrophe of 1096 for the simple reason that it took place in Mainz, the sight of the great carnage visited on this Jewish community eighty-four years later. There is, however, no real similarity between the events, and the chronological gap between them is too great to be overlooked. As for the portentous nature of the entire cluster of 1007–1012 incidents, the elimination of the element of martyrdom and suicide (except in Glaber's imagination) from the Holy Sepulchre and 1007 tales robs the events of any basis for comparison with the catastrophe of 1096, for martyrdom was the quintessence of the 1096 experience, as narrated in the sources at our disposal. Moreover, the conversionary campaigns of the early eleventh century were not only nonviolent but also engineered by the wielders of political authority, whereas the First Crusade massacres were perpetrated by various sectors of Christian society.

The threat by Archbishop Eberhard of Trier in 1066 to expel those Jews who refused baptism is the last episode of intolerance that usually appears in the litany of incidents that supposedly adumbrated the First Crusade. This story is told in the *Gesta Treverorum*, a twelfth-century historical work about Trier, which recounts that the local Jews prevented their expulsion by burning the archbishop in effigy on the day fixed for their fateful choice.[113] This attempt at forced conversion must have had some particular historical context, presumably political or social in nature, as can be assumed for the many similar episodes chronicled in the early Middle Ages, including that of Archbishop Frederick of Mainz in 938–939.[114] However, the context of the Trier incident remains a mystery, frustrating efforts to establish the meaning and significance of the strange affair. The Jews' reaction harks back to sources about the Jewish custom of crucifying images of Haman-Jesus on Purim and may be either truth or legend. Blumenkranz flatly dismisses the tale as "nothing more than the product of a later author's imagination."[115] Baron, however, believes that there is some truth to the story, on the bizarre grounds that Bishop Alduin of Limoges enjoyed scant success in 1010, in the episode narrated by Ademar.[116]

Conclusion

The attack by French crusading knights on the Jews of Spain in 1063 is—finally—an event that bears a clear resemblance to what was to transpire in 1096. A large number of armed Europeans setting off to engage the infidel in religious warfare equated the Jews with the enemy and molested those Jews who lay in their path.[117] The efforts of the archbishop of Narbonne and the bishops of Spain to save the Jews in this confrontation were also to find their counterpart in the First Crusade.

Nevertheless, the Jews of Europe could hardly have perceived the incident as an early warning of approaching calamity, for a broad range of sources depict normal, even friendly, relations between Jews and Christians in this period. For instance, Jews and Christians must have dined together, or the prohibition decreed by the Council of Metz in 888 would make no sense. Anecdotal evidence of both Jewish apostasy and conversion supports this image of intense social interaction, bordering on intimacy.[118]

Small wonder, explains Baron, that in 1096 the Jews were caught off guard.

> In retrospect the events of 1096 appear as but a culmination of anti-Jewish trends gradually building up among the Western masses over several generations. But these hostile manifestations were geographically and chronologically so disparate and apparently so unrelated to one another, their immediate effects so local and temporary, that their threatening portents would have escaped the attention of Jewish leaders even if the latter had not wishfully lulled themselves into a false sense of security. Not all of these disturbances became known even to informed persons in distant communities, and they could be largely discounted as the result of some specific, more or less accidental causes.[119]

The charter of Speyer Jewry in 1084 indicates that the Jews of the Rhineland *were* on their guard and took political-legal precautions to protect their persons and property. There are therefore no grounds for Baron's censorious comment that the Jews "wishfully lulled themselves into a false sense of security." This statement reads like an allusion from hindsight to the Jews of Nazi Germany. Indeed, Baron referred to the incidents of 840–1096 as "Rumblings of Hostility" only in the expanded version of his history, after ignoring the period in his 1937 edition.[120] One cannot help but wonder, therefore, whether the harbinger approach is an example of what David Nirenberg has termed the teleological historiographical response to the Holocaust.[121] This was clearly the case for James Parkes, who—*during* the Nazi period—referred to the medieval incidents as "Coming Storms."[122] Whether the victims could have anticipated what lay ahead and taken action was clearly a sensitive issue in the aftermath of the Final Solution. Croce is famous for the aphorism that "all history is contemporary history," and in our case, too, the object of our study turns out to be the historians as much as or more than the subjects of their investigations.[123]

Three   Martyrdom

In the spring of 1096 armies of crusaders made their way across Europe to wrest the Holy Land from the Muslims. As they passed through the Rhineland, they slaughtered the Jews in city after city. Faced with the choice of *Tod oder Taufe* — death or baptism — hundreds of Jews chose death, giving rise to a legacy of martyrdom that inspired descendants for a millennium. The portrayal of Ashkenazic Jewry as a society completely devoted to the law and spirit of Judaism rests in part on the record of their mass martyrdom, initially in 1096 and in countless subsequent instances of persecution in central and eastern Europe. For its martyrological legacy and for its impact on the image of Ashkenaz, the First Crusade slaughter really is, in Yitzhak Baer's formulation, "the prototype of all the mass persecutions of the Middle Ages and even of modern times."[1]

All Jews killed because they were Jewish can be considered martyrs, but the key to the heroic image of Ashkenazic Jewry is the assumption that in 1096 the victims spurned an offer of baptism. Haim Hillel Ben-Sasson expresses this notion as follows: "Because every Jew was offered the choice of converting to Christianity, and there were those who apostatized and hoped to return to Judaism, the *voluntary sacrifice* of the martyrs appears in bold relief."[2] For Ben-Sasson it is clearly important that the martyrs of 1096 acted voluntarily; he implies that the presence or absence of choice is crucial for the proper evaluation of their behavior. Shmuel Shepkaru puts it even more starkly: "Without the individuals having the opportunity to make a *choice* between death and life, the basic characteristics of martyrdom are absent."[3]

Almost all other historical accounts of the 1096 massacres present the same picture. Jacob Katz and Salo Baron agree that the martyrs faced the alternatives of death or conversion.[4] Norman Cohn believes that there was "no doubt" that "a Jew could always save both life and property by accepting baptism."[5] Avraham Grossman states that the martyrs took their lives and those of their wives and children "primarily because of the concern that the Gentiles would baptize them against their will."[6] Haym Soloveitchik asserts that the Jews of Ashkenaz "committed suicide rather than have baptism forced upon them, rather than be dipped in what they called 'contaminated waters.'"[7] Robert Chazan writes that the purpose of the attacks on the Jews of Worms, Mainz, and Cologne "was to eliminate entirely the Jews—preferably by conversion, or, failing that, by slaughter."[8] Jeremy Cohen agrees that the Jews of Ashkenaz were "compelled by their attackers to choose between conversion to Christianity and death."[9] Anna Sapir Abulafia declares that the "hordes" approached the cities with Jewish populations, "voicing their intention of killing any Jew who would refuse to be baptized."[10] Jonathan Riley-Smith claims that "everywhere attempts were made to force Christianity on the Jews, who had heard that the crusaders intended to offer them the choice of conversion or death."[11] Gavin Langmuir states categorically that "Jews were not killed if they would accept baptism."[12] Ben-Zion Netanyahu concurs that in 1096 German Jewry "in the great majority of cases chose death rather than conversion."[13] Citing Hebrew and Latin sources alike, Jean Flori asserts that the crusaders "did not seek to kill the Jews, but rather forcibly to convert them."[14] Aryeh Grabois avers that the Latin sources confirm the report of the Hebrew texts that the crusaders' goal was to forcibly convert the Jews.[15] Benjamin Kedar presents forcible conversion as the central element in the persecutions of 1096.[16]

The principle of Occam's razor would suggest that if the crusaders murdered the Jews, murder must have been their primary intention. The Jews' meager efforts at armed resistance proved futile, and when crusaders wished to convert Jews, they seem to have done so forcibly, offering no options. The Hebrew narratives say that direct force is exactly what the crusaders applied to the Jews of Regensburg in order to convert them. The only exceptions to this pattern were those cases in which Jews killed themselves before falling into the hands of their enemies. In short, if the attackers slaughtered Jews, it makes sense to posit that this was their purpose.[17]

Why the crusaders sought to murder Jews remains a puzzle. One approach, suggested by Israel Yuval, emphasizes the centrality of the theme of vengeance in the thinking of both Jews and Christians in 1096. Yuval claims that "vengeance" is to be understood in its peculiarly German context—*Blutrache*, referring to the exaction of justice through the spilling of blood.[18] Similarly, Riley-Smith states that the crusaders saw themselves as ending a thousand-year vendetta. This view is eloquently expressed at the beginning of the crusade epic *La Chanson d'Antioche*. Jesus, at the time of his actual crucifixion, is told, "It would be most just, moreover, if you should be avenged on these treacherous Jews by whom you are so tormented," to which he replies, "A thousand years from today . . . will come a new race which will take revenge on the death of its father."[19] Yet, if vengeance was indeed the crusaders' motivation, it seems unlikely that baptism was their intention, because converting the Jews would have put vengeance out of reach, as when a soldier surrenders on the battlefield; the crusaders would have had the Jews' souls but not their blood.[20]

The notion that the martyrs had the opportunity of spurning conversion resonates in the medieval Hebrew chronicles of the events. These texts describe the large-scale slaughter of the Jews of Worms, Mainz, and elsewhere and also dwell at length on personal anecdotes, in which victims reject the offer of baptism (see later discussion). The Hebrew tales give the impression that martyrs generally faced a choice, but there is every reason to read the tales with skepticism and caution, because the glorification of the martyrs is the chroniclers' central theme and purpose.

The Hebrew narrators consistently highlight the voluntary sacrifice of individual martyrs and their rejection of conversion. They enlarge on the destruction of the Jewries of Worms and Mainz and gloss over the wholesale apostasy of the communities of Regensburg, Metz, Kerpen, and Trier.[21] The choice of what to emphasize or soft-pedal may reflect the narrator's greater or lesser acquaintance with the course of events in the various communities; this would skew the overall picture. The personal anecdotes also distort our view, by focusing on the experiences of a small number of people. In Baron's succinct formulation, "The Hebrew chronicles underplay the number of the weak-kneed, and stress only the acts of heroism on the part of the resisters."[22]

What underlies this pointed presentation? Avraham Grossman and Jeremy Cohen claim that voluntary apostasy presented a real and powerful threat to German Jewry during the twelfth century, the period of the chronicles' composition. Grossman maintains that the Hebrew narratives were intended to strengthen the public's Jewish identity, which was eroding.[23] If so, the writers would have had every reason to highlight the repudiation of conversion in 1096, even if murder was truly the order of the day.

Taking a different tack, Ivan Marcus suggests that for twelfth-century Jewry the mass suicides and infanticides of 1096 represent a desperate attempt by the martyrs to establish a sense of superiority over the crusaders, by maintaining control over their own destiny.[24] The succeeding generation would enjoy a greater sense of spiritual superiority if the martyrs chose death over life than if their only choice was between suffering martyrdom at their own hands or at the hand of the enemy.[25]

Methodology

The difficulty of disentangling a historical event from the tendency of its narrator is emblematic of the methodological challenge posed by the Hebrew narratives of the First Crusade. Apart from the problem of accounting for the narrators' goals and slanted reporting, some, if not all, of the sources were written and edited decades after the events, and this inevitably affects one's perspective of past deeds.

The responses to these challenges range from almost complete rejection of the tales as historical sources to their nearly literal acceptance. Marcus sees in them tales of a literary-mythic nature: "fictions of a particular Jewish religious imagination." The aim of the chronicler, in Marcus's view, was to justify the sinful acts of suicide and murder perpetrated by the Jews in 1096, and toward this end the chronicler depicted the Jews as acting "only after exhausting all conventional religious and political alternatives." This is why Marcus believes that historical data related in these texts cannot be accepted at face value; they are merely means to an end.

Cohen agrees that the tales cannot be accepted as accurate depictions of what transpired, but he stops short of describing them as literary fictions. He regards the tales as inspired by actual events but posits an unbridgeable gap between event and tale. All that is left to the reader is to study the representation of the First Crusade in the narratives, with the symbolism and "narrative games at play."[26]

Chazan sees the texts as too complex to be dismissed as didactic and hagiographical exercises. For one thing, the texts supply a mass of concrete detail regarding the identity of individuals and places, more than would seem to be required of a fictitious account. Moreover, some of this information undercuts the main theme of glorifying the martyrs. Chazan acknowledges that the sources are tendentious and need to be read critically, but he maintains that to dismiss them altogether would be like throwing out the baby with the bathwater.[27] This approach makes sense, for the wholesale rejection of the historicity of sources that purportedly report historical events implies an equally wholesale rejection of the critical-historical enterprise.[28]

Furthermore, the rejection of the historical interpretation of the chronicles is ironic, because it is based on an impossibly high standard of proof. Cohen rejects as fiction any report that cannot be corroborated by another source.[29] Thus a positivistic methodology serves to undermine a positivistic reading! The alternative would be to accept a lower standard of proof and to evaluate any particular report for its relative plausibility.

We are left with the challenge of crafting a methodology that makes it possible to weigh the sources cautiously and sensibly. Basing the analysis on a broad range of sources is fundamental to such an approach, and so in the following discussion I take account of Latin as well as Hebrew sources. Naturally, the Latin sources are no less tendentious than the Hebrew ones, for they express open hostility to Judaism and thus need to be read critically. In addition, the relatively detailed Latin narratives condemn the excesses of the First Crusade in the Rhineland and see them as the reason for the destruction of this force in Europe, far from the Holy Land; this tendency also renders their version of the incidents suspect of distortion. All in all, however, the Hebrew and Latin sources agree, reinforcing the credibility of each.[30]

The principle of the broad base applies equally to the Hebrew sources, and so my analysis will use the two main narratives: the longer one, associated with Solomon ben Samson, and the shorter one, known as the Mainz Anonymous.[31] I will not, however, examine the sizable corpus of liturgical poems on the massacres, because events reported in this type of text are described in vague language and are heavily laden with literary allusions and symbolic imagery such that, apart from basic questions about their historicity, even reconstructing their particulars poses formidable and often insurmountable difficulties.

Minimizing guesswork and dealing only with what the sources actually say is a second methodological principle. This dictates my focus on the events of Worms and Mainz; relatively full and detailed narratives are available for these two cities, and they are the focus of both the Hebrew and Latin sources.[32] Minimizing the guesswork also underlies my decision not to explore the apostasies of Regensburg, Metz, Kerpen, and Trier. These experiences were no less important historically than the suicides and homicides, and, what is more, they support the argument that the crusaders could have baptized the Jews by force if this had been their intention. Still, the chronicles supply little information about the cases of mass apostasy, and so they must remain peripheral.

The same consideration excludes the fate of French Jewry at the hands of the crusaders from our purview, because the corpus of sources concentrates on the fate of the Rhineland communities.[33] The same is true for communities east of the Rhine, although some sources are available about their travails in 1096, particularly the chronicle of Cosmas of Prague. Admittedly, the proposed approach excludes a large number of Jews affected by the crusade, but the sources do not permit a detailed examination of their experiences.

I also have a historiographical reason for focusing on Worms and Mainz. Whether or not the behavior reported there was representative of other communities, the large-scale martyrdom in these cities came to symbolize Ashkenazic culture in the collective Jewish national memory. This is presumably attributable to the large number of victims cited in the reports, to the shocking descriptions of their suicides and murders, and to the image of these Jewish communities as the largest and most famous in the Rhineland.

The following discussion, then, will not do justice to the 1096 tragedy in its entirety. If, however, we find that in the tales of the two principal encounters, in Worms and Mainz, the assailants' primary intention appears to have been slaughter rather than conversion, then the martyrs' image will have to change: Their deaths will still constitute sanctification of the divine name, for they lost their lives on account of their Jewish identity, but the absence of choice will render their sacrifice less heroic.

The Hebrew First Crusade narrators make extensive use of motifs from biblical and postbiblical Jewish literature, such as the binding of Isaac, and this further complicates the task of separating historical data from literary-religious topoi.[34] The safest course is to rely on information of a neutral nature, and certainly on tales or details that appear to contradict the narrators' tendency, while assuming a skeptical stance vis-à-vis discourse that seems designed to support it. A central point here is that, although describing the crusaders as bent on converting the Jews lionizes the victims, which is the narrators' overall tendency, nevertheless the chroniclers generally depict the assailants as bent on murder, and this bolsters their credibility.

The critical evaluation of tendentious material applies in unequal measure to different types of evidence. When a chronicle relates an act, such as the armed resistance of the Jew Qalonymos and his fighters, it seems unlikely that the account is utterly fictitious. But the tale is told with descriptions of the protagonists' feelings, and these are suspect; although the storyteller may have had access to oral or written traditions about actions, feelings are a private matter, on which hearsay cannot be accepted. Even here, however, the chronicles may preserve a frame of mind shared by the society of protagonists involved in or touched by a particular incident. The only measure for the critical evaluation of this kind of information is the extent to which the purported mind-set furthers or contradicts the narrator's overall direction; testimony that supports the writer's inclination may or may not be accurate, but contradictory data are less suspect of manipulation or outright fabrication. Finally, narratives often attribute utterances or verbal exchanges to various protagonists. This historiographical technique dates back to ancient Greece, and readers were expected to understand that the purpose of the rhetoric was to convey values or feelings that the writer considered appropriate to the scene described, rather than actual, historical speech acts. The Hebrew narratives of the First Crusade use the same convention, and hence their rhetoric also must be seen as the projection of the narrators' understanding rather than as evidence of what was actually said.

Inconsistency is another major methodological obstacle to the assessment of the Hebrew chronicles. Accounts often contradict each other, and sometimes themselves, with regard to the attackers' purpose. Some sources, in both the Latin and Hebrew chronicles, testify that the crusaders' primary and principal intention was to baptize their victims, not to kill them, even in Worms and Mainz. Cohen describes these contradictions as "simultaneously valid, alternative readings" and reminds us that because "historical memories allow for multiple, ostensibly contradictory interpretations . . . these stories embody the conflicted perspective of the survivors who told them."[35] Chazan proposes that, rather than strain to harmonize contradictory dicta, a better strategy would be to focus on behavior patterns that appear repeatedly and more or less consistently.[36] This will be the approach that I use in what follows, and it is akin to the adage that sometimes one cannot see the forest for the trees; the forest contains many trees, of many species, but it is described as a whole, by its overall contours and colors.

Latin Sources

The 1096 massacres were not extensively reported in contemporary Latin annals, but the chroniclers did note them. The scope of the discussion varies widely, from extremely brief and stark notices to more detailed and perforce more complex reports.[37] The sources fall into four groups, based on the extent and content of their reportage. In general, the Latin sources emphasize the ferocious and nearly total annihilation of Rhineland Jewry. They mention that there were Jews who accepted baptism, but they do not provide numbers and are unclear about whether the Jews did so before or after their brethren were slaughtered.

The first group of sources are as laconic as telegrams. The *Annales Blandinienses* state simply that the Jews were killed, adding only the adjective *tumultuarie*, indicating that the acts were not planned or foreseen (at least by Christians) and possibly that they took only a short time.[38] The *Annales Corbeienses* add only a reference to location, indicating that the Jews "of Mainz and various locales" were killed.[39] In the *Annales Brunwilarenses* we read that the Jews of Cologne were also attacked and that the assailants were pilgrims.[40] None of these sources help us determine the attackers' purpose or whether they proposed baptism before or after the carnage.

The second group of texts is also laconic, but a number of sources give the impression that the crusaders sought to baptize the Jews, killing only those who refused. The *Annales Augustani* state that the Jews were forcibly baptized, annihilated, or took their own lives; the issue of choice was not raised.[41] The *Annales S. Albani Moguntini* (*Wirzburgenses*) report that in 1096 "Jews" were compelled to accept baptism and that an enormous massacre was perpetrated against those who refused; 1,014 persons were slaughtered in Mainz, including women and children.[42] A nearly identical report appears in the *Annales Hildesheimenses*.[43] Sigebert of Gembloux (ca. 1030–1112) notes that the crusaders forced the Jews in the cities to accept the Christian faith and killed those who did not convert.[44]

Other writers portray the crusaders as preferring homicide to conversion. The chronicle of Frutolf, Prior of Michelsberg (d. 1103), and of Ekkehard of Aura (d. 1125) states that approximately 12,000 crusaders, "as they were led through the cities of the Rhine and the Main and also the Danube[45] . . . either utterly destroyed the execrable race of the Jews wherever they found them (exercising slavish devotion to Christian zeal even in this manner) or forced them into the bosom of the Church."[46] Writing in 1143–1146, Otto of Freising states that Emicho, at the head of 12,000 crusaders, either destroyed the Jews wherever he found them or forced them to enter the Church.[47] These sources, or perhaps this shared historiographical tradition, presents murder as the default and baptism as secondary and less important.[48]

The third group of sources provides clearer and more detailed versions than those surveyed thus far. Bernold of St. Blasien (Schaffhausen), writing in 1050–1100,[49] relates that in Worms the Jews fled to the bishop and asked to settle in his quarters; the bishop agreed but saw safety only in baptism. "Persuaded by the devil and by their own obstinacy,"[50] the Jews killed themselves the moment they entered the bishop's chamber, "while our people [i.e., the bishop's men] waited for their answer."[51] Here the offer of baptism preceded the violence, making it plain that neither the bishop nor the Jews expected the crusaders to offer an alternative to death; both assumed that rejection of the bishop's offer would cost the Jews their lives.[52] A relatively late source, Sigebert Auctarium Aquicinense, writing after 1150, reports that some of the Jews killed themselves "out of zeal to preserve their ancestral law," which seems to imply that they expected to be forcibly baptized rather than killed.[53]

According to the *Annalista Saxo*, the First Crusade massacres resulted from the crusaders' declared eagerness to avenge Christ from the "gentiles," namely, the Muslims, or else from the Jews. In Mainz the crusaders killed approximately 900 Jews, sparing neither women nor children. The Jews had fled with their treasure[54] to Ruthard, the local bishop, but neither he nor his numerous soldiers could rescue them, because (he says) Christians generally did not want to fight other Christians on behalf of the Jews. The building was stormed, and "all were killed—however many Jews they encountered there." This carnage took place before Pentecost. The text depicts the sight, "terrible to behold," of "many and great heaps of murdered victims carried away on wagons from the city of Mainz." The graphic account of the slaughter in Mainz is followed by a reference to similar events in Cologne, Worms, and other cities of Gaul and Germany, with the offhand note that there were also "a few Jews" who took refuge in baptism.[55]

This account seems reliable, for the description of the wagons loaded with bodies is as specific and clear as only an eyewitness account can be.[56] More important for our purposes, this text makes no mention of an offer of baptism having been offered before the onslaught; on the contrary, it explicitly presents vengeance as the attackers' motive.[57] The chronicle makes brief and casual mention of those who converted and were saved, and this much is generally agreed; the issue is whether baptizing the Jews was the primary purpose, and it is plain from the *Annalista Saxo* that the crusaders were bent on destruction.[58]

A fourth body of Latin sources criticizes the crusaders for their immoral behavior. These sources depict the participants as a rapacious, undisciplined mob that committed acts of depravity, fornication, pillage, and violence. This moral bankruptcy provides an explanation for the Rhineland contingent's failure to reach the Holy Land: Its misconduct is held responsible for its destruction at the Hungarian frontier.

The central text in this group is that of Albert of Aachen. Written in the early twelfth century, on the basis of oral testimony (*ex auditu et relatione*), it is distinguished by its geographic and chronological proximity to the events and also by its great detail—greater than in all the other Latin sources.[59] Albert writes:

> I do not know if it was because of a judgment of God[60] or because of some delusion in their minds,[61] but the pilgrims rose in a spirit of cruelty against the Jews who were scattered throughout all the cities, and they inflicted a most cruel slaughter on them, especially in the kingdom of Lotharingia, claiming that this was the beginning of their crusade and service against the enemies of Christianity.[62]

Cologne was the first German city to experience the pogrom. Here the Jews were slaughtered by "the citizens" (*a ciuibus*), not by crusaders.[63] The attackers killed and wounded many Jews, destroyed their homes and synagogues, and divided their substantial monetary assets. Some Jews fled but were discovered and massacred.

Having heard of the slaughter of their coreligionists, the Jews of Mainz sought refuge at the hands of Bishop Ruthard. They entrusted him with "priceless treasures,"[64] and he admitted them to his palace. Emicho and others there "consulted together"[65] and, after sunrise, attacked the Jews, who made a futile effort to resist. About 700 Jews were slaughtered, including women and children.[66]

> The Jews, indeed, seeing how the Christian enemy were rising up against them and their little children and were sparing none of any age, even turned upon themselves and their companions, on children, women, mothers and sisters, and they all killed each other. Mothers with children at the breast—how horrible to relate—would cut their

throats with knives, would stab others, preferring that they should die thus at their hands, *rather than be killed* [emphasis added] by the weapons of the uncircumcised.[67]

A few escaped and a few accepted baptism.[68]

Albert later notes that these crusaders failed to reach the Holy Land because they had slaughtered the Jews "rather from greed for their money than for divine justice, since God is a just judge and commands no one to come to the yoke of the Catholic faith against his will or under compulsion."[69] Albert's reference to greed contradicts his previous reference to the assailants' religious motive. Moreover, greed as a motive does not suffice to explain the crusaders' behavior; Albert describes them as stabbing small children of every sex and age with their swords,[70] which would hardly have been necessary if they only lusted for gold.

Albert describes no choice, no options. First he writes that the crusaders equated killing the Jews with crusading and says nothing of baptism. In Cologne, Albert relates, none were offered the chance to save themselves. In Mainz, baptism was the prerogative of the few who escaped the massacre; it was not offered initially, as an alternative to death. Moreover, in Albert's narrative the Jews express no awareness that baptism is in the offing, falling upon one another after seeing that their assailants were "sparing none of any age."[71]

Two relatively late sources, written in the second half of the twelfth century, resemble Albert's account and may have drawn from it, but they diverge precisely on the question at issue here, with one of them explicitly saying that the crusaders sought to baptize the Jews and the other referring only to murder. The *Annales S. Disibodi*, written in Disinbodenberg in the bishopric of Mainz, follow Albert in citing immoral behavior—fornication and the massacre of the Jews—as the principal reason for the assailants' downfall.[72] Unlike Albert, this chronicle says that the crusaders intended to convert the Jews. This narrator relates that, despite the offer to save their possessions and lives by embracing Christianity, almost all the Jews were killed; a substantial number were "torn to pieces (*diripiebantur*) by Christians. Compelled by this frightful anguish, the Jews fell upon themselves and annihilated (*interemerunt*) the wounded[73] by turns with their own knives. Men did not spare wives and relatives; mothers slaughtered sons and daughters."[74] The text is clear that conversion was offered, but it emphasizes slaughter, whether at the hand of crusaders or Jews.

William of Tyre (ca. 1130–1185), on the other hand, is clear. Regrettably, he is also late and writing from a great distance. He opens his account of the "excesses" perpetrated against the Jews by saying that the crusaders failed to heed the authority of the noblemen[75] but rather "ran to and fro promiscuously, committing all kinds of lawless deeds at their own sweet will." Rather than proceeding on their journey, "they turned aside to mad excesses"[76] and

> cruelly massacred the Jewish people in the cities and towns through which they passed, for the latter, having no reason to fear anything of the kind, took no precautions.[77] These outrages occurred especially in the cities of Cologne and Mainz,[78] where Count Emicho, a powerful nobleman, well known in that country, joined the pilgrim bands with a large following. . . . This [the route through Hungary, which was the shortest] was entirely closed because of the insolence and outrageous excesses which those pilgrims who had gone on ahead so often and undeservedly perpetrated upon the inhabitants of that region.[79]

Like Albert, William depicts the crusaders as homicidal and does not mention a baptism option.

Clearly on the question at hand the Latin sources are equivocal. Those written closer to the time of the events deserve greater credibility, and almost all the early sources, namely those written before 1150, indicate that the crusaders' primary and principal objective was murder: Albert of Aachen, Ekkehard of Aura, Bernold of St. Blasien, and Otto of Freising. Sigebert of Gembloux is the only early writer who does not fit this pattern.

Another yardstick is the amount of detail provided by a given text. The more information a source provides, the easier it is to evaluate it, regardless of how tendentious it may be. This criterion buttresses the argument made here. The first group of sources say nothing on the subject; most of the texts in the second group indicate that conversion is the primary goal, but those in the third and fourth groups emphasize murder. Overall, the details point in the direction of slaughter—rather than baptism—being the assailants' intention.

The most conservative conclusion to be drawn from analysis of the Latin sources is that the historiographical consensus requires reexamination. The Hebrew sources, which are far more detailed, show even more clearly that those who killed the Jews merely did what they set out to do, namely, to slaughter the Jews. More important, the Hebrew narratives pull the various sources together, by explaining why the attackers sometimes offered baptism when they could have done as they pleased.

Hebrew Sources

Annihilation

The Hebrew sources emphasize slaughter, and they are credible on this point because they would have highlighted the heroism of the martyrs by depicting the Jews as rejecting an offer of baptism and submitting to martyrdom voluntarily. Instead, the narrative of Solomon ben Samson offers two similar versions of the pattern of thought that led the crusaders to the decision to annihilate the Jews.[80]

> Behold we journey a long way to seek the idolatrous shrine and to take vengeance upon the Ishmaelites, while the Jews dwell among us, whose ancestors killed and crucified Him [Jesus] for no reason. Let us take vengeance upon them first; "let us wipe them out as a nation; Israel's name will be mentioned no more" [Ps. 83:5]. Alternatively, let them be like us and acknowledge the son born of promiscuity.

> Why are they occupied with doing battle against the Ishmaelites in the vicinity of Jerusalem? Indeed among them is a people that does not acknowledge their faith. What is more, their ancestors crucified their deity. Why should we let them live, and why should they dwell among us? Let our swords begin with their heads. After that we shall go on the way of our pilgrimage.[81]

Here the primary purpose is unquestionably annihilation, rooted in the desire for vengeance.[82] The second version does not even mention conversion; the first adds a baptism option, but this contradicts the sense of the passage and its authenticity is therefore suspect. Even if it is genuine, conversion is presented as a concession, not a principal goal.

A similar privileging of bloodshed is imputed to Godfrey of Bouillon, Duke of Lower Lorraine, who swore that "he would not depart on his journey without avenging the blood of the Crucified with the blood of Israel and that he would not leave 'a remnant or residue' [Jer. 42:17] among those bearing the name Jew."[83] Count Ditmar is also reputed to have said that he would not leave Germany without killing at least one Jew.[84] These reports of the words and sentiments of Godfrey and Ditmar cannot be accepted as factual, but they testify to the Jews' perception—as mediated through the chroniclers—of the crusaders' mind-set on the eve of their departure for the Holy Land. Ditmar's more modest ambition appears to be an attempt to fulfill the promise allegedly circulating in the Rhineland that "anyone who kills a single Jew will have all his sins absolved."[85] Godfrey's rhetoric was bloodthirsty, even genocidal, but theoretically he could have wiped out the Jews through forced baptism; Ditmar's purpose was solely and unequivocally homicidal.

These reports jibe with a number of formulations in the account of the mass murder of the Jews of Worms, as told in the Mainz Anonymous. The townspeople promise the Jews their support, vowing to put to death anyone who murders a Jew; their vow reflects the expectation that the threat was of death, not baptism.[86] The townspeople quickly abrogate their commitment following an accusation that the city's Jews had murdered a Christian and contaminated the local water supply.[87] At this point, both crusaders and townspeople are made to say, "Behold the time has come to avenge him who was crucified, whom their ancestors slew. Now let not 'a remnant or a residue' escape, even 'an infant or a suckling' [Jer. 44:7] in the cradle."[88] Obviously the rhetoric placed in the mouth of the townspeople merely expresses the narrator's perception of the Jews' interpretation; they believed that the townspeople had formed the intention to annihilate them, in revenge for the Crucifixion.[89]

The narrative of the slaughter in Mainz, in both versions, is the longest and most detailed of the tales told in the Hebrew narratives, and it generally confirms the proposed historiographical revision. The writer begins by reconstructing the mind-set of the Jews and crusaders shortly before their catastrophic encounter. The Jews, having heard about the destruction of the communities of Speyer and Worms, cry out, echoing Ezekiel 11:13: "Ah Lord God of Israel! Are you wiping out the remnant of Israel?!" They upbraid God for delivering them into the hands of the uncircumcised "for destruction."[90] Their enemies taunt them: "Where is your promise?[91] How will you be saved? Behold the wonders that the Crucified does for us."[92] The narrator then observes, "All of them came with swords to annihilate us." The Jews lose heart and propose mass suicide, saying: "If only we might die by the hand of the Lord, rather than *die* [emphasis added] at the hands of the enemies of the Lord." Rabbi Baruch ben Rabbi Isaac, "a venerable scholar," tells his fellows of a sign that "we will not be able to be saved."[93] Hearing this, the Jews fall on their faces and exclaim, "Ah Lord God! Are you wiping out the remnant of Israel?!"[94] The Jews solicit the aid of Bishop Ruthard, and he and the burgrave promise, "We shall either die with you or live with you."[95] The chronicles compare the Jews of Mainz to the residents of Sodom and Gomorrah, the symbol of total annihilation.[96] All these motifs and expressions emphasize the crusaders' intention and the Jews' expectation that the object of the assault was death.

The confrontation begins with the admission of Count Emicho (of nearby Flonheim) and his forces to the city. No resistance is offered, and the crusaders see this as providential: "All this has the Crucified done for us so that we might avenge his blood from the Jews,"[97] or, in another version: "Now let us avenge the blood of the Crucified."[98] Some Jews do battle but are easily overcome. Others prepare for death: Rabbi Isaac ben Moses, their spiritual leader, "extends his neck" and is promptly decapitated. Others wait for death with him and are soon dispatched.[99] The narrator upbraids the heavenly bodies: "Why did you not withhold your light from shining on the enemy who intended to blot out the name of Israel?"[100] Still others retreat into the inner recesses of their refuge in Ruthard's keep[101] and decide to kill themselves, saying, "For the moment the enemy will kill us . . . but we shall remain alive; our souls [will repose] in paradise."[102] The great mass killing then ensues. When the crusaders burst in, they kill all those that remained alive, leaving neither "a remnant nor a residue."[103]

In sum, the chronicler tells us that the crusaders are determined to avenge the Crucifixion by annihilating the Jews.[104] This applies to the expectations attributed to both the crusaders and the Jews, and at all stages: before, during, and after the massacre. The Jews elect to die by their own hand rather than be killed by the enemy, but an option of baptism is neither anticipated nor offered.

Some statements in the Hebrew narratives suggest that the crusaders' primary intention is baptism, not slaughter, and that this is perceived as such by the Jews. Both Hebrew chronicles have the crusaders say that the Jews must "accept their abominable faith or else they would destroy us, from infant to suckling."[105] Likewise, when the Jews of Mainz decide to kill themselves, military resistance having failed and hope of survival vanished, they are said to have exclaimed, "Look and see, God, what we do for the sanctification of your great Name, rather than abandon you for a crucified one."[106] And in Xanten the Jews' pious leader exhorts his flock to martyr themselves "lest the impure defile us."[107]

These utterances suggest that there was an alternative to *Tod oder Taufe*, contrary to the argument presented here. They illustrate the complex nature of the sources, which have other internal contradictions. In such a state of confusion it is safer to trust the authenticity of statements that run counter to the narrator's overall tendency; accordingly, in this case preference would go to formulations that do not offer the Jews the choice of baptism. This also seems warranted because these last expressions are exceptions, contradicting the rest of the account of the Worms and Mainz confrontations. And ultimately baptism is not proposed; when the crusaders storm the Jews' hideout, they slaughter them indiscriminately.

Paradigms of Choice

Regardless of intentions and expectations, it is plain from the sources, Latin and Hebrew alike, that there were Jews who apostatized and survived, whether their baptism was coerced or voluntary. This is true not only of the Jews of Regensburg, Kerpen, and the like, who converted en masse, but also of individuals in Worms and Mainz. The Hebrew sources present a series of personal anecdotes in which individual Jews are offered baptism and nobly refuse. These tales occupy a great deal of space in the overall account and may have given rise to the impression that the Jews generally had a choice. But the anecdotes appear in only two types of scenarios, neither of which supports this interpretation.

In one case the crusaders penetrate the Jews' hideout and kill almost everyone (except those who had already killed each other and themselves), and only then, having slaked their bloodlust, do they offer baptism to a handful of survivors.[108] These circumstances hardly indicate that the crusaders sought to baptize the Jews.[109]

This is how the story of the Worms and Mainz massacres is told. The crusaders urge the "remnant and residue" to convert, pointing to the heaps of Jewish corpses lying naked in the streets to underscore the hopelessness of their situation. In Worms, according to the narrative of Solomon ben Samson, after the great slaughter, "the enemy stripped them [the slain] and dragged them about. There remained only 'a small number' whom they converted forcibly and baptized against their will in their baptismal waters."[110] The Mainz Anonymous offers a similar description, emphasizing the demoralization of the survivors: "When those who remained saw their brethren naked, they then acceded to them [the attackers] under great duress, for the crusaders intended to leave not a remnant or a residue. . . . There were those of them who said: 'Let us do their will for the time being.'"[111]

The Mainz Anonymous then presents three personal anecdotes in which Worms Jews martyr themselves rather than convert, and in two of them slaughter clearly precedes conversion. When precisely Isaac ben Daniel is offered baptism is not clear,[112] but Simhah ben Isaac ha-Kohen is told, "Behold, all of them have already been killed and they lie naked."[113] And an "important woman" named Minna is exhorted, "Behold you are 'a capable woman' [Prv. 31:10]. Know and see that God does not wish to save you, for 'they lie naked at the corner of every street,' unburied. Sully yourself [with the waters of baptism]."[114]

The pattern of baptism following carnage appears again and with even greater clarity, in the report of the massacre in Mainz.

> Subsequently they threw them through the windows naked, heap
> upon heap and mound upon mound, until they formed a high heap.
> Many of the children of the sacred covenant, as they were thrown still
> had life and would signal with their fingers: "Give us water that we
> might drink." When the crusaders [to'im; literally, errant ones] saw
> this, they would ask them: "Do you wish to sully yourselves?" They
> would shake their heads. . . . The crusaders then killed them.[115]

And the pattern also applies to David ben Nathaniel the sexton and his wife. The two had hidden in the courtyard of a local priest, and after the killing the priest urges them to save themselves by becoming Christian.

> Behold there remains in the courtyard of the archbishop and in the courtyard of the burgrave "neither a remnant nor a residue." They have all been killed, cast out, and trampled in the streets, with the exception of a few whom they have baptized. Do likewise and you will be able to be saved . . . from the hands of the crusaders.[116]

The alternative is presented after the massacre, and in fact the argument for baptism is punctuated by and predicated on the sight of the corpses strewn about. Thus Samuel ben Na'aman, who remained in his house along with a few others after the other residents had fled, is invited to save himself through conversion after the mass slaughter but refuses and is killed.[117] Similarly, the narrative of Solomon ben Samson records that following the great slaughter in the chambers of the archbishop of Mainz, the archbishop sends an emissary to Qalonymos, the military leader of the Jews, urging him to save himself and his band by converting.[118]

The narrative of Solomon ben Samson also tells the tale of Abraham ben Asher, one of a group of Jews who hid in a forest near Mainz. Called to save himself through baptism, Abraham asks, "Is there anyone here who knows if there remains from all my household or my family even one?"[119] No one knows and Abraham elects to die, presumably because he despairs of finding any surviving family members. Abraham's own case fits the pattern of baptism being offered after the massacre, but equally important, his question shows that, without knowing precisely what has transpired, he expects the attackers to kill, not convert.

Not all the anecdotes fit the pattern described. According to Solomon ben Samson, Isaac ben David, the *parnas*, or communal leader, of Mainz, and Uri ben Joseph are baptized against their will "when the community was killed."[120] The circumstances of Uri's baptism are unclear, but of Isaac we read that he accepts baptism to save his two children, after his wife is killed and his mother wounded.[121] This seems to conform to the scenario of baptism after slaughter.[122]

A second paradigm concerns the setting in which baptism is offered rather than its timing. As a rule, the clashes between Jews and crusaders involve large numbers of both groups, but sometimes a small group of crusaders encounters a small number of Jews—sometimes only one—to whom they might then offer a chance to survive. Typically these "close encounters" occur in secluded locations, away from the prying eyes of the crusaders' zealous companions. In some cases the assailants are acquainted with the Jews they encounter and are anxious to spare them. The intimate circumstances appear to blunt the attackers' religious zeal and to restore their humanity.

Often the close encounter is a subset of the paradigm of conversion after slaughter. In the case of Abraham ben Asher, for example, baptism is offered after the vast majority of the Jews are killed. In cases like this, the enemy offers conversion both because vengeance has already been achieved and because of the humanizing effect of the close encounter. But the close encounters also appear at the height of the assault, especially those that occur in obscure places, and then the paradigm is crucial for explaining the inconsistency in the crusaders' behavior and hence also the contradictory formulations in the Hebrew chronicles.

We find the close encounter in both Worms and Mainz and environs. In Mainz, David ben Nathaniel the sexton and his household are urged to accept baptism when they are discovered hiding in the courtyard of a priest.[123] Attackers urged Samuel ben Na'aman to be baptized, on discovering him and his immediate family at home.[124] Two women, Guta and Scholaster, are hiding in the courtyard of a certain townsman "at the time when the saintly ones were killed in the courtyard of the archbishop."[125] Samuel ben Isaac ben Samuel of Mainz is caught while fleeing the carnage.[126] Abraham ben Asher is discovered in the forest along with other Jews, and the enemy "gathers against" him and presses him to convert because he is well-known and "pleasant" (na'im).[127] Similarly, Minna of Worms is entreated to convert after her hiding place is discovered by people who know and like her.[128] The narrators' emphasis on the generosity displayed by the enemy in these cases highlights how statistically insignificant they are.

There is, however, a special case, an important exception to the rule that the Jews of the Rhineland communities expect death rather than forced conversion. The references, in the Latin sources, to the indiscriminate slaughter of women and children indicate that these writers considered such behavior out of the ordinary.[129] Nevertheless, Albert of Aachen is clear that the Jews expect their children to be killed, for he reports that they slaughtered their young, "preferring that they should die thus at their hands, rather than be killed by the weapons of the un-circumcised."[130] The Hebrew chronicles, however, make it plain that the Jews expect the enemy to baptize their children, not kill them.[131]

The pious Rachel of Mainz urges her accomplice to have no mercy on her four children, "lest these uncircumcised come and seize them alive and they be raised in their error."[132] Similarly, Moses ben Helbo, also of Mainz, tells his sons to choose between hell and paradise, both of which yawn before them, immediately before the enemy's as-sault;[133] hell means Christianity, not death. Isaac ben David, the *parnas* of Mainz, explains his conversion as follows: "I did not accede to the enemy except to save my children from the hands of the wicked and so that they not be raised in their error."[134] We learn that the Jews' concern is well founded: "for they [the crusaders] had seized the children that remained, 'a small number,' saying that perhaps they would be raised in their error."[135] It therefore seems that when the survivors of the Worms massacre agree to convert out of a desire to "save our children from them," they mean that conversion would save their children from bap-tism rather than from death.

Some Latin sources express concern that the Jews might slaughter their children to prevent them from being forcibly baptized. These sources date from no earlier than the thirteenth century and appear to have been inspired by the martyrdom of 1096. These texts indirectly lend support to the claim that during the First Crusade the Jews of Ash-kenaz viewed their children as a "special case."[136]

The special case of the children is important for evaluating the his-toricity of the Hebrew narratives. It would make sense to posit that the writers described the crusaders' intentions retrospectively, in light of their deeds, and therefore these sources would seem to be useless as evidence for the assailants' original intention. But, as we have seen, the sources leave no doubt that Jews of all ages were killed, and thus the Jews' fear that the enemy would convert their children rather than slaughter them was without foundation. The narrators must have known this, and yet they made no attempt to align intentions and actions. By reporting a mistaken expectation, the narrators testify that they did not seek to revise the historical record with the benefit of hindsight but to honestly and accurately represent what actually occurred. The special case of the children reinforces the credibility of the Hebrew sources, particularly on the question of the priority of slaughter over conversion with regard to the adult population.

Conclusion

The Hebrew and Latin texts report that the crusaders were motivated by the desire to avenge the Crucifixion through bloodshed and thus massacred the Jews of Worms and Mainz, man, woman, and child.[137] They record the baptism and survival of a small number of Jews but mostly describe these cases as exceptional. The Hebrew narratives present the personal anecdote, in which conversion is offered, in one of two basic sets of circumstances: after nearly all the Jews have been killed, in a close encounter, or in a combination of these two scenarios. These paradigms serve to explain the enemy's decision to spare certain individuals, and they are probably responsible, at least in part, for the impression that conversion was generally the assailants' purpose. The special case of the children is the exception to the rule that the Jews expected to be killed and did not anticipate an offer of baptism.

There was, it seems, only one choice facing the Jews of Worms and Mainz: death at their own hand or at that of the enemy. The Hebrew narratives depict the crusaders as bent on bloodshed, not baptism, and the victims knew this and elected to wrest from the enemy at least this minimal degree of power and control.

Four   Survival

The story of the First Crusade slaughter in the Rhineland, as told by medieval chroniclers and later by modern historians, has focused on those who suffer martyrdom, whether at the hands of Christians, fellow Jews, or themselves. This mass martyrdom came to epitomize the willingness of Ashkenazic Jews to die for their faith. This is the ideal known as *Kiddush ha-Shem*, the sanctification of the divine name. The collective suicide of 1096 showcased the Jewish people's devotion to their faith and hence the victory of Judaism over Christianity. Paradoxically, then, the carnage was a source of solace for generations of Jews, for their ancestors' fortitude and steadfastness made them proud and reinforced their own religious identity.

Why not leave it at that? Because 1096 is not only the story of the final act of self-immolation but also the story of the terror and conflict that must have preceded it. "How," asks Jeremy Cohen, "could they not have had hesitations, second thoughts, and misgivings?"[1] Medieval chroniclers and modern historians soft-pedaled this painful stage and highlighted the legacy of martyrdom, but although this elevated the victims to the plane of sainthood, it also robbed them of their humanity. Restoring the authentic pallor of those final days, hours, and moments of agony enriches rather than tarnishes the memory of 1096, because it makes it possible not only to admire the protagonists but also to understand them.

The sources also emphasize the heroism of the martyrs by homogenizing them into a community of fanatics. The following passage, from Robert Chazan's seminal work, is representative.

> The descriptions of mass martyrdom emphasize the involvement of
> all elements in the community and all age groups. . . . The acts of self

sacrifice in 1096, however, were not limited to those with little to lose. The wealthiest members of the community willingly gave themselves up to death as did those in the very flower of youth. . . . Youngsters are often portrayed as anxious to join in the acts of martyrdom. . . . Perhaps most striking is the involvement of the intellectual luminaries. . . . Thus every level of Rhineland Jewry is portrayed as committed to martyrdom—poor and wealthy, old and young, little known and widely respected.[2]

As this passage indicates, the Hebrew chronicler of 1096 generally flattens the narrative by effacing nuance and diversity. This immediately suggests that the critical reader ought to be alert for hints of heterogeneity in the conduct and emotional state of the Jews. This form of critical discourse, which has just begun to receive scholarly treatment,[3] promises to yield new perspectives on and insights into the way the First Crusade massacres were perceived and narrated, especially regarding victims who were not martyred. In this chapter I sketch some of the social dynamics of 1096 in which elements of Jewish society express ambivalence toward martyrdom.

Some of those who do not embrace martyrdom are ultimately martyred, either by Jews or by their enemies, whereas others save themselves through flight or apostasy.[4] Yet even among those Jews who willingly give their lives, there are those who do so for nonideological reasons. As Cohen notes, one ought not to assume that the acts of martyrdom recorded in the Hebrew chronicles "proceeded from that ideology of *qiddush ha-Shem* with which the chronicles explained them."[5] The desire to preclude humiliation and torture might have been such a reason. The pressure to conform to the collective will of one's relatives, peers, and leaders would likely also weaken the instinctive will to survive. The combinations of circumstances and considerations that resulted in martyrdom were myriad and varied, and when we take account of them, the story of the First Crusade massacres becomes vivid and textured. Thus my purpose in this chapter is to identify vestigial traces of conflict—in sentiment as well as behavior—in the 1096 experience and to explore their multifarious modes of expression.

The Hebrew chronicles about the atrocities of 1096 glorify martyrdom and downplay unheroic conduct, and hence statements and an-

ecdotes that convey the martyrological message are particularly likely
to reflect exaggeration or outright invention on the part of the chronicler. For example, the chronicler avoids reference to fear of death, and
Chazan aptly notes that he is "not interested in the broad range of
human motivations involved in the martyrdoms"[6] because dwelling on
them would defeat his primary purpose, namely, to glorify the martyrs.
The chronicler grinds his ax openly in the following passage, which
concludes the report of the chronicle of Solomon ben Samson about
the martyrdom in Mainz:

> These pious ones did not say to one another: "Have pity on yourselves."
> Rather they said: "Let us spill our blood on the ground like water,
> and let it be considered by God like the blood of the gazelle and the
> deer[7]. . . . Let the reader of these words not say that only those whom
> we have specified here sanctified the Name of the Lord of heaven. Also
> those for whom we have not specified here their names and the deeds
> which they did at their deaths sanctified the holy and glorified Name.[8]

The chronicler emphasizes that the martyrs did not hesitate to give
their lives for Judaism and that those whose stories are not reported
acted in a similar fashion. Taken together, these two ideas reflect his
need to obliterate emotional responses and behaviors unfavorable to
martyrdom. However, the assumption that all living beings cling to life
forces the critical reader to reject this portrait of 1096 as an accurate reflection of the Jews' state of mind. Significantly, the chronicler himself,
notwithstanding his agenda, occasionally leaves traces of a reluctance
for martyrdom and of the resultant conflict, as we shall see.

The chronicle contains short, sweeping summaries of the fate of entire Rhineland Jewish communities, and these are of little use to the
present investigation. But the succinct accounts are almost always followed by detailed narratives about the fate of small groups (usually martyrs) or individuals. The chronicler describes the (inevitably pious) state
of mind of the protagonist at the time of a certain action and sometimes
includes an account of his or her words. These more focused anecdotes
merit careful, critical examination, for they contain traces of conflict.

This interpretive strategy illuminates aspects of the narratives that contradict the chronicler's martyrological bias, rendering them less suspect of
tendentious manipulation and thus more credible, but we remain unable

to determine with any certainty whether or not a behavior or emotion narrated in the tales occurred purely on the literary-mythological plane or perhaps also on the social-historical playing field. Indeed, there is no reason to formulate a single, global evaluation of the truth claim of the narratives, for it may well be that some stories reflect the historical record of events more precisely than others, even though the less accurate ones may present a more accurate image of the impressions and values formulated and articulated by the survivors. The focus of the following discussion, therefore, is not what took place but rather the ambivalence to martyrdom that can be detected even within the fabric of the chronicles; the fact that these chronicles clearly project a powerful martyrological message renders this finding all the more striking and paradoxical.

The idea that the Hebrew narratives subtly convey ambivalence toward martyrdom alongside tales clearly intended to glorify it has already been noted. Haym Soloveitchik observes that the martyrdom of the First Crusade, specifically the killing of Jews by Jews, suicides, and homicides, stands in diametric opposition to talmudic law and begs justification, which would provide a rationale for the composition of the Hebrew Crusade chronicles, with their apologetical, nay hagiographical, tendency.[9] Going further, Cohen maintains that subtle expressions of ambivalence in the martyrological tales reflect the trauma of the survivor generation, with the attendant ambivalence toward both martyrdom and survival.[10] This basic approach to the narratives is the point of departure for the following analysis of the survival experience.

The Root Story

Patterns of conflict or dissent from martyrological behavior emerge most sharply when the protagonists are studied in groups rather than as isolated individuals or families. Because analysis of each group in turn would entail repeated narration of particular passages or anecdotes, a single tale will serve as a "root story," a model for the discussion of the behavior of various groups in other anecdotes. I first identify a form of thought or behavior in the root story; I then locate this thought or behavior in another anecdote or two from the chronicles, to show that the root story presents a pattern rather than an isolated incident.

The root story I have chosen is the narrative of the martyrdom of the Jews of Mainz "in the chambers," namely, within the archbishop's palace.[11] The chronicler relates that the Jews of Mainz hear awful tales of the fate of their brethren in Speyer and Worms and therefore hold out little hope of survival. A substantial number of them seek refuge in the archbishop's palace. A great battle rages at the palace gates, but the enemy prevails, pours through the gate, and kills Jews in the courtyard, including Rabbi Isaac ben Moses, "uprooter of mountains," who "extends his neck" and is decapitated.[12] Other Jews remain seated in the courtyard and do not flee inside the palace.

Those in the chambers observe the events in the courtyard and begin putting each other and themselves to death.

> There women girded their loins and slaughtered their sons and daughters, and also themselves. Many men, likewise, gathered strength and slaughtered their wives and their children and their little ones. . . . The virgins and brides and bridegrooms gazed through the windows and cried out loudly: "Behold, our God, what we do for the sanctification of your great Name."[13]

"Rachel" orchestrates the murder of her four children.[14] She tells a woman friend not to have mercy on her children and asks her not to kill her son Isaac before Aaron, lest Aaron see his brother die. Nonetheless, one of the women friends promptly slaughters Isaac, who dies without a sound. When Aaron witnesses his brother's death, he cries out to his mother, "Do not slaughter me!" and hides under a cabinet. Rachel leaves him momentarily to slay her daughters, Bella and Madrona, and then returns to drag Aaron from his hiding place and slaughter him too. Judah, the children's father, cries out when he sees his four children die and throws himself on his sword.[15]

Unheroic Conduct

Judah's behavior is a glaring example of inner conflict. Although we are not told that the slaughter of his children is perpetrated without his knowledge and consent, he fails to act or react until the deed is done. His passivity or paralysis is therefore a striking expression of ambivalence to martyrdom. This interpretation fits the nature of his suicide, which is presented as a reaction to the slaughter of his children rather than as an act of martyrdom.[16]

A lack of unanimous support for martyrdom can be inferred in the case of Shemaryah "the pious" of Moers and his wife and three children. This family finds refuge among gentile acquaintances; these, however, hand them over to enemies, who seek to forcibly baptize them. Shemaryah acquiesces but requests a night's leisure and lodging; he rises in the dead of night to slay his wife and children.[17] His decision to kill his family members in their sleep implies that he did not expect them to embrace martyrdom.

Actually, Shemaryah himself turns out to be less of a hero than he appears at first glance. After killing his family, he attempts to slaughter himself as well but faints and is found on the ground in the morning, alive and well. The gentiles who discover him invite him to convert, but he proudly refuses and eagerly awaits death, telling his enemies that he has waited for this moment all his life. They then bury him alive, with the expectation that at some point he will change his mind and accept baptism. He enters the grave they have dug and lays there, with his dead wife to his right and his children to his left, and the family is then covered with earth. At this point the narrator attenuates Shemaryah's heroism a bit, by reporting that, although Shemaryah does not abandon his faith, he shouts and cries out for the rest of the day and the following night, lamenting himself and his family.[18]

A more explicit expression of conjugal conflict over martyrdom appears in the record of the martyrdom in Worms. Meshullam ben Isaac announces his intention to slay his only son, Isaac, whom his wife Zipporah bore at an advanced age.[19] Unlike Rachel, Zipporah affirms her maternal instincts to the last and begs her husband to kill her first, thereby sparing her the sight of her son's execution.[20] Meshullam does not heed his wife's request and slays his son, but he then proves incapable of murdering Zipporah or himself; he takes her outside, where both are killed by the crusaders.[21]

Meshullam, like Rachel, is every inch the martyr, and also like her, his spouse is not. Other anecdotes in the chronicles are more equivocal; some martyrs, like Judah in the root story, willingly exit this world but are not motivated to do so by religious zeal. Both Jacob ben Sullam and Samuel "the Elder" ben Mordecai urge those standing in their vicinity to observe their action, and each then fatally stabs himself. Yet Jacob and Samuel operate from different motives. Samuel may have been motivated, at least partly, by the dread of dying unnoticed, as he seems to have lacked a family of his own. We are told that Jacob was not born to a Jewish woman and that his family was not highly esteemed; as he is about to commit suicide, he reminds his witnesses that up until that moment they had scorned him.[22] Jacob appears to use his martyrdom as a mechanism for raising his social status and thereby exemplifies the nonideological martyr.

Jacob's story is echoed by the martyrdom of the anonymous convert of Xanten, who slaughters himself only after ascertaining from the head of his community that in the world to come he would "sit with us in our circle," that is, enjoy social recognition and integration. The community leader tells him that following his martyrdom, "[he] shall be a true convert," implying that up to that point he had enjoyed a limited degree of acceptance in the Jewish community. This, rather than a crisis of faith, seems to have been the root of Jacob's ambivalence to martyrdom as well as the key to his ultimate decision to link his fate with that of the community.[23]

We read that the narrator hears of the martyrdom in Xanten from eyewitnesses, and a few lines later we are told that "all" went joyfully before the glorious Lord, like a bridegroom from his bridal canopy."[24] This sort of contradiction, which is fairly common in the Hebrew narratives of the First Crusade, trumpets consensus and leaves it to careful readers to probe for the survivors' stories.[25]

In the narrative of the events in Trier, unheroic conduct is depicted as the rule rather than the exception. We read that the bishop valiantly attempts to save the Jews, but when he senses that the crusaders will ultimately turn against him, he directs his efforts toward convincing the Jews to apostatize. They refuse, which is heroic enough, but do not kill themselves. The bishop then decides to demoralize them by having "two or three" Jews killed; these include Asher ben Joseph (the community sexton), Meir ben Samuel (a youth), Abraham ben Yomtov, and a young girl. Of these victims, only Meir is described as embracing martyrdom voluntarily. The martyrdom of the young girl is noted without detail, indeed without even her name. Abraham ben Yomtov does not merely refrain from choosing martyrdom; falling on the ground, he produces a lengthy and bitter lamentation about God's abandonment of Israel and passionately repudiates the principle of divine justice, which lies at the heart of the chronicler's record of the First Crusade experience.[26] The crusaders then lift him up and lead him outside for execution. The chronicler includes Abraham ben Yomtov in the roster of martyrs, depicting him as "faithful and saintly and righteous and beloved of heaven," but his behavior is that of an antihero.[27]

Social Context

In the root story those within the chambers witness the violence in the courtyard, including the martyrdom of their rabbi, Isaac ben Moses. They must have realized that the enemy was about to penetrate their sanctuary and felt fear and despair. Presumably these emotions were accompanied by a certain amount of social pressure. This is inevitable when a group of people who live in fairly close quarters and know each other fairly well find themselves together in a stressful situation. This sort of intimacy characterizes the Jews of medieval Ashkenaz, where communities were small.[28] As there was no hope for survival, the only choice was between death at the hands of the enemy or death at the hands of a "friend," namely, a relative, friend, or oneself.[29] Under the circumstances, one would expect those favoring active martyrdom to take the lead and to exert pressure on others to go along with their plan of action. The more passive group would find it difficult to stand up to the "activists" and to refuse to cooperate in the collective martyrdom.[30]

This consideration also applies to the rabbis and important Jews seated in the courtyard with Rabbi Isaac ben Moses. The Mainz Anonymous says nothing about their fate and state of mind, but the chronicle of Solomon ben Samson describes them collectively as sitting and weeping with their necks stretched out and exclaiming, "When will the marauder come, so that we may accept upon ourselves the judgment of heaven?"[31] Clearly they were impatient for the end to come, but would it not be more natural for their impatience to reflect anxiety rather than zeal?

The precise description of the social and physical setting of these martyrs helps to explain the rhetoric imputed to them, and it suggests that they experienced conflicting feelings. On the one hand, they probably felt constrained to imitate the bravery of their rabbinic leader. They would also have sensed pressure from each other, with no one daring to propose a withdrawal to the relative safety of the inner chambers. Finally and perhaps most important, the men in the courtyard must have also been aware that those inside the chambers were watching them through the palace windows. Under these circumstances, whether or not those in the courtyard were eager for martyrdom, they were understandably rooted to their seats, not daring to abandon their position and join those cloistered within. These considerations would have applied to Isaac ben Moses as well as to his flock.

This kind of reconstruction cannot be termed factual if factuality requires that the narrator report the presence of ambivalence and inner conflict on the part of the protagonists. Rather, the truth claim of the observation rests on the reliability of the narrative's description of the physical and social environment in which the events allegedly took place, for these constitute "neutral" data, information that in and of itself neither advances nor prejudices the chronicler's tendency. If we accept the depiction of the social and physical setting of the men in the courtyard, that image forms the basis for the reconstruction of their state of mind, provided that the feelings we impute to them can reasonably be considered to have necessarily resulted from their conditions. For instance, assuming that Jews really were sitting in the courtyard with Rabbi Isaac when he was killed, it seems inconceivable that they would not have felt constrained to maintain a brave front, given the social circumstances. Therefore the emotional forces at work must have produced inner conflict and ambivalence toward martyrdom, notwithstanding the protagonists' purported zeal for martyrdom.

What of the observers, those hiding within the chambers? Were they also propelled toward martyrdom by powerful social pressures? From the physical and social environment described in the tales, it would appear so. The scene of the mass martyrdom of Mainz took place "within the chambers," namely, in closed rooms. This was an intimate community, in which anonymity was unavailable, and once the activists expressed their intention to commit homicide and suicide, and perhaps already had begun doing so, it would have been difficult for the passivists among them to balk or demur.

Once again, the neutral description of the physical and social conditions renders the existence of social constraints a necessity and hence an assumed fact. Yet here we can avail ourselves of direct testimony. The root story depicts a process of commitment, a kind of chain reaction, rather than a single, spontaneous moment. The structure "women girded their loins. . . . Many men, likewise, gathered strength" indicates plainly that women led and men followed.[32] Moreover, although the chronicler does not describe hesitation or dissent, he pointedly writes "many men," rather than "all the men," implying that some men could not bring themselves to participate in the slaughter. Yet neither could they bring themselves to halt the slaughter or even to protest.

Eliezer ben Nathan offers an interesting variation on this description: "Tenderhearted men also mustered their strength and slaughtered their wives . . . etc."[33] The phrase "tenderhearted men also" could mean that men are generally more tenderhearted than are women, because the chronicle emphasizes the leading role played by women. Alternatively, the phrase could mean that not only did the stouthearted men slaughter their families but the more timid did so as well. Both versions and interpretations concede the presence of men who were reluctant to follow the lead of the martyrologically minded, yet the fact that women were the driving force behind the slaughter made it difficult for men to adopt a less pious course.[34]

The tales of the martyrdom in the bishop's palace in Worms offer further evidence of the role of social context in the martyrdom scenes. These martyrs, we are told, sanctify the divine name publicly, extending their necks. The key word here is *publicly*, literally "before the eyes of all" or "before the eyes of the whole world."[35] Eliezer ben Nathan also emphasizes the public nature of their martyrdom in the following line from the poem he intersperses at this point in his narrative: "Publicly in every region, they sanctified my God the King."[36] The reference to the public nature of the scene cannot refer to the presence of Christian observers, because talmudic law assigns value only to what Jews witness; in Jewish law the presence of Christian witnesses does not justify the forfeit of one's life and hence is insignificant.[37] The emphasis on the public nature of the martyrdom in the bishop's palace in Worms highlights the role of social context in the scene described. People extended their necks not only *while* others were watching but also *because* others were watching. The presence of the "heads of the community"[38] among the "public" can only have increased the pressure felt by the protagonists.

Nonetheless, we read that most of those present in the bishop's palace in Worms resist the social pressure. The chronicler notes that, in addition to those who submit passively to martyrdom, "there were some of them that took their own lives." This evidence of diverse forms of behavior implies the absence of consensus, which is why the chronicler immediately flattens the description with the following summation: "All of them accepted the heavenly decree unreservedly." The impact of this effort at homogenization is blunted by the addition that a few of those present are baptized "forcibly" and survive.[39]

Social context is also important for understanding the story of the martyrs of Xanten. The head of this community exhorts his fellow congregants, seated at his dinner table on a Friday night, to slaughter each other and themselves; they unanimously assent.[40] Like the root story, this is a scene of social intimacy, in which it would have been difficult for those present to express reluctance.

The story of the Jews of Moers presents yet another instance. After a vain attempt to convince the local Jews to apostatize and thus save the city from the crusaders, the mayor has the Jews imprisoned. The Jews are incarcerated individually to prevent them from killing each other, as everyone knew had happened elsewhere.[41] The next day, the Jews are evicted from the town and flee in all directions; some are cut down by the crusaders, and the survivors hide in a nearby forest.

The mayor may well have imprisoned the Jews individually for the reason stated by the chronicler.[42] But this policy probably had the additional effect of increasing the chances that individual Jews might be induced to apostatize. The mayor could have deduced this from the fact that up to that point the Jews had twice refused to apostatize and that on both occasions they had acted as a group, with the pressure that that entails. Yet even if this consideration did not cross his mind, its social significance is readily apparent.[43]

Young People

Young people are heroes in some of the martyrological anecdotes recounted in the chronicles. In Trier, a young woman, "comely and charming," is approached by her aunt and asked whether she wishes to die with her. She assents, and the two women bribe the guard of the palace for permission to leave, walk to the town bridge, and plunge into the river and drown. The aunt is the protagonist here, but the young woman is her enthusiastic follower.[44] In the story of the martyrdom in Trier, Meir ben Samuel, a youth, is the only member of the community to embrace martyrdom, actually stepping forward to answer the bishop's call for volunteers.

Yet a series of other personal histories form a pattern that highlights the particularly severe constraints attributable to young people who find themselves in extreme peril: pressure from parents, relatives, and communal leaders as well as from peers. They might also be expected to feel frustration, rage, and sorrow at the imminent and abrupt deprivation of their future, of the chance to build a life. Both of these powerful forces would be particular to the experience of young people facing death, whatever their ideological convictions.

The presence of these feelings is spotlighted in the root story: "The virgins and brides and bridegrooms gazed through the windows and cried out loudly: 'Behold, our God, what we do for the sanctification of your great Name.'" The narrator's decision to emphasize the behavior of the young people indicates that at that poignant moment something differentiated them from the adult population. Did they relegate decision and action to their elders, and were they therefore simply waiting passively to be slaughtered? Was their cry really a declaration of faith, or perhaps a lament for their youth? The poetic depiction by Rabbi Abraham—"pure maidens wail bitterly"—appears to support the latter reading, by its use of the adverb *bitterly*.[45]

The classic example of the young person's ambivalence or conflict is Aaron, the son of Rachel in the root story. We are told that Isaac is small, young, and good-natured, and so he is easily put down. Aaron is no longer young enough to be dispatched quietly, but neither is he sufficiently mature to face up to his mother's desperate choice. Social constraints seem to be powerfully at work, namely, his mother's approval and that of the other women around him, but these cannot outweigh his fear of death. His is a rare cry of protest "tolerated" by the Hebrew chroniclers, apparently on account of his youth.

Aaron's sisters, Bella and Madrona, cooperate in their martyrdom; we are told that they even sharpen the knife used on themselves. Of course, it would have been hard for Bella and Madrona to protest; in addition to the social constraints exerted by parents and adult nonrelatives, the two siblings would have likely felt sibling rivalry, either by a competitive desire to please their parents or to outdo each other in piety.

Sibling rivalry also may have been a factor in the cooperative behavior of Helbo and Simeon, the two sons of Moses ben Helbo, which appears in the narrative of the martyrdom within the chambers. The father asks the sons whether they prefer paradise over hell or vice versa; they express a preference for paradise, extend their necks, and are killed by the enemy (!), as is their father.[46] Like Bella and Madrona, it would have been hard for these children to rebel against their father's exhortation, especially when the power of his will was coupled with the social pressures exerted by siblings on each other.[47]

Paradoxically, siblings, in addition to experiencing feelings of rivalry, can also identify with each other to a remarkable degree, enabling one sibling to draw support from another's resolution. In a kind of chain reaction, the second sibling then reinforces the first sibling's conviction, as well as his or her own. This dynamic of reinforcement, as well as rivalry, may be found in the behavior of the two pairs portrayed so far; each sibling reinforces the other's desire to do the right thing rather than succumb to fear and weakness.[48]

The martyrdom of two young men, Samuel ben Gedaliah and Yehiel ben Samuel, is the centerpiece of the martyrdom in Wevelinghofen, and it reflects the dynamics presented thus far. We read that "some of the pious" climb a tower overlooking the Rhine and hurl themselves into the river, for the Name of God.[49] Allegedly, Samuel and Yehiel also intend to drown themselves but are unable to do so; they lament their fate, specifically the fact that they would never "see seed go forth from us"[50] or grow old. Later, the town's remaining Jews, those "who did not go up on the tower," discover those who had hurled themselves from the tower and drowned as well as the two youths, who are still very much alive. Among the discoverers is Yehiel's father, Samuel, who exhorts his son to extend his neck and be slaughtered, which he does.[51] Samuel ben Gedaliah is put to death by Menahem, the sexton of Cologne, at Samuel ben Gedaliah's request, so that Samuel ben Gedaliah not witness his friend Yehiel's demise.[52] The sexton then kills Yehiel's father, also at the latter's request, and the sexton finally falls on his own sword.

These events are replete with unheroic conduct. The largest group of nonmartyrs includes, of course, those who choose not to climb the tower in the first place.[53] Prominent among the reluctant martyrs are the young Samuel and Yehiel, the central protagonists, who prove incapable of killing themselves and who voice nonmartyrological feelings. Their lament over the fact that they would never "see seed go forth from us" or grow old is a particularly striking expression of the young person's ambivalence to martyrdom in 1096.

It is uncertain whether Samuel and Yehiel intended to die but suffered remorse at the last minute or whether they never intended to die with the pious ones but rather chose to leave town in search of seclusion and survival. At any rate, these youths suffer martyrdom only after they are discovered by the side of the river, and in this case *post hoc ergo propter hoc* may not be a fallacy: Yehiel's father's exhortation would hardly have been necessary if the two boys were ready to die. Also, the chronicler writes that Yehiel accedes to his father's wishes,[54] an expression that scarcely connotes martyrological fervor. Finally, in summing up the story, the chronicler implies Yehiel's reluctance to die when he praises Yehiel's father Samuel more highly than the others: "How great was the strength of the father, whose mercy was not aroused for [the] son!"[55]

In "Ilna,"[56] as in Wevelingofen, the youth are reluctant victims. The chief protagonist is Judah ben Abraham, for whom the chronicler expresses the most profuse praise, apparently to allay contrary feelings aroused by the following anecdote.[57] Sarit, a lovely young woman, sees the community's members slaughter each other and attempts to flee the scene. However, Judah seizes her and tells her, "Since you are not permitted to be wed to my son Abraham, you will not be wed to any other, to the foreigners."[58] From this point on Sarit is passive, except that she cries. Judah lays her down in Abraham's bosom—we are not told whether she resists—and then slaughters her along with Abraham.[59]

The window is a significant prop in Sarit's story. Sarit is frightened by "what she saw through the window, outside," and later Judah "took her outside the window" or "removed her from the window."[60] In the root story young women of marriageable age also "gazed through the windows."[61] In general, these windows may be allusions to Jeremiah 9:20: "Death is come up into our windows." More specifically, however, the act of standing by the window during the hour of slaughter connotes passivity: either passive acquiescence—at best!—or perhaps reluctance, as is clear in the case of Sarit.[62]

The ambivalence to martyrdom particular to young people finds additional expression in their preference for resistance. The chronicle of Solomon ben Samson lists a number of the members of Qalonymos's band of fighters, and most of them are referred to by the honorific *Mar*, meaning mister: Abraham ben Asher, Samuel ben Tamar, Seigneur, Isaac ben Samuel, Isaac ben Moses, Helbo ben Moses.[63] This title generally indicates low social status, which was the natural lot of the young.

The other fighter depicted in the chronicles is Simhah ben Isaac ha-Kohen of Worms, described as "the young man." Simhah sees that he is being led to the baptismal font and stabs to death a nobleman, the bishop's grandson, and continues to assault others until his knife breaks and he is killed. The chronicler notes that this youth's behavior is unusual: "[He] did what the rest of the community did not do, for he killed three of the uncircumcised with his knife."[64] But what Simhah does not do is commit suicide or suffer martyrdom passively.

Sefer Hasidim offers some testimony to the notion that young people were particularly ambivalent about giving up their lives. We read that the Jews of Mainz delay the crusaders' assault by throwing money out the window, whereupon the attackers' chief halts the attack, reasoning that the delay gives the young people and the wicked time to flee, leaving only the elderly and pious.[65] The assumption that the young people would opt to flee rests, I maintain, not only on their physical fitness but on their will to live, for the assumption that the young were reluctant martyrs in 1096 resounds in the Hebrew narratives.

Another *Sefer Hasidim* anecdote is all about ambivalence. Two "pupils" hide to escape murdering gentiles. At night, one elects to walk out into the open and be killed for the sanctification of the divine name, in emulation of the public martyrdom of the Palestinian sage Haninah ben Teradion.[66] The other youth remains in seclusion and reminds his companion that in that same incident Haninah was castigated for endangering himself.[67] This story is but an exemplum, with hardly a nod at historicity, but it belongs here nonetheless because, although ambivalence toward martyrdom was widespread, if not universal, it is associated here with young people in particular, which reflects a pattern that runs like a thread through the First Crusade chronicles.

Separation of Families

In the root story, Rachel and her husband Judah appear to differ over the appropriate course of action, and indeed on a number of occasions spouses make different choices. In the case of Qalonymos and his band of armed men, the separation of spouses seems perfectly natural, because women did not fight, and it does not reflect conflict between spouses. In other situations, husband and wife may have separated to enhance the family's chances of survival. However, this consideration is nowhere articulated, and in at least some cases the couples probably disagreed over the best response to the crisis. This, then, is a second type of situation that expresses ambivalence or conflict about the available choices during the First Crusade.

The chronicles make no attempt to recount the fate of all the members of a given family, and an anecdote or remark sometimes leaves the reader wondering what happened to other family members. For instance, in Speyer, "there was there an important and pious woman, and she slaughtered herself for the sanctification of the [Divine] Name. And she was the first of those who slaughtered and were slaughtered in all the communities."[68] One wonders what became of the rest of her family, for the text gives no indication that she was unattached.

More often the reader deduces that families were separated by piecing together snippets of narrative. Isaac ben Samuel is one of Qalonymos's fighters.[69] Although he fights and later flees with the Qalonymos band, his son, Samuel, flees to Speyer but is killed en route.[70] This is typical of stories in which families meet the crisis apart from one another. The reader is left with an incomplete picture of the family's intentions and actions, specifically of how the fate of one family member relates to that of others.

To the example of Isaac and Samuel's family one can add the stories of Guta and Scholaster of Mainz. The chronicle of Solomon ben Samson reports that these two women are in the courtyard of a townsman until "the enemy" forces them out of doors.[71] The crusaders and burghers crowd around them and demand that they apostatize, but they extend their necks and are slain.

Guta is the wife of the venerated Rabbi Isaac ben Moses, who is decapitated in the courtyard in Mainz. Scholaster's husband is Isaac ben David, the *parnas*, or communal leader, of Mainz, who saves his mother and children by accepting baptism. It seems more likely that Guta and Scholaster are in the townsman's courtyard by choice rather than by chance, but it is uncertain whether their behavior signifies dissent from that of their husbands. In Guta's case we may conjecture that her husband sees martyrdom as a man's prerogative but views women as obligated to save themselves and their children. But this explanation does not seem to fit Scholaster's case, whose husband Isaac submits to baptism rather than suffer martyrdom.[72] It therefore appears that Scholaster and Isaac agreed about the need to survive but not about the way to do so.

Abraham ben Asher belongs to Qalonymos's military force, which flees to the forest after its abortive attempt to defeat the crusaders in combat. Abraham is surrounded by Christian acquaintances, who urge him to accept Christianity, presumably out of a friendly desire to save his life.[73] Before responding, he inquires about the fate of his children and the members of his household, but none of those who confront him can enlighten him on that score. Their reticence seems to destroy his will to live, for he promptly rejects the offer of life and is dispatched. Like other members of Qalonymos's band, Abraham separates from his immediate family and remains ignorant of their fate. We are not told whether this is accidental, whether they separate to improve their chances of survival, or whether Abraham is the only member of his family to reject the option of martyrdom, at least initially.[74]

In Cologne most of the Jews flee to the homes of gentile acquaintances before the crusaders' arrival. However, Isaac ben Eliakim purposely remains behind and seeks martyrdom; we are told nothing about the fate of his family members and can assume that they fled.[75] Solomon, the husband of "Rebecca," leaves Cologne for the home of a gentile acquaintance, but Rebecca tarries in order to carry off her precious possessions, and this costs her her life.[76] This is a rare case indeed, in which a couple's separation is plainly the result of their inability to agree on a single course of action. Neither of them seeks martyrdom and neither cuts a heroic figure, but they are a classic example of the separation of families in 1096, which apparently implies ambivalence or conflict among family members over the best response to the great crisis.[77]

Conclusion

The story of Isaac ben David the *parnas* and his family exhibits most of the patterns and dynamics suggested earlier and serves as a summary. Isaac saves his mother and children by converting to Christianity, even though his wife Scholaster has already been killed.[78] He later suffers remorse and is therefore determined to sacrifice himself in an act of expiation. He tells his mother of his intention, and she makes him swear not to carry it out, but he is determined. Like Moses ben Helbo, he asks his children whether they wish to be sacrificed; they answer, "Do what you will with us!"[79] This reply suggests resignation rather than enthusiastic cooperation. Isaac then declares that "our" God is the only true God, which is apparently intended to inspire them to greater devotion. In this Isaac fails, for although the children allow him to lead them to the synagogue and slaughter them in front of the ark, there is no record of any declaration of support on their part. Isaac then returns home and sets fire to his home, leaving his mother to burn to death, no doubt against her will.[80]

This scenario exhibits unheroic conduct, conflict between family members, the separation of families, and the particular predicament of the young. One cannot help but wonder why the chronicler chooses to present it, given his clear general tendency to glorify martyrdom, even at the price of effacing nuance and downplaying ambivalence and conflict. The case of Abraham ben Yomtov of Trier, the antihero, is even more extreme, for not only does the chronicler note Abraham's reluctance for martyrdom but he even records his sorrowful soliloquy.

The inclusion of "inconvenient" material cannot be accidental. It may reflect a desire on the part of the chronicler to relate as complete an account as possible, supporting the view that the chronicles are basically factual. Cohen views the tale of Isaac the *parnas* as a prominent example of the ambivalence to martyrdom conveyed by the narrator, often obliquely and esoterically, to address the conflicting feelings of the survivors and their descendents.[81] On the plane of cultural values, the chronicler may be signaling that the term *martyr* is applicable to anyone who is deprived of life on account of his or her Jewish identity, whether or not the victim behaves bravely. This approach would increase the didactic power of the narrative, by enabling the audience to empathize with the protagonists rather than merely idolize them. Our exploration, then, fleshes out an element embedded in the tales by the chronicler's own design and may perhaps achieve the effect he intended.

Five Apostates

From the pioneers of nineteenth-century Europe to the present, scholars of Jewish history have used a "rhetoric of excellence" to characterize the Jews of medieval Europe, imputing to them unswerving devotion to Jewish law and unstinting fidelity to their religious identity. The persistence of this rhetoric has an element of cognitive dissonance, for the severe and variegated challenges to Jewish identity in their own age did not lead latter-day historians to question the heroic image of their medieval forebears and to suppose that they too enjoyed only partial success in the struggle for the survival of Judaism. On the contrary, it has been important to convey that medieval Jewry was characterized by consummate faith and communal solidarity, unsullied by the skepticism and assimilation of the modern era.

The rhetoric of excellence has been described by Avraham Grossman in the following terms:

> The Judaism of early Ashkenaz is often described in the scholarly literature in idyllic terms, as a society whose members were punctilious in their observance of the commandments. . . . This description stems from three sources: the reality which seems to emerge from the liturgical poetry composed in those days . . . ; the great esteem expressed by the German Pietists for these ancestors; and especially, the heroic martyrdom of many members of these communities in the First Crusade, which is described in extravagant terms in the chronicles of those events.[1]

This portrait recognizes that medieval texts, both prose and poetry, are the source of the modern characterization of the Jews of Ashkenaz as paragons of religious devotion. I would go a step further and contend that it is widely applied not only to the founding fathers of Ashkenazic Jewry but also to the Jews of medieval Ashkenaz in general.

It is the Jews of Ashkenaz, of Franco-Germany, who are characterized as steadfast and spiritually pristine, as opposed to those of Sepharad, the Iberian peninsula. The contrast between these two ethnic blocs is rooted in the historical record of their responses to conversionary pressure: The Jews of Ashkenaz, the sources report, overwhelmingly chose death over baptism in the First Crusade, whereas those of Sepharad apostatized in the tens of thousands in the century leading up to the 1492 expulsion (on the Iberian experience, see Chapter 8).

This approach is characteristic of Yitzhak Baer and appears in almost all his writings on medieval Judaism.[2] For Jacob Katz too, the record of Ashkenazic fidelity under pressure is primarily why "the Ashkenazi Middle Ages outshine all other periods of Jewish history as an epoch of heroic steadfastness. Everything known to us points to the assumption that the proportion of those who stood the test, compared with those who failed to do so, was greater in the Ashkenazi Middle Ages than in any other period of Jewish martyrdom."[3]

The crux of the heroic image of Ashkenazic Jewry, then, is the mass martyrdom of the Rhineland communities, as related in detail in the Hebrew narratives and liturgical poetry. These texts make fleeting mention of Jews who survive by accepting baptism, but for these writers the First Crusade is not primarily their story.

Since the 1980s historians have begun questioning the reliability of these narratives as sources of information about what occurred. Simon Schwarzfuchs challenges the number of victims cited in the medieval texts.[4] Ivan Marcus questions whether the Hebrew narratives can teach us anything at all about what actually happened during the crusader onslaught.[5] The significance of apostasy has been among those aspects of the First Crusade tragedy to be reevaluated. Kenneth Stow speculates that in addition to the martyrs, "there were also hundreds of converts in Ashkenaz, far more even than the Jewish chronicles concede."[6] Avraham Grossman claims that those forcibly converted in 1096 numbered in the thousands and cautions against taking the Hebrew sources at face value.[7] The claim that apostasy was a central feature of the 1096 attacks undergirds Jeremy Cohen's interpretation of these events.[8]

The argument of these scholars rests on the fact that in 1097 Henry IV issued an edict sanctioning the return of the forced converts to Judaism; this edict triggered a written complaint by the antipope Guibert of Ravenna (Clement III) to the bishop of Bamberg.[9] This hypothesis is based on the assumption that the emperor would not have issued an edict in response to a problem of negligible dimensions. This is debatable, because the problem facing the Church and the secular authorities was the reversion of the forced converts after the violence subsided. Throughout its history the Church regarded heresy as a severe threat, and Henry might well have acted whether the number of renegades numbered in the dozens, hundreds, or thousands.

What do the medieval sources actually say about the scope of apostasy in 1096? The narrative edited by Solomon ben Samson, which is the most detailed and expansive of the Hebrew sources, reports isolated cases of forced baptism. There were also a few large-scale incidents of forced conversion; in Regensburg, we read, all the Jews were herded into the Rhine and baptized.[10] It was probably the experience of one of these communities that inspired the tale told in *Sefer Hasidim*, an anthology of exempla of a pietistic bent compiled in Germany in the late twelfth and early thirteenth century.

> When there was a persecution the community said: What shall we do?
> The rabbi said: Do as I do! He took a woof and warp [i.e., an object in
> the shape of a cross] and carried it, so that the gentiles would not kill
> him, and they forced him [to apostatize] with the members of his city.[11]

But these tales are terse and marginal, whereas the narrative focuses on martyrological tales, which are elaborate and heavily laden with pathos and religious significance. Baer notes that the liturgical poet too, in memorializing the persecutions of medieval Ashkenaz, "does not mention the cases of treachery . . . and itemizes the histories of each and every victim."[12]

The only premodern historian to acknowledge the greater significance of apostasy in the events of 1096 is Gedalya ibn Yahya, a sixteenth-century Spaniard writing in Italy. Ibn Yahya relates that the First

Crusade left more than 5,000 dead in France and Germany and "apostates without number."[13] These figures seem inflated, but what matters is the relative size of the two groups, for Ibn Yahya acknowledges that there were far more apostates than fatalities. Still, one cannot help but wonder whether the historical experience of his own ethnic community in the fifteenth century played a role in tilting the balance in his report from martyrdom to apostasy.

Solomon ben Samson reports that after the wave of violence had passed, the apostates reverted to Judaism.[14] Focusing on the writers of our sources and their twelfth-century audience, Stow maintains that "Albert of Aachen condemned marauders like Emicho of Flonheim so sharply just because a major after-effect of Emicho's attacks on Jews in 1096 was to create hundreds (at least) of Judaizing apostates."[15] Stow offers no grounds to abandon the accepted view that Albert savages Emicho and his band for their immoral behavior in order to explain the ignominious failure of this particular crusader band, but his suggestion reflects the recent tendency to grant greater prominence to apostasy in the history of the First Crusade assaults.

Avraham Grossman also shifts the focus from text to context and asks what created the need for the martyrological ethos espoused by the narrators (in poetry as well as prose) of the First Crusade catastrophe. He suggests that their message offered a sorely needed injection of religious faith at a time when many Jews willingly abandoned their Jewish identity. "The problem of apostasy," he claims, "was one of the central problems with which the Jewish communities of those days were confronted."[16] Similarly, Cohen claims that "among these converts to Christianity and among their children . . . we must seek the impetus for the composition of the chronicles, the mentality that nourished their tales of *qiddush ha-Shem*" (i.e., martyrdom).[17]

The importance attached to apostasy in the recent historiography of the First Crusade, particularly with regard to its place in twelfth-century Jewish society, largely undergirds the following review of the nature of Jewish apostasy in medieval Ashkenaz. I argue that the prevailing vision of the nature and scope of apostasy in medieval Ashkenaz is a romantic one. Here, the writers would have us believe, Jews rarely apostatized and then only under extreme duress, only to revert at the earliest opportunity. Portrayals of the medieval Jewish community ignore or downplay the renegades, who drop out of the annals of Jewish history as though they ceased to exist. This also is a reflection of the rhetoric of excellence rather than of the reality of life in the Jewish communities of northern Europe in the Middle Ages.

The etiology of apostasy also has served the heroic image of Ashkenazic Jewry. Apostasy, we are taught, represents the failure of medieval Jews to stand up to the conversionary forces of their environment, be they economic, social, or psychological. Such forces surrounded and bombarded them every day, and they stood in perpetual need of effective means with which to fend off the cultural aggression of their predatory neighbors. I would replace this model with one of symbiosis. The interaction between Jews and Christians in medieval Ashkenaz was not, I believe, a never-ending *Kulturkampf*, in which apostates represent instances of the Jews being vanquished in religious warfare. Rather, medieval Jews crossed the Jewish-Christian cultural divide with ease, signifying that the gap was not nearly as wide or the boundary as high as we have been led to believe.

Numbers

The rhetoric of excellence about Ashkenazic Jewry has numerous components, first and foremost that apostates were few. This notion, like the other components, rests on medieval sources. Agobard of Lyons, the nemesis of Narbonese Jewry in the early ninth century, complains that "in spite of all the humanity and kindness we display towards them, we do not succeed in bringing over one of them to our faith."[18] In the twelfth century Guibert of Nogent admits that the sincere, ideological conversion of a Jew "in our days is unusual."[19]

How common was apostasy in the high Middle Ages? Jacob Katz wrestles with the question and concludes, "Our sources do not allow us to come to a conclusion concerning either the absolute or the relative numbers of Jews who embraced Christianity in the Ashkenazi community of the Middle Ages."[20] Conceding that the rabbinic literature of medieval Ashkenaz abounds in cases dealing with apostasy, Katz views this abundance as indicative, not necessarily of the large scale of apostasy but of its significance for the Jewish community.[21] Katz does not elaborate, but his caution is probably rooted in the methodological principle that thorny issues, such as apostasy, merit extensive treatment in legal sources even when they are statistically insignificant. In Cohen's formulation, "The law had to account for the isolated as well as common occurrence."[22]

Salo Baron also ponders the dimensions of apostasy in medieval Ashkenaz and offers no simple answer.

> How effective was the Christian mission? Of course, statistical data, even those for individual countries and periods, are extremely sketchy. Bishop Stephen of Tournai was not guilty of understatement when, in asking the almoner of Philip Augustus for a subsidy for a recent convert from Leon, he wrote: "It rarely happens that a member of the stubborn uncircumcised [sic] people converts himself faithfully and is reborn in the new Church." Nonetheless, at times the number of baptized Jews, particularly in Mediterranean countries, was far from inconsiderable. . . . Even among steadfast German Jewry, apostates are mentioned from time to time, particularly in the "Book of the Pious."[23]

In using the phrase "even among steadfast German Jewry," Baron subscribes to the image of the superior devotion and fidelity of Ashkenazic Jewry. Elsewhere, Baron writes that "such conversions [i.e., ideological] must often have taken place *even in the more staunchly orthodox* [emphasis added] communities of northern France and Germany, and many more in the Mediterranean countries."[24] For Baron, then, the Jews of Ashkenaz truly were more steadfast than those of other regions, but at the same time he concedes that apostasy was not a totally negligible social phenomenon.

Haym Soloveitchik concedes that "people did convert—a good number of them." But in his view what characterizes Franco-German Jewry in the high Middle Ages was "the absence of religious alternatives. . . . Conversion as a cultural phenomenon was not perceived as being an actuality."[25] Soloveitchik offers the intriguing suggestion that even if Ashkenazic Jews apostatized in large numbers, the self-image of this community remained as positive and firm as ever, and thus his understanding of the significance of Ashkenazic apostasy is diametrically opposed to that of Grossman, for whom the Jews of Ashkenaz viewed apostasy as a dire threat.

Grossman admits that "due to a dearth of sources about apostasy in those days [the eleventh and twelfth centuries], it is impossible to establish the precise dimensions of apostasy in the Jewish society of that time," but he concludes, "Clearly the number of apostates was fairly large."[26] Elsewhere he asserts that "the problem of apostasy, voluntarily or under duress, was one of the central problems with which the Jewish communities of those days were confronted."[27] Most pertinent is Grossman's comment that the number of apostates in Germany and France in the high Middle Ages was "greater than was once thought."[28] The past generation of scholars have indeed acknowledged the presence of apostasy as a significant element of medieval Ashkenazic life, although none has pointed out the origins of the previous tacit, contrary assumption in the rhetoric of Ashkenazic excellence.

A barometer of the numbers issue is the following remark, attributed to Jacob ben Meir of Ramerupt, known as Rabbenu ("Our Rabbi") Tam (d. 1171): "More than twenty bills of divorce involving apostates were executed in Paris and [île de] France."[29] Katz interprets this text to refer to isolated instances of apostasy rather than to a single large group, but he draws no conclusions about the overall scale of the problem.[30] The difficulty is that Rabbenu Tam's statement does not present a time frame, and it is therefore impossible to know whether the incident he relates was common, rare, or possibly even unique. Grossman, on the other hand, derives that apostasy was still a big problem in the twelfth century. Twenty apostates, he explains, reflect a widespread phenomenon when we take into consideration the minuscule size of European Jewish communities in the twelfth century, which generally numbered a few dozen families. He also observes that there were undoubtedly some apostates who did not write bills of divorce, whether because they were unmarried, because their wives converted with them, or because they simply opted not to cooperate.[31]

Rabbenu Tam goes on to relate that "it happens every day" that apostates divorce their Jewish wives. This phrase, even if it is an exaggeration, seems to settle the matter in favor of frequent crossover between the Jewish and Christian communities. Curiously, however, the remark has gone unnoticed in scholarly discussions, which seems to reflect prior assumptions about the extremely modest scope of apostasy in medieval Ashkenazic society.

Even if apostasy was not something that "happens every day," the volume of legal sources about the apostate's right to inherit seems to indicate that this was an important problem and one that could not have been altogether uncommon. The charter issued by Henry IV in 1090 to the Jews of Speyer and Mainz prohibits apostates from inheriting their parents' estate.[32] Clearly this clause was drawn up at the behest of the Jewish constituency, which might have insisted on it even if apostates were few. However, the issue was also of concern to the Church, as is evidenced by the inclusion among the decrees of the Third Lateran Council of one that allows Jewish converts to inherit.[33]

The view that apostasy was rare, a view articulated by medieval writers and echoed in modern historiography, has begun to give way in the past generation to greater recognition of its presence in and significance for medieval Jewish life. However, the impact of this shift for the romantic image of Ashkenazic Jewry has been blunted in two ways: by maintaining that it compared favorably with that of Spain (or, in Baron's idiom, with "Mediterranean countries") and by classifying the Franco-German apostates as predominantly the victims of coerced baptism.

Coercion

A second component in the mythical depiction of Ashkenazic Jewry is that its (few) apostates were almost all forcibly baptized rather than being true converts to Christianity. The following generalization by Baron illustrates this mode of discourse: "Whatever the cumulative effects of voluntary baptisms may have been, they were indubitably far surpassed numerically by those of mass Catholicization under duress, especially during massacres and expulsions."[34] This assessment is unsubstantiated, but more important for our purposes is that Baron's image of the proportion of coerced to voluntary apostates makes room for apostasy without destroying the image of Ashkenazic fidelity.

Given the obvious significance of the distinction between voluntary and forced conversion, it is all the more remarkable that medieval sources tend to play down this issue. Their failure to attach enormous significance to the distinction catches the modern reader by surprise and highlights its tendentious import. Thus, in contrast to Ephraim Kanarfogel's contention that "halakhists had to consider the intention . . . of the apostate," it is the rarity of such discussions in the halakhic literature of medieval Ashkenaz that is striking.[35]

The Hebrew terms for apostate, *mumar* and *meshumad*, nicely illustrate the confusion. Solomon Zeitlin claims that before the Hadrianic persecution of the second century CE, the Hebrew term was *mumar*, meaning one who changes his religion (from the root *m-u-r* for "change"); *meshumad* refers to a victim of persecution, that is, a forced convert, for it derives from the root *sh-m-d*, which expresses destruction. Zeitlin explains that the distinction vanished at some later stage and that *meshumad* came to refer to voluntary apostates as well as to victims of coercion.[36]

Simhah Goldin locates the shift at the time of the First Crusade, before which, he avers, *mumar* was the preferred term. He posits that this preference connotes a relatively liberal attitude toward apostasy on the part of the Jewish leadership and laity alike. Following the 1096 catastrophe, however, the survivors supposedly took a harder line on deviant behavior, particularly apostasy, and this new attitude is allegedly reflected in the new preference for the term *meshumad*.[37] This theory is not supported by philological evidence. In fact, *mumar* does not fall out of use, and the two terms are used interchangeably before and after the First Crusade.[38] This interchangeability signifies the absence or insignificance of a distinction between coerced and voluntary apostasy in the thinking of the rabbinic leadership of Franco-German Jewry in the tenth to twelfth centuries.

The classic example of the conflation of coerced and voluntary apostasy is the case of the son of Gershom ben Judah of Mainz (d. 1028), known in rabbinic literature as Rabbenu Gershom, "the Light of the Exile." Gershom is arguably the greatest spiritual and communal leader of medieval Ashkenaz. That this apostasy could have been anything but coerced strikes modern scholars as inconceivable, and they therefore at-

tach the story of Gershom's son to that of the persecution of Mainz
Jewry in 1012.[39]

What precisely happened in Mainz is unclear. A Latin source reports
that Henry II expelled the Jews of Mainz in that year, and Gershom
himself composed a Hebrew poetic lament, which recounts in powerful, if allusive, language that at a particular point in time his community faced the alternatives of conversion or expulsion. Jews are found
in Mainz shortly after they were supposedly expelled, and this has led
some scholars to suspect that the threatened expulsion was never implemented, but this is uncertain (see Chapter 2 for a discussion of this
episode).

How have modern historians grappled with this confusing set of
events? Heinrich Graetz paints the following picture:

> During this persecution [1012] many Jews became Christians, either
> to save their lives or their possessions. Among them was Gershom's
> son. When the latter died a Christian, his hapless father observed the
> mourning ceremonials for him as for one who had died a Jew. Simon
> b. Isaac . . . succeeded in staying the persecution, and even in obtain-
> ing permission for the Jews to settle again in Mayence. Those Jews
> who had been compelled to submit to baptism now gladly returned
> to their religion, and Gershom protected them from the scorn of their
> brethren on account of their temporary apostasy, by threatening to ex-
> communicate any one who reproached them.[40]

Graetz's account synthesizes the information reported in the sources
mentioned earlier and more. His portrayal of Simon ben Isaac is predicated on the statement in the Mainz *memorbuch* that Simon "exerted
himself on behalf of the communities and annulled decrees [of persecu-
tion]."[41] Graetz also uses sources (to be discussed shortly) concerning
Gershom's son and concerning an edict reportedly issued by Gershom.
The result is a much fuller picture of the alleged decree and its connection to Gershom's son; the instrumental role purportedly played by
Simon ben Isaac in the ultimate return to the status quo ante is a tour
de force of historical reconstruction by Graetz.

Victor Aptowitzer's version of the story, which is less precise than
Graetz's, injects the novel element of martyrdom. By and large, he
writes, the Jews of Mainz passed through the crucible of martyrdom

successfully, but a minority, including Gershom's son, were incapable of making the supreme sacrifice. This presentation is anachronistic, for no incident in the history of medieval Ashkenaz before the First Crusade precipitated the death of large numbers of Jews. Aptowitzer reports the reversion of the forcibly baptized and accepts the assumption that only sudden death prevented Gershom's son from joining their number, writing that "he died before he *managed to* [emphasis added] repent."[42]

James Parkes treads essentially the same path. Gershom's son, we read, "was baptized, *apparently by force* [emphasis added], and died a Christian." Parkes also sets the son's apostasy in the context of a "wave of indignation against the Jews," which forced many Jews to the baptismal font, only to have them revert once the danger was past. For Parkes, such a reconstruction accounts for Gershom's benign attitude toward reverting apostates (about which more later).[43]

In a more recent treatment of the episode, Avraham Grossman offers the familiar presentation but couches it in more cautious terms. He adds Elhanan, the son of the selfsame Simon ben Isaac, to the list of hapless forced converts but concedes that the link to the persecution of 1012 is uncertain.[44] Grossman notes that, according to Hebrew sources, Gershom mourned his son for two weeks, twice the customary period, because he died as a Christian, or in the familiar idiom, "before he was able to return to the bosom of Judaism."[45]

A closer look at the sources concerning Gershom's mourning illustrates the manipulation of this story by both medieval rabbis and modern historians. Our earliest source of information is Isaac ben Moses of Vienna (d. ca. 1250). Having explained that one does not mourn villains who die unrepentant, this scholar adds the following caveat: "However, in times of destruction,[46] I heard from my teacher, R. Samson [of Coucy], that Gershom mourned for fourteen days for his son that apostatized."[47] Isaac does not impute to his teacher the assumption that Gershom's son was forcibly converted; Samson merely reports the apostasy and Gershom's exceptionally lengthy period of mourning. It is Isaac who fills in the blanks with the phrase "in times of destruction" and presents the apostasy as involuntary.

Later authorities are more cautious. Meir ben Barukh of Rothenburg (d. 1293) writes, "I heard from Isaac of Vienna that Rabbenu Gershom mourned for his son that apostatized, but he told me that one ought not to draw any conclusions from this, for he [Gershom] did so out of an excess of sorrow, since he [the son] did not merit [the good fortune] to repent."[48] Here Isaac reports the fact of the apostasy without stating whether it was coerced or voluntary. The final clause also is significant, for it contains the germ of the notion that Gershom's son would have reverted had he lived. Yet this interpretation is unwarranted; saying that an apostate "did not merit [the good fortune] to repent" does not relate to a particular individual or to the circumstances of his apostasy but merely assumes that, given the opportunity, anyone in his right mind would revert to Judaism.[49]

Another component in the story of Gershom's son, of equal import for our purposes, is the apocryphal detail that he apostatized with his mother. This notion first appears in the text in which Mordecai ben Hillel (d. 1298) relates the story of Gershom's son thirdhand.[50] Apostates generally had their children baptized, and were this true in the present case, there would seem to be grounds for the assumption that the apostasy of Gershom's son was involuntary and perhaps also for the conviction that he would have reverted at a later date. But this element of the story is an easily explained error. In the text cited earlier, Isaac ben Moses of Vienna presents the story of Gershom's son in his ruling that one does not mourn for a person who commits a capital offense and dies unrepentant. Isaac adds that there are those who hold that one *does* mourn the death of a 1- or 2-year-old child who apostatizes with his mother, "for a child placed in water, what difference does that make?—it is as if he did not apostatize."[51] The proximity of the comment about the child who apostatizes with his mother to the story of Gershom's son suggests that Mordecai ben Hillel conflated the two scenarios. Perhaps he did so because the rule about the child apostate offers a halakhic explanation for Gershom's baffling behavior.

That Gershom's wife apostatized has also been inferred from the contents of Gershom's marriage contract, which, amazingly, has survived. The document is dated 1013, and it states that Bona, the bride, is a widow. Several scholars, including Ben-Zion Dinur, deduce that this must have been a second marriage, for Gershom's first marriage would probably have been to a maiden, who would have been more valuable on the marriage market than a widow. Coupled with the date of the contract, the notion that Gershom's first wife apostatized during the persecutions of 1012 virtually suggests itself.[52]

This is pure speculation, invited by the paucity of the period's sources. Stripped of the presumed link to the alleged persecution of 1012, of the assumption that only untimely death prevented the reversion of Gershom's son, and of the notion that Gershom's son was the involuntary victim of his mother's apostasy, all we are left with is the story of an ordinary case of apostasy, which was exceptional only because the apostate was the son of Ashkenazic Jewry's charismatic rabbinic scholar and communal authority. Moreover, Gershom's behavior belies the notion that his son's apostasy was coerced, for a father could be expected to grieve more deeply over the death of his apostate son if the apostasy were voluntary than if it were forced, given that he died as a lost soul rather than as merely the victim of persecution.

The absence of a distinction in medieval texts between coerced and voluntary apostasy also emerges from the documentation of a ban attributed to Gershom, which threatens with excommunication anyone reminding a reverted apostate of his sin. The ban reads, "Not to shame the penitent ones [by] mentioning their sin," with no qualifying phrase to apply this rule exclusively to victims of forced baptism.[53] A variant formulation reads, "Not to shame a coerced person and a penitent one, by mentioning his sin to him in any way."[54] Here the issue of coercion is mentioned, but it is unclear whether the decree refers to one or two categories of people, that is, exclusively to reverted victims of forcible baptism or perhaps also to penitent voluntary apostates. Both options are plausible. One can easily understand why members of the Jewish community might remind a voluntary apostate of his error, but the same might be true for those who accepted baptism in times of persecution, for, notwithstanding their reversion, their apostasy might continue to rankle, given that other Jews either suffered martyrdom or managed to escape both death and forced baptism.[55]

The ambiguity in the precise formulation of Gershom's decree persists in eleventh-century discussions. A responsum of Solomon ben Isaac of Troyes (d. 1105), known famously as Rashi, tells the tale of two families that bait each other with insults and curses. The community orders them to desist, and one family explicitly refuses. A member of the other family promptly reminds his adversary "that he had been polluted during the period of destruction. Then one of them stood and told him: 'Do not mention [it], for this has been the subject of a decree,' and he did not mention who had decreed about it. And now it has been learned that Rabbenu Gershom decreed that anyone who mentions this shall be excommunicated."[56] The protagonist that mentions Gershom's ban seems to have thought, or at least contended, that it refers to coerced apostates, because he uses the expression "during the period of destruction." The difficulty is that the meaning of the phrase depends on one tiny letter; with the Hebrew letter yod in *BYMY HShMD*, the phrase refers to a period of persecution and hence to coercion, but without it the phrase reads *BMY HShMD*, meaning "in the waters of destruction," a common euphemism for the baptismal waters, free of any element of persecution and coercion. The confusion in this case is, I think, typical of the absence of unequivocal distinctions in the high Middle Ages between coerced and voluntary baptism, which suggests that to eleventh-century Jews such a distinction was unimportant or unclear. Modern scholars tend to emphasize it, because they see it as the key to Ashkenazic Jewry's sterling reputation.

The brilliant analysis by Avraham Grossman of two contradictory rulings by Gershom is a case in point. At issue is the right of a penitent apostate of priestly descent to perform the priestly blessing in the synagogue. In one text Gershom trumpets the importance of allowing such a person to return to his original status: "If he was a penitent person, one should not say to him: 'Remember your former deeds,'" that is, his apostasy. This is his position, although the renegade was sufficiently devout as to become a Christian clergyman![57] However, in another responsum on the same subject Gershom issues the opposite decision.[58] Grossman proposes that the first case deals with a coerced apostate and the second case with a voluntary one, toward whose predicament Gershom was less sympathetic.[59]

Grossman's attempt to harmonize Gershom's contradictory responsa cannot be sustained. On the level of common sense, the proposed scenario is simply beyond belief, for one must assume that any adult apostate (forcibly baptized children are a different story) who becomes a clergyman must have converted to Christianity voluntarily. There is also the matter of the actual text. The medieval debate about whether a Jew of priestly descent who has performed idolatrous worship may subsequently officiate in Jewish religious ritual is based on the talmudic debate between the amoraic scholars Nahman and Sheshet: Nahman ruled that he may, whereas Sheshet ruled that he may not.[60] For medieval authorities the issue is participation in the priestly blessing, not the sacrificial cult. Maimonides sees no reason to deviate from Sheshet's position,[61] but his European colleagues, Gershom (in his lenient responsum) and later Rashi, equate apostasy with physical disability, which does not bar a priest from performing the priestly blessing, provided that the handicap does not affect his hands. They also note that the talmudic discussion refers to the priest's participation in the sacrificial cult rather than to activities conducted outside Jerusalem.[62]

Where is the crucial distinction between voluntary or involuntary apostasy? Grossman locates it in Gershom's stringent responsum, which argues that because Sheshet expressly refused to differentiate between voluntary and involuntary apostasy, a fortiori the priest in the case at hand—who apostatized voluntarily—may not perform the priestly blessing; conversely, Grossman reads Gershom's lenient ruling as ignoring Sheshet's ruling because it deals with a case of coerced apostasy.[63] This is a forced interpretation of Gershom's contradictory responsa, one that is neither apparent from a straightforward reading of the sources nor shared by medieval scholars.[64] Rashi allows a penitent priest-apostate to resume his priestly status and functions whether or not his apostasy was coerced.[65] Only much later, in sixteenth-century Safed, does Joseph Karo introduce the distinction between voluntary or involuntary apostasy into the legal literature once and for all.[66]

The absence of a clear distinction between coerced and voluntary apostasy emerges from other sources as well. The First Crusade narrative attributed to Solomon ben Samson records the self-immolation of Isaac ben David, the *parnas* of Mainz, and it states that two days before being martyred, Isaac and one other fellow "had been saved for hell, as the enemy sullied them [with the baptismal waters] against their will."[67] This formulation damns coerced apostates along with voluntary ones, indicating that its writer made no distinction between the two categories.

A second case is that of Benedict of York, who was forcibly baptized in 1189 but later reverted. The chronicle of Roger of Hovedon reports that "he was a stranger to the common burial-ground of the Jews, even as of the Christians; both because he had been made a Christian, and because, like a dog to his vomit, he had returned to his Jewish depravity."[68] If this tale is to be believed, reversion did not necessarily lead to reintegration into the Jewish community, at least in this case.

Both of these sources are roughly contemporaneous with *Sefer Hasidim*, which offers another powerful illustration of the same phenomenon. *Sefer Hasidim* contains the tale of two brothers who apostatized. Wondering why such a tragedy should befall a particular family, a scholar determined that it was the result of the sin of their ancestor, who, as rabbi of a certain community, led his entire congregation to the baptismal font during a time of persecution.[69] As Alfred Haverkamp notes, what matters here is the linkage of voluntary and coerced apostasy; succumbing to coercion is seen as a sin, for which one pays with the *voluntary* apostasy of one's children, particularly if one also causes others to sin.[70] The text suggests that, although the rabbi and congregation acted against their will, their decision to live was an act of weakness. The tale seems to rest on the assumption that capitulation under duress is the result of a predisposition to apostatize, stemming from a flabby religious commitment. The distinction between voluntary and coerced apostasy is thus muddied and barely perceptible.

The absence of a clear distinction between voluntary and coerced apostasy colors ecclesiastical legislation as well as Jewish sources. Jews baptized by force were particularly likely to revert, and thus it was common sense for Innocent III to declare, in 1201, that those "who never consented, but wholly objected, accepted neither the impress nor the purpose of the sacrament" were not to be considered Christians.[71] But this formulation did not include those who accepted baptism to avoid slaughter, for they—so the Church determined—acted voluntarily.

Perhaps it was the realization that capitulation in the face of the threat of death does not constitute voluntary conversion and virtually guarantees reversion that motivated a French priest to lead forced converts from Germany to France during the Second Crusade so that they could revert to Judaism.[72] It may have been this consideration, coupled with a hefty bribe, that inspired William, bishop of Sens and Chartres, to arrange for the release of "the lads that were forced [to convert]" following the Blois incident of 1171.[73] But these were isolated instances, infinitely outnumbered by the large volume of cases in which coerced apostates were constrained from reverting to Judaism by the threat of prosecution for heresy.

Reversion

Much of the ecclesiastical legislation on reversion, and on baptized Jews in general, gives voice to the suspicion that Jewish conversion was insincere or at any rate impermanent. Burchard of Worms's *Decretum*, dated 1012, deals extensively with this problem: Converts may be forcibly prevented from reverting to Judaism; they must not consort with Jews, for fear that they might revert; lapsed converts are to be treated harshly. These laws can be traced to the seventh-century Councils of Toledo, but presumably they were relevant to the situation in eleventh-century Germany.[74] And Church legislation indicates that this concern was perennial. For example, in 1215 the Fourth Lateran Council declared, "Some . . . who have come to the baptismal font voluntarily have not departed completely the old self so as to put on a more perfect one. Since they retain remnants of their former rite, they confound by such a mixture the decorum of Christian religion."[75]

Jews express a similar concern that reverting apostates might retain traces of their Christian lifestyle, and here also whether the initial apostasy was voluntary or coerced does not enter into the equation. Even the loyalty to Judaism of the forcibly baptized is not taken for granted, particularly if they remained among the gentiles for "many days."[76] This applies to the case of Benedict of York, and it is crucial to the tale of Elhanan, the son of Simon "the Great" of Mainz, who is baptized as a child and rises through ecclesiastical ranks to become pope. Eventually Elhanan orchestrates a reunion with his father and confesses his desire to revert but asks him whether repentance is still possible, given the length of time he has spent among the gentiles.[77] Ephraim Urbach gives gloomy expression to the time factor when he writes, "Apostasy, which struck even the families of the leaders, aristocrats and affluent, began under duress but ended with voluntary [conversion]."[78]

Predictably, then, another component in the myth and rhetoric of Ashkenazic excellence is that all their (few, coerced) apostates revert to Judaism at the earliest opportunity. Katz, for example, makes the sweeping declaration that forced apostates made every effort to revert, as they did in 1096.[79] Reversion is the key to the issue of coerced versus voluntary baptism, for nonreversion or delayed reversion undermines the edifice of coercion that underpins the glorious reputation of Franco-German Jewry.

The issue of immediate or delayed reversion is not the brainchild of modern historians but is found in medieval sources. In the context of his strenuous effort to excuse the apostates, Solomon ben Samson maintains that the community of Regensburg reverted "immediately following the departure of the enemies of God and performed great acts of penitence, for what they did they did under great duress, for they could not stand up to the enemies and the enemies did not wish to kill them."[80] In Metz also we read that the conversion lasted only "until the days of wrath had passed," after which the apostates reverted to Judaism "with all their heart." This is certainly what is presented, and it is presented with certainty, but the narrator's emphatic language betrays anxiety about the loyalty of these (or any) apostates.

Solomon ben Samson also introduces another apologetical element; his narrative concludes with words of praise for the apostates, whom, he insists, did not deviate from the dietary laws and "only rarely went to their place of worship." Moreover, we read that their Christian neighbors knew of the insincerity of their conversion and that these apostates observed the Sabbath laws in full view of the Christian populace.[81] Clearly it was important to exhibit fidelity to Judaism before reversion, both actively, by continuing to observe the commandments, and passively, by neglecting Christian rituals.[82]

Prereversion behavior is a crucial issue in a responsum by Rashi.[83] Asked whether the testimony of a reverted forced convert is admissible in a proceeding of Jewish law, Rashi replies that it would be, if it were known that the witness, before his reversion, only violated Jewish law under compulsion; otherwise, he could not testify about what he had witnessed while an apostate, even though he ultimately reverted "properly." Rashi's yardstick is neither whether apostasy was forced nor whether reversion was prompt but rather the apostate's religious conduct before reversion. With no apologetic ax to grind, Rashi can easily imagine that a coerced apostate might willingly transgress the commandments, even the Sabbath.[84]

These remarks betray awareness that any delay in reversion would likely be interpreted as a sign that the act of apostasy had not been involuntary. This is remarkable, given that the apostates were known to have accepted baptism at the point of a sword, but it seems reasonable when we bear in mind that those who apostatized during the First Crusade lived as Christians for up to a year; only in 1097 did Henry IV issue his edict permitting their reversion.[85]

Given that the 1096 apostasy lasted at least for the better part of a year, Solomon ben Samson's observation that the apostates rarely attended Christian services and continued to observe the commandments makes sense, and one can also understand why among the Jews of Ashkenaz some might have been skeptical about their true religious identity. Indeed, Solomon ben Samson indirectly acknowledges the problem in his concluding admonishment: "Whoever speaks ill of them [the apostates], it is as if he spoke ill of the Divine Presence."[86]

The Mainz Anonymous puts this suspicion in the mouths of those among the Jews of Worms who escape the initial crusader attack. They comfort the less fortunate, who accepted baptism, by expressing solidarity with them, but then conclude with the warning, "Do not turn away from the Lord."[87] These ominous words give voice to the suspicion that apostasy, even under threat of death, testifies to one's level of devotion, or perhaps that even a devout person might spiral downward from coerced conversion to despair and ultimately fail to revert when the danger was past.

That the apostates of the First Crusade were not viewed by their memorializers as totally blameless emerges from the account of the fate of the Regensburg community, which concludes with the prayer, "And may our Rock grant us atonement for our sins."[88] Similarly, concerning the Metz apostates, Solomon ben Samson's chronicle ends with the prayer that God absolve his people's iniquities. These must have included the acts of apostasy, for we are told that the apostasies were the consequence of "the multitude of iniquity and culpability."[89] These statements articulate the belief that apostates are sinners who need to atone even though they acted under extreme duress, because only the shortcomings of one's previous religious conduct can explain the occurrence of something so awful. Here the boundary between voluntary and coerced baptism is effaced on theological grounds.

The issue of immediate or delayed reversion crops up again in a responsum in which Rashi is asked whether one ought to abstain from wine handled by forced converts until these return to Judaism and remain Jewish for "many days" and their repentance (i.e., reversion) is public and well-known. Speaking of these penitent apostates, Rashi's interlocutor notes that "we do not know them well and have not seen [evidence of] their repentance." All the same, Rashi replies vehemently that to abstain from their wine would shame them and that coerced apostates could never bring themselves to offer idolatrous libations, that is, to participate in Christian religious worship. Rashi links the issues of reversion and coercion. The penitent apostates in question, he writes, are blameless, "for everything they did, they did on account of [fear of] the sword,[90] and they turned away [from Christianity] as soon as they could."[91] The question posed to Rashi testifies to the prevalent confusion about the halakhic significance of the distinction between forced and voluntary apostasy. Rashi emphasizes the element of coercion, and indeed this is an exception to the indifference generally exhibited by medieval authorities. However, by affirming that these apostates were quick to revert, Rashi grants the premise that the allegiance of a forced apostate remains suspect until he or she returns to the fold.[92]

Elsewhere Rashi writes of "all the forced converts" that "their heart inclines towards heaven, for their end testifies to their beginning, that they left and returned when they found salvation."[93] This is not a ringing endorsement of the eternal loyalty of the forcibly baptized.[94] On the contrary, Rashi shares the conviction that one can be sure that a forced convert's heart inclined toward heaven only after his or her return to the fold, when "their end testifies to their beginning"; until such time, an apostate is an apostate, whether baptism was voluntary or coerced.

That Rashi did not take reversion for granted is also apparent from his interpretation of the passage in Proverbs about the "strange woman" from whom one needs to be saved (Prov. 2:16–19). Rashi equates this enigmatic figure with the Church, and on the phrase "All who go to her cannot return" (Prov. 2:19), Rashi makes the following pessimistic observation: "All who apostatize, after they are tainted with heresy, do not return."[95] The absence of any distinction between coerced or voluntary apostasy resounds loudly in this categorically dismissive remark.

Vacillation regarding the appropriate posture toward reverting apostates, even those whose conversion was forced, is powerfully expressed in the following responsum, attributed to Rashi.[96] The issue is whether one may drink with a reverted apostate. Grounds are brought for a lenient ruling regarding apostates who, as Christians, did not violate the Sabbath laws, but what about forced converts who publicly transgressed these regulations and whose complete and final reversion is as yet uncertain? Rashi rejects the view that equates transgression of the Sabbath with idolatry and insists that "when they undertook to publicly return to the awe of our Rock [i.e., to Judaism], they are [again] permitted." The most striking feature of this text is the conflation in the question of voluntary and coerced apostates, with no halakhic distinction between the two categories.

In the responsum about the wine of penitent apostates, Rashi uses the phrase "these forced apostates that have just arrived." In rabbinic parlance the expression "recent arrivals" sometimes refers to a recent occurrence (based on Deut. 32:17), and hence it could mean that these apostates reverted recently. If, however, Rashi meant the phrase literally, he would then have been testifying to the migration that seems to have frequently accompanied reversion.

Fear of prosecution for heresy was a good reason for lapsed converts to leave their city and settle elsewhere. In a letter dated 1286, Pope Honorius IV complains that among those converts who revert, some move to another town, but many others do not and live openly with Jews and as one of them.[97] The practice of relocation also finds expression in Hebrew sources, such as the responsum by Rashi (to which allusion has already been made) concerning an apostate who is baptized in one place and later reverts elsewhere.[98] It is also telling that the priest who facilitated the reversion of forced converts during the Second Crusade escorted them from Germany to France.[99]

This anecdote contains a telling ambiguity. Ephraim writes that the reverting apostates were to remain in France "until their baptism would be forgotten." Obviously one concern would be that the ecclesiastical authorities might persecute them as heretics. But an apostate might also migrate to avoid the opprobrium of fellow Jews. Relocation granted reverting apostates a new start, for one's former confreres had long memories and were not necessarily quick to forgive, even when the sin of apostasy was committed under duress.[100]

The sources cited illustrate plainly that Ashkenazic scholars of the high Middle Ages share the historians' concern with the speed with which forced converts reverted, but with a significant difference. Whereas historians emphasize that reversion was virtually immediate, medieval scholars (in their halakhic texts) do not voice this assumption; nor do they take it for granted that victims of coercion zealously observe the dictates of Jewish law before their reversion. To a surprising extent, and in contrast to most modern historical presentations, medieval rabbis portrayed their constituents warts and all.

Disappearance

"Many Jews," wrote Solomon Zeitlin, "mourned for seven days if one of their kin adopted another religion as they would if a member of their family had died."[101] Yosef Hayim Yerushalmi does not discuss mourning rites, but he paints the same picture of the apostate's disappearance: "The apostate in the Middle Ages left not only the Jewish faith, but the Jewish quarter, his family, his friends. Whatever the theoretical attitude that might be taken toward him in theology and jurisprudence, considered from a *sociological* point of view his rupture with the Jewish community was generally complete."[102] Similarly, Gerald Blidstein writes that "the complete 'de-Judaizing' of the apostate was a view held more by the unlearned than by the rabbinic authorities; the former judged matters, after all, by visible reality rather than by texts—and, in reality, the apostate *had* burned all bridges."[103] These scholars reflect the widely held conviction that in the eyes of his family and community an apostate ceases to exist. This idea portrays the medieval Jewish community as pure, if scarred; there may have been a few apostates, but they departed the scene. The resultant image is of a homogeneous community of devoted believers.

The idea that apostates cease to exist, and hence that one must mourn for them at the time of their apostasy as if they had died, is common today, and its source is probably the case of Gershom's son.[104] Isaac ben Moses of Vienna states that Gershom mourned "for his son that apostatized," which could mean that Gershom mourned at the time of his son's apostasy, a novel practice that might have set a trend. However, the sources on Gershom's son are clear that Gershom went into mourning following his son's death rather than at the time of his apostasy. The popular notion is therefore baseless, and moreover it was unknown in the Middle Ages.

Another source cited by historians but also erroneous is the remark by Jacob ben Meir Tam that it is customary not to mourn the death of an apostate, but this scholar says nothing about mourning at the time of the apostasy and on its account.[105] Echoing the sentiment, but more to the point, is the explication offered in *Sefer Hasidim* of Jeremiah 22:10, which reads, "Do not weep for the dead and do not lament for him; weep rather for him who is leaving, for he shall never return to see the land of his birth." The pietist writes:

> The text juxtaposes "Do not weep for the dead" and idolatry: when a Jewish apostate dies, one does not cry or eulogize him. "Weep rather for him who is leaving" the Torah of God, to become an apostate, "for he shall never return," and shall die. And if he returns and then dies, one weeps over him. And when he apostatizes, it is appropriate to weep: when the body is lost one [generally] cries, *a fortiori* when the soul is lost.[106]

Weeping is, of course, a classic expression of mourning, and thus this passage might be construed as a source for the custom of mourning the act of apostasy, even though *Sefer Hasidim* does not refer explicitly to the laws of mourning and although it was not deemed an authoritative legal text.

Another passage in *Sefer Hasidim* offers a different basis for the notion of the disappearance of the apostate. We read that one whose father apostatizes is not called to read from the Torah as the son of his father but rather as the son of his paternal grandfather, and he must also sign contracts as such. Furthermore, if both his father and his father's father are apostates, he should use the name of his paternal great grandfather.[107] The elimination of any reference to the apostate father conveys that in a certain sense he ceases to exist.

Yet another source might be the talmudic law that anyone who hears a fellow Jew curse God must rend his garment. Apostasy might be considered tantamount to cursing God, and in Jewish law the tearing of the clothes is a central component of the rites of mourning. One could therefore deduce from this rule that mourning is the appropriate religious response to the act of apostasy.[108]

It is no accident, I think, that the medieval sources fail to document the practice of mourning rites for apostates at the time of their apostasy or to provide a clear rationale for their observance; the reason, I suggest, is that apostates did not disappear. Whether we situate them on the Jewish end of the Christian social spectrum or on the Christian end of the Jewish social spectrum is semantic quibbling. Apostates were part of the panorama of Jewish society, and they interacted with their former coreligionists on a daily basis, whether for economic or social reasons.

The serial apostates, namely, Jews who apostatize and then move back and forth between their old and new religious identities, offer a special model of Jewish-apostate interaction, although we know nothing about how common a phenomenon this was. A famous case, told in a thirteenth-century text about an incident that purportedly occurred in 992, is that of Sehok ben Esther, an apostate who wanders from town to town in northern France, posing everywhere as an indigent Jew and receiving alms from the local Jewish communities. Ultimately he takes up residence in Le Mans, in the home of his sisters, who surely knew of his apostasy.[109] True or not, the tale was meant to be believed and hence is evidence of social norms.

We also read of an apostate who purportedly "repented [i.e., reverted], not with a complete heart but with a deceitful repentance, like that of those worthless people, who roam the towns, sometimes appearing as Jews and sometimes strengthening themselves by means of the laws of the gentiles."[110] Similarly, an early thirteenth-century source reports the dilemma concerning an apostate who "went from place to place, and in one city he publicly avows his belief in idolatry, and in another city he enters the House of Israel and says that he is a Jew, and we do not know whether he is a Jew or not."[111] From Eudes Rigaud, the archbishop of Rouen, we learn of a serial apostate whose repeated changes of heart appear to have been sincere. He was burned in 1266, having converted from Judaism to Catholicism, "reverted from the Catholic faith to Judaic depravity, and once again baptized, had once more reverted to Judaism, being unwilling afterwards to be restored to the Catholic faith, although several times admonished to do so."[112]

There are also apostates who, although they do not revert, maintain close ties with their Jewish friends, relatives, and community, and this is even more important for the issue of the apostates' presence in medieval Jewish society.[113] Apostates have several reasons for doing so, including economic expedience. As Jacob Katz explains, "Since taking interest was forbidden between Jews only (Deut. 23:21), the apostate who severed himself from his brothers was to be regarded as a 'stranger,' to whom the prohibition did not apply." Rashi rejects this approach, in keeping with his pathbreaking strategic decision that "although he has sinned, he is still Israel," which means that an apostate permanently retains his legal status as a Jew, but the approach is accepted by other scholars, both before Rashi and after him.[114] Moreover, evidence does exist that among the Jews of medieval France lending money at interest to apostates was an accepted custom.[115]

That frequent social interaction between Jews and apostates was normal is evident in the famous responsum of Jacob ben Meir Tam (discussed earlier) about the twenty bills of divorce issued in Paris.[116] Here Rabbenu Tam states that Jews routinely refer to apostates by their Jewish names, even if they know their Christian ones, demonstrating that in twelfth-century France Jews and apostates were in constant contact and that the apostates cannot be said to have disappeared. The Rabbenu Tam text also says something about the apostate's mind-set, or at least Rabbenu Tam's understanding thereof. Regarding the rule that if a person has two names, both are to appear in his bill of divorce, Rabbenu

Tam writes that this is true only when the husband habitually uses both names, and hence it would not currently apply: "Here, however, he does not normally use his non-Jewish name, but rather the Jewish name with which he grew up all his life, up to the present time."[117] This scholar is sure that an apostate clings to his Jewish cultural baggage even after his religious convictions have altered.

Support for this expectation is found in the *Sefer Hasidim* texts about apostates who give charity to the Jewish poor[118] or to the local rabbi.[119] We read that one may pray for the soul of an apostate who performs deeds favorable to the Jews.[120] The story is also told of an apostate who offers to contribute money toward the acquisition of a Torah scroll. The community is instructed to refuse the offer, partly for fear that he may demand its return at some future time and partly for fear of shaming his family whenever people say, "This is the Torah scroll of that apostate." However, the passage concludes, "Sometimes the family is honored when people say: 'Although he is an apostate, his heart inclines heavenward,' and then they should allow him to give it."[121] That the writer of this passage could entertain the existence of such pious apostates is impressive evidence of the continued involvement of the apostate in Jewish social and religious life.

Another *Sefer Hasidim* passage contemplates the dilemma of whether or not to accept aid from apostates who attempt to help the Jewish community by offering to save Jewish books from a fire on the Sabbath or by burying an unidentified deceased person. Cognizant of the ambivalence a Jew might feel in such a situation, the text nonetheless declares that the assistance should be accepted, unless the apostate's behavior has been so deplorable as to result in a communal decision not to bury him as a Jew following his death.[122] The end of this passage is its most striking feature, for this decision implies that in less extreme cases apostates were buried as Jews, which would obscure for eternity the social boundary between them and the Jewish community.

Jews and apostates also engage in intellectual exchange. Thus *Sefer Hasidim* instructs its readers: "If one hears a good explanation or a good question or answer from a Christian or from an apostate or from someone who causes others to sin, he should not tell others anything in his name."[123]

Needless to say, interaction was not always friendly (see my later discussion regarding the term *minim*). One of the letters about the Blois incident concludes with a warning to erase the passage about the austerities adopted by the Troyes community in memory of the martyrs, "lest it be seen by apostates and delators," who presumably read Hebrew and might gain access to the text in question and use it against the community.[124] Whether for lucre or out of spite, some apostates, it was feared, might abuse their familiarity with the community and bring about potentially disastrous consequences.

Suspicion of apostates also surfaces in the story told in *Sefer Hasidim* about an apostate who asks three scholars their opinion concerning his dilemma: He intends to return to Judaism but has little money. The gentiles trust him, meaning that they are unaware of his infidelity, and he would like permission to take a substantial sum of money from them before returning to Judaism.[125] One scholar grants permission and another refuses it, each for his own reason. The third scholar recommends that none of them answer the question, lest the apostate report to the authorities that the rabbis were responsible for his reversion. In the end, we are told, the apostate did indeed make this accusation.[126] This tale need not be accepted as historical, but it testifies eloquently to the Jews' ambivalence toward apostates as well as to the zeal with which the Church prosecuted "Judaizing."[127]

In light of the fairly free interaction between apostates and Jews, the case of the priest-apostate discussed in Rabbenu Gershom's contradictory responsa merits reconsideration. Eidelberg suggests that the stringent ruling refers to an apostate who had not repented, but this strikes Grossman as absurd: "If he were still an apostate, what doubt could there have been in the respondents' minds? Is it conceivable that he might be allowed to perform the priestly blessing or read from the Torah? And what ever is he doing in the synagogue?"[128] Then Grossman hedges and admits that this view cannot be summarily dismissed, and his caution seems warranted: The Jews of medieval France and Germany may have entertained the possibility that a priest-apostate might seek to officiate in the synagogue or read from the Torah without having shed his Christian identity.

Apostates, then, did not disappear from Jewish society but were rather

a ubiquitous and perennial component. This has an important implication for Rashi's visionary policy, which, we now understand, reflects not
an ideal but a reality. In medieval Ashkenaz the apostate really was "still
Israel." We have seen evidence that apostates remained in close contact
with Jewish relatives and associates, and we have sources that present
tales of what I have termed serial reversion. Rashi, it seems, was right.[129]

Etiology

The Jews of twelfth-century Germany are alleged to have been "beset by
varying sorts and degrees of doubt concerning the worth, viability, and
future of their faith." Jeremy Cohen makes this argument, based on the
Hebrew narratives of the First Crusade, the memoir of the apostate Hermann of Cologne, and passages from *Sefer Hasidim*. This atmosphere of
religious doubt, Cohen notes, reflects the depth of Jewish involvement
in European culture, for as Gavin Langmuir argues, twelfth-century
Christians also agonized about the truth of their faith.[130]

This image matches Avraham Grossman's perception of the etiology of the wave of apostasy that swept through the Jewish society of
twelfth-century Germany. Inquiring into the purpose of the writers
of the First Crusade narratives, Grossman avers that "the chroniclers
sought to describe the act of sacrifice as heroic, in order to encourage
the weak and strengthen weak knees."[131] In attempting to explain why
Germany's Jews experienced a weakening of the knees in this particular
period, Grossman proffers a panoply of corrosive forces.

> The difficult and protracted exile weakened the resistance of many
> Jews and was an important factor in the weakening of their determi-
> nation and their ability to defend themselves. . . . The tragic events
> of the First Crusade . . . coupled with the intensification of Jewish-
> Christian polemic, made these questions [of the exile and redemption
> of the Jewish people] even more significant for the Jews of northern
> and central Europe.[132]

These spiritual pressures are essentially those alluded to by Cohen.

Whether or not apostasy among Ashkenazic Jewry truly had risen to
alarming proportions, it is clear that some apostates were not driven to

baptism by a crisis of faith. Indeed, historians have long recognized that there were apostates of various stripes. Grossman writes that among the apostates "some apostatized as a result of economic and social pressure and some under the influence of Christian propaganda."[133] The Jews of Ashkenaz, he maintains, faced "mounting pressure, of various kinds—political, economic, social and especially religious."[134] This taxonomy can be boiled down to the categories of ideological and venal apostasy: Ideological apostates are those whose conversion is as sincere as Paul's and Augustine's, whereas venal apostates are those who opt for baptism for social, economic, psychological, or other reasons.

Which category predominated? The rhetoric of Ashkenazic excellence would seem to require that ideological apostasy was extremely rare, and indeed Jacob Katz seems to be swimming upstream when he observes, with a vaguely belligerent air, "Christian sources tell us of many Jews who accepted Christianity through conviction, and we have no reason to doubt this." Katz also writes that "some genuine conversions must have occurred at a time when the whole of society lived in a state of religious tension," a minimalist formulation designed, so it seems, to overturn a contrary consensus or predisposition.[135]

Katz's views represent a revision of the commonly held view that in Ashkenaz apostasy was overwhelmingly venal. In Haym Soloveitchik's formulation, some converted "from conviction, some from desire for advancement, and some, probably most from sheer weariness" (whatever that means).[136] Admittedly, venal apostasy also challenges the image of Ashkenazic perfection, but to a lesser degree.

Medieval Hebrew sources give the distinct impression that apostates were mostly venal rather than ideological. Examples are legion. The *Sefer Nizzahon Yashan* (Old Book of Disputation), of thirteenth-century Germany, states that a Jew became an apostate (*nishtamed*) "to enable himself to eat all that his heart desires, to give pleasure to his flesh with wine and fornication, to remove from himself the yoke of the kingdom of heaven . . . cleave to sin and concern himself with worldly pleasures."[137] This is a classic description of the venal apostate, albeit grotesquely exaggerated, but more important, it refuses to acknowledge ideological apostasy and reflects only a type of apostasy that is both casual and venal.

In the previous source *nishtamed* obviously refers to venal apostasy, and hence a *meshumad*, from the same root (*sh-m-d*), would be a venal apostate; conversely, medieval Ashkenazic texts tend to refer to ideological apostates as *minim*, or heretics.[138] We find this pair of terms elsewhere in *Sefer Nizzahon Yashan*, in a passage about the length of the exile: "It is because of the heretics (*minim*) and apostates (*meshumadim*) among us that we must suffer the exile until that appointed end, for all Israel are responsible for one another. This will last until they are almost all destroyed and then they will repent."[139] Obviously *minim* and *meshumadim* refer here to different categories, but how do they differ? We have seen that *Sefer Nizzahon Yashan* describes the *meshumad* as one devoted to "worldly pleasures," namely, the venal apostate, and by process of elimination, then, it would appear that *minim* are ideological apostates.[140]

The term *minim* appears fairly often in medieval Hebrew anti-Christian polemical literature and Jewish biblical exegesis, both of which present interpretations "as a response to the heretics (*minim*)."[141] It is often assumed that medieval writers used the term in reference to Christians, but *minim* may refer to ideological apostates rather than to "old" Christians. Aside from the philological evidence, such people were simply more likely to engage in polemical exegetical exchanges with Jews than were Christian commoners or even clerics.[142]

Venal apostasy receives a great deal of attention in *Sefer Hasidim*. We read of a villain who threatens to apostatize if his request for charity is not granted;[143] of a father and son who sit in judgment, and the son urges his father to bend the law, lest the (undeserving) litigant apostatize;[144] and of a son who threatens apostasy after his father upbraids him for having committed adultery.[145] Exasperated fathers are warned that ill-behaved children will apostatize if one lashes out at them, "Go apostatize!"[146] Katz labels the apostates in these scenarios the "iniquitous sons."[147]

A large group of venal apostates are those who sought economic and social advancement. These apostates were sometimes susceptible to financial inducements to revert, but it was this type of apostate whose reversion was particularly suspect because, in Baron's words, "one could never be too sure of their honesty, since many a relapsed convert sought other than spiritual solace."[148] The Church also felt the sting of the problem of venal apostasy, namely, the lingering doubts about the fidelity of these converts. In 1169 Pope Alexander III wrote that converts "despaired easily and might be compelled to forsake the Christian faith on account of indigence and the lack of assistance, thus returning to their former religion like the dog to his vomit."[149] Borrowing the idiom, the Council at Tours (1233) warned that unless Christians gave generously, "poverty should compel converted Jews to return to their vomit."[150] More significant than the choice of idiom, however, is the formulation that converts despair easily (*facile desperant*), which reflects the fluidity of traffic—particularly of venal apostates—across the Jewish-Christian frontier.

Pope Innocent III voiced similar concerns. In 1199 he wrote to the bishop of Autun about the importance of supporting converts, lest "the shame of poverty, which they are not accustomed to bear easily, force them to look back (*retro aspicere*) to the abandoned Jewish perfidy."[151] That very year a papal letter to the abbot of a convent in Leicester states:

> Care must be taken that they [converts] should be solicitously provided for, lest, in the midst of other faithful Christians, they become oppressed by lack of food. For lacking the necessities of life, many of them, after their baptism, are led into great distress, with the result that they are often forced to go backward because of the avarice of such as are possessed of plenty—yet scorn to look at the Christian poor.[152]

Within the broad category of venal apostasy we also find the romantic apostate. *Sefer Hasidim* tells the tale of a young man who threatens to apostatize unless he is allowed to marry the girl who has won his heart.[153] Isaac ben Menahem, of eleventh-century France, consults his teacher, Eliezer ben Isaac "the Great," about whether two young Christian men may be allowed to enter the Jewish community. Apparently, both of the parents of these youths were apostates. Their mother's first husband had died without issue, whereupon she underwent *halizah*, a ritual that releases her brother-in-law from his levirate obligation. She then married someone else, but he also died without offspring. Once again she faced the obligation to bear her (second) brother-in-law's child, but instead she opted to apostatize and promptly married her initial levir-repudiator, who also apostatized. The two wed as Christians and had the two boys, who grew to adulthood and sought to join the Jewish community. This was problematic because Jewish law forbids a levir from marrying the woman he has repudiated, which might render the children bastards, whose presence in the community could not be tolerated.[154] This is obviously a case of romantic apostasy, because the double apostasy was necessary only because Jewish law prevented the couple from marrying.

The link between romantic apostasy and reversion is explicit in a case from thirteenth-century France, reported by Isaac of Corbeil, a scholar with ties to the German pietists. We read of a female apostate who has a Christian lover; she repents and reverts to Judaism, whereupon he converts to Judaism and the two seek to marry. Isaac refuses permission but admits that he "found this [decision] exceedingly difficult, for fear that they might revert [to Christianity]."[155]

Not only do medieval sources present more evidence of venal than ideological apostasy, but they also expressly posit that apostasy is predominantly venal. Rashi and other European authorities accept the assumption, based on talmudic, midrashic, and gaonic sources, that women who apostatize do so for romantic or erotic reasons. Female apostates who revert are therefore prohibited from reuniting with their Jewish husbands, for they are presumed to have had a sexual liaison with a non-Jew.[156] Similarly, in a case cited earlier concerning a serial apostate seeking recognition of his Jewish identity, the rabbis of northern France decide to accept his claim, because they assume that his earlier protestations of faith in Christianity were motivated purely by his "evil inclination"—that is, they were venal and hence insincere—whereas his current declaration of faith in Judaism is believable, "since our faith is an honest, good, correct and true one."[157] Because the idea that one could choose Christianity in good faith strikes these luminaries as patently absurd, their working assumption is that any apostate must be a venal apostate.

Modern historiography, on the other hand, tends to spotlight the implosion of religious identity on the part of the ideological apostate and portrays apostasy as an act of immeasurable pathos. The gravity with which historians address the topic of apostasy meshes with their somber descriptions of Jewish-Christian relations in medieval Europe and seems to be a function thereof. I treat this subject extensively in Chapter 7, and here I would only add that medieval sources typically describe venal apostasy as casual (such as in the model of the iniquitous sons or in the phenomenon of serial reversion) and relations between Jews and their Christian associates as generally free and easy.

What requires reexamination, then, is not only the nature of apostasy but also its etiology, the climate in which it took place. If the atmosphere was one of perpetual conflict between the two religious communities,[158] apostates are exceptions to the rule of Jewish survival, which assumes a heroic and glorious character, consonant with the myth of Ashkenazic excellence. And this picture is certainly not altogether misguided. Doubtless some apostates acted out of a sense of spiritual defeat, demoralized by the reality of exile or by the triumphalist propaganda of the Catholic Church. This threat must have been perceived as significant, for it spurred Franco-German Jewish thinkers of the twelfth and thirteenth centuries to compose anti-Christian polemical tracts and to lace their biblical exegesis and liturgical poetry with statements about the falsehood of Christianity and about its oppressive character.

All the same, the sources marshaled in this chapter present a less idealized image of the place of apostates and apostasy in the medieval Jewish communities of France and Germany. How many apostates there were during the first quarter of the second millennium remains unknown, but coerced apostates do not necessarily outnumber voluntary ones, and the distinction is generally unimportant to medieval rabbis. Even coerced apostates do not always revert, or do not necessarily do so promptly, and there is also the phenomenon of serial reversion. Apostates do not vanish but are rather a fixture of medieval Jewish society, with whom members of the Jewish community interact freely and often without ill will. And although some individuals apostatized because they became convinced of the truth of Christianity, other individuals' apostasy was venal. These apostates hurdle the Jewish-Christian divide with ease, as if they do not consider it terribly significant.[159]

Taken together, these elements present an alternative image of apostasy and, by extension, of the character of the Jewish community and the nature of Jewish-Christian relations in medieval Ashkenaz. The image of Jews and Christians separated by an enormous spiritual and cultural gulf and locked in a state of unremitting confrontation and hostility is replaced with one of unrestricted social and cultural inter-course, with the two communities separated by a low barrier of beliefs and taboos.[160] Of course, both of these pictures of Jewish-Christian relations are caricatures, but they provide useful models for elucidat-ing some of the tendencies of modern historiography and for pursuing alternative interpretations.

The low-barrier model also offers a context in which, I would argue, Jews were more likely to apostatize, and for this reason it seems more compelling. I think people are generally ill-disposed to perform a de-sired behavior in an atmosphere fraught with feelings of conflict, pres-sure, and guilt, but they might elect to do so in a calm environment, in which they do not see the behavior as terribly charged.[161] This offers a more convincing context in which to situate the statement by Joseph Qara, a leading Jewish Bible scholar in twelfth-century France: "The desire to follow in the error of their way is like a burning fire in my heart."[162]

Six   Deviance

Apostates lie on the extreme end of the scale of fidelity to Judaism, and as we have seen, the image of Ashkenazic Jewry as pure necessitates their excision from the portrait of the Jewish collective. It remains, then, to examine the religious behavior of the bulk of Franco-German Jewish society, to assess the degree of its obedience to Jewish law and rabbinic leadership.

The reputation of Ashkenazic Jewry for universal and total observance antedates the modern period. Israel Isserlein, a leading fifteenth-century Ashkenazic scholar, blandly asserts, in the name of Shalom Neustadt, that "the Torah is upheld in Ashkenaz more than in other lands because [here] they take interest from the gentiles and do not need to perform labor, which enables them to have free time for Torah study; and whoever does not study, assists those who do from the profit [that he makes]."[1] The main point here, for our purposes, is the speaker's claim that German Jewry is more committed to the Torah than any other Jewish ethnic group. Admittedly, Isserlein's explanation refers to study rather than observance, but he does not make this distinction, and he probably thought that the two were intertwined.

In modern Jewish historiography a classic expression of the notion of the absolute commitment of Ashkenazic Jewry to religious observance is the formulation by Yitzhak Baer: "The Ashkenazic Jews seemed to be the purest embodiment of the people of God. The rule of the Torah, in theory and practice, was manifested there to the utmost degree."[2] I have already noted that Baer's view of medieval Ashkenaz includes ideas found in the work of earlier scholars, and this holds true for the subject at hand. Heinrich Heine relates that Rabbi Abraham of Bacherach, his fictitious creation, "observed the most trivial rites with painful consci-

148

entiousness."[3] Similarly, Heinrich Graetz contrasts the asceticism and pietism of Ashkenaz, as well as the dialectical talmudism of France, with the worldliness and hedonism of Spain to produce an image of scrupulous halakhic observance without parallel in the medieval world.

This theme runs like a thread through modern studies of medieval Jewish culture. Irving Agus makes much of a statement in *Kol Bo*, an anonymous fourteenth-century halakhic compendium. Referring to the community of Troyes, the text states that "the small (*qetanim*) among us listen to the great (*gedolim*)."[4] For Agus, this text proves that "for the first time in history a corporate group approached the ideal of 'a nation of scholars, a holy nation (a rephrasing of Exodus 19:6).'"[5] He concludes, "That the members of an entire group of communities should attain such a high cultural level was a phenomenon that never existed anywhere else; it constituted a unique situation. . . . The forefathers of Franco-German Jewry constituted a rare and highly select society, a group of individuals sharply distinguished from and radically different than, any such aggregate of Jews that lived in any other place or time."[6]

This is an extreme formulation of a fairly prevalent portrayal of Franco-German Jewry in the high Middle Ages, one that is rarely subjected to critical examination. In the following discussion, which is based on rabbinic sources, I depict the level of obedience to rabbinic authority among the Jews of northern Europe as partial rather than absolute or even nearly so. The rabbinic literature of the period depicts a broad spectrum of deviant behavior—deviant in the assessment of the rabbinic writers of our primary sources. I look at a variety of nonhalakhic behaviors and take note primarily of the less than total conformity to rabbinic norms. Righting the record on this matter is important for the reconstruction of medieval Ashkenaz as a society of mortals rather than saints. It also narrows the gap between medieval and modern Judaism.

The Tenth Through Eleventh Centuries

The deviant behavior manifest in Ashkenaz during the early years of the tenth- to eleventh-century diaspora was different in nature from that which followed in the twelfth century and beyond. It is only in this early phase that we encounter, in the rabbinic literature of the period, evidence of the brazen contravention of Jewish law. We find incidents in which these misdeeds are accompanied by acts of violence or threats, leveled not only at fellow members of the community but also at its rabbinic and lay leaders, when these attempt to respond.[7]

The rabbinic literature of this period is meager compared to both that of the Islamic realm and that of twelfth- and thirteenth-century Europe. The evidence of deviant behavior is particularly striking in proportion to the relatively low number of surviving records. This must mean that the problem was vexing, and it may also signify that it was common. In a few instances the sources indicate plainly that the problematic behavior in question is relatively widespread. Thus a responsum attributed to Gershom ben Judah (i.e., Rabbenu Gershom, fl. ca. 1000), the doyen of Ashkenazic Jewry in its formative years, reports that "there are people who are suspected of swearing falsely," and he asks whether the community can take extreme measures to compel witnesses to tell the truth under oath.[8] This seems to have been a social ill, not a lone occurrence.

Another example, cited in a responsum of Joseph Bonfils (Tuv Elem) of Limoges, a contemporary of Gershom, concerns a community that excommunicates a group of miscreants, but a neighboring community blatantly disregards the sanction. Bonfils deplores this behavior as irresponsible, commenting that "nowadays it is impossible to compel villains [to comply] by any means other than excommunication and monetary penalty, and one who abrogates [these sanctions] causes transgressions to increase."[9] This was a society with a wayward element that those in authority found difficult to rein in. In neither of these texts can the number of culprits be determined, but they are too numerous to be depicted as isolated individuals, and thus we have a smattering of evidence of wrongdoing on a fairly large scale.

Yet the volume of deviant behavior is not Bonfils's point; he is explaining that a Jewish tribunal must not ignore or invalidate decrees passed by communal governing bodies, because the decree is the only available instrument of communal authority, since it punishes violations with either a monetary penalty or excommunication or both. Communal authority is, in fact, the issue in both incidents and in numerous other cases from the same historical milieu. And no wonder, for this period witnessed the emergence of the Jewish community as an autonomous self-governing body, exercising a measure of social control. Naturally, as the governing body emerged, constituents would sometimes defy the authority of the fledgling institutional leadership when they thought they could do so with impunity. Thus both cases involve a power struggle, and it is noteworthy that both Gershom and Bonfils are convinced that only the application of maximal force could conceivably coerce the recalcitrant to accept the yoke of communal discipline.[10]

That the misdeeds were performed publicly may simply reflect effrontery on the part of the protagonists, which would make sense in view of the immature state of the community's development; this is certainly the impression given in the documents. It may be, however, that the villains in these cases were convinced of the rectitude of their deeds, which would raise an important point, namely, the extent of the indeterminacy of Jewish law at this historical juncture. Although it is not uncommon to find Jews contesting halakhic authority while confident of the probity of their actions, this phenomenon may have been especially common in the tenth and eleventh centuries, before the code of appropriate conduct became increasingly homogenized, as the various fields of human activity were mapped out by legal codes and manuals of ritual. At this early stage in the history of halakhah, many policy decisions were still open questions and thus were partly contingent on political conditions. Thus whether an action was ruled halakhic or deviant depended in part on the extent of rabbinic and communal authority.[11]

Yet another case from this formative stage of Ashkenazic Jewry concerns a community member with whom several Jews continued to associate even though he was excommunicated for fiscal impropriety with the funds of orphans. The respondent writes that those fraternizing with the offender are also to be excommunicated, "for they transgress intentionally and treat excommunications frivolously, and aid and abet wicked people in hiding the money of orphans. . . . They are to receive lashes and to desist in the future."[12] This rabbinic document deals not only with the problem of the appropriate response to this particular criminal behavior but also with the challenge of safeguarding and nurturing communal authority, which was still in an early stage of development.

The twelfth and thirteenth centuries evince a drop in the incidence of the flagrant defiance of communal authority, which probably means that the legitimacy of communal authority had largely ceased to be an issue.[13] This suggests that if normative behavior was more the rule in Ashkenaz than in other centers of Jewish population, this may have been due to the greater ability of the local community to impose communal discipline. This would not be altogether surprising, given the intimate nature of these communities—their small size and close family ties—compared with the large communities of the Islamic realm, such as Baghdad, Fustat, or Córdoba.[14] In Ashkenaz malfeasance would be noticed straightaway: There was no anonymity, and ostracism was a powerful social sanction. With a comparatively high level of social control, the wonder is not that we find so little nonnormative behavior in medieval Ashkenaz but that we find any at all.[15]

The First Crusade

The Hebrew narratives of the First Crusade massacres relate what were arguably the most appalling violations of Jewish law in all of Jewish history, namely, the acts of mass murder and suicide perpetrated by the Jews of the Rhineland during the crusader onslaught. One can hardly conceive of a more egregious breach of the sixth commandment, which under the Oral Law prohibits suicide as well as homicide.

The Bible does not prescribe the conditions in which surrendering one's life is the right or wrong decision. The Talmud records a policy decision taken by a group of tannaitic scholars at Lod, obligating Jews to die rather than perpetrate idolatry, but this regulation is immediately hedged with a series of caveats, and the decision to opt for martyrdom over apostasy in 1096 is, at the least, questionable from a halakhic standpoint.[16] What is more, although the Lod ruling might justify the passive submission to slaughter, the Jews of Ashkenaz actually killed others and themselves, and this cannot be grounded in any biblical or talmudic source. The desire to convince readers of the moral and religious rectitude of the 1096 martyrdom in the face of its nonhalakhic character has thus been seen as a primary goal of the Hebrew sources of those dreadful events.[17]

That the heroic martyrdom of the First Crusade was a gross violation of talmudic law was pointed out by Haym Soloveitchik. In view of the Lod decision, Soloveitchik attributes the mass martyrdom to "religious intuition," an instinctive sense of what ought to be done. Rather than probe the sources of this type of knowledge, Soloveitchik simply presents it as the alternative to behavior rooted in halakhic texts.[18]

The notion that Jews sometimes contravened talmudic law in favor of some other standard of behavior was mooted by Jacob Katz. Katz notes the phenomenon in his study of the "Shabbes Goy," the time-honored practice of having a non-Jew perform for a Jew on the Sabbath a task that would constitute a profanation of the Sabbath if performed by a Jew, such as lighting a fire. With respect to the Shabbes Goy, rabbis throughout the Middle Ages and early modern era prescribed a relatively convenient policy, whereas the laity clung to a more stringent course. This counterintuitive model forces Katz to conclude that the Jewish masses seem to obey a "ritual instinct" that enables them to chart a path among a broad range of options and directs them to choose now a lenient behavior, now a stringent one.[19]

Soloveitchik uses a similar concept in his study of gentile wine in medieval Franco-Germany, another case in which the common attitude and practice was rooted not in talmudic and halakhic literature but rather in a deep-seated sense of what is right. Here this sense was directed by an irrational loathing, and so Soloveitchik labels the Ashkenazic attitude a taboo, which resembles ritual instinct in the absence of a textual base but has a different conceptual foundation.[20]

The Shabbes Goy and gentile wine behaviors are deviant in a special and paradoxical sense. Instead of focusing on the form of deviance characteristic of modern Jewish society, in which Jews transgress a precept because it is burdensome, Katz and Soloveitchik spotlight cases of supererogatory stringency. Medieval deciders generally condone these behaviors, but they remain deviant nonetheless, because rabbinic legal theory postulates that normative conduct is rooted in the Written and Oral Law.

The case of 1096 is thus the ultimate example of supererogatory stringency. Here the assumption of an unnecessary hardship, one not prescribed in the Bible or in talmudic literature, involves the taking of life, which (as Soloveitchik explains) is no less than murder. Yet even with such high stakes, the martyrs followed their "religious intuition" or "ritual instinct" and did what seemed right, in flagrant violation of the norm prescribed by talmudic law.

The deviant nature of the First Crusade martyrdom may be related to the fact that women, and not men, were the first to martyr themselves and their family members, setting the example that swept through the crowd of fellow Jews and inspired them to follow suit. This, at least, is what is reported in the Hebrew narratives of what transpired.[21] Whatever the narrator may have intended to convey by this observation (which he formulated somewhat emphatically), one historical explanation for the leading role of women would spotlight the religious life and the education of Jewish women in medieval Europe.[22]

Men and women held fundamentally different conceptions of the nature of Judaism and of the Jewish way of life, because as a rule only male children were exposed to the canonical talmudic and posttalmudic legal literature. Girls were sometimes instructed in the modest corpus of precepts traditionally identified as particularly female obligations: the laws of menstrual purity, the bread offering (*hallah*), and the ritual lighting of candles on the eve of the Sabbath and festivals. For the most part, however, girls acquired rudimentary instruction about Jewish ritual life and mores from their mothers in the course of daily living. Hence girls could not have shared the notion that Jewish law is rooted in a textual source or tradition (at least in theory), which made it easy and natural for them to adopt behaviors that seemed right, even when these lacked a textual base.[23]

That women were completely ignorant of rabbinic literature was axiomatic for the tosafists, the leading rabbis of twelfth-century France, who ask whether women can fulfill the commandment to recite Grace After Meals when the opening formula is recited by men. The text explicitly states that the question rests on the assumption that women do not understand what is being said. It goes on to specify that, whereas ignorant men are able to fulfill the commandment, women cannot, "for they understand nothing at all."[24]

It is therefore understandable that we find Jewish women in medieval Franco-Germany practicing a variety of ritual behaviors that were textually rootless. The practices are attested in rabbinic documents, in which rabbis grapple with their legitimacy, in response to either queries from others or their own ruminations. These women's behaviors constitute a large and significant part of the deviant behavior we will be examining in the discussion to follow.

Women's Law

The nonrabbinic behavior exhibited by women in medieval Ashkenaz does not involve flouting or disregarding rabbinic dictate and authority but rather shows adherence to a different code of behavior, one with a frame of reference that is not strictly rabbinic. This comes as a surprise, for it is generally supposed that medieval Jewish society was exclusively rabbinic (except for the Karaites), whereas medieval Ashkenazic women seem to see Judaism as far more heterogeneous and flexible and as allowing them virtually unlimited autonomy. In a number of instances and realms, women leave the rabbis puzzling over practices they cannot trace to a canonical source and hence cannot legitimate. Time after time, rather than attempt to quash the deviant behavior, the deciders usually throw up their hands and accept it.

One of the most widely discussed deviant behaviors exhibited by women concerns the wearing of jewelry on the Sabbath. Ele'azar of Worms (d. ca. 1230) testifies that women wear all sorts of jewelry in public on the Sabbath, including gold and silver rings, gold chains, and earrings, despite an explicit talmudic prohibition.[25] The reason given for the talmudic proscription is that women might remove their jewelry for their friends to admire and, by holding them as they walk, violate the injunction against carrying an object in the public domain on the Sabbath.

This is concrete evidence not only of deviant behavior (vis-à-vis talmudic law) but also, and more important, of behavior that is at one and the same time deviant and normative. These are not Karaite women, and yet they habitually perform an action that any educated person would have to regard as a profanation of the Sabbath, one of the most sacred commandments. Another issue, of course, is the authority of the contemporary rabbis, to which the women appear to be oblivious. This would have been socially unacceptable, except in the realm pertaining particularly to women. Apparently the exception covered all the activities and traditions that girls learned at their mothers' knee; these actions, it seems, were by definition legitimate, regardless of what the hoary books had to say. The rabbis, however, are puzzled by these women's laws, for they see law and ritual as necessarily grounded in talmudic literature. They therefore exert a great deal of effort to try to harmonize the deviant practice and the sources. This, as we will see, is a fundamental dynamic in the legal literature of twelfth-century France and Germany.

Eliezer ben Samuel of Metz, a disciple of Jacob ben Meir (Rabbenu Tam), resolves the contradiction between text and practice by declaring the talmudic ban on jewelry obsolete. He notes that the Talmud does not apply the prohibition to "important" women, who supposedly would feel no need to boast about their jewels, and he places all contemporary women in the category of important women.[26] Jewelry, he explains, is now so common as to no longer merit social attention, a state of affairs that would normally be characteristic only of important women. A tosafist gloss also observes that "our women do not display their jewelry and rings" and asserts that because jewelry is ubiquitous, it is no longer likely to lead to transgression.[27]

In like fashion, Eliezer ben Nathan of Mainz (Ra'avan), a contemporary, avers that fear of removal and carrying does not apply to an object the like of which is also owned by other women, because the object's novelty is what motivates the women to transgress.[28] He underscores this point with the observation that women wear jewelry on weekdays as well as on the Sabbath.[29] These analyses are illustrative of the efforts of rabbinic scholars in medieval Franco-Germany to justify an ostensible transgression by finding ways to align it with the corpus of existing legal principles and doctrines.

Rashi argues that earrings should be excluded from the talmudic ban on Sabbath jewelry, because, as he points out, women cover their ears with their head covering and are therefore virtually incapable of removing their earrings to show them off.[30] This comment on women's fashions does not appear in earlier sources, talmudic or gaonic, and indeed later scholars identify Rashi as its source; it therefore appears to be based on contemporary practice. Similarly, Rashi's student, Simhah of Vitry, permits earrings on the Sabbath because they are "well attached."[31] On the other hand, another source by Rashi (or his disciples) flatly forbids women from wearing jewelry on the Sabbath and says that "the ancients" had already been asked about the matter and ruled that they may not even wear jewelry that is well attached, such as earrings.[32]

Rashi's grandson, Rabbenu Tam, proposes a different rationale for the wearing of jewelry. Rather than assess the likelihood of women removing their baubles, he focuses on the legal status of the site and opines that at present, in twelfth-century France, the type of space that might normally be considered a public domain (in which carrying on the Sabbath is prohibited) really has the status of a *karmelit*, that is, a public space that nevertheless cannot be considered a public domain because an obstacle impedes free use of it by the public.[33]

Isaac of Dampierre, Rabbenu Tam's son-in-law and disciple, challenges this position, citing a talmudic discussion that permits carrying in a courtyard but not in a *karmelit*, implying that *karmelit* status would not solve the problem.[34] Eliezer ben Joel Halevi (Ra'avia), a German contemporary, finds fault with Rabbenu Tam's argument, because although the change in the status of the space removes the action from the category of a biblical transgression, carrying on the Sabbath is still a rabbinic proscription, which remains in place.[35]

The relationship between theory and practice is one of the most fascinating aspects of this case and others like it. Rashi, Rabbenu Tam, and Ra'avan discuss the issue from a textual perspective and pose possible grounds for justification of the female behavior, but they say nothing about how women understand their own mores. Ra'avia takes a bold step when he asserts, in the name of Rabbenu Tam, that "on this women rely nowadays to go out in things in which one may not go out into the public domain on the Sabbath."[36] This statement presumes that women base their behavior on a textual foundation, of which they are of course necessarily aware. On this point, I believe, Ra'avia is simply incorrect: Women were ignorant not only of the texts themselves but of the fundamental notion of text-based halakhah. This is a clear case of a scholar projecting his orientation on a group of people whose way of thinking is altogether different from his own. I should note, however, that this statement by Ra'avia is almost unique; medieval rabbis rarely express Ra'avia's assumption.

The jewelry case introduces the problem of compliance or authority, an issue that lies at the heart of the deviance question. Isaac ben Moses of Vienna (d. ca. 1250) rules that there are no grounds for permitting women to wear their jewelry on the Sabbath, because of the concern that they will remove and show it, and he continues as follows:

> Nevertheless, in our days the permission of this prohibition has spread everywhere and *they will not listen and will not believe* [us] to desist from the permissive practice to which they have become accustomed. [Therefore] we rely on the saying: "Leave Israel alone; better they should sin in error than intentionally," even when the injunction is biblical [rather than rabbinic]. . . . The Jerusalem Talmud states: "Just as one is obligated to say that which will be heard, so is one obligated to refrain from saying that which will not be heard,"[37] and on this matter we are unable to protest, *for we know that they will not receive [it] from us.* Therefore one ought not to reveal and publicize the prohibition, *for it is known that they will not receive [it].* Whoever is able to warn and to be careful, more power to him.[38]

Three times, no less, does Isaac of Vienna explicitly state that women simply refuse to yield to rabbinic authority on the matter of Sabbath jewelry. This is a fact of fundamental importance for understanding the position of Jewish law in medieval Ashkenazic life. Women obeyed their own law, which did not always overlap with the directives and norms prescribed by talmudic and halakhic literature. Nor were they automatically subservient to the authority of the rabbinic leadership of their community, the custodians of the ancient sources. There was a realm that lay beyond the rabbis' power, and the rabbis knew it and had difficulty coping with it.

The testimony of Isaac of Vienna about female noncompliance is not the only such source. Two generations later, Asher ben Yehiel was forced to make a similar admission, in mitigation of his own permissive ruling: "One must not forbid women their jewelry, *for they will not listen to us,* and 'leave the daughters of Israel alone—better they should sin in error than intentionally.'"[39] Clearly women had not grown more compliant by the late thirteenth century with respect to their jewelry, and neither had the rabbinic leadership formulated new options and strategies in the face of the recalcitrant behavior of their womenfolk.

As in so many cases regarding the problem of female deviant behavior, the rabbis of medieval France and Germany delve into the legal literature to locate a principle that could provide a halakhic foundation for the policy they deem inappropriate: de facto recognition of nonhalakhic behavior—not as an ideal response but for want of a viable coercive mechanism. Isaac ben Moses of Vienna locates the textual solution in the talmudic dictum "Leave Israel alone; better that they err unwittingly than intentionally."[40] He is hardly the first scholar to focus on this prooftext; another source has Rabbenu Tam invoke it in this very context, namely, to justify his decision not to prohibit women their rings on the Sabbath, "for they will not listen to us."[41] Isaac buttresses his policy decision with a second talmudic prooftext: "Just as one is obligated to say that which will be heard, so is one obligated to refrain from saying that which will not be heard."[42] Here again a passage from the Talmud itself enables medieval scholars to finesse the dissonance between the assumption of subservience to talmudic law and rabbinic authority on the one hand and the reality of noncompliance on the other.[43]

In theory, rabbis could be expected to wage a campaign to urge, if not coerce, women to accept their dictates. Yet this is precisely what they admittedly do not do. Eliezer of Metz and Eliezer ben Nathan state candidly that they mention the ubiquity of earrings to explain why no one protests the current female practice: "We rely on this reasoning *to refrain from protesting* the behavior of our women, who go out wearing their non-signet rings, soul-houses, and earrings: because they are important[44] and used to fine jewelry, and it is undignified for them to boast and display."[45] The scholars of France and Germany bear witness to their own silence and passivity, and it is this impotence that they feel compelled to explain and to justify.

Although he concedes the reality of noncompliance, Isaac of Vienna also pursues de jure solutions to the jewelry problem. He accepts Rabbenu Tam's *karmelit* argument, which effectively legitimates the prevailing female behavior, and claims that this argument was accepted by the scholars of Ashkenaz.[46] Isaac also cites the practical talmudic adage

"Go see what people do"[47] and notes that this motto can be exploited in the service of leniency as well as stringency.

The jewelry issue nicely illustrates the existence on a large scale of deviant behavior in medieval Ashkenazic society. This was not criminal behavior of the sort displayed in the tenth and eleventh centuries, when rabbinic and communal authority could be flouted almost with impunity by individuals bent on having their way. Women flout the norms of the text-based male culture of Jewish law and ritual because they have their own brand of Judaism, their own code of conduct. The jewelry case also reveals women exercising a large measure of control over their own conduct. The appearance of this autonomous female realm in the period's rabbinic literature signifies that it had social significance. Medieval rabbis describe their women as oblivious to men's law, an obliviousness described in some sources as casual and in others as militant. Although troubled, the rabbis avoid a showdown, issuing tepid responses that range from resignation to approbation.

In the pages to come I examine a range of other practices deemed deviant by rabbinic authorities, beginning with those peculiar to women. My purpose is to document fully and broadly the extent and range of deviant behavior in medieval Franco-German Jewry. The perspective is limited because the sources are always rabbinic documents, which invariably express disapproval of behaviors that the rabbis deem non-normative. Nonetheless, I attempt to describe these behaviors and also to examine the nature of the rabbinic response. This response assumes a fairly standard set of forms, with room for variation. The overall impression, and the main point, is that the volume of deviant behavior (from the rabbinic perspective) was substantial. This can only mean that this society was more heterogeneous and less disciplined or controlled than is often held to be the case.

The first set of deviant behaviors to be examined also falls under the category of women's law. It is a considerable corpus, which is not altogether surprising, given the proportion of women to men in the general population. To give the presentation greater coherence, I present the behaviors in two basic categories: those concerned with ritual acts performed at designated points in time, such as the Sabbath, and those pertaining to the female cycle of menstruation and ritual purification.

Sabbaths and Holy Days

During the high Middle Ages women enjoyed a day of leisure once a month, abstaining from domestic or economic tasks on Rosh Hodesh, the first of the Hebrew month. This is documented in the eleventh century in Rashi's talmudic commentary. Rashi's successors, the tosafists, state plainly that Rosh Hodesh is exclusively a women's holiday.[48]

A textual basis for the Rosh Hodesh holiday can be found in a passage from the Jerusalem Talmud, which lists a series of such women's holidays, including not only Rosh Hodesh but also Saturday night, Mondays, and Thursdays, and the eves of festivals.[49] Of course, Ashkenazic women were unaware of this or any talmudic source; they view the custom as their own. Moreover, instead of automatically adducing this prooftext, medieval scholars express confusion about the origins and hence also the legitimacy of the practice. Rashi, for example, reports hearing from his teacher that the holiday was a reward for female righteousness during the golden calf debacle.[50] This is an instance, and a fairly ingenious one, of the pattern of medieval scholars searching for explanations of baffling practices. This reflects their inability or refusal to acknowledge that women's law lay beyond the bounds of men's law and followed a different course: Women acquired it by observing their mothers. There is thus no gainsaying the deviant nature of the Rosh Hodesh moratorium.

A similar custom is reported in *Shibolei ha-Leqet*, a thirteenth-century halakhic compendium from Italy, which contains an abundance of material from Ashkenaz in the high Middle Ages. We read that "here women are accustomed to abstain from labor on Hanukkah." Apparently this also was a women's custom and thus also one rooted in some sort of female tradition rather than in written sources. Once again, the existence of a behavior without rabbinic sanction causes confusion, but its direction is different; rather than seek out a prooftext or an explanation, the writer of the passage (whoever he was) focuses on the right of subsequent generations to critique accepted behaviors. The argument, which is based on a dictum from the Jerusalem Talmud, is made that one ought not to permit an action that people perceive to be prohibited. The *Shibolei ha-Leqet* text then cites the view of "R. Ephraim,"[51] that this dictum pertains to an ignoramus (*'am ha-aretz*), and particularly to rustics (*benei medina*), who are not "children of Torah" (*benei Torah*), that is, well-versed.[52] This last comment is then elucidated on the basis of the talmudic dictum, in which a scholar tells people who are not children of the Torah that something is forbidden, and Rashi explains "because they are very lax" (*meqilei tefei*).[53]

This last section of the *Shibolei ha-Leqet* text means that rabbis ought not to permit women to perform labor on Hanukkah, because they perceive it to be prohibited. Given the context of Rabbi Ephraim's statement, his comment about children of the Torah must also refer to women, who were indeed not children of the Torah insofar as they lacked formal education. Rashi's comment about laxity provides an explanation for the policy statement of the Jerusalem Talmud, and the focus is on ignorance of texts. This speaks to the fundamental quality of women's law, which is rooted in tradition rather than in talmudic literature.

But the final component of Rashi's position is about laxity, which he associates with a dearth of learning. This is fascinating, because we have already seen that it is imprecise. In 1096 women's ignorance of the talmudic discussion of martyrdom allowed them to play a leading role in the mass martyrdom of Rhineland Jewry, and similarly, as Katz and Soloveitchik have shown, the simple folk displayed uncommon—irrational—zeal with respect to the issues of the Shabbes Goy and gentile wine.

Elsewhere, *Shibolei ha-Leqet* relates another women's labor moratorium, this time during the evening hours of the *'Omer* days, that is, the period separating Passover from Shavuot. The deviant character of this custom is evident in the presentation of this topic: "With regard to the women's custom . . . some attribute it to the fact that Rabbi Akiva's disciples died almost at sunset." The passage openly describes the rabbis' puzzlement in the face of this practice, which has no clear rationale or textual base, and it therefore offers two midrashic rationales.[54]

Medieval women make their own rules in other realms of Sabbath and festival observance as well. Eliezer ben Nathan (Ra'avan), one of the central rabbinic figures of mid-twelfth-century Ashkenaz, reveals that women would plait their hair on the Sabbath, even though the Talmud explicitly prohibits this activity. This is similar to the jewelry case, but unlike the moratorium in that case, the behavior in question here is not simply absent from the sources but rather explicitly prohibited. Ra'avan admits that women habitually plait, and he adds, "Even people living long before us did so and no one protested." He cannot help wondering how it is that the rabbis of earlier generations allowed a flagrant violation of a talmudic regulation. He thus implies that it must have been within the power of his rabbinic forebears to prevent the plaiting, which is probably no more likely than in Ra'avan's own time. Ra'avan, however, is not alone in assuming that a given popular practice must be justified because he could not conceive that the leaders of previous generations would have allowed any behavior that was prohibited by talmudic law.

Like other scholars we have seen, Ra'avan strives to locate some explanation for the absence of protest, which for him clearly implied legitimation. Typical of the mind-set of the age, Ra'avan frames the issue in a male-centered way, focusing not on the justification of the women's behavior but on the absence of protest by rabbis. Ra'avan suggests that possibly the plaiting was (and is) tolerated "because it was impossible for them to tie their hair without plaiting it." It is difficult to understand why plaiting should have provided the sole technique for female coiffure or why this would be considered a sufficient explanation. Ra'avan's explanation is thus a poignant expression of his perplexity vis-à-vis the halakhic authorities' toleration of a flagrantly deviant behavior.

At the passage's end, Ra'avan adds, "And leave them to transgress unintentionally, rather than willfully."[55] This is a crucial phrase for our discussion. Rooted in the Babylonian Talmud, it is cited repeatedly in texts about deviant behavior, always indicating the rabbis' inability to enforce their norms among the rank and file. Ra'avan assumes that his rabbinic predecessors enjoyed hegemonic authority, but the reality of deviant behavior forces us to conclude that this was an illusion and that the portrait of medieval halakhic behavior is more complex.

Less flagrant a nonnormative behavior for the scholars of medieval Ashkenaz and therefore less vexatious were time-bound obligations. Talmudic law exempts women from the performance of precepts of this nature, and this is tantamount to forbidding them, because the ritual observance of such a commandment involves the recitation of a blessing, that is, taking the name of God, which of course cannot be done in vain, that is, without a religious obligation. And yet a number of sources indicate unequivocally that the women of medieval Franco-Germany did nonetheless perform time-bound commandments.

This reality is expressed fairly early in our study period. Rashi attributes to his teacher, Isaac Halevi of Worms (d. 1070), the decision not to prevent women from reciting the blessing over the palm frond (*lulav*) and the tabernacle (*sukkah*) on the Festival of Tabernacles (Sukkot). As Avraham Grossman has noted, the formulation "not to prevent" can only mean that the initiative for this practice came from the women themselves and was met by Rashi's teacher with a studied passivity.[56]

Fifty or more years brought no change in the status quo. Ra'avan refers to the same two customs, *lulav* and *sukkah*, and duly notes the absence of protest on the part of earlier Ashkenazic halakhic authorities.[57] *Sefer ha-Asufot*, an Ashkenazic manual more or less coeval with Ra'avan, offers a slight variation: "I have also heard of women who would recite the following blessing . . . 'who commanded His people Israel [to perform] a certain commandment, to sit in the *sukkah* or to take the *lulav*.'"[58]

We also read about the practice in France. Rabbenu Tam reputedly legitimates the troubling phenomenon by noting that "they [women] were accustomed to doing and observing them," namely the blessings.[59] Rabbenu Tam's alleged explanation is a de facto legitimation at best and a tautology at worst; he explains (and ostensibly justifies) the fact that women recite blessings that in theory they ought not to recite by noting that this is their custom!

Isaac of Dampierre states that if "our women" seek to perform a time-bound commandment and to recite the blessing over it, we do not protest, even though they are under no obligation, and he explicitly removes the custom from the category of taking the name of God in vain.[60] The use of the possessive pronoun in "our women" must be significant; it posits a distinction between the women of contemporary France (or Franco-Germany) from women in other societies. This seems related to the rabbinic idea, raised in connection with jewelry, that all Ashkenazic women belong in the halakhic category of "important" women.

This notion is attributed to several tosafists.[61] The expression comes from the amoraic statement that an "important woman" must recline at the Passover seder.[62] Avraham Grossman maintains that it refers to women with economic and social connections with gentiles rather than to their level of moral and religious behavior.[63] In the same vein, it may be that "important" women, or for that matter men, are to be viewed as independent of and not necessarily loyal to rabbinic leadership.[64]

The theme of rabbinic passivity in the face of deviant behavior appears in numerous contexts, apart from those already cited. The tosafists also use the expression "we do not protest" when they confront the practice of women and children rolling nuts or apples on the Sabbath—a forbidden activity—"for it were better that they err unwittingly than intentionally."[65] *Mahzor Vitry*, a liturgical-halakhic compendium by a student of Rashi, tells the same story, but after writing that one ought not to protest, the writer adds, "except where it is known that they will accept [the criticism] from him, for 'leave Israel alone; it were better that they err unwittingly than intentionally.'"[66] This is an explicit admission that women did not—and were known to not—heed rabbinic directives and exercised a significant measure of autonomy from rabbinic authority.

The rabbis of medieval Ashkenaz also explain the current female autonomy by referring to them as "daughters of prophetesses," a talmudic expression stemming from a famous anecdote in which Hillel granted approbation to a popular custom.[67] Rabbenu Tam appropriates the expression for women rather than men when he addresses a question relating to the lighting of the candles on Friday night; although the act requires the recitation of a blessing, it seems pointless, because it is recited late in the day, when lights have already been lit in people's homes for illumination. Rabbenu Tam explains that the women's custom is to extinguish the lights and then light them again in order to perform a necessary action, over which the blessing can be recited. He adds, "I saw [this] with my own eyes, and I asked them [whether this was indeed their custom], and they said 'Yes.' And if they are not prophetesses, they are daughters of prophetesses."[68]

The "daughters of prophetesses" coda serves as Rabbenu Tam's seal of approval, but it also reflects his inability to locate a textual base or context for the custom. This text is fascinating because it is one of the rare occasions in which a rabbi actually confronts a woman and asks her about her seemingly deviant behavior. Rabbenu Tam turns anthropologist and goes into the field because he lacks the bibliographical tools with which to confront the issue at hand. Although Rabbenu Tam would never grant carte blanche approbation to the halakhic behavior of women, clearly he recognizes a realm of halakhic activity peculiar to women, about which they had to be trusted. This response was fairly common; whether or not they did so by choice, rabbis largely ceded turf to the female autonomous realm.[69]

Finally, on occasion medieval sources probe into time-related female customs not because they are halakhically problematic but simply because they have no textual basis. One of these is in the domestic realm: Women would draw water on Saturday night immediately after the conclusion of the Sabbath. Rather than cite a practical motive for this practice, an Ashkenazic source offers a midrashic explanation, concerning the well of the biblical Miriam, and concludes, "Every Saturday night one visits all the springs and wells, and whoever is ill and drinks water [therefrom] is immediately healed, even if his entire body is stricken with leprosy."[70] This explanation and folkloric tidbit date no earlier than the twelfth or early thirteenth century. Once again, the invocation of a legend to explain a contemporary behavior reflects its nonhalakhic character.

A similar domestic custom having to do with water is the practice, associated particularly with women, of pouring out all the water in the house following a death. Samson ben Zaddok, of thirteenth-century Ashkenaz, links this custom to the legend of Miriam's well; the loss of water at the death of someone dear is modeled after or analogized to the drying of Miriam's well at her death.[71] *Shibolei ha-Leqet* records that, following a death on the eve of Passover, "the women" wanted to throw out the water, but this posed a difficulty, because water would shortly be needed for the baking of unleavened bread. Isaac of Dampierre is alleged to have ruled that the water may be conserved, because the custom's raison d'être is trivial; its purpose, he avers, is simply to publicize the death, so that people would come and attend to the needs of the deceased.[72] Both of these water customs are intimately associated with women, and neither has roots in the talmudic-halakhic corpus. Thus, although these customs violate neither biblical nor rabbinic precepts, they are nonhalakhic. They are also deviant in that they exist beyond the bounds of rabbinic authority; neither Isaac of Dampierre nor anyone else had the power to stamp out these female traditions.

Women exercise halakhic autonomy with respect to fast days as well. The Kol Bo, a late medieval Ashkenazic halakhic compendium, records the "venerable" custom that women wash their heads on the ninth of Av in the late afternoon (following the afternoon service). The text immediately explains that the scholars of yore instituted this practice, and "they relied on" the legend that the messiah is due to be born on the ninth of Av.[73]

This practice constitutes a flagrant violation of the law (cited in the Kol Bo passage) that one may not wash for pleasure on the ninth of Av, a national fast day commemorating the destruction of the Temple. It is therefore unlikely that rabbinic scholars of any age gave it their blessing, particularly when its sole textual foundation rests in the realm of legend rather than law.[74] Furthermore, the phrase "they relied on" suggests that the proposed explanation represents a legitimation effort rather than an a priori prescription, as the Kol Bo would have one think. In all likelihood, then, this tradition is yet another instance of female deviant behavior, with a belated, feeble effort on the part of the rabbis to find a place for it within their textually oriented halakhic worldview.

In all the cases considered here the women say nothing in justification of their traditions; it is the men who puzzle over the deviant behavior and attempt to legitimate it. Indeed, one cannot help but wonder at the gap separating men from women, who seem to inhabit separate worlds. Rather than question the women about their behavior, the rabbis comb the sacred tomes in search of a prooftext. Obviously this strategy stems from the valid assumption that the women are unfamiliar with the sources and hence unlikely to produce a textual justification. The rabbis are willing to grant that the behaviors are fundamentally legitimate, but they see no point in confronting women about them, because women lack the tools with which to answer their question.

There is, however, an exception to this pattern.[75] A *Kol Bo* passage records that some women are known to have abstained from meat and wine from the seventeenth of Sivan to the tenth of Av, even though the officially prescribed period of abstinence is significantly shorter. The text then elaborates, "*They say* [emphasis added] that this is what they have received from their mothers, generation after generation."[76] Here it is the women who speak out in defense of their custom, and as one might expect, they offer the classic female justification—the oral tradition of mothers and daughters.

Menstruation and Immersion

That medieval women had their own norms concerning menstruation and immersion, norms that were not rooted in talmudic tradition and sometimes conflicted with it, comes as no surprise, because this was a peculiarly female sphere of activity. Scholars were intensively engaged in issues pertaining to female bleeding and spotting, but the culture of the Jewish woman's cycle of menstruation and immersion is far richer and more textured and extends beyond the confines of men's knowledge and control.

Some of the practices pertaining to menstruation illustrate the important point that deviant behavior should not necessarily be associated with transgression or, in other words, with falling short of the halakhic standard. It is deviant nonetheless because it exists independent of rabbinic authority and beyond male censure, but it does not reflect laxity, as Rashi suggests in a text cited earlier.[77] To illustrate, Rashi notes that some women refrain from entering the synagogue or touching the Torah scroll during their period of menstruation. This regulation is not found in the sources, and Rashi duly terms it "a groundless stringency."[78]

We also read, in the writings of Ra'avan, that women refrain from cooking and baking during the period of their menstrual flow. This custom is problematic, as Ra'avan explains, because these tasks are among a wife's domestic duties to her husband. Speculating as to its origins, Ra'avan theorizes that it stems from an error; at a certain point in the distant past, someone thought that a menstruating woman may not pour drinks, so as not to come into contact with her husband's food and render it unclean. From here to the conclusion that she may neither cook nor bake during these days of her cycle is but a short step. Ra'avan imputes the error to an imaginary scholar who must have imparted this mistaken information to women, who then propagated it among themselves. Ra'avan points out the error, explaining that the laws of purity and impurity are currently in abeyance and are therefore of no practical significance.[79]

Although Ra'avan believes that the abstention is wrong, at no point does he take vigorous action to combat it. This passivity or resignation is typical of what we have seen so far of the rabbinic reaction to deviant behavior on the part of women. Also typical is the kind of explanation Ra'avan proposes. Rather than ask women about their tradition, he assumes that it is rooted (however erroneously) in a halakhic source, and this assumption leads him to posit a male point of origin. This is unlikely and untrue to the nature of women's law as depicted in the sources studied thus far, as is Ra'avan's historical reconstruction. What is not unlikely, however, is Ra'avan's assumption that the practice is not recent, as is evident from his suggestion that the error crept in in the distant past.[80]

One of the most vehement protests against women's norms, attributed to Rashi, reads as follows:

> Some people refer to the seven last days [of a woman's menstrual period of abstinence] as her white days, because she washes in warm water and "whitens" herself with attractive clothing. And all of them[81] do not at this point separate themselves on account of impurity, and they eat and drink with their husbands, and perform for their husbands every service which a wife performs for her husband: pouring his drink, making his bed, and washing his face, hands and feet, during their white days. And this is a great evil . . . for she never leaves her state of impurity until she immerses herself. . . .
>
> Should you ask: Since the menstruant needs to immerse herself, what sort of purification do they perform in warm water? Know and understand that women invented this,[82] for during their period of impurity they would change their clothes and wear ugly clothing, so that their husbands would find them unattractive and not become accustomed to transgressing.[83] Then, after they ceased [menstruating], they

would wash and put on attractive clothes, because making themselves so unattractive was difficult for them. And when they saw [that the period was called] the woman's "white days," they began to say that these are the days of which the rabbis spoke, and they made it their habit, and women would serve their husbands in those days, and one may not behave thus . . . on account of the habit of transgressing. . . .

Worse still, since they became accustomed to washing themselves during their white days, they began doing so habitually, and they forgot the main cleansing performed immediately before the immersion that is performed as prescribed by law. . . . We are therefore commanded to eradicate this custom . . . for having made it their habit, they began saying that it is not these things that purify.[84]

Rashi is highly critical of the current female norms during the period between menstruation and immersion, specifically of two evils stemming (in his view) from a misunderstanding of the term *white days*. In halakhic literature this concept refers to the week-long waiting period that follows the cessation of the menstrual flow and precedes the woman's ritual immersion, after which she and her spouse may resume conjugal relations. The days of the waiting period are termed white in reference to the fact that the woman has stopped bleeding, but Rashi thinks that women associate the term with their own practice of washing in warm water and putting on fresh clothing at this point in time. He strongly opposes this custom, not because it is a misrepresentation of the term but because it poses halakhic pitfalls; women, he thinks, are overly intimate with their husbands during their white days, and their bathing and changing during this period could jeopardize their ability to immerse properly at the end of the period of abstinence. Because of this misunderstanding, women fail to realize the religious significance of the ultimate immersion and, by extension, of the final washing they must do immediately before that immersion, to remove any grit that might interrupt the contact of flesh and water.

Apart from documenting another set of female deviant behaviors, Rashi's text is special because it is an almost unique instance of active male opposition to women's law. Instead of expressing resignation, as rabbis do when they invoke the slogan "better that they err unwittingly than intentionally," Rashi issues a clarion call for resistance to these norms. Clearly, some behaviors were so unacceptable as to impel rabbis to respond, however rarely this may have occurred.

Rashi offers an etiology of the dangerous white days customs, and Israel Ta-Shma perspicaciously observes that this was his way of attacking their validity: "The power of custom," Ta-Shma explains, "lies in its not having a history."[85] This tactic is available, however, only when the writer (in this case Rashi) can speak with authority, that is, when the custom springs up within historical memory; customs believed to be ancient, such as cooking and baking during menstruation, are virtually unassailable.[86]

Immersion practices bring this section to a close. Ra'avan allows women to immerse in water that flows through the city in pipes, provided that the water "crawls" at least a minimal distance on its own after being conducted through the pipes; a minimal crawling distance would suffice to remove the water from the category of "drawn" water (she'uvin), which may not be used for ritual immersion. Ra'avan instructs his interlocutor not to publicize his lenient ruling, because he may be mistaken. Significantly for our purposes, Ra'avan adds that if women are already accustomed to using this kind of water, there is no need to actively discourage them from continuing to do so, because "it is possible that if you tell them they will not listen." He concludes with the familiar formula, "Leave them alone, to err unwittingly rather than intentionally."[87] This case is a bit unusual, in that Ra'avan does not explicitly state that women actually observe the norm that he is scrutinizing, but the important point here is the admission of male powerlessness to sway women from their female traditions, which is a classic element of deviant behavior.

A more typical female custom is that of submerging three times, rather than once, during ritual immersion. As usual, scholars labor to assign it some sort of rationale. In typical fashion, the writer of Sefer Hasidim seeks a textual foundation and offers a midrashic solution, citing three biblical prooftexts that include the verb for cleansing.[88] He concludes by proposing that on the eve of Yom Kippur, when men undergo ritual immersion, they too should submerge three times.[89] This is a rare instance of a scholar recommending a female tradition to the male public, although it is not surprising, given the book's pietistic bent.

The same norm is documented by Abraham ben Nathan of thirteenth-century Lunel, who raises the possibility that the practice is not exclusively Ashkenazic. This writer offers a different rationale from that of *Sefer Hasidim*, although his explanation is also gender conditioned, that is to say, male oriented. He suggests that the custom was the brainchild of contemporary scholars, who thought that although women might fail to perform a satisfactory immersion if they submerged themselves once, one of three attempts was bound to be successful. This is an effort at historical reconstruction, such as Rashi's hypothesis regarding the white days.[90]

Immersion is rendered invalid when any substance interrupts the complete contact of skin and water. Thus, if a woman has hairs that are glued together, some portion of her hair will not come into contact with water. Nonetheless, Ra'avia declares that women may immerse themselves under these circumstances, because removing the hairs would jeopardize the woman's health. He makes the following observation:

> I investigated [and discovered] that there are women who have [this condition] and immerse. "Leave them alone: if they are not prophetesses, they are daughters of prophetesses," for they grew up among Torah scholars and it is impossible that they did not ask them. Additionally, my father and other scholars lived in Köln and I knew for certain they [women] used to immerse themselves in this condition [and] I did not hear anyone protest. And at the time it did not occur to me to discuss this with them and learn their opinion. Now, in my old age, however, I have been asked about this and I am inclined to permit it. And it is stated in the Jerusalem Talmud: "If you see an uncertain [*rofefet*] law, see how the public behaves,"[91] although the case at hand is not an uncertain law.[92]

Ra'avia acknowledges that the custom is not new and that the rabbis of previous generations did not challenge it, although he finds this puzzling. For him, the absence of protest is an indication that the practice is legitimate, although we have already seen that this assumption is baseless. Ra'avia errs also, as he does in the jewelry case, in assuming that women must have consulted with Torah scholars before undertaking the proposed course of action. This is a classic instance of gender-conditioned thinking, one that women would not have entertained, as the many topics surveyed so far make clear.

The categories of immersion and holy days converge in the following case. A tosafist passage, in the name of Samson ben Abraham, notes that women may cut their nails on the intermediate days of festivals, and it offers justification. At issue here is the talmudic statement that one may not use a tool to cut one's nails on these days.[93] A more detailed discussion, in *Shibolei ha-Leqet*, makes it clear that the tosafist statement was more than theoretical, for here we read that Isaac (!) ben Abraham wonders at the female practice of doing so before immersion, in the face of the talmudic prohibition. Unlike the tosafist passage, it is clear from this text that the custom is problematic because women use a knife, which is explicitly ruled out by the relevant talmudic source.

In a model of tosafist dialectic, the *Shibolei ha-Leqet* speaker proffers a distinction between the talmudic source and the situation under discussion, which allows him to permit the use of a tool. He then weighs the relative legitimacy of using a knife or a scissors and concludes that a scissors should probably be considered the classic tool for nail paring. This results in the identification of the scissors as the forbidden utensil, with the result that the exceptional use of a knife is then found to be legitimate.

The last words of the *Shibolei ha-Leqet* ruling are telling: "One ought not to prohibit [this], for it is a permitted custom, since there is no custom that has no [legitimating] proof."[94] This last phrase is not lifted from talmudic literature or medieval predecessors; it represents the speaker's own conviction of the power of dialectic to resolve discrepancies between behavior—no matter how deviant—and the textual tradition. The flexibility of the tosafists extended, as we have seen, even to the legitimation of murder and suicide in 1096 and would certainly extend to lesser transgressions, such as those surveyed in the preceding section.

My discussion of women's law concludes with the well-known problem of Jewish women and gentile men finding themselves alone together in an intimate setting. The tosafists struggle with the talmudic rule that a woman may not be alone with a gentile man because, as they point out, "it is impossible that she not be alone with a gentile for a single hour" (i.e., a short time).[95] Avraham Grossman asks, correctly, why this should be "impossible" if it is outlawed by the Talmud. He concludes that, Talmud or no Talmud, the position of Jewish women in medieval European society effectively ruled this out, but it is unclear why men could not control this aspect of their social reality.[96]

Nevertheless, that women habitually found themselves in such a compromising situation with gentile men, regardless of the talmudic prohibition, cannot be denied. Ra'avia discusses the case of a woman who was assaulted after taking a trip in the company of two men, neither of whom was her husband. Ra'avia notes that "every day women go with two or three men, and they [the women] see that the Torah scholars do not protest. They do not know that it is forbidden, for they cannot assume that people are lawless. . . . And they [the women] assume that every man is upright until he behaves like a lawless person [*paritz*] or a thief."[97] Ra'avia allows the woman in the case at hand to remain with her husband, contrary to talmudic law, from which Grossman infers that the norm's prevalence forced the rabbis to disregard talmudic law.

This is yet another instance in which we find Ra'avia expressing the assumption that women act out of ignorance, implying that they would correct their behavior if people in authority would instruct them properly. The medieval reality, however, was otherwise: Women are indeed ignorant of the textual tradition, but their behavior is rooted in their alternative culture rather than in ignorance. This is also why women frequently refuse to mend their ways, even when chastised, although Ra'avia fails to acknowledge this as well. Indeed, the more common dynamic is that rabbis choose not to confront the aberrant behavior because they recognize that female behavior is beyond their control.

Male Deviant Behavior

The abundant examples of deviant behavior in the female Jewish society of medieval Ashkenaz can be understood, as I have suggested, through the existence of a discrete female oral tradition that is distinct from and often at variance with talmudic tradition and largely independent of rabbinic authority. In this section I explore deviant behavior among the male Jewish society of medieval Ashkenaz and argue that it was no less characteristic of men than of women. This is significant, because here the category of gendered thinking and behavior cannot explain the severe limitations of rabbinic authority and talmudic tradition. Women's law is a reality in medieval Ashkenaz, and yet the problem of deviant behavior cuts across the sexual divide, for reasons I will examine. Early in the discussion, I looked at the deviant behavior of the early stage of Ashkenazic communal development, before the authority structures were in place, when people thought that they could defy their leadership and flout social and religious norms. The following discussion is limited to a later period, mostly from the twelfth century through the middle of the thirteenth century, when in fact blatant defiance disappears from the sources, and the rabbis are depicted as powerful communal leaders.

Before surveying some of the medieval sources on male deviance, we might usefully inquire into the semantics of deviance. What terms do rabbis use to describe people who engage in nonhalakhic behavior, and what can these terms teach us about the morphology of medieval Ashkenazic society?

A tosafist gloss observes, "Everywhere we see that converts are not as punctilious as Jews in their observance of the commandments."[98] This comment challenges the talmudic statement that converts are excessively punctilious and zealous in their performance of religious obligations. It would therefore appear that converts were visible enough to warrant a sociological observation about their conduct and that the tosafists (or at least this particular tosafist) found it wanting.

The tosafists do not harmonize their own experience regarding converts with that expressed in the talmudic source.[99] Interestingly, Rashi, in his commentary on this same passage, accepts the Talmud's observation and suggests that the converts' problematic behavior is rooted in their ignorance of Jewish law. In this respect, converts might be compared to women.

Medieval rabbis use a few epithets to denote those who habitually flout halakhic discipline. One such term is *reqim*, or worthless people. A student of Rashi's reports, in his master's name, that although Rashi would be inclined to permit Jews to derive financial benefit from gentile wine, he was reluctant to publish his viewpoint "lest the worthless ones become accustomed to this and regard the matter lightly."[100] Clearly the worthless are regarded as frivolous in their religious conduct, ever ready to seize on a lenient ruling to shirk a burdensome precept.[101]

Ephraim ben Isaac of Regensburg records a case in which someone bought books from "the worthless ones who wander around the kingdom."[102] It came to light that the books were stolen, and when the original owners sued for their return, the rabbis forced the new owners to return them without compensation.[103] Here the worthless are actually criminals, but Rabbi Ephraim would probably have applied the term more liberally, to include people without strong moral or religious scruples, a characterization that could also apply to the previous source.[104]

A third usage, which has its own particular nuance, appears in *Sefer Hasidim*. A passage relates that, although all the needy members of any community are entitled to receive food or alms from the townspeople, Torah scholars receive a larger portion than "the worthless simple folk." Here *reqim* is conflated with ignoramuses.[105]

Simple folk (*'am ha'aretz*) is a talmudic term, not a medieval one, and it always refers to a sector of the population that is unlearned, although not necessarily disobedient. The sources from medieval Ashkenaz testify to the presence of such a sector and, by definition, to a certain tension between the learned and the unlearned, although not necessarily to a crisis of leadership.[106]

How unlearned is unlearned? Commenting on the Talmud's discussion of the role of the interpreter in the synagogue, who traditionally rendered the biblical lection into Aramaic, Rashi explains, "The interpreter's job is to recite for women and simple folk, who do not know the holy tongue."[107] It is impossible, however, to determine whether Rashi intended his explanation to refer only to the reality of the talmudic age or perhaps also to his own society. Eliezer of Metz attests that even the simple folk are able to recite the doxology on their own, including the biblical verses contained therein.[108] Similarly, Zedekiah Anau, author of *Shibolei ha-Leqet*, observes that "no commoner in the world does not know [the Passover haggadah] a little: he reads a little, sometimes in the book, sometimes out of the book."[109] Anau means that even an illiterate, or someone who knows no Hebrew, can master the liturgy, a reality as true today as it was then.

The size of the simple folk sector in Ashkenazic Jewish society is difficult to ascertain. Rashi asks Isaac Halevi of Worms, his teacher, whether he issued a certain stringent ruling because he viewed his own community as composed of rustics (*benai kefarim*) and simple folk, who stood in need of a "fence," or safeguard. The master responds in the negative, pointing out that there are among the community's members a number of learned men who know the law and can distinguish forbidden actions from permitted ones.[110] The significant formulation here is that there are learned people "among" the membership, which acknowledges that the uneducated constitute a significant presence in or percentage of the constituency.

The tosafists present a different image of the level of literacy in their society. Rabbinic law mandates that the Torah scroll be rolled shut before the recitation of the blessing over the Torah, so that the masses (*hamon*) not say that the blessings are written in the text of the Torah. The tosafists add, however, that "if one did not do so, no matter, for simple folk are not so common nowadays."[111] Clearly the writer of this dictum views his own society as fairly literate and knowledgeable, a view that is of a piece with the assumption that even customs that appear deviant must have a textual base. Whether the objective situation had changed or whether the tosafists appraised it differently cannot be determined.

A couple of passages reveal the existence of tension between rabbis and commoners. Rabbi Yossi, a second-century Tanna, posited that judges must accept the testimony of simple folk.[112] Elhanan ben Isaac of Dampierre, an English tosafist, affirms this ruling and adds that "we are concerned about enmity," which lays bare the gap and tension between rabbis and simple folk. Rabbi Elhanan was undoubtedly focusing on contemporary conditions rather than offering a universal halakhic comment, for he adds that "this is why *nowadays* [emphasis added] we count an ignoramus towards a group recitation of Grace After Meals [despite Talmudic dicta to the contrary]."[113]

Further testimony to this kind of tension appears in a remark by Isaac ben Moses of Vienna, who writes that, although a scholar of ordinary ("Israelite") lineage ought to be called to read from the Torah before a commoner and even before one of priestly lineage, this hierarchical principle is currently ignored for the sake of peace "because the studious have dwindled in number and the simple folk have multiplied. . . . Nowadays, we receive their testimony [in a judicial proceeding] for the sake of peace."[114] Taken together, the dicta of Elhanan and Isaac ben Moses reflect the social significance of the simple folk as a sector, and they portray a state of tension between them and the rabbinic leadership. Whether this issue was becoming increasingly problematic over time is unclear.[115]

The term *paritzim*, or the lawless, is also deployed in the rabbinic literature of medieval Franco-Germany to denote those who habitually flout Jewish law.[116] Rabbenu Tam uses it to refer to self-serving types, who manipulate situations and individuals to their own advantage. Regarding his ordinance against threatening with excommunication one who derogates a bill of divorce, Rabbenu Tam writes that people can agree among themselves to deal with such an excommunicant for a specified period of time only, not indefinitely. This is justified, he explains, "because this has caused controversy to increase in Israel, since the lawless draw [people] near or [cause them] to move far away,"[117] meaning that they exploit the act of excommunication to elevate or degrade the social status of others.[118]

Sefer Hasidim refers to the lawless in a number of passages. One text asserts that a Jewish woman may masquerade as a gentile if she hears that Jewish lawless men are going to assault her. She may also take other measures, including calling for non-Jews to come to her aid, even if this should cost the lawless man his life.[119] This type of lawless man is a cold-blooded desperado, who shows no mercy in the pursuit of nefarious objectives.

Other *Sefer Hasidim* texts depict a gentler type of rogue. Giving alms to the lawless, warns one text, is tantamount to giving them "the fees of whores."[120] Elsewhere we read of a child who associates with lawless youths. Challenged about this by his father, the son replies that he has been drawing them to the study of Torah. Seeing that the young men want to play at dice, the son suggests that they play at biblical verses instead: One fellow recites a verse, and the next participant must recite a verse that begins with the final word of the previous fellow's verse.[121] In these exempla the lawless are associated with whoring and dice, the everyday vices of the dissolute, rather than with heinous crimes. This is also the tenor of the comment, in a third passage, that "the lawless say the blessings and praises quickly";[122] although the speaker portrays the lawless as rushing through the prayers, at least he assumes that they bother to recite them.[123]

Medieval Ashkenazic rabbis did not suffer fools, another category associated with deviant behavior. Rabbenu Tam upbraids Joseph of Orleans, his disciple, for writing that one may not alter a custom for fear of casting aspersions on earlier generations. With his notoriously caustic wit, the giant of Ramerupt remarks that *minhag*, or custom, when written backwards spells *gehinom*, namely Gehenna, "for if fools (*shotim*) behaved thus, scholars have not."[124] This last phrase establishes a dichotomy between scholars and fools, whose behavior Rabbenu Tam rejects as nonhalakhic.

The use of the epithet *fools* or *foolishness* in connection with customs that incur rabbinic disapproval has a long history. The defining characteristic of a foolish custom is that it is well-intentioned rather than deliberately transgressive. This is a different variety of deviant behavior, but it falls under that general rubric nonetheless. Once again it is the acerbic Rabbenu Tam who skewers the "foolish custom" (*minhag shtut*) of equipping a child with a Pentateuch so that he can then be counted as an adult, to enable the community to reach a quorum for prayer.[125]

Medieval rabbis associate fools with actions that are not only well-intentioned but also actually acts of piety, however misguided. This is the concept of the "pious fool" (*hasid shoteh*). Rashi describes a type of usurious transaction that is rather dubious, as it involves two Jews, contravening the famous biblical prohibition of usury (Deut. 23:21), but he rules that it is in fact legal and refers to one who refrains from collecting the amount due him in such a situation as a "pious fool."[126]

The defining characteristic of the pious fool, however, is not just that his piety is unwarranted but that his efforts to excel lead him into error. To illustrate, Rashi has harsh words for ascetics (*perushim*) who fast on both Thursday and Friday when Purim occurs on a Sunday, so as to link the fast of Esther as tightly as possible to Purim; of such people Rashi cites the verse "a fool walks in darkness" (Eccles. 2:14), because they misrepresent the status of the fast of Esther, acting as though it were biblically ordained.[127] For the noblest of motives, these ascetics violate the prohibition against fasting on a Friday, the eve of the Sabbath, and hence they merit the humiliating designation.

Perushim are often called *Hasidim*, and the pious fool, as a type, also appears in *Sefer Hasidim*. Predictably, here it is a badge of honor: "Whatever you can do, but refrain from doing out of embarrassment, because they will call you a pious fool (*hasid shoteh*), think to yourself as follows: Were you in a time of persecution, you would be killed for a minor infraction . . . , *a fortiori* shall I overcome my [Evil] Inclination, which is within my power."[128] This speaker recognizes the association of the pious fool with unnecessary stringency; indeed he embraces it, but he would not identify it with transgression.[129]

The rabbinic literature of medieval Ashkenaz preserves a cornucopia of source materials on male deviant behavior. In terms of topics, the sources divide fairly neatly into two categories: Jewish-Christian relations and religious ritual. The following survey highlights some of the same themes touched on with regard to women's law, as well as others. The main point is that the authority of talmudic tradition and rabbinic leadership was never more than partial in medieval Ashkenaz, for men as well as women, and this realization narrows the gap separating them from those of the present day.

Jewish-Christian Relations

From the early days of Jewish settlement in Ashkenaz, Jews were accustomed to conducting commercial relations with their gentile neighbors on non-Jewish holidays, including Sunday, in flagrant violation of talmudic law.[130] Rabbenu Gershom advises against raising an outcry, for he sees no hope of compliance: "Their livelihood depends on their [Christian] merchandise, and most of the days of the year are their festivals . . . such that their [the Jews'] livelihood would be destroyed unless they do business on their [Christian] festivals, and they would transgress intentionally. Rather, 'leave Israel—better that they err unwittingly than intentionally.'"[131] This is a rather bald admission of the limited fidelity of the Jewish rank and file to religious dictates.

Later scholars may have been unaware that Gershom and other early Ashkenazic authorities tolerated this violation for lack of choice, because they turn to the task of rationalization. Rashi legitimates the practice "on account of enmity" (*mishum evah*), meaning fear of alienating the gentile constituency.[132] A standard formulation in this era reads, "On what did the world rely" to permit this or that prohibition?[133] This question spurs Samuel ben Meir (Rashbam, Rashi's grandson) and Rabbenu Tam (Rashbam's brother) to offer one or more theoretical justifications.[134] The legitimation exercise reflects the conviction, noted earlier, that even ostensibly nonhalakhic norms must be rooted in talmudic tradition.

The "better that they err unwittingly" adage was adduced in connection with dietary laws also. Rashi holds that wine poured from a barrel for an idolatrous gentile is considered "libation wine" and is therefore prohibited; this was also the status of any wine that remained in the barrel, because it was "joined" to the libation wine. But Rashi refuses to force his position on the public, citing the "better . . ." adage. We are explicitly told that the prohibited behavior is legion and that people will not exercise caution, meaning that they would not obey.[135]

Isaac ben Moses of Vienna informs us that rabbis did not always meet violations of the dietary code with equanimity. He reports having seen his teacher, Ra'avia, administer lashes to people who ate bread baked by gentiles on the Sabbath.[136] This testimony seems to refer to a repeated occurrence rather than a single incident, both because the speaker uses the imperfect tense and because he refers to people, in the plural. It implies both frequent breaches in halakhic discipline and at the same time a high degree of halakhic discipline. It was this discipline that enabled Ra'avia to confront the transgressors rather than fall back on the "better . . ." adage, which was wielded when rabbis thought that their authority was weak.

There is also a case of dietary norms violating the law in the direction of excessive stringency. Isaac ben Judah, Rashi's teacher, admits that there is no fundamental prohibition against eating foods cooked in gentile vessels, but he insists that it is impossible to abrogate this prohibition, because it has become universally accepted and must therefore be tolerated.[137]

A responsum attributed to Rashi challenges the legitimacy of the "better . . ." adage as a halakhic strategy, because it flies in the face of the biblical injunction to reprove offenders. The respondent concedes the point and agrees that one must make the law known to the public as well as to those who might accept reproof and mend their ways; he reserves the right to remain passive, however, with regard to those "most strongly bound" to the violation, who are convinced that the norm is legal and who would not heed words of protest.[138]

Twelfth-century authorities continued to wrestle with the problem of whether and when to reprove and challenge their flock for malfeasance. The tosafists repeat the doctrine that one ought not to rebuke offenders when they are sure to disregard the rebuke.[139] Ra'avia formulates one of the clearest policy statements on this issue.

> Regarding anything to which they are accustomed, and if we protest they will not listen, leave Israel alone—better that they err unwittingly than intentionally, whether the prohibition is rabbinic . . . or biblical. . . . For just as one is commanded to say that which will be heard, so is one commanded not to say that which will not be heard, such as when it is clear to him that he will not be heard, and they [the public] also think that it is permitted. However, if they act intentionally and transgress, one must upbraid even one hundred times[140]. . . . And if they act unintentionally, one must guide them on the path of righteousness, on the chance that they will listen, given that their fathers did not train them to conduct themselves in this way.[141]

This is a programmatic passage rather than empirical evidence about the nature and scope of deviance in Ra'avia's particular social context. Still, it is difficult to imagine that it was entirely divorced from his social experience, and this also emerges from other evidence. Ra'avia stakes out a middle ground between reproval and apathy and advises reproof when the aberrant behavior is flagrant, in the sense that the transgressor knows that it is nonhalakhic. Ra'avia's formulation closes with the assumption that deviant behavior could not possibly be rooted in oral tradition. We have already seen that this is not the case and that in fact all sorts of practices that contravene talmudic law were rooted in a nontextual tradition, particularly the customs of women.

Sefer Hasidim also addresses the question of rebuke. A passage that comments on the verse "a time for silence" (Eccles. 3:7) instructs readers to refrain from rebuking people when it is evident that they will not accept criticism, for "better that they err unwittingly than intentionally." By contrast, it is "a time for speech" when one can protest effectively.[142] Elsewhere, this time regarding the commandment to rebuke offenders (Lev. 19:17), *Sefer Hasidim* declares, "We are obligated to rebuke transgressors, and to whiten their faces from [their] transgressions until they beat us and revile us and curse us."[143] The violent language may be hyperbole, but it powerfully evokes the presence of a recalcitrant constituency.

Another stock phrase in discussions of deviant behavior, apart from the "better . . ." adage, refers to the Jewish people as "prophets, sons of prophets." One text that uses this formula relates to mortuary ritual. Rashi relates that there are those who refrain from reciting the liturgical composition known as the "justification of the divine judgment" (*zidduk ha-din*) at a funeral when the funeral takes place on Friday afternoon; the rationale is that one must not impinge on the commandment to delight in the Sabbath. Rashi admits that he knows of no grounds for such a stringency but adds that "the Israelites are scholars, the sons of scholars, and 'if they are not prophets, they are the sons of prophets,'[144] and the custom that they learned from their fathers is [considered] Torah, to which nothing is to be added and from which naught is to be detracted."[145]

The "prophets" adage is a powerful affirmation of the authenticity and legitimacy of customs, including those that appear aberrant when measured against the talmudic corpus. It represents, in a sense, the institutionalization of deviant behavior. It is the opposite reaction to the three attitudes mentioned thus far: passivity ("better . . ."), reproof, and physical measures, such as Ra'avia's lashing of transgressors. When faced with a challenge to a halakhic norm, a scholar might prefer one policy to another for many reasons; in the case at hand one must recall that the "justification" custom is, as Rashi points out, a stringency, meaning that it does not threaten the halakhic edifice. This may have made it easier for him to be supportive and to prefer the "prophets" adage to the "better . . ." one.[146]

Real estate transactions are the last case to be considered here under the category of Jewish-Christian relations. Selling and renting houses to idolaters is prohibited under rabbinic law, because of the biblical injunction "You must not bring an abhorrent thing into your house" (Deut. 7:26). Nevertheless, people did this all the time. Barukh ben Isaac of Worms, a student of Isaac of Dampierre (fl. ca. 1200), says as much: "We now normally rent houses to gentiles, and also bring gentiles inside when they are ill or on other occasions, and I wonder on what this practice is based?"[147] Isaac of Vienna simply depicts the rampant violation: "Nowadays people do not refrain from lending and renting houses to non-Jews, even though they bring idolatry inside."[148]

The typical response is to offer textual rationales, as a tosafist passage proceeds to do.[149] Ra'avan provides a halakhic rationale and does not seem to find the custom especially galling.[150] On the other hand, Eliezer of Metz and Isaac of Vienna note that, even when one may rent houses to idolaters, one may not rent them dwellings, because they bring idolatry inside, in violation of the biblical injunction.[151] This "distinctione" enabled these two scholars to supply at least partial legitimation for what they perceived to be a religious taboo.

Religious Ritual

The largest block of deviant behaviors in the category of religious ritual concerns the commandments to don *tefillin*, wear ritual fringes (*tzitzit*), and fix a *mezuzah* to the doorpost. These precepts are taken for granted in the life of today's observant Jews, but such was not the case in medieval Ashkenaz.

Sources on this problem are abundant. Rabbenu Tam remarks that "less than ten years ago there was narry a *mezuzah* in the entire kingdom."[152] Speaking about *tefillin*, a tosafist text notes that "our grasp of this commandment is weak."[153] *Mahzor Vitry* obliquely testifies to the inadequate fulfillment of the *tefillin* obligation when it instructs readers about the order in which they are to be donned "if one has *tefillin* and wishes to don them."[154] A tosafist gloss of Judah Sir Leon of Paris seeks to discover "on what did the [people of the] world rely, to abstain from donning *tefillin*?"[155] His student, Moses of Coucy, preaches about the need to don *tefillin*, contrary to common practice.[156] A *Sefer Hasidim* exemplum observes that "many good people (*tovim*) would like to wear *tzitzit* and don *tefillin* but abstain on account of embarrassment."[157]

These sources seem to refer to simple neglect rather than to aberrant custom. Joseph "Bekhor Shor" of Orleans (ca. 1110–1185) supplies a different sort of explanation.

> The nations of the world say that the words of Moses are allegory. . . . Among our own people, too, I have heard people express doubt about *tefillin*, *mezuzah* and the covering of [a slaughtered animal's] blood, for they say that [the verses] "and it shall be as a sign upon your hand and as a symbol on your forehead" [Exod. 13:16], "inscribe them on the doorposts of your house and on your gates" [Deut. 6:9] resemble "let me be a seal upon your heart, like the seal upon your hand" [Canticles 8:6], that you remember me always, and it is not a seal on your arm and heart in the literal sense, and neither are these literally *tefillin* and *mezuzot*.[158]

Bekhor Shor's portrayal of the popular mind-set is difficult to accept, because allegory did not have substantial impact on the Jews of northern France, although Bekhor Shor's interpretation is corroborated by Samuel ben Meir, a contemporary French exegete.[159] It is interesting nonetheless that this Bekhor Shor talks about behavior that is rooted in an ideological stance rather than on either weakness or wickedness.[160]

Another approach attributes the problem to excessive orthodoxy. A tosafist text suggests that people avoid *tefillin* because of uncertainty about the rules for when they should or should not be donned. This anxiety was supposedly rooted in the concern to prevent oneself from becoming unclean, and it resulted in the new custom of donning *tefillin* for the morning prayers only.[161] Zedekiah Anau's *Shibolei ha-Leqet* observes that the general public (*ha'olam*) does not regularly don *tefillin* and muses that this may be because they are unsure whether to follow the (Bekhor Shor) *tefillin* regulations of Rashi or those of Rabbenu Tam.[162] A *Sefer Hasidim* passage on excessive stringency lampoons a pietist whose quest for an ever higher level of punctilious observance leads him to falter in something so simple as the donning of *tefillin*. The text concludes with the moral that performance of the commandments is perforce imperfect and offers the consolation that "the Torah was not given to angels."[163] This direction of interpretation seems peculiar: One who frets over the fine points of the religious commitment would be unlikely to respond to the problem by altogether abandoning observance of the precept.[164]

Evidence for the neglect of *tzitzit* is equally plentiful. Rabbenu Tam and Isaac of Dampierre write that currently people do not all wear *tzitzit*, and they therefore warn against shrouding a deceased person in *tzitzit*, for this would only highlight his shame. Nor should one distinguish between those who did and those who did not wear *tzitzit* in their lifetime, for this would bring humiliation upon the families of the less worthy.[165] Ra'avan also wonders how it is that "most Jews" do not wear *tzitzit* every day, considering the importance of this commandment. He replies, as do other scholars, that the obligation rests only on people who are accustomed to wearing a four-cornered garment, which in his society is simply not done.[166] This is a model of tosafist dialectic, for it provides a formal solution, but although it excuses the deviant behavior, it fails to explain it.[167] We are left with an image of a Jewish society that casually ignores fundamental elements of everyday religious life.

Synagogue ritual is another realm in which the Jews of medieval Ashkenaz exhibit deviant behavior of different sorts. Using the classic formulation, "on what did they rely . . . ?" Rashi expresses wonder at the popular custom of reciting the time blessing (*she-hehiyyanu*) over the palm frond on the second day of Sukkot, a custom he views as absolutely baseless.[168] Similarly, a tosafist gloss asks how it is that, on the intermediate days of festivals, "everyone has been accustomed" (*nahagu ha-'olam*) to read the same text for the fourth person called to the Torah that was read for those who preceded him, because one is normally required to read the Bible in a linear, consecutive fashion, without repeating what has been read; no answer is provided.[169] Ra'avan responds to a query about the basic contradiction between the talmudic prohibition against reciting portions of the Written Law and the universal custom of including biblical lections in the daily liturgy.[170]

Ephraim ben Isaac of Regensburg, in a letter to Joel ben Isaac Halevi of Bonn,[171] strongly deplores the custom of having a cantor who reads from the Torah recite the blessings as well and declares that God will punish anyone who is able to protest but refrains from doing so. He adds, "I am unable to protest, for they say that their ancestral custom has the status of the Law of Moses, as you wrote. And on *Simhat Torah* I left the synagogue in anger, for I heard the cantor skip more than forty times. . . . And you can protest, and if you do protest, you will merit fame and glory in the supernal yeshiva."[172] This is important testimony to the limits of this particular rabbi's authority and, more important, to the public's ability to stand up for its traditions in the face of severe disapproval. Needless to say, the custom under discussion here is not a female tradition, and it is one of many cases in which men also practice norms that are nonhalakhic, causing rabbis to search for rationales and shun confrontation. Thus, although women had their own nontextual traditions, men did as well; neither had a monopoly on deviant behavior.[173]

A crystal clear illustration of the similarity between the position of men's and women's customs is the following statement by Ra'avan about clapping at weddings held on the Sabbath, which violates the talmudic dictum that one may not produce sound on the Sabbath.[174]

> Nowadays people normally clap at weddings, and earlier authorities (*ha-rishonim*) did not protest, on account of the rule—"Leave Israel alone, to err unwittingly rather than intentionally," for the earlier authorities knew that they would not refrain from doing so on account of their protest. Alternatively, they may have instructed them that this behavior is permitted when performed in an unusual manner . . . and eventually they clapped also in the usual fashion and the scholars were then unable to prevent them from doing so. It is also possible that they felt no need to protest, even though clapping might be considered a violation of the commandment to rest on the Sabbath, because one is commanded to clap for a bride and groom.[175]

Ra'avan offers three explanations for the current behavior, beginning with the possibility that it truly is aberrant but that the rabbis of yore were powerless to effect change. He then posits a historical explanation, according to which earlier scholars offered a halakhic option, which eventually got distorted and fell into desuetude, leaving scholars impotent to effect change.[176] Finally, Ra'avan suggests that esteemed predecessors legitimated the practice in its current form. The striking feature of this text is Ra'avan's assumption that behaviors are always processed, if not ratified, by rabbis, who, at the least, make a policy decision to refrain from intervening when they sense that their protest will go unheeded. This is the pattern we have seen all along, in Ra'avan and other writers, and it presents an image of Ashkenazic society as less disciplined and more heterogeneous than its reputation has led us to believe.

Ra'avan does not always cede to popular custom. He writes that a woman who gets her period before her wedding ceremony must observe the rules of menstruation and immersion like other women. Some people, he has heard, rule leniently on this matter and excuse women from waiting seven additional "clean" days after the cessation of the menstrual flow, but Ra'avan debunks this view and calls for the correct policy to be publicized, to prevent transgression. This is not, he insists, a case of "better that they err unintentionally than willingly," for the biblical penalty is *qaret*, excision from the Israelite nation. He therefore advises "erecting a fence," enacting measures to make sure that the errant practice is eradicated; in practical terms, he explains, this means threatening offenders with excommunication.[177]

Although Ra'avan presents a picture of a male-dominated society, in which men define appropriate behavior, it is of course equally plausible that the source of the norm he is describing is female, particularly because it concerns menstruation and immersion, traditionally a feminine realm. This, however, cannot be assumed, for Ra'avan does not say as much. The behavior presented here is deviant not only because it flies in the face of talmudic law but also on account of the element of noncompliance. In what we know to be a rare move, Ra'avan decides to push for strenuous action, but he informs us that the situation could just as easily stimulate the opposite response, of "better that they err unintentionally than willingly," which is the cry of the defeated.

Ra'avan is equally proactive regarding conjugal sex during mourning. When a death occurs, a bereaved man may not conduct relations with his wife. To prevent temptation, certain other forms of contact between spouses are forbidden as well. Thus a wife may not wash her husband's face, hands, and feet, as she normally would; this rule applies not only after burial, when the period of mourning officially commences, but also from the moment of bereavement.[178] However, Ra'avia maintains that washing is the only restriction, whereas other kinds of touching are permitted, "for they do not tempt one to intercourse." Ra'avia considers total abstention from contact "a mere stringency," meaning one with no compelling rationale. Furthermore, he draws an analogy from bereavement to menstruation, when physical contact between spouses is also restricted, and claims, "had not the people observed this custom," there would be no need to prohibit all contact. Still, he concludes, "it is better to distance oneself [from transgression] and to erect a fence, and one ought not to permit [this behavior], because one might be led into error."[179] It is the unnecessarily stringent behavior of "the people" that forces Ra'avia to "erect a fence" in the case at hand.

The Talmud offers little hard and fast law concerning the laws of mourning, and it is therefore not surprising that this was fertile ground for popular custom. The Talmud states that Purim overrides the laws of mourning, and Rashi observes that this premise cannot be based on the law that one does not eulogize the deceased on Purim, because this latter rule is universally disregarded.[180] He proceeds to offer an explanation, but the crucial point here is Rashi's acknowledgment of the universal disregard of talmudic law.

Priestly gifts is another area of religious ritual in which we find aberrant behavior. Jewish law commands one to offer a portion of produce to a person of priestly lineage, but in medieval Ashkenaz, it seems, this law fell into abeyance. Rashi suggests two possible explanations for why "the people began regarding the matter lightly."[181] The dynamic suggested in this formulation is more important for our purposes than the explanations themselves: the fact that "the people" choose their own halakhic path, without reference to the canonical literature and without consulting rabbinical authorities.

Judah ben Qalonymos of twelfth-century Speyer still wonders—in the classic formulation—"on what did they rely nowadays, to refrain from giving presents to priests," indicating that the custom had not entirely been uprooted. He adds, "I heard that before the great slaughter of 4856 [i.e., 1096] they used to give [them] in Mainz." Perhaps this writer provided the historical insight to explain his own perplexity, but it might also have been an explanation: He may be proposing that the destruction of the Mainz community led to the neglect of this precept, as a result of the large number of victims from the ranks of either the priests themselves (as Rashi suggests) or perhaps of rabbinic leaders, who could have steered the community back on course.[182]

Talmudic law prohibits writing on the intermediate days of festivals. The tosafists condemn the widespread custom of writing in the round (*be'ogel*),[183] a practice apparently predicated on the assumption that this unusual form of writing would not be considered writing at all and thus not covered by the proscription.[184] This norm represents a creative attempt on the part of the general public to uphold the law, not to flout it, but it is nonetheless significant that the tosafists admit their helplessness in the face of a contemporary popular practice.

I conclude the present discussion with two cases involving the talmudic dictum that forbids a scholar from permitting an action that people perceive to be prohibited.[185] Isaac ben Dorbello, a twelfth-century scholar, relates that he had allowed mourners to bathe on the last day of their week of mourning, provided that they sat in mourning for part of the day. A colleague, Isaac ben Jacob ha-Lavan of Prague, told him that, although this is undoubtedly the law, he had never dared to publicize a ruling that permits something held by commoners (*benei medinah*) to be forbidden, even when the popular practice is erroneous and even if one is certain that the public would change their custom once the error was revealed. Dorbello adds that the talmudic adage about not permitting something perceived to be prohibited applies when people know that a behavior is not halakhically mandated, but it may be corrected when the practice is observed out of ignorance, so long as one can be confident that the public will indeed alter their behavior once the law is explained to them.[186]

It is apparent from this document that commoners are guided only in part by talmudic tradition and rabbinic leadership. Unnecessary stringencies, then, can be considered a type of deviant behavior, for they too are nonhalakhic. So long as the stringencies are within the law, rabbis are reluctant to challenge them, because of the talmudic adage. This type of behavior is also deviant because of the element of noncompliance, which lurks behind the rabbis' refusal to intervene. The anecdote underscores the impression that when formulating rules for normative behavior, the threat or fear of noncompliance was ever part of the rabbis' calculation.

The second case involves Rashi, who allegedly taught his students that animals are to be considered kosher (i.e., slaughtered in accordance with Jewish law) unless a flaw has been identified in the slaughtering process. The narrator of this anecdote then reports that he questioned Rashi what the law would be if a slaughterer removed an animal's lung before it could be examined for perforations (which, if found, would render it inedible). We read that Rashi grew angry with the speaker for asking a difficult question, but when he calmed down, he whispered to him, in the language of the Talmud, "One may not publicly permit things which are permitted, if others have been accustomed to viewing them as prohibited."[187] Here, again, the rabbis accept the fact that it is not entirely they who steer the course of Jewish tradition and that from their perspective, it is not all that uncommon for the ship to stray.[188]

Images of Deviance

The sources surveyed in the preceding sections are culled from the printed halakhic literature of medieval Ashkenaz and as such are not new discoveries. It remains to examine how they have been perceived and how their scholarly representation fits in with other aspects of the image of Ashkenazic Jewry. In general, that image has been one of unswerving fidelity to Jewish law, and I think it requires revision. All the same, in recent years discussion of nonhalakhic behavior has been anything but monolithic, and in the pages to follow I explore positions staked out by historians of the past few decades.

Irving Agus represents the classic view of the purity of Ashkenazic faith. Agus presents a responsum by Isaac ben Menahem, a contemporary of Rashi, to his student, Ele'azar ben Judah. The medieval redactor of the responsa collection notes that Rashi disapproved of the decider's reply and "uprooted" it. The subject is an arrangement of dubious legitimacy, in which a Jew and a Christian share ownership of a pair of oxen, such that the oxen can plow seven days a week, because on each

partner's day of rest the oxen are legally the property of the other partner. The respondent writes:

> I do not want to be asked such questions, for it were better that Israel
> err unwittingly than intentionally, regardless of whether the transgres-
> sion is biblical or rabbinic in nature; for the extension of Yom Kippur
> is a biblical ordinance and [nevertheless] women eat as soon as dark-
> ness falls and we say nothing.[189] Therefore, if they come to consult
> you, it were well to issue a ruling, to point out to them what is true
> and right, but if they do not come to consult you, it were better to put
> a hand to your mouth.[190]

Isaac ben Menahem responds with the passivity we have seen time and
again when popular custom flagrantly contradicts talmudic law and the
rabbinic authority judges that its roots are too deep to be uprooted.
Agus reacts with a highly idealized image of Ashkenazic Jewish life.

> The women transgressed a Scriptural prohibition, but were not cen-
> sured for it; for they would not desist even when censured. This is
> indeed astounding. We possess overwhelming evidence of the fact that
> the Jews of this period were very strict in their observance of religious
> law, that they were under tremendous social pressure to show zeal and
> devotion even to the minutiae of the law. Apparently the women were
> an exception to this rule. The piety and devoutness of the men were a
> result of the intensive study of Bible and Talmud to which they were
> exposed for many years in their youth and for large portions of their
> days in later years. It was also fostered by the social atmosphere in the
> synagogue, where they spent many hours of their lives. The perfunc-
> tory education of the women, however, and their exclusion from a large
> part of the educational and social activities of the synagogue, often
> tended to form a serious chasm between the men and the women.[191]

The fundamental element in Agus's vision is his assumption that in this
particular Jewish society observance was nearly absolute. He is thus
duly astounded to discover a rabbinic admission that these Ashkenazic
women could be expected to remain obdurate in the face of rabbinic
censure. This is the basic conception that stands in need of revision.

Agus offers other perspectives as well on the absolute fidelity of medieval Ashkenaz. Referring to the economic conditions of medieval
commerce, he argues that the Jews of Franco-Germany were zealous of

their reputation for scrupulous observance because their economic survival depended on it: "Under the 'system of trustfulness' that dominated the commercial life of the Jews of the period . . . a person's reputation for honesty, piety and 'fear of heaven,' was his most important asset, for the enhancement of which he labored diligently every day of his life. He could not afford to lose it completely, due to a single misstep."[192] This is a sociological explanation for widespread halakhic compliance, having to do with social control rather than saintliness and with almost no bearing on the issue of rabbinical authority.

Agus also introduces a slightly different version of the impact of social control on medieval Ashkenazic society in his efforts to explain the perceived discrepancy between male fidelity and female lawlessness. He locates this in the difference in their education and in the impact of study on male piety, as opposed to the women's ignorance and consequently their lesser devotion. Talmud study, he avers, not only affected men intellectually but also created a setting in which the social pressure to conform was powerful and in which aberrant behavior became increasingly difficult and unlikely.[193] That women were not partners in the move from oral tradition to talmudic canonicity is beyond doubt, and this is clearly important for understanding the issue of women's law. This should not, however, lead to the assumption that women were less devout than men, for the source of their tradition has no bearing on the depth of their faith. One need look no farther than the martyrdom of the First Crusade, in which women played a leading role, to grasp that women in medieval Ashkenaz were as committed as men to their ancestral religion.

Other scholars have inferred from the sources cited that northern European Jewry was experiencing a decline in the level of faith and observance. Regarding the neglect of *tefillin*, *tzitzit*, and *mezuzah*, Louis Rabinowitz claims, "It is clear . . . that prior to our period [the twelfth–fourteenth centuries] there was a general neglect of these outward and distinctive observances."[194] Taking a similar tack, Ephraim Urbach suggests that there were "signs of collapse." He notes the increasing prevalence of Christianity, which I believe means that Christianity was exerting increasing pressure on European culture, and he links this observation with one about a drop in halakhic fidelity: "Those who were lax in the observance of the commandments were not few in number, and Rabbenu Tam mentions that 'just ten years ago there was narry a *mezuzah* in the entire kingdom.'"[195]

Jacob Katz explicitly rejects the thesis of decline and argues that the nonobservance of *tefillin* and *mezuzah* was "a custom that struck roots in a period when Franco-German Jewry was not supervised by rabbinic scholars." He portrays Joseph of Orleans's remark about the allegorical interpretation of *tefillin* as a latter-day apology for popular custom (namely, neglect), as he does the mental gymnastics of the tosafists, who used dialectic to align practice with theory.[196] Katz's approach is a major revision insofar as it recognizes deviant behavior as real and as deserving a place in the overall characterization of Ashkenazic Jewry.

But Katz's revision goes only so far, for he assumes that once rabbinic leadership was established, deviant behavior was severely curtailed. This assumption is not accompanied by supporting evidence. Furthermore, the notion that rabbinic leadership arose at some point in the high Middle Ages is imprecise; as is well-known, the early Jewish settlers in Germany, beginning in the early tenth century, numbered rabbis and laity alike. Earlier, I cited evidence of bold acts of malfeasance in the tenth and eleventh centuries and noted their decline in succeeding generations. Most of the sources surveyed in this chapter are from the later period, namely, the "long" twelfth century, and show no signs that deviant behavior was on the wane. These findings may seem contradictory at first blush, but they are both true, because only the early transgressions were criminal, in the sense that their perpetrators knew them to be sinful; the widespread deviant behavior documented here was popularly believed to be legitimate, which is also why it was slow to yield to the pressure of rabbinic authority.

The notion that deviance reflects the weakness of rabbinical authority, although true, implies a monolithic conception of Jewish law, in which on any given issue there is only one correct possible behavior. This point of view can be found in Jewish sources of all periods, but Jewish historical experience, including that of medieval Ashkenaz, tells the tale of heterogeneity. Judicial experts labor ceaselessly to craft a uniform code of conduct, but even people with a shared social or spiritual ethos tend to find a variety of ways to give it concrete expression.

Attention has shifted in recent years from the record of Jewish behavior to its image or representation. The oeuvre of Haym Soloveitchik
is replete with references to a self-image of Ashkenazic Jewry as excellent, that is, virtuous. This conviction, he argues, underpins the valiant
efforts of the tosafists to align aberrant practices with talmudic dictates.
Soloveitchik also claims that the Jews of Ashkenaz, rabbis and laity
alike, viewed popular practice as a legitimate and authentic source of
Jewish law, as an incarnation of the word of God.

Soloveitchik further asserts that this self-righteous perception, which
permeates the thought of the earliest Ashkenazic scholars, is not found
elsewhere in the medieval Jewish world, and its origins remain a mystery.[197] Elsewhere, however, he hypothesizes that the martyrdom of the
First Crusade was at least partly responsible for the widespread acceptance of the self-righteous perception, because it must have seemed inconceivable to later generations that such a "holy community," with its
thousands of martyrs, could routinely transgress.[198]

Soloveitchik suggests that four factors contributed to the self-image
of excellence. The first is "the simplicity of religious beliefs."[199] This may
be an oblique reference to the absence of philosophy, in contrast to its
allegedly pernicious impact on the Jews of Spain, in Yitzhak Baer's classic dichotomy. Whether or not this model ought to be accepted as true,
the nexus between this simplicity and the righteous self-image is not
mandated by logic and it remains unclear.

The second factor is undivided allegiance—the universal assumption
that the Ashkenazic community was and would always remain faithful, notwithstanding the existence of some apostates. The First Crusade
comes into play here, because this aspect of the Ashkenazic self-image
rests on the record of mass martyrdom in 1096.[200] The closest connection between the 1096 experience and faithful observance is the passage
from *Sefer Hasidim* that makes the argument that a Jew ought to meet
his quotidian religious obligations because, were he to live through a
period of religious persecution, obviously he would suffer death rather
than transgression, that is, baptism.[201] How widespread this image of
the First Crusade experience was in the twelfth century is uncertain;
recent scholarship has highlighted the significance of apostasy and has
downplayed the scope of the mass martyrdom. Moreover, the extent

of the impact of the German pietists on Ashkenazic society is another murky problem. A third problem with this argument is that it is tautological: The Jews of Ashkenaz, argues Soloveitchik, saw themselves as absolutely faithful to Judaism because they believed they are and would always be faithful to Judaism.

Soloveitchik's third factor is what he terms the "thickening of the heavenly yoke." We are told that the commoners increasingly heeled to talmudic law and that "tosaphist thought was percolating downward."[202] Our sources for this are limited to rabbinic literature, which can hardly be taken at face value.

More significant is the fourth factor, the "refusal to maximize allowances." The germ of this notion can be found in Jacob Katz's suggestion that medieval Jewry had a "ritual instinct," which impelled the public to reject permissive rulings as well as proscriptive ones.[203] Soloveitchik pursues this line of inquiry and sees in this pattern "the workings of a religious intuition alongside of which the written word pales."[204] This argument leads to a conclusion very much in conjunction with the argument of this chapter, for both religious intuition and ritual instinct are explanations that justify deviant behavior. We have seen that the Jews of medieval Franco-Germany adhered to a code of behavior that was, to a surprising extent, autonomous and recalcitrant rather than submissive to talmudic and rabbinic authority.

Soloveitchik concedes that "there were murderers, lechers, apostates, informers, thieves, Sabbath violators in Ashkenaz, no less than in Sefarad," and he asks, "Have we not painted an idealized portrait of Ashkenaz?"[205] The foregoing discussion suggests that this question must be answered in the affirmative. Soloveitchik then asks whether "Ashkenaz" had an idealized image of itself. No sources exist to answer this question with respect to the rank and file of Ashkenazic Jewry, but it would appear that the tosafists did subscribe to the idealized portrayal. Over and over they labor to harmonize aberrant customs with talmudic rulings, and it is axiomatic to their discussions that the perplexing practices are fundamentally legitimate.

The central argument presented thus far has been that, from a critical-historical perspective, the tosafists' axiom is insupportable. Could they have misjudged the unscholarly public? With respect to women, such a blind spot is conceivable, and perhaps women really did enjoy a large measure of halakhic autonomy. I have noted the rarity of Rabbenu Tam's attempt at fieldwork in his efforts to understand female behavior, and the sources do seem to indicate a strange but fundamental disconnect between men and women when it comes to halakhic tradition. And yet, other texts reveal the twelfth-century luminaries puzzling over the same type of conundrum regarding their male coreligionists, which suggests that the issue cuts across the male-female divide and has a broader context.

The tosafist project and methodology offer a possible explanation. A good deal of talmudic discussion involves the efforts of amoraic scholars to supply textual rationales for lawless practices, and these rabbis were motivated by the conviction that customs may be bizarre, but they must have some sort of authentic and legitimate base, be it midrashic or logical. A classic expression of this attitude is the well-known apothegm uttered when a rabbi concedes that he is at a loss to rule on a given halakhic dilemma: "Go see what people do." What we are witnessing in the twelfth century, then, is a new, medieval, cycle of talmudic methodology, devoted, as it was in late antiquity, to aligning deviant practice with canonical, textual law. This being the case, the relationship between this exercise and the tosafists' actual conception of the mindset of their nonrabbinic contemporaries cannot be fathomed from their own dialectical exertions, for that is all these passages represent.

What is more, not only do the tosafists engage in dialectic to reconcile aberrant practices with talmudic law, but they also do so to align contradictory and mutually exclusive talmudic dicta, which do not necessarily deal with actual deviant behavior. As with Abelard's *Sic et Non*, the tosafists' efforts at reconciliation are part of the scholastic revolution, which was about book learning more than actual behavior. This removes the tosafist alignment project even further from the plane of social reality and situates it more firmly in the realm of their theoretical enterprise.[206]

It is also possible that in Germany it was objectively difficult to recognize behavior as deviant. From its inception in the tenth century, this particular diaspora is characterized by a plethora of local custom.[207] Practices normative in one community or region were unknown or nonhalakhic in another, and in such an environment the rabbinic leadership might not be sure to recognize nonhalakhic behavior when they saw it.

The lack of uniformity in the stock of religious practices found in the Jewish communities of Franco-Germany explains the enormous respect accorded custom in the Ashkenazic halakhic system during the tenth and eleventh centuries.[208] Thus, for example, Rabbenu Gershom responds to a question about *ma'arufia*, an arrangement in which a Jew has a Christian as his exclusive client, in a monopoly relationship; Rabbenu Gershom is careful to note that his interlocutor's question implies that he lives in a community in which this concept and arrangement are either unknown or unrecognized.[209] The great halakhic diversity characteristic of this region necessarily prevented communities from laying down the law to one another. Thus anyone raised in this environment was used to the idea of discrepant halakhot or practices and would not automatically attribute variation to heterodoxy.

This custom-oriented halakhic outlook was gradually replaced, in the period in question, by text-based law, specifically talmudic precept. This shift precipitated a crisis in the minds of the lawyers, who previously tolerated behavior that was ostensibly nonhalakhic, because of the elasticity of the concept of custom. However, this elasticity diminished when Jewish law became talmudocentric, and there were new limits to what one could justify, and this development catalyzed the tosafists' alignment project.

The tosafists' efforts to locate ancient sources for medieval deviant behavior are echoed in our own day in the scholarly investigations of Israel Ta-Shma. Ta-Shma speculates that in the Land of Israel, Italy, and Ashkenaz it was accepted that women not wear their jewelry out of doors, not as a safeguard to prevent them from carrying their baubles in the public domain but because, following the view of Rabbi Meir, the Tanna, women may not wear jewelry outside the home even on weekdays, because they should present themselves attractively only to their husbands, inside the home. Ta-Shma hypothesizes that this absolute prohibition was abandoned at some point in the early Middle Ages, and as a result the Sabbath regulation also fell by the wayside, which is why the women of medieval Ashkenaz allowed themselves to go about adorned.

Ta-Shma concedes that in medieval Franco-Germany the rationale for the jewelry prohibition was different: Here scholars argue that the biblical prohibition no longer exists, for there is no longer such as thing as a "public domain," because the definition of this term requires that such an area contain a population of 600,000 or more pedestrians (and possibly 600,000 Jews!). Nevertheless, scholars living in medieval Ashkenaz admit that the rabbinic prohibition remains in effect and that the problem of the definition of public domain does not really solve the problem, and hence they are left to fall back on the alternative of preferring error to intent.[210]

The assumption that Ashkenazic behavior was based on ancient and authentic lost traditions also informs Ta-Shma's understanding of the women's custom of bathing in warm water and changing clothes after the cessation of the menstrual flow. Ta-Shma asserts that this represents the survival of an old Palestinian tradition that was unknown to medieval scholars but evidence of which survives in the Cairo genizah.[211] Perhaps, but for the eleventh-century Franco-German reality this is irrelevant, because Rashi evinces no awareness of an ancient tradition for this custom but rather explains that "women invented this."[212]

Ta-Shma also notes that *Liqutei Pardes*, a work of Rashi's school, portrays the intermediate bath as proper and legitimate behavior and stresses that this legitimation was a halakhic rather than a popular development, meaning that it was wrought by rabbis, specifically Rashi.[213] This hypothesis exposes Ta-Shma's conviction that custom must have been grounded in halakhic tradition and, by extension, was also subject to rabbinic authority.[214] Ta-Shma's interpretation of the white days practice contradicts Rashi's own sociological explanation, but more important, the Jews of medieval Ashkenaz, rabbis and laity alike, generally held a different conception of the nature of custom; they accepted the existence of a significant corpus of behavior that must be considered deviant, in the sense that it was not rooted—or was not perceived to be rooted—in talmudic tradition or subject to rabbinic authority. The rabbis' frequent citation of the adage "better they should sin in error than intentionally" is the classic illustration of this medieval Ashkenazic reality.

Seven Christians

The accounts of the First Crusade massacres present Jews and Christians at sword's point, with hatred and blood spurting forth in equal measure. It would be difficult to conjure a more radical description of the abyss separating the believers of both faiths. From here to the Nazi destruction of European Jewry seems but a short and almost comprehensible step.

Such a polarized image of Jewish-Christian relations accords with the portrait of Ashkenazic Jewry as absolutely faithful to Jewish law and belief and hence as a community with few incidents of apostasy and blindly obedient to rabbinic authority. In previous chapters I reexamined these aspects of the medieval Ashkenazic diaspora, and a fresh assessment of the ties between Jews and Christians will contribute further to this attempt at a fresh characterization.

Leading twentieth-century scholars offer a wide variety of images of Jewish-Christian relations. Ephraim Urbach's characterization of the literary legacy of Isaac of Dampierre, one of the leading tosafists, epitomizes the gloom-and-doom approach to our subject: "For the most part we find echoes of the Jews' difficult struggle with the medieval Christian society about their legal status, their livelihood, their right to live and even their right to be buried after death."[1] Elsewhere Urbach describes the Jews and Christians of medieval Ashkenaz as "two societies living in a state of complete mutual negation, in which every meeting between them is one of disputation and polemic, replete with insults and curses."[2]

Other portrayals of Jewish-Christian relations are a bit more sanguine. Jacob Katz concedes that relations were tense but adds a caveat.

> At times the antagonistic notions concerning Jews abated and normal human relations sprang up between neighbours, partners, and partici-

pants in some common undertaking. Yet behind such "natural" relationships there always lurked the ideology of separateness based on the religious conceptions of both the Jewish and Christian groups.[3]

Irving Agus also presents a nuanced picture: "Contact often resulted in the development of a feeling of trust, and even of friendship, between the persons involved. This feeling of trust and friendship in the heart of a non-Jew toward a particular Jew, however, did not completely erase, in the heart of the former, his feelings of suspicion, prejudice, and resentment toward the Jews as a group."[4] Agus highlights the discrepancy between the attitude—by both Jew and Christian—toward individuals and the attitude toward the collective but agrees with Katz that, notwithstanding evidence of friendly relations, alienation and even hostility were never entirely absent from interfaith encounters.

The following idyllic picture, by Yitzhak Baer, is among the rosiest:

The medieval condition of exile should not be described simply as a maelstrom of abominable murders and extortions. The judicial and economic relations between Jews and Christians were based on legal foundations which were almost never discontinued and nowhere entirely so. . . . Similarly, the social connections between Jews and Christians were never terminated. In times of persecution it was common for Jews to find refuge in the homes of gentile acquaintances. Despite the religious antagonism, we know of touching examples of tolerance and friendship from the middle ages. . . . These examples lead one to conclude that in medieval times the groundwork was laid for the relations of support and friendship found between Jews and Christians in the good modern times, which have since disappeared."[5]

In the closing sentence Baer waxes nostalgic about the tolerance and friendship of the Middle Ages against the backdrop of the Holocaust.

Spearheading the school of thought that downplays the hostility between Jews and Christians and stresses the cordiality of quotidian life is Salo Baron, whose call to correct what he termed "the lachrymose conception of Jewish history" bears directly on our theme. Baron decries the tendency of modern historians to follow the example of sixteenth-century chronicles and portray medieval Jewish history as a litany of persecution. The past, he concedes, had its share of tragedies, but the

Jews of medieval Europe enjoyed a relatively high degree of political and legal protection compared with the general populace.

As a corollary to Baron's thesis, I would add that the social and cultural ties linking Jews and Christians as partners in the European experience are no less important than the episodes marking ruptures of these neighborly relations. And they were no more than episodes: the Rindfleisch massacres of 1298 marked only the second incident of large-scale violence against Franco-German Jewry in the half millennium since the rule of Charlemagne.

The range of portraits of our theme is a function not only of climate change in modern culture but also of ambiguity in the sources. Jewish texts condemning Christian belief or behavior actually imply a reality of conviviality and intimacy on both the social and cultural planes, and the same is true for Christian sources. Both the explicit and implicit messages are true. In medieval Ashkenaz Christians and Jews engage each other on a day-to-day basis, on many levels and with varying degrees of warmth, from violence and hostility to amicability, friendship, and even intimacy. At the core of their relationship lies the contradiction between human interaction and religious difference, with one or the other coming to the fore depending on the circumstances and finding expression in the historical materials. At bottom, however, we find that even in the most grim moments of the Jewish-Christian encounter, when Jews and Christians roundly condemn one another in word and deed, they remain partners in the life and culture of Europe, sharing ideas and ideals.[6]

Social Engagement

Discussions of Jewish-Christian relations generally survey the range of activities that brought Jews and Christians together, with the general purpose of demonstrating how much contact the two populations had.[7] We read mostly about economic contacts of one sort or another. Commercial relations predominate, with the Jew offering the gentile desirable products, especially wine, and gradually gravitating toward money lending. Christians are also employees, with women serving as domestic servants and wet nurses and men supplying labor in the family business as well as in the home. Both Christian men and women participate in the preparation of food and drink.

Most of our information comes from rabbinic documents about the legal complications caused by interaction with outsiders. For instance, wine libation (*yeyn nesekh*), when Jewish wine is rendered undrinkable because a gentile has touched it, is the subject of voluminous rabbinic discussion.[8] However, there are limits to what can be derived from this kind of literature, because these are legal sources, written not to portray social networks but to address pressing halakhic problems. Of necessity, then, the documentation is heavily weighted toward thorny situations and has little to say about less problematic forms of Jewish-Christian social intercourse. This is an obvious reason for the emphasis on economic rather than social ties, both in medieval sources and modern historiography.

The case of Jewish-Christian relations also illustrates why it is difficult to assess feelings and attitudes from halakhic texts. Were rabbinic authorities to define Christians as idolaters, life in medieval Europe would have been impossible, because talmudic law severely restricts social and economic interaction between Jews and idol worshippers. For instance, a Jew may not conduct business with an idolater on the latter's religious festival or even on the three days preceding or succeeding the festival; because Sunday is the Christian day of worship, it would seem that one may never do business with a Christian.[9]

An obvious solution was to draw a distinction between contemporary gentiles and those of former days, and one finds a dictum of this nature in the Talmud: "Gentiles of other lands are not idol-worshippers; rather, they observe the custom of their fathers."[10] Gershom ben Judah of Mainz (Rabbenu Gershom) uses this statement as the basis for his decision to allow trade with Christians;[11] Rashi relies on it to permit the consumption of wine touched by Christians.[12] The tosafists of twelfth-century France extend this idea and suggest that Christianity is not all that different from Judaism. The Talmud rules that one may not create a partnership with a gentile, lest a future dispute impel the gentile to take an oath, which would contravene the biblical prohibition against causing an idolater to utter the name of his deity (Exod. 23:13).[13] A tosafist gloss strips this talmudic passage of practical significance with the observation that when Christians refer to

God, they mean the creator of heaven and earth; they are therefore not to be deemed idolatrous and partnerships with them are legal.[14]

This solution was plainly the convenient and necessary one for the Jews of twelfth-century France, but we are no closer than before to determining whether these tosafist scholars actually considered Christianity idolatrous. Although it seems inconceivable that Rashi and the tosafists would concoct a legal position that contradicts their genuine, fundamental convictions, their approach to the problem—here and elsewhere—is atomistic and formal rather than essential and ideological. Rabbinic rulings and interpretations address practical social problems rather than convey their candid impressions of the Christian faith, which is why they are of limited utility as historical sources.

If the rhetoric of the medieval lawyers seems to paint an overly rosy picture of Christianity, other sources more than compensate for this distortion with a torrent of anti-Christian vitriol. Here is an example from the portrait of the departure of the crusaders for the Holy Land presented in the Mainz Anonymous, the shorter of the two medieval Hebrew narratives of the slaughter of Rhineland Jewry in the First Crusade:

> There first arose the princes and nobles and common folk in France, who took counsel and set plans to ascend and to rise up like eagles and to do battle and to clear a way for journeying to Jerusalem, the Holy City, and for reaching the sepulcher of the Crucified one, a trampled corpse, who cannot profit and cannot save, for he is worthless.[15]

The stream of invective accompanying the reference to Jesus is typical of the language used throughout this text. Later, at the height of the drama, when the Jews of Mainz slaughter each other in the bishop's palace, they cry out, "Look and see, God, what we do for the sanctification of your great Name, rather than exchange your divinity for a crucified one, a trampled and wretched and abominable offshoot, a bastard and a child of menstruation and lust."[16] This narrator cannot mention Jesus and Christianity without the use of insulting euphemisms, conveying ridicule and abomination. It is difficult to imagine that this language does not reflect the way the Jews of Ashkenaz felt about Christians and Christianity when they pondered the ghastly events of 1096. The hostile rhetoric implies that Jews and Christians were separated by a chasm of unremitting and unbridled religious antagonism.

Still, other elements in the Crusade narratives tell a different tale. Jews find refuge in the homes of sympathetic gentiles. David ben Netanel the beadle and his family are hidden by a priest, as are Shemaryah of Moers and his wife and three children.[17] A townsman shelters two women, Guta and Scholaster.[18] Sometimes we are told explicitly that Christians think highly of their Jewish neighbors. For instance, the attackers beg Abraham ben Asher to accept baptism and live, "for he was a well-known and pleasant person."[19] Similarly, the townspeople refer to Mina as a "woman of valor," and hence they implore her to renounce Judaism and save herself.[20] These incidents fly in the face of the nature of Jewish-Christian relations implicit in the vituperative rhetoric of the narratives.

The obloquy used by the narrators of the First Crusade narratives has its paradoxical side. Clearly the texts were composed in the pursuit of a particular end, and, as we have seen with regard to apostasy, that end seems to have been the fortification of Jewish identity: If the story stresses the importance of religious fidelity, so the argument goes, the storyteller is probably using it to shore up the flagging commitment of his generation.[21] The same logic would seem to apply to abusive rhetoric: If the narrator finds it necessary to insult the sacred symbols of Christianity, he must be facing what seems to him excessively intimate intercourse between Jews and Christians.

This is not entirely to dismiss the value of the abusive rhetoric as evidence that Jews viewed Christianity with scorn; in order to have impact, the text would have to strike its audience as authentic and meaningful. To derive that Jews and Christians were divided by a gulf of hostility, however, would be going too far. Both the biting rhetoric and its inverse, namely, the identity crisis, despite the apparent tension between them, must reflect a single, complex historical reality.

Whether Jews vented their aversion to Christianity solely in the relative safety of Hebrew writing, accessible for the most part only to believers, or perhaps also in verbal exchanges with real Christians is debatable. In the 1096 tales we find Jews hurling insults against Christianity as they expire, and although there is no way of affirming the truth of these reports, it is at least believable of someone who has chosen death over baptism. Can the same be said of one involved in a less fraught exchange?

This question has aroused discussion regarding the anti-Christian polemical works compiled in thirteenth-century Franco-Germany, such as *Sefer Nizzahon Yashan* and *Sefer Yosef ha-Meqanneh*, in which an imaginary Christian interlocutor is habitually treated as a fool and his beliefs are ridiculed. One text of this kind is the following conversation, reported in *Sefer Nizzahon Yashan*, between a king ("Henry") and a rabbi ("Qalonymos") following construction of the Speyer cathedral. The king asks the rabbi in what way the Temple of Solomon was greater than the new cathedral, and, after the king swears that the rabbi can speak with impunity, the rabbi responds:

> Regarding the time when Solomon completed the building, see what is written: "And the priests were unable to stand and minister because of the cloud, for the glory of the Lord had filled the house of the Lord" (1 Kings 8:11). In this case, however, if one were to load a donkey with vomit and filth and lead him through the church,[22] he would remain unharmed.

The king replies, "If not for my oath, I would have you decapitated," which is the narrator's way of indicating that Qalonymos's barb hit its mark.[23]

This conversation is almost certainly imaginary; more realistic exchanges, including the following, appear in *Sefer Yosef ha-Meqanneh*, written in France in about the same period:

> My father, Rabbi Nathan, was once riding with the archbishop of Sens. Along the way, the archbishop dismounted next to a bush to urinate. Seeing him do so, my father, too, got off his horse next to an abomination [i.e., a cross] and urinated on it. The archbishop saw and was angry, and said to him: It is wrong to do thus, to make a cross stink. My father retorted: On the contrary, you have behaved foolishly [Gen. 31:28]. You urinated on a bush, upon which God bestowed His presence purely for salvation; regarding that upon which you say your awe-inspiring one was tortured, stank and rotted it would be appropriate for you to expose yourselves and defecate.[24]

This account includes the particulars of the reported conversation: the participants, their location, and the precise chain of events. The anecdote seems factual because it is so concrete and because, content aside, it is the kind of casual exchange one can readily imagine between a Jew and a Christian in the course of daily life. Because the incident involves the narrator's father, we can also infer that it occurred fairly recently.

Scholars have differed in their approaches to anti-Christian rhetoric. Bernhard Blumenkranz views it as a reaction to the oppressive conditions of medieval Jewish life.

> Conditions of life for the Jew were harsh, and this harshness showed through in his manner of argumentation, whether offensive or defensive. Even his jokes turned easily into macabre farce, and his ironical smiles became twisted grimaces. The very tone of Jewish propaganda itself warned those to whom it was directed of what would await them if they paid heed to it: a state of ceaseless struggle.[25]

A different perspective sees the aggressive posture as a reflection of the Jew's pride and sense of superiority. Supposedly, this Jewish pride was the legacy of the Jews of Provence, who negotiated with Charlemagne and Louis the Pious from a position of strength, a posture that their Ashkenazic descendants maintained until the First Crusade persecutions.[26] Evidence of Christian proselytes, albeit few in number, seems to support this image. A priest named Wecelinus seems to have converted to Judaism in approximately 1012, and the Hebrew 1096 narratives refer to a proselyte named Jacob ben Sullam and to another, anonymous proselyte in Xanten.[27]

Nor did the First Crusade put an end to the image of a proud, aggressive posture. Of the Jews of twelfth-century Champagne, Emily Taitz affirms, "Jews appear to have conducted themselves with the assurance that they belonged in France and were secure in their privileges. . . . In Champagne, as in all of northern France, Jews made no attempt to keep a low profile."[28] Christians composed anti-Jewish polemical tracts in the twelfth century, writes David Berger, because "they faced a genuine, vigorous challenge from a proud and assertive Jewish community."[29]

This image dovetails with the portrayal of medieval Jews in modern historiography as culturally superior to their Christian neighbors, in that allegedly more of them were literate and educated and they were respected for their access to important bodies of knowledge, especially medicine and astrology. This was still true in the thirteenth century, as the writings of Aquinas illustrate, and it was only during the Renaissance, when Jews began seeking knowledge from gentile masters rather than the reverse, that their pride was humbled and their self-image began to erode.

Alternatively, we might suppose that the Jews of medieval France and Germany were not likely to be as outspoken as they appeared. Urbach writes that the Jew's natural need for vengeance could not be satisfied in real life and could find only literary expression.[30] If so, the insulting remarks such as those quoted earlier were simply wishful thinking: what a Jew might have liked to have said but did not dare.

The synagogue poetry of medieval Ashkenaz is another genre that contains abundant deprecatory references to the Christian faith and particularly to the harshness of life under the infidel's thumb. A famous example is Simon ben Isaac's *Groan of a Prisoner* (*Enqat Assir*), composed in eleventh-century Germany, in which the poet bemoans the misfortunes of life in exile:

Robbed, exploited and harassed,
the goblet of poison drained,
wandering, universally despised.[31]

Like a ewe struck dumb[32]
reproached and shamed,
not knowing why.[33]

As in the case of halakhic writing, here too it is uncertain how rhetoric correlates with the conditions of Jewish life, because collective self-portraits such as this one were a literary convention and do not necessarily reflect a downturn in the Jews' fortunes. Still, the language of lamentation must have spoken to the spirit of the Ashkenazic Jew or it would have become utterly sterile and eventually would have been abandoned. This, then, is an example of Ashkenazic anti-Christian rhetoric that must be taken seriously, if not literally.

The problem of rhetoric and realia surfaces also in references to the principle of enmity (*evah*) in medieval Jewish law.[34] Following the deaths of the archbishops of Magdeburg in 1012 and 1051 and of the archbishop of Cologne in 1075, the Jewish communities of these cities participated in the funerary rites for the deceased officials.[35] These incidents may reflect affection for the departed, particularly because high Church officials were often the Jews' political patrons.[36] On the other hand, the Jews may have felt constrained to participate or risk being considered hostile and disloyal. The Cologne affair occurred on a Saturday, when Jewish law prohibits mourning, and this makes it seem unlikely that the Jews acted freely. By the same token, the consideration of enmity, namely, concern for their safety and political future, would justify suspending the Sabbath prohibition, which supports the supposition that the Jews took part in the public display of grief for fear of retribution of one sort or another.[37]

Enmity is also the principle behind a tosafist ruling that allows a Jewish traveler to receive a gift of beer from a hospitable host who happens to be an idolater, that is, a Christian. The text also warns against drinking beer in the home of an idolater, based on the talmudic report that two amoraic scholars, Papa and Aha, refrained from doing so.[38] The warning seems to imply the existence of good fellowship between Jews and Christians; otherwise it would be gratuitous. Yet one cannot be sure; the tosafists may simply be teasing out an inference latent in the talmudic anecdote with no real bearing on current conditions.

A better known anecdote about gentile gifts concerns Rashi, whose neighbor entered his courtyard and produced a gift of loaves[39] and eggs on the eighth day of Passover, ostensibly to be eaten that evening, at the conclusion of the holiday. This posed a problem, because Passover was not over and the food could not have been kosher for Passover. Rashi recounts that the gift was actually presented to his wife, who promptly sent for him. He ruled that the eggs could be stored until after nightfall, at which point he ruled that they could be eaten. He was unable, however, to accept the gentile's bread gift; the latter offered to deposit it with neighbors, but Rashi demurred.[40]

The story bespeaks cordial relations between Jews and Christians and a particularly friendly attitude on the part of the Christian neighbor. Rashi's reaction and that of his wife are more complex; apart from dealing with the halakhic dilemma, they also had the delicate task of managing their relationship with the friendly non-Jew. Rashi's responsum does not mention the terms "on account of enmity" or "for the sake of peaceful relations," but this consideration lurks in the background of the discussion. Even when facing what is obviously a friendly act, the medieval Jew remains mindful of the possibility of mistrust, and the gap separating him from the Christian yawns wide.[41]

In the case of the archbishops, enmity may have provided a halakhic justification for the suspension of normative practice. Enmity also serves in that capacity in rabbinic discussions of whether one may conduct business dealings with gentiles on their idolatrous festivals, contrary to Jewish law. As mentioned, if Sundays were deemed idolatrous festivals, commerce with Christians would be impossible and Jewish life in Europe would be unsustainable. Thus we find both Rashi and his grandson, Samuel ben Me'ir (Rashbam), formulating a more lenient approach to the problem, ruling that one may effect transactions with gentiles on their festivals "on account of fear" (Rashi) or enmity and fear (Rashbam).[42]

Yet this halakhic stance does not prove that relations between Jews and Christians were strained, because the case at hand involves legal experts. Aligning contemporary reality with the principles of Jewish law was the rabbis' stock in trade, and toward that end they marshal arguments and concepts with versatility and creativity. This is not to claim that Rashi and Rashbam acted disingenuously; the cogency of a halakhic stance depends on its credibility as a reasonably accurate reflection of social reality. Nonetheless, Rashi and Rashbam were presenting legal arguments, and these are a form of rhetoric formulated for a particular legislative or judicial purpose rather than for the sake of historical representation. They tell a truth within their own generic boundaries, but a gap remains between their narrative and a nonrhetorical rendition of the scene (if such a thing were conceivable). Thus whether or not enmity and fear were of great concern to Ashkenazic Jewry remains uncertain.

To offer another example, Jacob ben Meir of Ramerupt (Rabbenu Tam), the intellectual giant of twelfth-century French Jewry, rules that a Jew may derive financial benefit from the error of a non-Jew, because non-Jews are presumed to be liars.[43] This assumption may rest on contemporary experience, but it echoes a talmudic and biblical prooftext with no bearing on the actual qualities and conduct of medieval Christians.[44] Nevertheless, it is unlikely that Rabbenu Tam would feel justified in invoking a talmudic principle that completely contradicts the reality of his own age. At the least, his stance affirms the existence of a significant social and cultural gap between Jew and Christian.

The twin concept of enmity is peaceful relations ("for the sake of the paths of peace"), a mishnaic expression that also appears in the rabbinic literature of medieval Europe.[45] Peaceful relations is the tosafists' explanation for the Jewish custom of offering food gifts to impoverished Christians on the Sabbath, contrary to the letter of talmudic law.[46] A thirteenth-century source recounts that a gentile from Regensburg who had fallen ill is convinced that he will die unless he obtains wine; he asks a Jew to send him some wine, explaining his dire need. This occurs on a Jewish festival, when normally such an action would be forbidden by Jewish law. The Jew asks his rabbi, Isaac ben Moses of Vienna, whether or not to accede to the request and is told that an exception can be made for the sake of peace.[47] The interpretive dilemma raises its head in this case, as well. On one hand, this is a story of congenial relations between Jew and Christian, for clearly the ailing non-Jew had some expectation that the Jew would comply. On the other hand, by invoking the principle of peaceful relations, Isaac ben Moses was conceding that a negative response might yield unpleasant or even dangerous results, which undercuts the friendly image of Jewish-Christian relations.

The same problem emerges from the rabbinic ruling that one may not cause gentile female servants to expect to receive a monetary present on Purim, although the giving of such gifts had become customary. Still, "for the sake of peace," the rabbinic authority does not order communities to desist from this practice if it has become normative.[48] The giving of the Purim gift per se is open to opposing interpretations: Clearly it is a friendly or neighborly gesture, but we cannot know whether it is offered purely in the spirit of good fellowship or possibly as a calculated act of diplomacy, for the sake of future relations and with an eye toward a possible downturn.

The more pessimistic view of the concern for enmity and peaceful relations seems appropriate to scenarios in which Jews express apprehension about the non-Jew's possible response to Jewish behavior. A case of this nature in Rashi's milieu involves a firstborn animal, which according to Ashkenazic tradition may not be eaten, and so Rashi instructs the owner to slaughter the animal and bury it. He does so, but in a bizarre way, burying part of the animal in Rashi's house (or on his property) and part in that of the owner, and we read that this was "so that it will not be noticed, lest they say it was done for the sake of witchcraft."[49]

A similar fear of the witchcraft accusation leads the Jews of northern Europe to abandon the practice of overturning the bed as a sign of mourning.[50] For the same reason, the Jews of Ashkenaz suspend the custom of walking barefoot as a sign of mourning, both with respect to personal mourning, when a mourner returns from a funeral, and to national mourning, on the Ninth of Av (Tisha b'Av), the anniversary of the Temple's destruction.[51] This concern differs from that of enmity, but it does express the same kind of insecurity—the insecurity of someone who knows that he is perceived as alien. Thus it reflects the Jews' perception of the limits of their socialization in gentile society.

Insecurity would explain why medieval Jews avoid behaviors that might arouse derision on the part of their Christian neighbors. For instance, according to the Talmud, a mourner must wrap himself in a cloak, covering his head and face, but this custom is held in abeyance in Rashi's time for fear that the gentiles would ridicule it.[52] Moses of Coucy, of thirteenth-century France, writes, "I saw this observed in Spain, but in these kingdoms it is not customary, because it causes great laughter, for the gentiles laugh at us, as do the domestic maidservants, the slaves and the lads."[53]

Fear of derision differs slightly from enmity. Enmity reflects apprehension, which implies a sizable cultural gap between Jews and non-Jews, but the desire to avoid derision may be an opposite indication. It may appear that medieval Jews avoid derision because they fear the consequences of arousing animosity, which would fit an image of Jewish-Christian relations as polarized and tense. Paradoxically, however, it may be that medieval Jews feel slighted by gentile derision, which would mean that their avoidance of derision signifies the depth of their acculturation in European society.

Avoiding derision could take the form of behavior designed to make a favorable impression. A rabbinic source studies the circumstances in which one ought to perform ritual immersion following nocturnal emission. The initial discussion is about whether this rule would apply to Yom Kippur, when normally bathing is proscribed. The respondent responds in the affirmative and adds, "Similarly, all year one ought to immerse himself for the sake of cleanliness and for the sanctification of God's name before the gentiles."[54]

Some sources express admiration for Christian behavior. An eleventh-century responsum treats the case of a husband who is sued because he divorced his wife but refused to pay her the sum stipulated in their marriage contract, on the grounds that only after their wedding did he discover that she was a leper. The respondent, Rashi, rules that he ought to take pity on her and take her back, "for even among those who deny God we have seen many who do not distance themselves from their wives . . . and similarly also women [who do not distance themselves from] their husbands."[55] "Those who deny God" could only be Christians, for Jewish miscreants are not presumed to deny God, and thus we see Rashi pointing to Christians as models of desirable behavior for the Jewish community. This would not be conceivable if relations between Jews and Christians were particularly tense or hostile. On the other hand, Rashi's use of the word *even* situates the gentiles on a lower ethical plane than the Jews, which gives expression to a sense of apartness and innate Jewish superiority.

Christians serve as a foil for Jewish ethical behavior in a *Sefer Hasidim* passage as well: "In some places the gentiles judge truthfully and the Jews do not, because there are few Torah scholars there, and those who come there from other places where people behave disreputably incline them [local scholars] to behave as they do."[56] The focus of this dictum is the need for an improvement in Jewish justice, and the reference to the non-Jews is a device intended to highlight the shortcomings of the Jews; the text implies that under normal circumstances the Jews, rather than the gentiles, would be expected to judge truthfully. As in the previous instance, the use of the Christian as a model testifies to congenial relations between Jews and Christians but also to the firmness of the barrier between them and to the assumption of gentile inferiority.

Elsewhere, *Sefer Hasidim* holds up the knight as a model, without injecting the element of Jewish superiority.

If one faces evil tidings, he should contemplate the knights' behavior: they go to war to display their bravery and do not flee the sword, for they are ashamed to flee, and they are killed and wounded solely on account of shame, and receive no reward from their lords when they die in war. Thus, "He may well slay me, yet will I trust in him" (Job 13:15), and I shall worship him not for the sake of receiving a reward.[57]

This text combines the motifs of the knight's bravery and selflessness to produce an ideal image, one that may have been influenced by Arthurian legend or perhaps by the military orders founded in the wake of the First Crusade.

A similar *Sefer Hasidim* passage throws a slightly different light on the image of knighthood. It opens with an exhortation to exercise cunning for the sake of the honor of God. Knights are cited as an illustration of this principle, because they risk death for their own honor, to avoid being deemed cowardly: "so that they not feel ashamed."[58] Here the speaker emphasizes the knights' fear of shame rather than their bravery, but his main point is the importance of honor, and it is therefore clear that the knights are being praised rather than denigrated.

Looking beyond rabbinic literature to the Christian environment, we encounter sources that are no less ambiguous and paradoxical. A central theme in Church legislation concerning Jews, beginning in the earliest stages, is the importance of curtailing social interaction between believers and Jews. Thus Church councils from the early fourth century enjoin commensality with Jews, for fear that such encounters might undermine the Christian's religious belief and commitment. Of even greater concern was the prospect of Christian women having sex with Jewish men. This was seen as an act of betrayal and pollution and a violation of the Augustinian principle that Jews must occupy a position subordinate to Christians.[59]

These concerns are aired over and over throughout the Middle Ages, raising the question of their significance as evidence of existing social relations. It would appear that social exchange and sexual relationships must have been common enough to be deemed worthy of papal attention, which would offer a powerful statement about the intimacy of Jewish-Christian relations in medieval Europe. And yet, legal systems and bureaucracies have their own internal procedural dynamics and create their own version of reality, which does not necessarily correlate with that of the street, table, or bedroom. The Catholic Church habitually promulgated laws time after time, making no reference to particular contemporary circumstances, as though the reality of the fourth century were still in place a millennium or so later. The election of a new pope would be reason enough to reissue traditional legislation, and this was also true of kings and other sovereigns.

This dynamic also applies to laws expressing fears of Jewish malevo-lence and influence, which reflect the atmosphere characteristic of the early centuries of the nascent religion rather than the era of its domina-tion of Latin Europe. It is therefore difficult to draw conclusions from this kind of Church document about the medieval intercourse across religious boundaries. One can assume that a medieval commensality law is merely the traditional, pro forma renewal of a hoary measure or posit that it must still reflect the true nature of Jewish-Christian interac-tion on each occasion of the law's renewal. The former interpretation implies that Jews and Christians were not necessarily deeply involved in each other's lives; the latter implies the exact opposite.

This methodological conundrum would of course not be relevant to the promulgation of a new kind of measure. The charter negotiated in 1084 between Rudiger, archbishop of Speyer, and the town's new Jew-ish settlers is such a document. It presents a list of the Jews' obligations and privileges, each of which is then a kind of snapshot of the condi-tions prevailing in 1084, at least on the level of expectations. We find the kind of intimate intertwining of Jewish and Christian lives mentioned earlier, with Christians employed by Jews in various capacities at home and at work. This is particularly noteworthy because Rudiger is not only the sovereign of Speyer but also the region's highest clerical official.

Rudiger's statement that he decided to build a wall separating the Jewish quarter from the rest of Speyer "so that the Jews not easily be troubled by the commotion of the masses"[60] commands attention in the present context. This measure makes it plain that life in the Rhineland was not altogether free of tension with the gentile community. The text does not identify a particular segment of the Christian population as posing a threat, or its underlying causes, but clearly violence was con-sidered a real possibility.

This is also plain from a ruling by Rashi about ritual immersion. Normally, at the end of a woman's period of menstrual impurity, she must perform ritual immersion at night, but Rashi rules that she may do so in the daytime, that is, on the following day, "if she fears that [gentiles] will harm her."[61] Rashi offers some examples of dangerous situations: "for example, in places where they pursue them with sticks or rocks, or other fears and dangers, or where there is reason to fear burglary or night terror."[62] In the rabbinic literature of this period the reference to those who pursue others with sticks or rocks can only indicate non-Jews, and clearly religious identity is at the heart of violence of this type. Yet Rashi seems to refer here to acts of petty violence, which are more an annoyance than a mortal danger.

Barukh of Worms, a thirteenth-century scholar, offers a more sanguine comment on the civility of non-Jews. He states categorically that the idolaters of today, namely, the Christians, are less prone to lawless behavior than those of antiquity, because previously the Jews were multitudinous and owned land and were therefore subject to theft and lawlessness.[63] The social theory underlying this generalization is intriguing, but the main point is the assumption that medieval Jews are safer than their ancestors were.

Another new kind of measure is the requirement, legislated in 1215 at the Fourth Lateran Council, that Jews wear a distinguishing sign on their outer garment so that innocent Christians do not mistake them for Christians and unwittingly have illicit intercourse with them. The new law implies not only that close social or personal ties between Christians and Jews were possible, and even common, but that Jews and Christians were so alike as to be indistinguishable by external criteria. That this was true across Latin Europe is indicated by the adoption of the Jewish badge idea in numerous lands.[64]

At around the same time that the Fourth Lateran Council issued its statutes, the Jewish communities of the Rhineland published a set of ordinances, first among which is a ban on gentile apparel.[65] Clearly the Jewish communal leaders who formulated and signed this document felt as threatened as did their clerical counterparts by the intimate mingling of Jews and Christians.[66] This impression is supported by the coeval appearance of these regulations in *Sefer Hasidim*, in a passage that provides halakhic detail to implement the prophet Isaiah's vision that "their offspring shall be *known* [emphasis added] among the nations" (Isa. 61:9).[67]

The sartorial regulations illustrate that for the Jews of medieval Ashkenaz the trappings of daily existence were largely those of the general European environment. The residents of any given region were familiar with the local language or dialect, as Rashi demonstrates in his use of French terminology to explicate obscure biblical and talmudic terms. For instance, when the disgruntled Israelites hanker after the foodstuffs of Egypt, which they lovingly enumerate, Rashi explains that the biblical term *qishu'im* refers to *cucumbres* (Num. 11:5). This use of French is clearly a convenient expository device—How would one describe a cucumber?—and may be insignificant as an expression of cultural identity, just as dress is fundamentally utilitarian and does not bear intrinsic symbolic significance.[68] It may be, however, that willy-nilly cultural overlap creates a sense of a shared identity, at least to some degree, even if this solidarity surfaces only when both populations are threatened by a third party. If so, Rashi's *cucumbres* may say something about his Frenchness and that of his audience.

A more conscious expression of the level of acculturation is the Jews' use of non-Jewish names. This was particularly common for daughters, such as El'azar of Worms's martyred wife Dolce and elder daughter Bellette.[69] Although the choice of names from beyond the Jewish heritage was certainly not intended as an ecumenical statement, it was a choice, unlike dress and language, which were automatic and therefore less impressive as expressions of cultural identity.

A high degree of participation in European culture is also manifest in the realm of entertainment. In the late twelfth century we find a Jewish *Minnesinger* (i.e., troubadour), named Süsskind of Trimberg. Some works of Hebrew literature resemble Christian works, such as *Mishlei Shu'alim*, an anthology of fox fables by Berekiah ha-Naqdan of thirteenth-century London.[70] In the social realm, a tosafist gloss notes the custom of young men jousting on horseback at weddings in front of the groom. It establishes that should one of the combatants accidentally damage his adversary's clothing or horse, he would not be liable for financial compensation because the activity was not a spontaneous act; it was conducted for the sake of bringing merriment to the groom, which is a religious obligation.[71] Clearly twelfth-century Jews share the popular appreciation of the joust as a form of sport and entertainment.

By engaging in jousting, the Jews express their identification with the upper ranks of society, the knights and nobles. Isaac of Dampierre testifies to this value, but more in a legal than a social sense: "We have seen in this region that the Jews enjoy the standing of knights (*parashim*) wherever they wish, and they are free by royal law, [namely] that no ruler shall seize the Jews' land when they leave his city, and such is the custom throughout the kingdom of Burgundy."[72] The issue here is legal standing, and the master talmudist notes the relatively high degree of mobility and protection enjoyed by the Jews of northern France compared with many of their Christian neighbors in both urban and rural environments.

These texts suggests that medieval Jews were familiar with the mores, values, and ideas of their Christian neighbors, but what were their sources of information? One avenue for transmission was the non-Jews resident within the Jewish home. *Sefer Hasidim* warns parents not to allow Christian domestics to sing Christian lullabies to the children at bedtime because this would violate the biblical injunction against causing idolaters to utter the names of their gods (Exod. 23:13).[73] What is more, this text is followed by one that forbids a parent to pacify an infant with non-Jewish songs, signifying that the parents themselves know these songs and would be tempted to sing them to their children, as no doubt their parents or nannies had done for them.[74] The right to employ Christian nursemaids and domestics dates to the earliest days of European Jewish settlement; it is stipulated in the 825 charter of the Jews of Lyons as well as in the 1084 charter of the Jews of Speyer. It appears, then, that Jewish children imbibed Christian lore and mores from early childhood, in many cases at their nursemaid's breast.

Children are also the focus of a Jewish ceremony closely and clearly associated with Christian images and doctrines. Beginning in the twelfth century, Hebrew sources from Germany and France attest that Jews practice the following initiation ceremony when their sons begin their formal education:

> When someone brings his son to study the Torah, the letters are written on a board. . . . Three loaves of choice flour with honey are kneaded. . . . Three eggs are cooked for him. Apples and other kinds of fruit are brought to him. . . . He is brought to the synagogue and fed

the honey loaves, the eggs and fruit. The letters are read to him. Then it [the board] is covered with honey and he is told: "Lick!" He is then returned to his mother with his nose covered [with honey].[75]

In other, parallel sources, biblical verses as well as the Hebrew alphabet are inscribed on the board and eggs. Either way, the ritual equates the word of God with honey and bread, which the Jew is expected to ingest with delight. Ivan Marcus sees this rite of passage as a response to the Eucharist, in which the believer consumes the host, that is, Jesus's body, which is equated with the divinity. The honey represents the manna eaten by the Israelites in the desert (Exod. 16:31), which is identified by midrashic literature with the Torah and by Church doctrine with the host.[76] Evidently, the initiation rite expresses the Jew's familiarity with Christian dogma and praxis and is a kind of counter-Eucharist, a polemic against Christianity. The paradox is that it simultaneously expresses both intimacy and rejection.[77]

Intellectual Intimacy

In the realm of ideas, the extent of the Jews' participation in the culture of medieval Europe is evident and unambiguous. A powerful and paradoxical example is the martyrological ideal expressed in the Hebrew narratives of the First Crusade. In the tales of mass murder and suicide, the protagonists are made to articulate the very ideal attributed to their killers, the crusaders—namely, the decision to value faith above life itself.[78] In this sense Robert Chazan refers to the Jewish martyrdom of 1096 as a "counter-crusade."[79] What is more, the narrators of these episodes must have realized that the martyrs, by dying at their own hand, express greater religious zeal than their foes; although the crusaders risk death by embarking on the holy war, the Jews embrace death with open arms and accept it as a certainty.[80]

The paradoxical notion that the Hebrew narratives of the 1096 persecutions reflect contemporary Christian values is fundamental to Jeremy Cohen's interpretation of these texts. One of Cohen's most powerful readings of this sort concerns the description of the slaughter of the four small children of a woman named Rachel, at her initiative and possibly her own hand. In an exceptionally heartrending moment, the attackers come upon Rachel as she is seated, wailing over her slain children, two of whom she enfolds in her left sleeve and two in her right.[81] On the symbolic level, Rachel stands for the biblical matriarch, of whom the prophet Jeremiah says, "Rachel weeps over her children" (Jer. 31:14). For Cohen, Rachel also represents the Church (Mater Ecclesia), or Mother Mary, the grieving mother (Mater Dolorosa) prefigured in the Old Testament by Rachel.[82]

This is but one example of Cohen's general approach to the Hebrew First Crusade narratives. Cohen maintains that the narrator has a fairly intimate acquaintance with Christian doctrine and imagery, that he expects his audience to share his level of knowledge, and that he would choose to use Christian imagery to tell his tale of woe. For some of the tales told in the Hebrew texts the Christian element seems obvious, even unavoidable, such as the allusion to the Last Supper in the tale of the martyrdom at Xanten, but the association of Rachel with Mater Ecclesia is forced and less compelling.[83] On the other hand, the association of the Rachel of 1096, and hence also of the weeping Rachel of the Bible, with the Mater Dolorosa seems plausible. The connection is explicit in the Gospels (Matt. 2:18), and the Gospel according to Matthew was indeed known to some twelfth-century European Jews.[84] In addition, scholars maintain that awareness of the image and plight of Mother Mary rose dramatically in this period, raising the likelihood that the image penetrated Jewish society.[85]

That Jews and Christians shared a similar mind-set is strikingly apparent in two tales found in the Hebrew narratives of 1096. First we encounter the tale of the miraculous goose, believed by the crusaders to be their divinely inspired guide to the Holy Land.[86] This is immediately followed by a story attributed to Barukh ben Isaac. Barukh relates to his listeners, in the synagogue, that he knows with certainty that the community cannot be saved, for on the previous night he and others heard a loud noise that sounded like weeping and wailing come from the synagogue. Thinking that fellow congregants had assembled for an impromptu prayer session, Barukh and a companion hurried there. Finding the door shut and the building empty but still hearing the loud voice and the weeping, they conclude that the synagogue itself must be the source of the wailing, a miraculous occurrence that could only mean that destruction was unavoidable. To the twelfth-century audience, the wailing synagogue and the crusading goose were supernatural occurrences and thus, by definition, portents that supremely important events were in the offing. Perhaps the most impressive indication of cultural sharing here is the juxtaposition of the Christian and Jewish miracle tales in the Hebrew narrative. The total rejection of Christianity is a leitmotif of the Hebrew First Crusade sources, and yet we find in them a single pattern of thinking characteristic of both Jew and Christian.

In the towns of medieval Europe, both Jews and Christians developed political structures of self-government in the high Middle Ages, and this too has been viewed as a reflection of the Jews' Europeanization, although scholars have disagreed about the direction of cultural influence. Yitzhak Baer argues that the Jewish development was rooted in ideals expounded in talmudic literature in late antiquity, and consequently he emphasizes the chronological priority of Jewish self-government over that of the medieval commune. Aryeh Grabois counters that the development of the Jewish community parallels that of the urban parish of northern France, and he highlights the emergence in the twelfth century in both institutional structures of the *parnasim* or *boni viri*.[87] Clearly the revival of the medieval town, beginning in the tenth century, stimulated the development of governing structures. Because the Jewish and Christian bodies came into existence to fill the legislative and judicial needs of the new urban dwellers, it is understandable that they assumed similar forms, and their parallel development expresses the extent to which the two groups shared a single social and cultural experience.

The twelfth and early thirteenth centuries were an especially creative period for Franco-German Jewry in the intellectual and spiritual realms, and the most notable achievements of this diaspora bear witness to the Jews' participation in contemporary trends. The main intellectual current to find expression in Jewish writings is what is known as the twelfth-century Renaissance. Hebrew writing in several disciplines and genres reflects the period's intellectual awakening in general as well as some of its particular forms of expression. This is most apparent in the fields of law and Bible study.

The Jews of northern France, and to a lesser extent of Germany, produced a substantial corpus of glosses, known as Tosafot or addenda;
these glosses comment on the Babylonian Talmud or on Rashi's commentary thereto. Typically a question is posed (usually anonymously),
often by noting a contradiction between two dicta on a given topic.
The contradiction is resolved by positing a conceptual or legal distinction between the two talmudic formulations, such that they are seen to
refer to discrete situations. One may posit, for example, that Text A provides a general rule, whereas Text B refers to a particular circumstance
to which the general rule would not apply; the opposite argument is of
equal utility in resolving contradictory rulings.

At times the root of the problem is located in deficient texts. For
instance, contradictory positions can be ascribed to different authorities rather than to a single individual. When confronted with a discrepancy between talmudic law and prevailing custom, the tosafists
sometimes cite a change in living conditions to justify contemporary
practice without challenging the authoritative source. These and other
methods enable them to harmonize opposing positions and to arrive
at accommodation or alignment. Jacob ben Meir (Rabbenu Tam), the
pioneering leader of the tosafist school, trumpets the new approach:
"Even when the Talmud states in one place that a person is liable and in
another that he is not, we resolve the problem well."[88]

The tosafist glosses bear an obvious literary affinity to the literature
of the legal glossators of Bologna on the *Corpus Iuris Civilis*. Like the
glosses, the legal texts are constructed in a question-and-answer format,
with "Should you say . . . ?" followed by "One might say . . ." Apart
from the formal similarity, the French Tosafot represent the same kind
of scholarly endeavor as the glosses of Bologna, for both parse an ancient and authoritative text to establish its internal consistency and to
arrive at accommodation between the ancient source and contemporary
mores.[89] This is essentially the project of the scholastics, as exemplified
in Abelard's *Sic et Non*. That this resemblance was not lost on contemporaries is plain from the warning in *Sefer Hasidim* not to engage in
"the gentile science of dialectics."[90]

Ephraim Urbach expatiates at length on the similarity between the
methods applied by the tosafists and the scholastics, particularly the

glossators, but sees their approaches as analogous only up to a point. He stresses that the scholastics, especially Abelard, took pride in humiliating their masters, whereas Rabbenu Tam demanded only that others acknowledge the truth of his point of view.[91] In addition, Urbach emphasizes that dialectic emerged not only in the field of law but also in theology and philosophy; among the Jews, however, the Tosafot are its only expression, and the tosafists express no interest in theology or philosophy.[92] Third, whereas the glossators were attracted to Roman law because the German emperors viewed themselves as heirs to the Roman empire, the tosafists were motivated purely by intellectual and halakhic considerations rather than political ones.[93]

Urbach also observes that there is no evidence that the tosafists and scholastics were in direct contact, much less that either benefited from the other's achievement. He concludes, "Rabbenu Tam did not need to learn the talmudic methods which he perpetuated and developed from either the scholastics or the glossators."[94] Rather, Urbach sees the tosafists as using the hermeneutic of the Sages of late antiquity, who used similar tools to reconcile conflicting traditions and dicta in the heritage of the Oral Law.[95]

Isadore Twersky challenges the notion of the historical influence of the scholastics on the tosafists, or vice versa, on various grounds. For instance, Twersky maintains that it is the work of the talmudic scholars of Provence, rather than those of northern France, that bears a methodological resemblance to that of the scholastics. Furthermore, Twersky observes that Urbach pursues two alternative interpretations of the tosafist enterprise, pointing toward historical influence while also insisting that analogous development is all that can be demonstrated.[96] Twersky notes that Urbach could have cited numerous Jewish parallels to the scholastic enterprise from far-flung eras and locations rather than focusing on twelfth-century France.[97]

Urbach's conundrum is rooted, I believe, in his conception of Jewish-Christian relations in medieval Europe. Urbach insists that "the Jews distanced themselves from them [i.e., Christians] and from the deplorable and negative behaviors displayed in their daily life."[98] He characterizes the Jewish and Christian societies of medieval Ashkenaz as "two societies living in a state of mutual opposition and contradiction, in which every encounter is one of conflict and polemic, replete with insults and curses, while at the same time they maintain judicial systems, deploying similar methods and remarkably identical modes of expression."[99] This gloomy image of Jewish-Christian relations leaves Urbach trapped between a phenomenological explanation and a historical explanation of the supposed analogy between tosafists and scholastics.

That rabbis and theologians really did interact in twelfth-century France is beyond doubt in the realm of biblical exegesis. Hugh of St. Victor, a cathedral school in Paris, was convinced that the Bible could be understood properly only in its original language, and he pioneered the study of Hebrew as the means to attain the "*Hebraica veritas*." Without rejecting or devaluing the Christological interpretation of the text, Hugh and his disciples, Andrew and Richard, concentrated on the Bible's *sensus litteralis*. Their aim was to arrive at a more accurate text, free of the Vulgate's distortions, and to attempt to understand the Bible in terms of its own language and modes of expression.[100] Here the direction of influence is not open to question. It is clear that the Christian exegetes sought out the correct text of the Bible based on the Hebrew textual tradition. This circle of exegetes, known as the Victorines, aired their findings in Bible commentaries, and their methodology was continued and developed by generations of Bible scholars, such as Herbert of Bosham, Peter the Chanter, and Nicholas de Lyra.

Two examples illustrate Victorine literalism. Jacob the patriarch, on his deathbed, prophesies that "the scepter shall not depart from Judah nor a lawgiver from between his feet until Shilo come and unto him shall the gathering of the people be" (Gen. 49:10). "Shilo" is obscure, giving rise to the Christological interpretation that the verse is a cryptic announcement of Jesus's mission and of the ultimate replacement of the Jews as the Chosen People. Hugh, however, identifies Shilo as the site of Saul's coronation, without referring to Jesus or to the verse's venerable history as a prooftext for Christianity. Similarly, Christians have traditionally identified Jesus as the veiled subject of the fifty-third chapter of Isaiah, which describes the "suffering servant" of the Lord, whose torment and death atone for the sins of others. Nevertheless, in Andrew's commentary the Jewish people, exiled to Babylonia, collectively represent God's suffering servant, and once again no reference is made to Jesus, his mission, or his fate.

Not only were Hugh and his students eager to learn Hebrew and to acquire the Hebrew text of the Bible, but they also investigated the Jews' exegetical tradition. We thus find explicit references in the Victorines' commentaries to the interpretations of Rashi, Rashbam, and other twelfth-century Jewish exegetes. Nicholas de Lyra, a thirteenth-century Franciscan, mentions Rashi on almost every page of his *Postilla Litteralis*, and he is also familiar with the work of Rashi's predecessor, Moses the Preacher (*ha-Darshan*). Nicholas also refers several times to the views of Maimonides, whose *Guide of the Perplexed* was already available in Latin.[101]

The exegesis of the Jewish scholars of northern France was singularly well suited to the needs of Hugh and his disciples, because they also focused on the literal sense of the biblical text. This was the heyday of *peshat*, the plain meaning, which involved heightened awareness of corrupt manuscripts, careful scrutiny of biblical language, and the judicious use of historical, sociological, and anthropological insights to explicate thorny expressions and passages. The French commentators varied in their conception and use of *peshat*, but their concentration on the literal-historical plane dominates Jewish biblical exegesis in northern France until the mid-thirteenth century, by which time the creative phase of French Jewry had passed its zenith.[102]

For Jews, literalism undercuts the Christian method of prefigurative interpretation and is thus an obvious response to Christological exegesis. Beyond this, however, an anti-Christian polemical strain can be discerned in the interpretations offered by the Jewish literalists of France. This is especially noticeable in Psalms, Canticles, and other biblical books that were popular subjects of Christological interpretation, but it is found elsewhere as well.[103] At times the anti-Christian element is concealed, whereas at other times sallies are overtly directed at the *minim*, namely, the Christians.[104]

The following comment by Rashbam is illustrative. The Bible prohibits the mixing of species, in animals, plants, or textiles (Lev. 19:19). Rashbam explains that the various species were distinct at the time of Creation (Gen. 1:11), and the commandment serves therefore to preserve the natural order of things. He then adds, "And I told the *minim*: Wool is dyed and flax is not dyed, and God regards with disfavor a garment of two appearances; and they conceded the truth of my argument." A mixture of dyed and undyed threads in the warp and woof of a garment would produce distinct vertical and horizontal lines, forming the shape of the cross. Thus Rashbam demonstrates that the Pentateuch can be shown to reject the truth of Christianity by enjoining Jews from making the sign of the cross, even inadvertently. This example, which is not atypical of Rashbam's anti-Christian remarks, is interesting because he appears to concede the legitimacy of the prefigurative approach, but he does so only to prove the falsehood of Christianity.[105]

The marked presence of anti-Christian polemic in Jewish Bible commentary reflects a general increase in religious polemical writing in twelfth- and thirteenth-century Latin Europe. For Christians this was an age-old pursuit, which produced an extensive literature *adversus Iudaeos*, against the Jews.[106] Only now, however, did Jews begin assembling their own chrestomathies of arguments against Christianity, beginning with Jacob ben Reuben's *Wars of the Lord* (*Milhamot Ha-Shem*), written in twelfth-century France. Joseph ben Nathan Official's *Book of Joseph the Zealot* (*Sefer Yosef ha-Meqaneh*) followed in the thirteenth century, as did the *Old Book of Disputation* (*Sefer Nizzahon Yashan*), written at about the same time in Germany by one or more anonymous authors.[107]

These works and the *adversus Iudaeos* literature that they address revolve mostly around the Bible, with each side recording its own understanding of the biblical verse or passage under discussion and controverting the interpretation of the other. *Sefer Nizzahon Yashan* offers the following commentary on the verse "Hear, O Israel! The Lord is our God, the Lord is one" (Deut. 6:4):

> The heretics say in their arrogance: These three divine names [i.e., Lord, God, Lord] refer to the Trinity. One may respond that the answer is to be found in an adjoining verse: "You shall love the Lord your God with all your heart" [Dt. 6:5]. Here he omitted one of the names, reducing the number to two so that people should not err in saying there are three.[108]

In this passage and in the other contemporary anthologies of anti-Christian polemic it is usually the heretic that takes the initiative and the Jew that responds rather than vice versa. This passage is also typical in focusing on the Old Testament, which was sacred to both religions, although the Jewish works do contain some criticism of the Gospels as well. These texts do not clarify how much Latin the Jews knew, if any, but they attest that the Jews acquired some conception of Christian dogma and ritual.[109]

Apart from works devoted to the traditional tug-of-war over the Old Testament, a number of anti-Jewish polemical tracts of a speculative rather than exegetical nature were penned in the twelfth century. The most famous of these are Gilbert Crispin of Westminster's *Disputation Between a Jew and a Christian* and Abelard's *Dialogue of a Philosopher with a Jew and a Christian*.[110] These works condemn Judaism as based on authority (*auctoritas*), as opposed to reason (*ratio*), which they associate with Christianity. This set of values plainly reflects the rise of scholasticism and of systematic theology in Latin Europe.

Scholars are generally agreed that the dialogues described in these Latin works are literary creations rather than real social encounters.[111] The Jew seems to serve as a foil for Christianity, as the writer seeks to demonstrate the affinity of Christianity with rationalism and philosophy. Nevertheless, the civil tone of these rationalist polemics contrasts sharply with the disparaging rhetoric of the classical *adversus Iudaeos* literature. Crispin, for instance, writes that he and his Jewish colleague would converse in a tolerant and patient spirit so as to proceed "for the cause of faith and out of love to thee."[112]

The rationalist spirit of these treatises leads Amos Funkenstein to describe this historical juncture as one of intellectual intimacy between Jews and Christians unparalleled in medieval European history.[113] This generalization gains cogency if we widen our perspective to include the rise of literalist Bible exegesis in both the Jewish and Christian camps. The Victorine interest in Jewish biblical interpretation demonstrates not only the intersection of interests but also Christian interest in Jewish thought. The Jewish literalists, in addition to sharing an interest in accurate texts and biblical language, also display a rationalist bent. To illustrate, Rashbam is palpably uncomfortable with anthropomorphism: For "This is the finger of God!" (Exod. 8:15), he paraphrases "This is an epidemic!"[114] Rashbam also offers rational explanations of commandments, suggesting, for example, that the Bible proscribes particular foods because they are unhealthy.[115]

Taken together, the rationalist strain of religious disputation and the *Hebraica veritas* school of biblical exegesis suggest an atmosphere of academic exchange in which the search for truth brings Jews and Christians closer together than ever. Ora Limor terms the discussions conducted by Jewish and Christian exegetes in twelfth-century France

> an attempt by the learned to discover truth for truth's sake. . . . In this approach one can discern curiosity and a quest for knowledge that is almost scientific, insofar as the main goals of study and of the quest are the attainment of truth and the acquisition of knowledge. . . . The goal of both sides was, first and foremost, to exchange views for intellectual ends, and this is the great novelty of the twelfth century.[116]

This celebration of the shared atmosphere of academic scholarship echoes Funkenstein's generalization about the new intimacy of the twelfth century. But this perspective may be the anachronistic projection of a modern, secular, academic ethos on the medieval mind. Projects involving the attempt to acquire a more intimate acquaintance with Judaism may reflect not a new appreciation of Jewish culture but rather a new approach to a traditional end: the conversion of the Jews. If so, the literalism of the French Jewish exegetes might be viewed as a tactical response to a Christian conversionary move, because, as mentioned, literalism parries the thrust of Christianity's prefigurative hermeneutic.[117]

This perception of Victorine exegesis mirrors a common negative view of the relations between Christians and Jews in twelfth- and thirteenth-century northern Europe. Limor's explanation of the appearance of Jewish polemical writing in the twelfth century vividly illustrates this lachrymose perspective.

> Towards the end of the eleventh century there was a crisis in the relations between Jews and Christians in western Europe. The Jewish communities were attacked, both physically, during the wave of pogroms that accompanied the First Crusade, as well as religiously. . . . The numerous attacks by Christians against the Jews in their midst caused the Jews to lose self-confidence, and even to a significant number of cases of apostasy. It was not only the physical attack, but also the

Christians' conversionary efforts, and the need to confront the dogmas
of the "triumphant" religion that posed a real threat, and the Jews
were forced to confront this threat. One of the facets of this confrontation is the polemical literature. In this literature one finds answers
which seem to be directed outward, towards the Christian, and which
respond to questions which bothered the Jews inwardly as well.[118]

Limor's limpid formulation echoes Yitzhak Baer's assertion that
Rashi's Bible commentary couples anti-Christian polemic with a sustained effort to fortify contemporaries, whom he sees as demoralized
by the carnage of the First Crusade.[119] Similarly, Salo Baron writes
that the Hebrew chronicles of the First Crusade massacres were designed to combat the depression caused by the Church's missionary efforts; the writers of these works, he maintains, "sounded the keynote
of the 'lachrymose conception of Jewish history.'"[120]

Gavin Langmuir has set this sense of a spiritual malaise in the larger
context of a crisis of faith that beset Christians and Jews alike in the
eleventh and twelfth centuries, as a result of the new expectation that
beliefs be grounded in a rational and empirical worldview. The Jews,
Langmuir explains, were one of the sources of the Christian crisis, for
they rejected Christianity as irrational and as contradictory to the religion of the Old Testament, of which they were the uncontested masters.[121] Following Langmuir's lead, Jeremy Cohen writes that "doubt
fuelled the commonality of a medieval experience that Jews and Christians shared, perhaps despite themselves, even as they struggled to preserve distinctions between them."[122]

Jews were particularly vexed by the "argument from history," the
axiom that the temporal success of Christianity proves its truth. Western Christendom's triumphant posture rested on its demographic, economic, and social boom, which began in the tenth century and reached
mature expression in the initiative of the First Crusade and its successful execution, culminating in the 1099 conquest of Jerusalem. Jews
found the growth of European power threatening and were perplexed
by God's failure to demonstrate support for their own steadfastness.[123]
The source of this crisis was internal, rooted in the Jews' own perception of history rather than in Christian propaganda. And it is important that the argument from history was empirical and hence logically

compelling to a rational, thinking person of the Middle Ages. In this respect Jews and Christians found themselves in an identical quandary: Both felt constrained to embrace the new rationalistic mind-set even though it exposed weaknesses in their respective theological edifices.

The polar gap between the views of Jewish-Christian relations is rooted, then, not in the evidence but in its ramifications. The lively exchange of polemical sallies and biblical interpretations voices an insecurity to be found on both sides of the religious divide. The basic question is whether this insecurity signifies that a great distance separated Christian and Jew or perhaps the opposite. The latter approach might align Funkenstein's generalization about the new intimacy with the consensus (articulated by Baer and others) that twelfth-century Jews felt beleaguered: They felt beleaguered because it seemed that the frontier had come too close to home and their religious space had shrunk.

No wonder that both Jews and Christians were discomfited by the newfound respect for the epistemological potential of rational thought. Richard of St. Victor criticizes his colleague, Andrew, for being excessively attracted to Jewish exegesis and for citing the rabbis' interpretations even when they fly in the face of the Christological reading.[124] Likewise, the new Hebrew anti-Christian polemical texts may signal a reaction to proximity rather than to increased alienation.

This argument is essentially the same as the one deployed earlier regarding developments in the social arena. There also we find Jews and Christians legislating statutes designed to limit interfaith fraternizing, which expresses anxiety, and, as we have seen, Jewish apostasy was a reality of Ashkenazic society.[125] In the intellectual realm too, I would argue, evidence of insecurity and even hostility reflects intimacy, not alienation, for where there is distance, there is no threat and no cause for anxiety.

The argument can be extended beyond the intellectual realm to that of religious beliefs and values. Yitzhak Baer scrutinizes a wide variety of forms of environmental influence discernible in *Sefer Hasidim*, a work from Germany of the late twelfth and early thirteenth centuries, and these testify, in his view, to the immersion of German Jewry in the larger cultural sphere.[126] The assumption that the Jews of Franco-Germany were highly susceptible to "outside influence" contradicts his usual view of the cultural autonomy of Ashkenazic Jewry.[127]

Among the topics surveyed is Jewish self-government, which Baer portrays here as influenced by the development of the medieval European city.[128] The right of a community member to create a disturbance and halt the prayer service until his grievance is addressed (*'ikuv tephilah*) was derived, Baer asserts, from the Christian *interdictum*. Similarly, he traces to Catholic practice the custom of recording the names of martyrs and praying for their souls. More fundamentally, Baer links the Ashkenazic spirit of self-sacrifice to the Cluniac movement of religious revival.[129]

Scholars have critiqued many of the components of Baer's audacious and wide-ranging argument, and admittedly some of the forms he discusses are more telling than others. Thus the writers of *Sefer Hasidim* make use of the exemplum, a literary form they probably acquired by hearing the outdoor sermons of Berthold of Regensburg and other Franciscan preachers, but its adoption is merely utilitarian and does not indicate the penetration of Franciscan doctrine into the belief system of the Jewish pietists.[130]

In some cases, ideas in *Sefer Hasidim* do appear to stem from non-Jewish sources, but one is hard pressed to explain how the pietists gained access to them because they are unlikely to have read anything outside the Jewish canon, as currently defined. For instance, Judah ben Samuel, "the Pious" (*he-Hasid*), one of the book's primary architects, idealizes egalitarianism and advocates the communal allocation of property and the agricultural lifestyle. These ideals were realized by the new Premonstratensian and Cistercian orders, respectively, but Jews, as urban dwellers, had little contact with the rural and remote monasteries and convents of these orders. As the source of the pietists' egalitarian ethos, Baer proposes the writings of Lactantius and the Stoics of late antiquity, but he cannot explain how Judah the Pious could have acquired these ideas.[131] Baer also identifies the Stoics as the source of ideas expressed in *Sefer Hasidim* about the natural ecological relationship between animals and humans, and here also the links connecting the medieval Jewish pietist to the ancient Stoics elude us.[132]

The pietists' ideas about communal property, agriculture, and animal life are atypical of medieval rabbinic thought, which renders Baer's interpretation attractive, but the pietists' doctrine of atonement is even more impressive evidence of European cultural influence.[133] In *Sefer Hasidim* and other writings by the German pietists, the sinner confesses his sin to a wise man, who proffers penitential instruction. This doctrine clearly mimics Christian praxis and has no roots in Jewish law or custom.

The menu of penances is equally striking. There are four paths to atonement, two of which involve mortification of the flesh. *Mishqal* (measure) penance requires a sinner to suffer physical torment in equal measure to the delight he received from his transgressive act, and in *katuv* (scriptural) penance, the torment must be symbolically equivalent to the penalty prescribed in the Torah. An example of either *mishqal* or *katuv* penance would be the prescription that a repentant adulterer go down to the river during the winter, break the ice, and immerse himself in the freezing water up to his mouth or nose for the length of time he spent fornicating with his lover; in warm weather he should sit in ant hills.[134] *Mishqal* and *katuv* penance are unprecedented in Jewish law or thought, and they evoke the ascetic practices attributed to St. Francis of Assisi and his disciples.[135]

Other scholars locate immanent roots of hasidic ideals and practices in the mystical literature of late antiquity, primarily that of the *Hekhalot* (palaces) or *Merkavah* (chariot), rather than in the cultural interpenetration of Jews and Christians in twelfth-century Germany.[136] In recent years the focus on the synchronic context has shifted from the notion of historical influence to that of a shared historical setting. Haym Soloveitchik's allusion to the twelfth-century Renaissance is representative: "Underlying the movement of *Haside 'Ashkenaz* was the recent discovery of man and his hitherto unsuspected capacities."[137] Here we find Jews and Christians sharing the European cultural matrix and engaging in a single dynamic of intellectual and spiritual development.

Conclusion

The intense cultural interaction of Jews and Christians in medieval Ashkenaz finds succinct expression in the *Sefer Hasidim* entry declaring that "in every city, the custom of the Jews follows that of the gentiles dwelling with them in most places."[138] The Jews shared the landscape of northern Europe with their Christian neighbors, whom they knew as employees and clients, neighbors and friends, and sometimes enemies or lovers. Sharing the landscape involved inhabiting a single mental space as well, with its own lexicon of concepts and values, even when these were used as weapons to express hostility and establish distance.[139]

The barrier of religion stood out boldly in the two groups' perception of each other, with Jews characterizing Christians as idolaters and Christians characterizing Jews as Christ killers. We have explored numerous cases in which primary sources of various kinds stigmatize the Other as evil and dangerous, giving voice to intense feelings of fear and impotence that at times exploded into verbal or physical violence. The dark feelings were more than just a pose; they were real and led scholars to color the canvas of medieval Ashkenaz in somber hues.

But the relationship between Jews and Christians was more complex, with conflicting feelings and contradictory sentiments. The exertions by the religious leadership of both camps to distance their flock from the predatory unbeliever bespeak a reality of proximity and likeness. Medieval writing in a range of genres—sermons, exegesis, legislation, liturgical poetry—emphasizes difference, suspicion, and grievance, implying, *malgré soi*, that Jews and Christians engaged each other on every level of life. Inevitably, they continually negotiated and redefined the boundaries of their relationship, but a relationship it was, with intimacy and conflict, competition and mutual need, and a common pool of tastes and values.

Eight Sepharad

This book opened with a passage in which Nahmanides, the leading light of Aragonese Jewry in the mid-thirteenth century, explains to the rabbis of northern France that Maimonides attempted to save the Jews from Greek philosophy, to the perils of which his northern brethren had never been exposed. Nahmanides expresses the notion, which becomes fundamental to the historiography of medieval Jewry, that the image of Ashkenaz is bound to that of Spain, known as Sepharad (Obad. 1:20), and vice versa, and that the two diasporas are polar opposites: The Jews of Franco-Germany are presented as leading authentic and pristine Jewish lives, whereas the Jews of Sepharad are associated with worldliness and its corrupting impact.

The binary and dichotomous nature of a good deal of Jewish historiography along these lines reverberates through discussions of all the themes treated in the preceding chapters. I have examined Franco-German Jewry in isolation, for fear that a comparative approach might contaminate the resultant image of Ashkenaz, but I still need to confront the Ashkenaz-Sepharad relationship and to assess its significance in light of the foregoing discussion.

The upshot of this discussion is that medieval Ashkenaz and Sepharad need to be uncoupled in future studies of either realm. The infelicitous comparison seems to invite exaggeration and caricature and hinders efforts to reach a more profound understanding. Moreover, Nahmanides' statement illustrates the tendentious aspect of the comparison throughout Jewish history. Just as it enables him to apologize for Maimonides' philosophical oeuvre, so does it serve the efforts of sixteenth-century writers to explain the fall of Iberian Jewry. Leaping forward another 300 years, we find modern historians lavishing praise on the enlightened Sephardic diaspora while disparaging the ignorance and superstition of the Jews of central and eastern Europe. The romantic sensibilities of Yitzhak Baer and Gershom Scholem cause them to treat the culture of medieval Ashkenaz more sympathetically and that of Sepharad less so, labeling the Jews of Ashkenaz as authentic and pious and the Jews of Sepharad as intellectually and culturally sophisticated but also as enervated by a mix of hedonism and skepticism.

The major themes for comparison are those treated in earlier chapters, namely, martyrdom, apostasy, Jewish-Christian relations, and deviance. I attempt to shrink the gap between the two centers in both dimension and significance, largely by arguing that the dichotomy that often emerges from a comparison of the two diasporas is false. In some cases the comparison results from a skewed presentation in which undue emphasis is placed on part of the known information, whereas at other times it is simply misguided, such as the proverbial comparison of apples and oranges.[1] As I have hitherto played down the saintly and heroic qualities of Ashkenazic Jewry and emphasized their humanity, so too in the following portrayal will I strive to nudge the image of Sephardic Jewry toward the middle of the road of fidelity and orthodoxy. In both cases the end result is an image that is less of a caricature and more of a complex portrait.

Martyrdom and Apostasy

A surge of pogroms erupted in Castile on June 4, 1391, following the death of Juan I, when the kingdom passed to a regency until Juan's 11-year-old son, Enrique III, could reach the age of majority. This was clearly a moment of political instability, and the Jews' enemies, roused to action by the fiery sermons of the rabidly antisemitic priest Ferrán Martinez of Écija, attacked the Jewish quarter of Seville, killed thousands, captured thousands more for sale into slavery, looted and razed homes, and reduced most of the city's twenty-three synagogues to churches or rubble. Violence also broke out in Córdoba and other Castilian towns and in Valencia, Aragon, and Catalonia as well. Everywhere, the burghers swept through the *judería*, the Jewish neighborhood, and either killed the inhabitants or forcibly converted them to Christianity. The kings of these realms saw the attacks as treason and vainly attempted to prevent them and later to punish the assailants and restore the badly depleted Jewish communities.[2]

"Within two or three years from 1391," writes Benzion Netanyahu, "Spain's Jewish community, the largest in the world, was reduced by nearly one third—in both geographic and numerical terms, the greatest catastrophe that had hitherto befallen European Jewry."[3] The number of victims in the various communities is unclear. Hasdai Crescas of Saragossa, a rabbi and philosopher and one of Spain's most illustrious Jewish political leaders in this period, in a report to the Jews of Avignon, puts the number of Jews killed in the major communities in the hundreds: Palma de Majorca, 300;[4] Valencia, 250 or so;[5] and Barcelona, approximately 250.[6] Other accounts state that thousands, not hundreds, were slaughtered. Ortiz de Zuñiga, Seville's historian, states that more than 4,000 Jews were killed in Seville,[7] and José Amador de los Ríos, a nineteenth-century historian, maintains that more than 2,000 died in Córdoba.[8]

Among the victims were those who died at their own hands or at the hands of fellow Jews. A Hebrew elegy records that "the famous Judah" sacrificed his wife and children and that "Asher" likewise "sanctified the name of God, and did not betray His covenant" by preferring baptism to death.[9] These martyrs are thought to be descendants of Asher ben Yehiel, Toledo's illustrious rabbi in the early fourteenth century. The elegy also records the suicide of Israel al-Nakawa, a renowned thinker and poet.[10] Crescas writes that after the slaughter in Barcelona, the survivors took refuge in the city's tower, where numerous Jews sanctified the name of God, that is, were martyred, including his own son. Crescas adds that the martyrs included many who slaughtered themselves, jumped to their death from the tower, or stepped forth from the tower to be cut down in the street.[11]

In Gerona, states Crescas, a relatively large number of Jews died, many at their own hands, and only a few apostatized, but we know that this was unusual.[12] The story of 1391 is primarily that of the *conversos*, the apostates, who almost everywhere vastly outnumbered the killed.[13] Reuben ben Nissim Gerondi puts the number of apostates in 1391 at approximately 140,000. This breathtaking figure, which is probably an exaggeration, is intended to convey the dimensions of the phenomenon.[14] Crescas reports that although many of Seville's Jews sanctified the name of God, most converted; because he writes that Seville had 6,000–7,000 Jewish households, the apostates must have numbered more than 10,000 souls.[15] Crescas also states that most of Valencia's 1,000 or so Jewish families accepted baptism, or almost 1,800 apostates.

Other sources offer figures significantly larger than those cited in Crescas's letter to Avignon. Caspar Escolano, a local Christian chronicler, reports that there were 7,000 converts in Valencia.[16] Crescas also relates that in Barcelona all but the martyrs apostatized, and Graetz puts their number at 11,000, although he cites no source.[17] A royal document reports that in Madrid "everyone had become Christian" (*tornados todos christianos*), without producing a number, and a Hebrew dirge reports that "of the great and small of the pleasant community of Cordova not one remained that did not convert."[18] A Hebrew dirge about the pogroms mourns the mass apostasy of the Jews of Burgos and Cuenca in Castile and of Jaen, Ubeda, Baeza, and Carmona in Andalusia.[19] We read there of Cuenca:

A bandit came to Cuenca to destroy her and reduce her pride to
    destruction,
Her people in cowardice and weakness left the Creator and Maker
    of all.[20]

The pogroms are known to have sharply depleted the number of Jews resident in the larger cities and towns. From 1391 until the Expulsion in 1492, Spain's Jews resided mostly in rural villages. Many communities were permanently eradicated, especially in Catalonia, Valencia, and Aragon.[21] However, most of the Jewish townspeople had not died or fled; they had accepted baptism and remained. Notwithstanding the confusion over the precise dimensions of the wave of conversion in 1391, it is clear that in the final century of Spanish Jewish history the apostates, or *conversos*, were a significant presence in Spanish society, often living alongside their former coreligionists.[22]

The number of apostates in Christian Spain rose sharply once more in the wake of the disputation at Tortosa, in Aragon, which took place from February 1413 to November 1414, in the presence of Pope Benedict XIII. In this confrontation Christianity was championed by Geronimo de Santa Fe, who was known as Joshua ha-Lorki (of Lorca) before his own apostasy, when the Jewish faith was represented by twelve of Spanish Jewry's luminaries, including the renowned thinkers Joseph Albo and Profiat Duran, the poets Solomon Bonafed and Joseph ben Lavi, and other leading intellectuals.[23] The debate centered on the Christian claim that proof for the messiah's advent could be found in the rabbinic aggadah. This argument had already been articulated in the thirteenth-century disputations at Paris and Barcelona, and the Jews' spokesmen at Tortosa echoed their forebears' response that aggadic dicta are not canonical.

Geronimo de Santa Fe declared himself—and by extension Christianity—the victor, and even the Jews seemed to agree, for the Tortosa disputation triggered Spain's second massive wave of conversions, although only in Aragon, not Castile. The new converts included esteemed political and intellectual leaders of the Jewish community, including Don Vidal ben Lavi de la Cavalleria and the poets Joseph ben Lavi and Solomon da Piera, ben Lavi's teacher, who was over 70 at the time![24] This implosion of Jewish leadership demoralized the rank and file, and the result was a wave of apostasy of the dimensions of 1391 or greater. Abraham Zacut, writing a century or so after the Tortosa disputation, put the number of apostates at more than 200,000.[25]

At about this time conversion accelerated in Castile too, following the enactment of discriminatory laws in 1412 that forbade Jews to engage in tax farming and to hold government positions. The new laws also forced the Jews to identify themselves as such by their outer appearance and to take up residence in segregated quarters, remote from squares and markets; these regulations were designed to restrict social intercourse with unsuspecting Christians. Solomon Alami, a fifteenth-century moralist, describes the 1412 decrees in the following eloquent language:

> They decreed that they change their attire, and prevented them from engaging in commerce, [tax] farming and artisanship. . . . Those dwelling within their homes were driven out of the palaces of refinement and delight, to take up residence in graves. The worm of Jacob [Isa. 41:14],

those reared in purple have embraced refuse heaps [Lam. 4:5]; all citizens in Israel shall live in booths [Lev. 23:42], summer and winter, to abhorrence and reproaches [Dan. 12:2]. Most of the avaricious customs collectors departed thence, since they were forbidden farming and customs, for they had not learned a trade with which to support themselves. Artisans left, too, on account of the destruction, pressure and enclosure; seeing these events and tribulations, they were bowled over and unable to rise under these trials and changes.[26]

On the formal and theoretical plane, the legislation was no more than the implementation of Augustine's doctrine of toleration, which held that the Jews must be maintained in a humbled state, as proof of their rejection by God.[27] Likewise, the policy of restricting the social interaction of Jews and Christians dates back to the early centuries of Christianity.[28] Hitherto the secular authorities of medieval Europe—kings, nobles, and even bishops—had refrained from rigorously enforcing these policies, and this is what had now changed, for the new laws enjoyed royal support. In practice, the 1412 measures crippled the livelihood and social life of the affluent and powerful in Castilian Jewish society, and they also affected the humble, who were no longer allowed to provide Christians with their services as craftsmen or merchants of food and clothing. Stripped of economic options as well as political and social respectability, the Jews of Castile abandoned their faith in droves just as their Aragonese brethren were buckling under the conversionary pressure of the Tortosa disputation.[29]

The combination of violence and conversionary pressure reduced Spanish Jewry to its lowest ebb, not only through the demographic hemorrhage of apostasy but also in terms of the political, social, economic, and spiritual health of those who clung to their ancestral faith. Later in the century the conversionary pressure abated, and the final decades of Spanish Jewish history are a different story. Our concern is with the two-stage crisis of 1391 and 1412–1414 and particularly with the Jews' behavior under threat.

What stands out in the 1391 story is the preponderance of apostates and dearth of martyrs, and this experience contrasts starkly with that of the First Crusade in the Rhineland, in which *Kiddush ha-Shem*, sanctification of the divine name, occupies center stage. For decades historians have contemplated the meaning of the difference between the Spanish and German responses to persecution, viewing it as the key to understanding the nature of these two cultures. Historians have considered the apostasy of 1412–1414 together with that of 1391, even though Spanish Jews were not facing death in the early fifteenth century, because in both cases the Jews seem to have gone more or less willingly to the baptismal font.[30] Thus the subject for discussion has been the apparent erosion of faith in Spain, and scholars have sought to isolate features of Hispano-Jewish life that distinguish it from that of Franco-German Jewry, which supposedly weathered the paradigmatic crisis of 1096 in heroic fashion.

The most comprehensive effort to explain Spanish apostasy is a letter composed by Joshua ha-Lorki, a Jewish scholar, to Rabbi Solomon Halevi, a friend who apostatized in 1391 and assumed the name Paul of Burgos.[31] Ha-Lorki posits four possible motives for Halevi's apostasy, and these might be applied to the apostasies of 1391 and 1412–1414. The four motives can be reduced to opportunity, philosophy, history, and conviction.[32] Opportunity primarily refers to the prospect of socioeconomic gain, although ha-Lorki includes under this rubric the desire to have sex with Christian women. Philosophy does not connote a particular set of postulates so much as a skepticism caused by the study of philosophy. History, the third motive, means a demoralization brought on by the belief that persecution and exile will always characterize the Jewish national experience. The following lines from a poem composed in Spain in the early fifteenth century starkly illustrate this theme:

> The length of exile has exhausted us,
> such that we scarcely seek the mystery of your Name,
> but rather despair of hoping for sealed Ends.[33]

The history motive seems like a subset of the final one, conviction— that is, genuine religious conversion, such as that of Paul or Augustine. Although Jews who abandon Judaism for this reason have not become convinced of the truth of the myth of Jesus's birth and mission, their despair causes them to concede defeat and succumb to missionary propaganda.

Ha-Lorki's taxonomy fits into the classification of apostasy proposed earlier, as either venal or ideological: Opportunity is a venal motive, and history and conviction are ideological motives. Philosophy is clearly an ideological motive, but, curiously, in the case of Sepharad, it has been located on the boundary between the venal and ideological motives. Ha-Lorki links philosophy to opportunity when he suggests that a person's outlook can serve to justify a lifestyle of self-gratification.

Yitzhak Baer's sweeping interpretation of Spanish-Jewish history offers a similar mesh of venal and ideological motives. Baer claims that philosophy, which he calls "Averroism," served as an ideological platform for the hedonistic lifestyle allegedly led by the Jewish upper class, which supposedly involved widespread neglect of the commandments. According to Baer, the combination of Averroism and deviant behavior undermined the commitment of the upper class such that, under pressure to accept baptism, they capitulated. According to this explanation, the less affluent and cultured Jews simply emulated their leaders.[34]

Some have criticized Baer's interpretation, but his view continues to permeate studies of Ashkenazic and Sephardic history. The following examination of the thought and behavior of Spanish Jewry facilitates a critical evaluation of Baer's thesis. My argument is that the Jewish societies of Spain and Franco-Germany were both more alike and more different from one another than the historiographical record has shown. In previous chapters I have criticized the view that the martyrdom of 1096 reflects a society of saints, and in the following study I question the consensus that the apostasies of 1391 and 1412–1414 reflect a society corroded by Averroism and nonhalakhic behavior.

Averroism

Long after most of Spain passed from Muslim to Christian hands, Iberian Jewry maintained cultural links with the heritage of al-Andalus. The continued use of Arabic is one indication. As late as the mid-fourteenth century, Isaac Israeli, a rabbi of Toledo, wrote his works in Arabic, for which there was surely an audience.[35] The story of the translation into Hebrew of Maimonides' Mishnah commentary also illustrates this point. In 1296 an emissary from Rome named Simhah appeared before Solomon ibn Adret, Barcelona's preeminent rabbinic scholar, and asked for a Hebrew translation of the commentary, or at least for a copy of the Arabic original. Ibn Adret replied that local Jews did not know Arabic but that the Jews of Aragon might be able to help. The Roman found the commentary's various sections in Huesca and Saragossa and arranged for their translation. His search illuminates the continued presence of Arabic in most of Christian Spain, except perhaps for Catalonia.[36]

Baer's concept of Averroism alludes to the view of Ibn Rushd or Averroes, the twelfth-century Arab philosopher, that all true religions must be identical in doctrine, because truth is universal, and therefore that differences in religious ritual are insignificant.[37] This attitude attaches the greatest value to the intellectual quest for metaphysical truth, and it implicitly devalues the notion of precepts.[38] Baer maintains that the intellectualist bias is accompanied by an extreme Aristotelian position, such as the one expressed by the philosopher at the beginning of Judah Halevi's *Kuzari*: a belief in the absolute validity of natural law and consequently the denial of divine providence at the personal and national levels and hence also of reward and punishment.[39]

Baer draws support for his interpretation from Solomon Alami, a contemporary of ha-Lorki. In his *Ethical Epistle*, Alami attributes the misfortunes of his age to the shortcomings of Spanish Jewry, upon which he proceeds to elaborate. Alami lambastes those Torah scholars who seek to merge religion and philosophy, particularly for valuing speculation above proper action. In Alami's view, this preference for the pursuit of intellectual perfection over performance of the precepts ultimately led his countrymen to prefer apostasy to martyrdom.[40]

Shemtov ibn Shemtov also blames the downfall of Spanish Jewry on the philosophers' emphasis on intellection rather than action. Shemtov identifies the philosophers' denial of divine providence and reward and punishment as the context for their willingness to dispense with religious observance. Another important component of the Averroism thesis found in Shemtov's presentation is the notion that the better educated and more sophisticated members of Spanish Jewish society can be held responsible for the destruction of the simple folk, because the latter supposedly aped their betters.[41]

As the term *Averroism* suggests, the notion that a philosophical orientation weakens one's religious commitment dates back to the Middle

Ages and specifically to the ambient of medieval Islam. Here the Jews faced religious persecution in the twelfth century, at the hands of the Almohads, who rejected the traditional toleration of Jews and Christians in Islamic society. Faced with the alternatives of death or conversion, the Jews of Muslim Spain capitulated in droves.[42] Some twenty years later Maimonides penned his *Epistle on Martyrdom* for the benefit of Moroccan Jews who apostatized in a similar crisis. Maimonides mitigates their choice on the grounds that they were coerced but also counsels them to leave areas of persecution at the earliest opportunity, even at the cost of parting from family and property.[43]

No Averroist argument, effacing the practical differences between the monotheist faiths, appears in Maimonides' *Epistle on Martyrdom*, and there is no knowing what role, if any, the respect widely accorded philosophy in the Muslim world played in the mass apostasy of the twelfth century or in Maimonides' attitude thereto. What the Islamic ambient probably did contribute to Hispano-Jewish culture is the notion of *takiyya*, meaning prudence and dissimulation: Believers faced with the choice of apostasy or death ought to feign conversion while clinging to the true faith in their hearts until a return to the free practice of Islam becomes possible.[44] The collapse of Spanish Jewry during the great crises of 1391 and 1412–1414, and particularly the crypto-Judaism that ensued, lead one to suppose that the notion of *takiyya* held meaning for Spain's Jews even after centuries of life in a Christian environment. Although the concept of *takiyya* is theological rather than philosophical, it seems to dovetail with an Averroist view of religion. In any case, it may partly explain the Sephardic choice of apostasy over martyrdom.[45]

Shortly after the publication of Baer's monograph on the Jews of Christian Spain, Isaiah Sonne devoted an essay to a thoroughgoing critique not only of Baer's interpretation of the fate of Spanish Jewry but also of Baer's fundamental view of Jewish history.[46] Baer, he explains, sees Greco-Roman civilization and its European heir as rationalistic and Judaism as mystical. Sonne rejects this dichotomy, because "intuition and rational thinking form the rhythmical pulsation of the human spirit and are merely two facets of one and the same process."[47] Perforce both mental attitudes can be found in any person and in any civilization.[48] Although the association of Sepharad with rationalism and Ashkenaz with mysticism seems reasonable, Sonne insists that the universality of both tendencies precludes the labeling of Ashkenazic culture as authentically Jewish and the stigmatization of Sephardic Judaism as adulterated.[49] This is also why Sonne rejects Baer's preference for Ashkenazic over Sephardic Jewry, specifically Baer's thesis "that they alone remained loyal to the destiny and mission of the Jewish people, while the Spanish Jews were going adrift."[50]

Sonne's is the only frontal assault on Baer's entire historiosophical edifice, but there are also other grounds for doubting that Averroism, or philosophy in general, explains the apostasy waves of 1391 and 1412–1414.[51] A basic problem is the absence of writings that testify to the kind of thinking described as Averroistic; there are no self-styled Averroists, and it has not been possible to identify any Spanish-Jewish intellectuals as such.[52] A more general suspicion of the deleterious effect of philosophy on religious belief dates back to the Maimonidean controversy of 1230–1232 and 1303–1306, when the charge serves as a whipping boy in the hands of the traditionalist camp. Predictably, leaders of the rationalist camp, such as Jacob ben Makhir of Montpellier and Yedaiah ha-Penini of Béziers, trumpet the orthodoxy of their ancestors, who were schooled—they hasten to point out—in the standard philosophical curriculum.[53] Obviously the rationalist and traditionalist camps were grinding their respective axes, and the methodological point is that condemnations of philosophy were always partisan and hence tainted and unreliable testimony. The substantive point is that then it was also impossible to identify figures or works that embody or substantiate the charges against philosophy.[54]

Maligning philosophy also served the agenda of kabbalists eager to supplant the theological and ethical doctrines of Aristotelian and even Neoplatonic philosophy with their own. Shemtov ibn Shemtov, who gives perhaps the clearest formulation of the Averroism thesis, does so in the introduction to a book devoted to the merits of kabbalah.[55] This theme has a long history and is not strictly related to the crisis of the late fourteenth and early fifteenth centuries. In the early thirteenth century, Jacob ben Sheshet Gerondi blasts the devotees of philosophy for a lack of true religious feeling,[56] a sentiment echoed by Meir ibn Gabbai 300 years later.[57] The advantage to proponents of kabbalah from slurs cast against the devotion of philosophy's initiates vitiates in some measure the truth claim of such comments.

Ironically, there are grounds for thinking that kabbalah, rather than philosophy, undermined the faith and commitment of the educated elite and laid the groundwork for their apostasy. This is noticeable in the writings of several apostate intellectuals, primarily Abner of Burgos, a fourteenth-century kabbalist and apostate.[58] In addition, the sermons of Vicente Ferrer, who preached throughout Aragon and Castile in 1411–1412, suggest that at least some of the renegades were tempted by a fideistic spirit and an ascetic-pietistic way of life rather than by a rationalist posture and creed.[59] Although there is no way of gauging the impact of this mind-set on Spanish Jewry and hence on the apostasies of 1391 and 1412–1414, it serves as a stimulating corrective to the Averroism theory.[60]

The Averroism thesis also rests on questionable assumptions. Supposedly the vast majority of the apostates, who were simple folk, abandoned Judaism under the influence of their sophisticated and worldly leadership, namely, the aristocratic courtiers. This dynamic is assumed rather than proven: There is no evidence that the elite of Spanish Jewish society paraded their mores and worldview for the edification of the rank and file or that they exhorted the rank and file to adopt a lifestyle of diluted faith and observance.[61] Neither is it plausible that the behavior of the rich and powerful would motivate large numbers of people to make a life-altering decision affecting their family and progeny. However demoralizing the apostasy of rabbis and communal leaders may have been, it does not stand to reason that this was a significant factor in the mass apostasy of Spanish Jewry.

Another criticism is that the writings of the Spanish exiles in the sixteenth century fail to substantiate the argument that philosophy was a major factor in the spiritual collapse of Sepharad. This literature depicts the problem of history as more destructive than philosophy. Supposedly, the depressed political status of the Jews in exile and the humble nature of their form of religious worship contrasted poorly with the opulence of Christians and Christianity, demoralizing the Jews and leading them to apostatize. Moreover, the exiles' writings do not damn the courtiers as traitors to their people and their faith; on the contrary, they portray them as heroes for their efforts at court on behalf of the Jewish community.[62]

The record of Provençal Jewry also offers a challenge to the Averroism thesis. The Jews of southern France embrace religious philosophy with enthusiasm in the twelfth century, when it is made available to them in Hebrew by Spanish Jewish thinkers and translators, and yet they do not fit the Spanish model that pairs rationalism with an aristocratic class and lifestyle. Thus Isadore Twersky writes, "Provence had no entrenched courtier class and yet became the seat of rationalism."[63]

Finally, the Averroism thesis links the pernicious effect of philosophy to the ethical and religious conduct of Spain's Jews, but this argument is problematic on theoretical grounds. Even if we assume that the religious life of the proponents of philosophy was mechanical or even empty, one cannot assume that they would embrace Christianity in a time of crisis.

There are, however, grounds for positing a link between the intellectual and social life of the Hispano-Jewish elite, namely, the courtiers and aristocrats. Judah ben Asher and Menahem ben Zerah, who critique their society in the mid-fourteenth century, report that there are Jews who deny divine providence, miracles, and reward and punishment; unbelievers such as these are found among the wealthy and powerful elite, although not exclusively so. Yet this is not, strictly speaking, Averroism; these writers view astrology as a threat to proper belief, because of its implicit determinism.[64]

Astrology was popular with the courtier class in the heyday of the Andalusian era; like history, astrology offered a practical tool for political decision making, and Maimonides noted the danger latent in its implicit determinism.[65] Astrology was just as useful to fourteenth-century courtiers and even more so to scholars. The following lines from *Honor the Poets!* a poem by Samuel ibn Sasson, ben Zerah's compatriot and contemporary, illustrate astrology's popularity in the poet's milieu:

> Why do the stars in the heavens persecute the poets on earth,
> always causing them turbulence and exposing them to the accidents,
> to the point that I think to myself: Are they all focusing entirely upon
> them?
> Perhaps the heavenly host and stars above collectively take an oath

to bring them low.
Were it the will of the Lord of the world,
the wheel of heaven and its hosts would return to their aid.[66]

The popularity of astrology is also reflected in the scholarly literature of the time. *Minhat Qena'ot*, by Abner of Burgos, champions astrological determinism, and Abner's erstwhile colleague, Isaac Polgar, castigates him for denying free will.[67] The mid-fourteenth century saw the publication of Joseph ibn Wakkar of Toledo's harmonization of philosophy, kabbalah, and astrology as well as several supercommentaries on the biblical exegesis of Abraham ibn Ezra with an emphasis on astrology.[68]

Belles lettres also reflects the popularity of astrology and determinism. We find it in the *Tale of Efer and Dinah*, by Vidal Benveniste of Toledo, one of the most important works of Hebrew literature written in late-fourteenth-century Spain.[69] Efer is a wealthy old lecher who pursues the fair but poor Dinah. She finds Efer repulsive, but her father sees Efer's offer of marriage as the route to financial security, for himself as well as for her, and she agrees to the match. However, Efer is unable to fulfill his connubial obligation, which was a condition for the marriage. Fearing the embarrassment he would suffer when the reason for his divorce became public knowledge, Efer drinks an aphrodisiac to improve his virility but overdoses and dies.

The tale is presented as an allegory, instructing readers to subordinate their conduct to the dictates of wisdom rather than direct their lives toward the quest for riches and pleasure.[70] Matti Huss also detects a subtle emphasis by Benveniste on the belief in astrological influence on human existence, which Efer and Dinah's father express in terms of a radically deterministic view of life. In Huss's interpretation, Benveniste criticizes rich and poor alike for their belief that material success is a sign of divine approval.[71]

Here we find a link between courtiers (or affluent individuals, generally), philosophy (i.e., astrology, a branch of medieval science), and flabby religious observance, for determinism is seen not only in Benveniste's tale but also in numerous other works as a theoretical platform for nonobservance: If one's fate is predetermined by the stars, what point is there in punctilious observance of the commandments or in moral behavior generally? This line of thought would enable sophisticated aristocrats to justify their lapses and perhaps ultimately their apostasy. Astrological determinism would also appeal to simple folk, who could find in it an explanation for their life of toil and misery. This, then, is a philosophical framework that could explain the apostasy of Spanish Jews of all socioeconomic strata. Finally, the belief in astrological determinism accords with the notion that Iberian Jewry was demoralized by the argument from history, for it supplies an explanation for the travails of the Jewish people and the success of their enemies.

Deviance

Is the reputation of Spanish Jewry for lax halakhic behavior justified? "There were," acknowledges Haym Soloveitchik, "murderers, lechers, apostates, informers, thieves, Sabbath violators in Ashkenaz no less than in Sepharad,"[72] thereby emphasizing the contrast between the images of Ashkenaz and Sepharad. But the actual record of Hispano-Jewish behavior needs to be assessed in its own right. Were the Jews of Spain truly less devout than their northern European brethren?

The argument that Sephardic Jews strayed from the course of proper religious behavior has focused on sexual mores. Yom Tov Assis writes that Spanish Jewry "found itself characterized by sexual laxity unknown elsewhere in mediaeval Jewry."[73] Assis also claims that "adultery in Hispano-Jewish society was more frequent than elsewhere in the mediaeval Jewish world" and that "the fact that it occurred among Spanish Jews with such frequency reflected widespread sexual laxity."[74] Testing these hypotheses would require analytical tools capable of taking into account numerous factors, including the demographics of the communities being compared, the cultural differences between them, and the nature of the available documentation. No discussion of this level of sophistication has been attempted as yet, nor has the methodological difficulty of coping with any of these issues been addressed.

The reputation of rampant malfeasance is but an impression, albeit one based on a variety of sources, such as the poems of Todros ben Judah Halevi of Toledo (1247–after 1298). Like Samuel ha-Nagid and other bards of the eleventh and twelfth centuries, Halevi wrote erotic poetry, treating themes of beauty, love, and desire, including his liaisons with non-Jewish women. The following lines, for example, express his preference for Muslim, rather than Christian, women:

> The love of a maiden is no sin, and the desire of lad for maid is no evil,
> but it is right to desire the daughters of Arabs, even if she is not pretty and pure,
> and to distance oneself greatly from any Edomite girl, though she be radiant as the sun.[75]

Todros often writes in the first person, and so his poems have an auto-biographical flavor. This has made them seem to be particularly valuable testimony about courtier life, even though Todros operated within the accepted genres of Andalusian verse and used the accepted poetic conventions.

Vidal Benveniste's *Tale of Efer and Dinah* is another literary source that seems to reinforce the impression of Spanish Jewish courtiers as unbridled hedonists, and it was written close to 1391. Efer is the quintessential hedonist: "'Eat and drink!' he will tell you, and he pursued useless goals. Of morality he would hear nothing, and he did not fear God."[76] Thus we have Benveniste, a courtier-poet, writing a licentious tale for a sophisticated audience, who could be expected either to read the tale as pornographic entertainment or as a didactic mechanism for the propagation of a philosophical ethos.

How useful such literary sources are as reflections of social norms is uncertain. The patrons and audience of secular prose and poetry were the relatively wealthy and worldly Jews in Spanish society, who hob-nobbed with high-born and powerful Christians and wielded political, economic, and social influence beyond the confines of the Jewish community. In this regard, too, not much had changed since the period of Samuel ibn Nagrela, when power, pleasure, and poetry came together in a courtier class and culture. Nor is this persistence entirely odd, for as Spain passed from Muslim to Christian control, the new rulers largely retained the existing political and financial administrative structures, in which the Jews had been and remained a real presence. The Jewish officials thus continued to form a Jewish aristocracy, with social and cultural features akin to those of their Andalusian forebears.

The pleasures celebrated in the poetry of the courtier class in both Muslim and Christian Spain led modern scholars to associate the Jewish aristocrats with a lifestyle and ethos of hedonism, which appeared to them to conflict with the moral and religious code of rabbinic Judaism. Because the Andalusian poets included men whose orthodoxy seemed unimpeachable, such as the Nagid, Solomon ibn Gabirol, or Judah Halevi, scholars have debated whether the poetry ought to be understood literally or viewed as merely a literary exercise or convention.[77] However, no such debate has taken place over the reality of hedonism among the Jewish courtier class of Christian Spain, because medieval sources explicitly tag the Jewish upper class as hedonistic, as indeed ha-Lorki does in his letter. But how hedonistic the poets and their audience actually were in the late Middle Ages is a difficult question to answer; the Sephardic poets of this period were consciously aping the Andalusian masters of yesteryear, in genre and technique. There is therefore even more reason for skepticism about the social reality of their erotic verse than of the poems of Moses ibn Ezra and the like.

The argument that Sephardic Jews strayed from the course of proper religious behavior has also been partly based on evidence of promiscuity: documents attesting to the existence of Jewish prostitutes in Toledo and Saragossa and a responsum by Solomon ibn Adret, the country's foremost halakhic authority in the late thirteenth century, attesting that in Toledo a Jewish man fathered a child out of wedlock. There are also texts about cases of sexual relations between Jewish men and Christian women.[78] Joshua ibn Shu'eib of fourteenth-century Tudela also has harsh words to say about the "Zimris" in his community, who have intercourse with gentile women.[79]

The case based on this evidence is weak on methodological grounds. Prostitution generally reflects economic distress rather than a dearth of religious commitment. Lawsuits such as those brought before Ibn Adret happen in every Jewish society, and conclusions cannot be drawn from the occasional case about the moral fiber of a society. Sex between Jews and Christians is an early and perennial obsession with the Catholic Church, and in Spain as elsewhere prohibitions on relations were honored primarily in the breach.[80] And there are no clear criteria for determining whether Ibn Shu'eib's comment ought to be classified as timeless homily or pressing indictment, for he addresses this issue on the Saturday when the story of the biblical Zimri is read in the synagogue.

The taking of concubines, a common practice among the Jews of Christian Spain, is also cited as evidence of sexual promiscuity and ergo of moral and religious bankruptcy.[81] Usually the concubines were Muslims, because liaisons with Christians were forbidden, and Moses of Coucy, a French rabbi who toured Spain and looked askance at this practice, reports, "I preached at length to the Jewish communities of Spain and they removed many alien women in 996 [1236]."[82] The rabbi of Coucy may not have known that concubinage was acceptable in Islamic society and thus was part of Spain's Andalusian heritage and is no indication of licentiousness.[83] Furthermore, Menahem ben Zerah, whose critique of concubinage is a well-known source of information about this practice, does not criticize the institution per se; he objects to the practice of reciting a marriage formula to a concubine without writing a marriage contract for her. Thus his concern is for the concubine's legal and financial status, and nowhere does he equate concubinage with lechery and moral decline.[84]

Ben Zerah catalogues Spain's courtier class for a wide variety of shortcomings, apart from illicit sexual activity. We read that members of the upper class are less than punctilious in their fulfillment of the commandments: "They completely abandon the laws of prayer, blessings, permitted and prohibited food, Sabbath and festivals, laws concerning women and laws of wines."[85] But ben Zerah attributes their neglect to a desire for power and luxury rather than to an Averroist ideology, and indeed the link is neither inherent nor necessary.[86] What is more, we have seen criticism of lax observance among the Jews of medieval Ashkenaz also, and it is a commonplace of Jewish life in any place and time.

The courtier culture of Sephardic Jewry could hardly have been a necessary condition for improprieties of this nature, and there is no reason to assume that illicit trysts or relationships were characteristic of Sephardic Jewry in particular or specific to a certain juncture in Jewish history. Moreover, sexual misconduct is among the most common themes in *Sefer Hasidim* and the penitential literature of the German pietists.[87] The connection between sexual behavior and religion also makes no sense; there is no reason to attribute sexual infractions to an enfeebled commitment to the Jewish faith.

Nor are courtiers the only type of Spanish Jew to be censured for lax religious observance. Ibn Shu'eib divides Spanish Jewish society into four groups, based on their excellence in either Torah study or punctilious observance. "Corner sitters" (*yoshevei qeranot*) and "scoffers" (*letzim*) bear the brunt of his critique, as he applies to them the rebuke of simpletons, scoffers, and dullards found in the first chapter of Proverbs.[88] The term *corner sitters* is of talmudic rather than medieval origin and was understood to refer to simple, ignorant people who fritter away their time in idle chatter.[89] Elsewhere Ibn Shu'eib links corner sitters more closely with scoffers than with ignoramuses and describes both groups as neglectful of religious precepts and Torah study.[90]

Corner sitters are also criticized by Judah ben Asher, Ibn Shu'eib's contemporary and ben Zerah's teacher, who describes them as engaged in girl watching and scornful behavior (*divrei letzanut*).[91] In his ethical will Judah ben Asher warns his sons to avoid scoffers, but he does not seem to take scoffing too seriously, for he describes it as frivolous and, by implication, harmless rather than as heretical and dangerous.[92] Broadening the social critique to include corner sitters and scoffers as well as courtiers undercuts the Averroism thesis, because the idea that the upper class led the rank and file to the baptismal font becomes dispensable. It also becomes unnecessary to prove that particular elements in Spanish Jewish society were more inclined toward either martyrdom or baptism in 1391 and 1412–1414, an assertion not supported by the sources of those dark days.[93]

Judah ben Asher and Menahem ben Zerah also speak out against other vices found among the commoners and not especially among the community's more powerful constituents. Excessive swearing is a prominent fault; ben Zerah dryly comments, "If reprovers were to reprove them, they would swear that they do not swear!"[94] Improper synagogue behavior is another social ill; worshippers gossip and talk business when they should be praying.[95] More generally, ben Zerah observes that people perform their religious obligations in a perfunctory manner: "Even men of deeds [i.e., scrupulous observance] are unaware of what they do and why they do it, and this is even characteristic of very learned people."[96] Judah ben Asher catalogues other reprehensible activities as well: Jews use non-Jews to perform illegal acts on the Sabbath, and on festivals Jewish women are seen buying vegetables in the market. Cheating non-Jews and the use of weights by shopkeepers are also condemned practices. Judah ben Asher does not mention concubines, but he protests against the norm of conducting sexual relations with (Moorish) servant girls.[97]

Solomon Alami's *Ethical Epistle* also depicts a range of social ills. He complains that rabbis devote themselves exclusively to Talmud study, piling new laws one on another while ignoring the Torah's humble righteousness, saintliness, and holiness. Talmudists are castigated for disagreeing among themselves, which detracts from the honor of the Torah in the eyes of the public. Courtiers come in for criticism of their opulent lifestyle and for their alienation from their more humble brethren. Alami rails at congregants for dozing off during the preacher's oration and for their parsimony with alms.[98]

These failings can be found in practically any Jewish society, modern as well as medieval, including medieval France and Germany. We have already seen sources about the spotty performance of Ashkenazic Jewry, and the complaint of perfunctory, mechanical observance is precisely the sort of problem to attract the attention of the German pietists. *Sefer Hasidim* also shares the moralists' concern about sexual offenses, although these sources are unreliable indicators of what sorts of illicit behavior were actually practiced or how common they were.

Alami's epistle is also a problematic source because it is a treatise of ethical exhortation rather than a work of social history. Faultfinding is the stock-in-trade of preachers and homileticists, and human nature being what it is, one cannot stray far from the mark by castigating listeners or readers for being fond of power, honor, and creature comforts (including, and perhaps especially, forbidden women) and for cavalier religious observance and a dearth of spiritual feeling. Such sentiments are likely to hit home regardless of the audience's actual level of piety, and it becomes difficult to distinguish trenchant critique from trope.

The generic problem is equally evident in the social criticism voiced in the sermons of Ibn Shu'eib. Ibn Shu'eib expands on the dangers posed by the human hunger for physical pleasures, power, and honor. This passage is an elaboration on the statement in the Mishnah that "three things remove a person from this world—jealousy, lust, and honor," and one cannot be sure that it also describes real social ills.[99] Preachers of any age complain about their listeners' religious and moral shortcomings, and this becomes a topos, which perforce teaches us little about the social and spiritual conditions of the day.[100] In Spain, too, critical remarks about Jewish society were penned long before the catastrophe of 1391, and the writers of these texts tick off a fairly standard set of social and spiritual ills, without foregrounding philosophy.

Three Revisions

Of the various comparisons between medieval Ashkenaz and Sepharad, two studies view eschatology, along with martyrdom and apostasy, as a key to understanding the difference between the two societies and cultures. Gerson D. Cohen contrasts the responses of Franco-German and Spanish Jewry to crisis situations and, like Yitzhak Baer, sees philosophy as the differentiating factor. Cohen maintains that the Jews of Ashkenaz opted for martyrdom in 1096 because they believed absolutely in the divine vindication of their sacrifice at the End of Days. According to Cohen, however, the Jews of Spain, or of the Islamic realm generally, saw the world through the lens of Greek philosophy, and this prevented them from believing fully in divine reward and punishment. This was partly the result of an Averroist skepticism, but it also stemmed from the idea that salvation depends on intellectual achievement and is not guaranteed to everyone. The intellectualist flavor of philosophical culture also underlies crypto-Judaism, which posits that God evaluates conviction, not behavior. This attitude dovetails nicely with the Islamic concept of *takiyya*.

Cohen also embraces Baer's dichotomy between Ashkenaz and Sepharad, with Ashkenaz portrayed as authentic and Sepharad as sullied: "Quiescence and martyrdom sprang from a classical faith untroubled by rationalist doubts or scholastic distinctions between the intentions of the heart and the utterances of the lips."[101] Although this dichotomy is doubtful, as will be shown, Cohen identifies a cultural distinction between the Jews of Spain and the Jews of Franco-Germany that does ring true. He notes that messianic pretenders and movements arose in the Islamic realm but not in Latin Europe. Cohen explains that because the Jews of Islam played a role in government, they viewed redemption through the lens of political realism and therefore had an activist conception of the messianic scenario. In Christendom, however, and specifically in Ashkenaz, the Jews were not involved in political affairs, and so they had a mythical image of the End of Days and adopted a passive attitude toward messianism, which was largely limited to prognostication.

The dichotomy between political activism and passivity offers a novel explanation of the divergent responses to the threat of death in 1096 and 1391. The Jews of the Rhineland were not demoralized by the crusader threat, because they viewed major political developments as miraculously orchestrated by God from on high. Spain's Jews crumbled because they attached great importance to the role of human agency in history as a result of their historic involvement in political life. Thus the German Jew was primed to see the crusader threat as a *gezerah*, a divine decree, whereas the Spanish Jew focused on the plane of human activity: on the unbridled power of his all too mortal enemies and his own inability to prevail. By implication, philosophy is irrelevant to Cohen's question; if the courtiers played a crucial role, it was by virtue of the political culture they created rather than their intellectual life.

A weakness in this interpretation, and in Cohen's argument, is the assumption that martyrdom and apostasy represent active and passive responses, respectively. This is not always the case; whether one performs an action with an active or a passive attitude is a psychological and hence a subjective question. This point is made by Elisheva Carlebach, who also questions the exclusive association of martyrdom with Ashkenaz and apostasy with Spain: "Martyrdom was never alien to the Sephardic world, nor messianism to the Ashkenazic."[102]

The combined analysis of attitudes to redemption and martyrdom in Ashkenaz and Sepharad is also a primary theme in a study by Israel Yuval. Yuval breaks down traditional Jewish eschatology into two elements—vengeance and proselytization: At the End of Days God will avenge the suffering and death wrought on the Jewish people by its gentile enemies throughout history by killing them, and the nations of the world will recognize the error of their ways and turn to the worship of God.

Both elements are solidly grounded in talmudic and midrashic literature, but Yuval maintains that the Jews of Germany focused on the theme of divine vengeance, especially because they identified the Reich with Edom, the archenemy of the Jewish people in midrashic tradition.[103] Yuval sees this redemptive vision as responsible for the mass martyrdom of 1096, because the Jews of the Rhineland believed that the eschatological scenario would not commence until a predetermined amount of Jewish blood had been spilled; they therefore hoped that the sacrifice of their loved ones and themselves would precipitate the finale of human history, the destruction of Edom by God.

The proselytization theme, in Yuval's scheme, was characteristic of Hispano-Jewish theology, the Jews of Spain having inherited the religious tenets of al-Andalus and of the Jews of Islam generally.[104] The conversion of the non-Jews is a tame event compared with the cataclysmic scenario envisioned by the bloodthirsty Jews of Ashkenaz. Yuval's thesis does not explain the apostasy of Spain, but it explains why German and Spanish behavior differed so radically, by highlighting the eschatological significance of martyrdom peculiar to the German-Jewish belief system.

Yuval's rich and thought-provoking interpretation of Ashkenazic martyrdom and eschatology met with a barrage of criticism. A fundamental problem with his argument is that there is no evidence that the Jews of Worms, Mainz, and the other communities killed each other and themselves in order to trigger the vengeance component of the eschatological scenario.[105] Yuval's dichotomy between Ashkenaz and Sepharad has also been challenged, because both strands of Jewish eschatology, vengeance and conversion, can be found in the literature of both centers.[106] By extension, the suggestion that martyrdom came easily to German Jews, because they were obsessed with divine vengeance, but not to those of Spain, whose more civilized version of history's denouement involved the gentiles' ultimate enlightenment and conversion, is untenable.

The dichotomy between Ashkenazic martyrdom and Spanish apostasy is the target of Ram Ben-Shalom's study of martyrdom in 1391.[107] Ben-Shalom suggests that there were more martyrs in 1391 than has been recognized heretofore. He produces no new sources or figures but supports Haim Beinart's estimate that about one-third of Spanish Jewry was martyred in 1391, one-third apostatized, and one-third survived.[108] More compelling is his assertion that martyrdom was a central feature in Spanish Jewry's shared memory of the 1391 crisis.[109] Lest one maintain that Spanish expressions of the martyrological ethos reflect the cultural impact of the martyrdom of the First Crusade in Ashkenaz, Ben-Shalom demonstrates that it was a long-standing religious value among the Jews of Spain. He locates it, inter alia, in the poetry of Todros Halevi, and this blunts the argument that the fidelity to Judaism of Spain's Jewish aristocrats was crippled by their hedonistic lifestyle.[110]

Ben-Shalom's contribution creates a greater problem than it solves. Portrayals of the violence of 1391 ought perhaps to pay more attention to the martyrdom component, but this would not correct the image of Spanish Jewry as spiritually bankrupt; it would only defer the question to the next phase, namely, the large-scale apostasy that followed the Tortosa disputation and Castile legislation. The resultant scenario would be truly bizarre: We would now be expected to believe that the Jews of Spain were faithful unto death in 1391, only to collapse a generation later from the combined force of missionary exhortation, anti-Jewish polemic, and discriminatory legislation. Instead of puzzling over the response of 1391, we would have to explain a sudden nosedive in Hispano-Jewish religiosity in the generation or two separating the two crises.

Conclusion

Central to Ben-Shalom's thesis is the assertion that martyrology and patterns of response to threat were not all that different in Spain and Ashkenaz. He highlights studies that question the proportion of martyrs to apostates in the persecutions of the First Crusade as indicative of an analogous revisionist current in the study of medieval Ashkenaz. Ben-Shalom also notes my argument that, unlike in Spain, by and large the victims of the First Crusade were not offered a choice between death and baptism, and he embraces the conclusion that the Rhineland victims cannot be considered to have exhibited greater religious fidelity and heroism than their Spanish brethren.[111]

Ben-Shalom's argument in favor of a nobler image of Sepharad complements the image of Franco-German Jewry proposed in the present study. His portrait of the martyrological ethos as universal rather than particularly Ashkenazic sits well with the efforts made here and elsewhere to pay greater attention to apostasy in France and Germany, in daily life as well as in the First Crusade. In like fashion, my discussion of deviant behavior in Ashkenaz attenuates the contrast with the prevalent image of Spanish Jewry as lax in religious observance, and we have also seen that the social and cultural divide separating Jews from Christians in northern Europe was not nearly as wide as the stereotype of Ashkenaz would lead us to believe. In these respects the present exploration of Sephardic Jewry's response to the crises of 1391 and 1412–1414 and of the relevant historiography goes some way toward narrowing the gap between the regnant portrayals of the two centers. The result is at once a more pious and faithful Sepharad and a more human and less glorified Ashkenaz.

At the same time, it is important to note the enormous differences between the two societies and cultures, differences that complicate comparisons between their historical experiences. For one thing, the demographic structures of the communities of northern Europe and the Iberian peninsula differed widely. The urban centers of Spain had thousands or tens of thousands of Jewish inhabitants, as the data on 1391 illustrate, whereas those of France and Germany numbered in the dozens or hundreds. As a result, the French and German communities were far more intimate, with people knowing each other relatively well and inevitably exerting pressure on one another to conform to social and religious norms. Under the extraordinary circumstances of the First Crusade, this intimacy made it difficult for those closeted together in the palaces of Worms and Mainz to reject the martyrdom option.[112]

Intimacy also has implications for the issue of deviant behavior. Enforcing halakhic norms and communal legislation is more difficult in large societies than in small ones, because there is greater room for anonymity and alienation. Hence for infractions to appear in Aragon and Castile in larger volume than in the Rhineland and northern France is to be expected; on the contrary, the surprise is that deviant behavior is as robust in Ashkenaz as the evidence seems to indicate.[113]

Another significant demographic difference between the two diasporas is that in the north the Jews were the only religious minority, whereas in Spain there was also a minority of Moors. Other factors aside, this exclusivity would have made the Jew seem more alien to the average Christian in the Rhineland than he did to his Christian neighbor in the Iberian peninsula. The opposite is also true; the Sephardic Jew would have held a more pluralistic conception of European society than that of his northern confreres.

The social and economic structures of Ashkenazic and Sephardic Jewry were also distinct. Spanish Jewry inherited the Andalusian hierarchical model, with the Jewish community led by courtiers who held government positions and enjoyed political power. And the courtiers were numerous, making up an entire stratum of Spanish society. Ultimately, their number dictated their fate, for when these Jews opted for conversion in 1391 and 1412–1414, it proved difficult to integrate them into Spanish society because they were too numerous.[114] This led to the religious problem of crypto-Judaism, which was ultimately addressed by the Inquisition and the Expulsion.

None of this is relevant to the Jews of Franco-Germany, who had no courtier class, or for that matter any clear class structure. The society of the Rhineland communities was remarkably homogeneous, except for their founding families, who enjoyed an added measure of prestige. The absence of social stratification reflects the Ashkenazic communities' economic uniformity as well as their diminutive size. Although the Jews of Spain pursued a wide variety of occupations, those of northern Europe engaged almost exclusively in commerce and money lending, with Christians as clients. Some Jews must have been more successful than others, but the Jews of Franco-Germany as a whole had no stable class structure of affluent, middle class, and poor. The socioeconomic diversity of Sepharad and homogeneity of Ashkenaz must have shaped the attitudes of their respective constituencies toward the communal leadership and toward their sense of Jewish identity and solidarity, and this must have affected their resilience in times of stress.

Socioeconomic structure was particularly fateful for the Jews of Spain, because the riots of 1391, although they took the form of religious hostility, were also part of a broad social and political conflict in which the Jews played a major role by virtue of their unique relationship with the monarchs of the Spanish kingdoms. The rise of European monarchies involved a protracted power struggle between kings and nobles, for the king was essentially nothing more than a relatively powerful nobleman who amassed more land and subjects than his peers. The Jew was perceived as a symbol of royal power, and reluctant subjects sometimes expressed resentment of the yoke of the king's authority in the language of anti-Jewish agitation and violence. Resentment festered not only among the nobility but also among townspeople and peasants, who envied the Jews their economic and political power and hated them for the heavy taxes and customs duties they exacted on the king's behalf. They viewed Jews as parasites who, whether as moneylenders or tax farmers, sucked the blood of god-fearing Christians and got rich at their expense and under the king's protection.

These economic, social, and political forces exploded in peasants' revolts that broke out in England, France, and Italy in the fourteenth century. By this time the Jews had already been expelled from England, and so the peasants' revolt of 1381 did not take the form of anti-Jewish persecution. They did so, however, in France, in the Shepherds' Crusade of 1320.[115]

The Jew's image as a symbol of royal authority helps us understand why antisemitic attacks often accompanied a weakening of royal authority, as in 1328, when the death of Charles I of Navarre triggered assaults on several Jewish communities.[116] Similarly, the Jews of Castile suffered violence during the civil war of 1366, when the forces of Henry of Trastamara waged an insurrection against those of King Pedro the Cruel.[117] In 1391 also, as we have seen, the pogroms followed the death of King Juan I of Castile.

That the 1391 attacks were more than a religious outburst is also plain from the response of the government of Majorca, which took strenuous measures to prevent attacks, because it feared that the riots signified a peasants' uprising.[118] This is also evident from the slogan of the commoners of Barcelona in 1391: "The fat ones wish to destroy the little people."[119] In Barcelona the assault was a lower-class rising. The rioters set free the prisoners in the deputy's prison and threatened the houses of patricians. Following the destruction of the Jewish community, measures were taken to reduce taxes, and similarly in Gerona the rioters demanded that instead of collecting tolls at the city gates, people should be taxed in proportion to their wealth.[120] Throughout the Iberian penin-

sula the Jews were seen as royal agents, and they served as a convenient
outlet for frustration with political oppression and fiscal exploitation.
This sociopolitical constellation was absent in France and Germany,
which had no stratum of Jewish officialdom, and hence the violence of
1096 and 1391 differed widely in both its sources and goals.

Efforts to compare the mind-sets of the Jews of Spain and the Jews
of Franco-Germany are also complicated by the cultural differences between the two centers. The attempt to pin Sephardic apostasy on Averroism is unsatisfying, for the reasons stated earlier, but the Judeo-Arabic
legacy of Iberian Jewry did differentiate Spanish Jewry from the Jews of
northern Europe. Scientific learning, including astrology, was not to be
found in Ashkenaz during the high Middle Ages, and this may have had
some bearing on the spiritual collapse of 1391 and 1412–1414. The Arabic
notion of *takiyya*, or caution, was also part of the heritage of al-Andalus
and thus was alien to the Jews of northern Europe. The precedent of
the Almohade invasions and the principle of *takiyya* probably made the
decision to convert and go on living easier for those in Christian Spain
than for those in France and Germany.

The Sephardic ordeal is also distinguished from the Ashkenazic one
by sheer chronology. The First Crusade was a baptism of fire for Ashkenazic Jewry, which had been enjoying economic and political prosperity
for almost two centuries, with a few, sporadic incidents of antisemitic
agitation. The Spanish crisis, however, took place hundreds of years
later, and the ensuing centuries saw relentless missionary pressure,
declining political support, and rising popular animosity, all of which
sapped the Jews' morale and conviction.

Given the different political, social, economic, intellectual, and cultural complexion of Ashkenazic and Sephardic Jewry in the Middle Ages,
sweeping comparisons between the two centers cannot be meaningful.
The record of Spanish apostasy does not throw into relief the heroism
and authenticity of Ashkenaz, and neither does the story of the First
Crusade put the victims of 1391 to shame. These findings complement
the more nuanced image of Ashkenazic society and culture offered in
this study, in which although only some were heroes, all were human.

Notes

Chapter One

1. Saadia Gaon, of tenth-century Baghdad, in his Bible commentary, identifies Ashkenaz with the Slavic lands and Riphath with "Frangia," the land of the Franks. Samuel Krauss identifies the biblical Ashkenaz with northern Asia Minor and specifically with the Khazars in "The Names Ashkenaz and Sepharad," *Tarbiz* 2 (1932), 423–430 (in Hebrew). This is disputed by Jacob Mann in "Are the Ashkenazim Khazars?!" *Tarbiz* 3 (1933), 391–394 (in Hebrew). See also Avraham Grossman, *The Early Sages of Ashkenaz: Their Lives, Leadership, and Works (900–1096)*, 3rd ed. (Jerusalem 2001), 1n1 (in Hebrew); and *Genesis Rabbah*, 2nd ed., ed. Theodor-Albeck (Jerusalem 1965), v. 1, 343–344, 37:2–3. Cf. Jeremiah 51:27 and 1 Chronicles 1:6 and the commentaries thereto. Note the use of other terms by medieval writers in reference to Germany, such as Alemania.

2. Gerson D. Cohen, *A Critical Edition with a Translation and Notes of the Book of Tradition (Sefer ha-Qabbalah) by Abraham ibn Daud* (Philadelphia 1967), 88–89. See also the esteem for Rabbenu Tam expressed by Ibn Daud's contemporary, Abraham ibn Ezra, in his exchange of poems with the Frenchman: *Kovez Hokhmat ha-RABE*, ed. David Kahana (Warsaw 1894), 80–81. See also Ben-Zion Dinur, *Israel in the Diaspora* (Tel Aviv 1968), v. 2c, 83 (in Hebrew).

3. Marcus Nathan Adler (ed., trans.), *The Itinerary of Benjamin of Tudela* (London 1907), 2–5. There were significant cultural differences between northern and southern France in the twelfth century, but from Ibn Daud's perspective, both belonged to the realm of "Edom," that is, Christendom.

4. Letter to Pinhas ha-Dayyan, cited in H. J. Zimmels, *Ashkenazim and Sephardim* (London 1958), 268. See Itzhak Shailat (ed.), *The Letters and Essays of Moses Maimonides* (Jerusalem 1995), v. 2, 446 (in Hebrew). The reference to the Europeans' thorough search of the Talmud may signify that word of the new tosafist method of Talmud study reached Maimonides, regardless of the political explanation he provides.

5. See the references in Yom Tov Lipmann Zunz, *Ha-Derashot be-Yisrael ve-hishtalshelutan ha-historit* (Jerusalem 1947), 516n41; Zimmels, *Ashkenazim and Sephardim*, 269. See also the disdain for the literary talents of Ashkenazic rabbis expressed in Isaac Abarbanel's letter to Saul ha-Kohen (Venice 1573–74, fol. 11a) in H. H. Ben-Sasson, "Exile and Redemption Through the Eyes of the Spanish Exiles," in *Yitzhak F. Baer Jubilee Volume*, ed. S. W. Baron et al. (Jerusalem 1960), 220 (in Hebrew). On the intellectual superiority of the Sephardim to all other Jewish ethnic groups, see the comment by Elijah Capsali cited by Ben-Sasson in "The Generation of the Spanish Exiles on Its Fate," *Zion* 26 (1961), 24 (in Hebrew).

6. Joseph Kimhi, *Sefer ha-Galui*, ed. H. J. Mathews (Berlin 1887), 3; Ephraim E. Urbach, *The Tosaphists: Their History, Writings, and Methods*, 4th ed. (Jerusalem 1980), v. 1, 108 (in Hebrew).

7. Judah Alharizi, *Tahkemoni*, gate 18.

8. Judah Alharizi, *The Book of Tahkemoni*, trans. David Simha Segal (London and Portland 2001), 189.

9. Moses Maimonides, *Kovetz Teshuvot ha-Rambam ve-igrotav* (Leipzig 1859), II, 28a.

10. See Judah ibn Tibbon's introduction to his translation of Jonah ibn Jannah's *Sefer ha-Riqmah*, ed. Michael Wilensky (Jerusalem 1964), v. 1, 4.

11. Ibn Ezra, "*Nedod Hesir Oni*," in his *Kovez Hokhmat ha-RABE*, 25. See Abraham Melamed, *On the Shoulders of Giants: The Debate Between Moderns and Ancients in Medieval and Renaissance Jewish Thought* (Ramat-Gan 2003), 182–187 (in Hebrew).

12. Maimonides, *Kovetz Teshuvot ha-Rambam ve-igrotav*, pt. 2, fol. 40a, cited in Zimmels, *Ashkenazim and Sephardim*, 268. The translation, however, is mine.

13. On the literalist, anthropomorphic conception of God in the lands of Edom, see also Isadore Twersky, *Rabad of Posquières: A Twelfth-Century Talmudist*, 2nd ed. (Philadelphia 1980), 282–286. Moses Taku, of thirteenth-century Germany, lambastes the efforts of rationalist thinkers to neutralize the anthropomorphic conception of God. See his *Ketav Tamim*, ed. Joseph Dan (Jerusalem 1984), vii–xxvii.

14. Commentary on Proverbs 6:3, published by Israel Schwartz in *Ha-Shahar* 2 (1871), 209.

15. On this group of texts, see Yosef Hayyim Yerushalmi, *Zakhor: Jewish History and Jewish Memory* (Seattle and London 1982), 57–75.

16. Solomon ibn Verga, *Shevet Yehudah*, ed. Azriel Shohat (Jerusalem 1947), 120, no. 49. The identity of the "great big book" is not known.

17. Ibn Verga, *Shevet Yehudah*, 71, no. 26.

18. The three-day rule also appears in Ibn Verga's story of a persecution of Rome's Jews. See Ibn Verga, *Shevet Yehudah*, 94, no. 39. It is also known from the tale of the Ten Martyrs, as well as that of Rabbi Amnon of Mainz; see Ivan G. Marcus, "Un communauté pieuse et le doute: Mourir pour la Sanctification du Nom (Qiddouch ha-Chem) en Achkenaz (Europe du Nord) et l'histoire de Rabbi Amnon de Mayence," *Annales: Histoire, sciences sociales* 49 (1994), 1031–1047; and Israel J. Yuval, "The Historian's Silence and the Writer's Imagination: R. Amnon of Mainz and Esther-Mina of Worms," *Alpayyim* 15 (1998), 132–137 (in Hebrew). The historical origins of the three-day rule may be in the charter issued by Henry IV in 1090 to the Jews of Speyer and Mainz; see Robert Chazan, *Church, State, and Jew in the Middle Ages* (New York 1980), 61.

19. Ibn Verga, *Shevet Yehudah*, 91, no. 34.

20. Ibn Verga, *Shevet Yehudah*, 92, no. 36.

21. Ibn Verga, *Shevet Yehudah*, 71, no. 27. The persecutions of 1391 are discussed in detail in Chapter 8.

22. Shohat notes that Ibn Verga refers here to an event that took place in 1236 (Ibn Verga, *Shevet Yehudah*, 223).

23. Ibn Verga, *Shevet Yehudah*, 91, no. 35.

24. Ibn Verga, *Shevet Yehudah*, 72, no. 28.

25. Ibn Verga, *Shevet Yehudah*, 120, no. 49.

26. Cf. the remarks of an anonymous sixteenth-century Spanish refugee, who equated the experiences of suffering and persecution experienced by medieval French, German, and Span-

ish Jewry: Ms. Sassoon 560, 101–103, cited in Joseph R. Hacker, "The Responses of the Exiles to the Spanish Expulsion and to the Forced Conversion in Portugal," in *Jews and Conversos at the Time of the Expulsion*, ed. Yom Tov Assis and Yosef Kaplan (Jerusalem 1999), 241–242 (in Hebrew). Hacker also quotes Moses Galante, another Sephardic refugee, who writes that although many Jews suffered martyrdom (*"umah gam bi-gezerot Ashkenaz"*), nonetheless, not everyone was able to rise to the occasion (Hacker, "Responses of the Exiles," 243). This Hebrew expression is unclear: Galante's formulation might mean that the Jews of Ashkenaz were *particularly* noted for their martyrological achievements, or on the contrary, that *even* they met the challenge on certain occasions. Cf. 1 Kings 14:14.

27. Samuel Usque, *Samuel Usque's Consolation for the Tribulations of Israel*, trans. Martin A. Cohen (Philadelphia 1977), 192.

28. Usque, *Samuel Usque's Consolation*, 171; see also 172.

29. Joseph ha-Kohen, *Emek ha-Bakha*, ed. Meir Letteris (Cracow 1895), 56.

30. Me'ir ben Barukh of Rothenburg, *Responsa* (Prague 1608), no. 1022, fol. 160v.

31. Moses of Coucy reports that, as a result of his preaching on this theme, "they ousted many alien women in 996 [1236]" (*Sefer Mizvot Gadol*, negative commandment 112). See also Moses Nahmanides, *Writings*, ed. Charles P. Chavel (Jerusalem 1963), v. 1, 370 (in Hebrew). For the Zohar, see Isaiah Tishby, *The Wisdom of the Zohar* (Oxford 1989), v. 3, 1203; and Israel M. Ta-Shma, *The Halachic Residue in the Zohar* (Tel Aviv 1995), 35 (in Hebrew). Ta-Shma's assertion that Ashkenazic literature contains no mention of this problem requires correction in light of the passage from Ele'azar of Worms' penitential manual.

32. Todros Abulafia, *Gan ha-Meshalim veha-Hidot*, ed. David Yellin (Jerusalem 1932), v. 2, pt. 2, 85. See also Yitzhak Baer, "Todros ben Yehudah Halevi and His Time," *Zion* 2 (1937), 36–44 (in Hebrew).

33. Judah ben Asher of Toledo, *Zikhron Yehudah* (Berlin 1846), no. 91, fol. 44r. Baer asserts ("Todros ben Yehudah Halevi") that this text is also by Todros Abulafia.

34. Abraham Zacut, *Sefer Yuhasin ha-Shalem*, ed. Herschell Filipowski (London and Edinburgh 1857), pt. 4, fol. 76a. The word *jealous* in Hebrew must have seemed uniquely apt, because its numerical value is 151, which is also the Jewish year corresponding to 1391 CE. On vice in Spain, see Chapter 8.

35. See Samuel de Medina, *Responsa*, EH 203, cited in Zimmels, *Ashkenazim and Sephardim*, 274.

36. Maimonides, however, portrays "the people of *Rum*," namely Christendom, as adhering closely to talmudic law, rather than to latter-day customs and ordinances; see his commentary on mishnah, *Gittin* 5:8.

37. See David Messer Leon, *Kevod Hakhamim*, 63, cited in Ben-Sasson, "Exile and Redemption," 221.

38. Shmuel Feiner, *Haskalah and History: The Emergence of a Modern Jewish Historical Consciousness*, trans. Chaya Naor and Sondra Silverston (Oxford and Portland 2002), 47–48; Reuven Michael, *Jewish Historiography from the Renaissance to the Modern Time* (Jerusalem 1993), 115 (in Hebrew).

39. Feiner, *Haskalah and History*, 49.

40. Feiner, *Haskalah and History*, 112.

41. Solomon Maimon, *Lebensgeschichte* (Berlin 1792–1793), pt. 2, 4 (cited in Feiner, *Haskalah and History*, 36).

42. "Nahal ha-Besor," *Ha-Me'assef* 1 (1784), 2–3.

43. Feiner, *Haskalah and History*, 50–55. See also Moshe Pelli, *The Circle of* Hame'asef *Writers at the Dawn of Haskalah: The Literary Contribution of* Hame'asef *Writers to Haskalah (1783–1811)* (Israel 2001), 159–165 (in Hebrew).

44. *Ha-Me'assef* I (1784), 125.

45. Shimon Baraz, "Toledot Rabenu Mosheh ben Maimon," *Ha-Me'assef* 3 (1786), 19–27, 35–47.

46. Feiner, *Haskalah and History*, 52–53.

47. Tsemah Tsamriyon, *Ha-Meassef: The First Modern Periodical in Hebrew* (Tel Aviv 1988), 150 (in Hebrew).

48. In his biographical essays in *Bikurei ha-'Itim*, Rapoport also praises Hai Gaon, Nathan ben Yehiel, Hananel ben Hushiel, Nissim of Gerona, and El'azar Kallir as learned and as opposed to kabbalah. See Feiner, *Haskalah and History*, 112; and Ismar Schorsch, "The Emergence of Historical Consciousness in Modern Judaism," *Leo Baeck Institute Yearbook* 28 (1983), 423. In genres other than biography, scholarship of northern European thinkers did proceed; see, for example, Rapoport's letter on Simon Kara in *Kerem Hemed* 7 (1843), 4–18.

49. Feiner, *Haskalah and History*, 126.

50. Michael, *Jewish Historiography*, 133–149. See also Raphael Mahler, *Hasidism and the Jewish Enlightenment: Their Confrontation in Galicia and Poland in the First Half of the Nineteenth Century*, trans. Eugene Orenstein (Philadelphia 1985), 31–67.

51. Jacques Basnage de Beauval, *L'histoire et la réligion des Juifs depuis Jésus Christ jusq'à present*, 5 vols. (Rotterdam 1706–1707); Solomon Maimon, *Autobiography*, trans. Moses Hadas (New York 1947), 96. See Lester A. Segal, "Jacques Basnage de Beauval's *l'Histoire des Juifs*: Christian Historiographical Perception of Jewry and Judaism on the Eve of the Enlightenment," *Hebrew Union College Annual* 54 (1983), 303–324; Jonathan Elukin, "Jacques Basnage and the *History of the Jews*: Anti-Catholic Polemic and Historical Allegory in the Republic of Letters," *Journal of the History of Ideas* 53 (1992), 603–630; Amnon Raz-Krakotzkin, *The National Narration of Exile: Zionist Historiography and Medieval Jewry*, Ph.D. dissertation (Tel Aviv University 1996), 19–27 (in Hebrew); and Adam Sutcliffe, *Judaism and Enlightenment* (Cambridge 2003), 81–89.

52. See Basnage, *Histoire et la réligion des Juifs*, bk. 1, 12, cited by Segal, "Jacques Basnage de Beauval's *l'Histoire des Juifs*," 309. See David N. Myers, "'*Mehabevin et ha-tsarot*': Crusade Memories and Modern Jewish Martyrologies," *Jewish History* 13 (1999), 52.

53. See Basnage, *Histoire et la réligion des Juifs*, v. 5, bk. 7, ch. 11.

54. Basnage, *Histoire et la réligion des Juifs*, v. 5, bk. 7, ch. 8, 1628–1631. Basnage's account is riddled with inaccuracies, but these are not our concern.

55. Basnage, *Histoire et la réligion des Juifs*, v. 5, bk. 7, ch. 8, 1859–1860.

56. Michael, *Jewish Historiography*, 196–205; Michael A. Meyer, *The Origins of the Modern Jew* (Detroit 1979), 157–182, esp. 161.

57. Heinrich Graetz, *Geschichte der Juden*, 2nd ed. (Leipzig 1900), v. 11, 414.

58. Isaac Marcus Jost, *Geschichte der Israeliten seit der Zeit der Maccabäer bis auf unsre Tage* (Berlin 1826), v. 6, bk. 9, 50.

59. Jost, *Geschichte der Israeliten*, v. 6, bk. 9, 55.

60. Jost, *Geschichte der Israeliten*, v. 6, bk. 9, 220.

61. On Jost's treatment of the First Crusade massacres, see Nils Roemer, "Turning Defeat into Victory: *Wissenschaft des Judentums* and the Martyrs of 1096," *Jewish History* 13 (1999), 68–69.

62. Jost, *Geschichte der Israeliten*, v. 6, bk. 9, 229.

63. Jost, *Geschichte der Israeliten*, v. 6, bk. 9, 229.

64. Jost, *Geschichte der Israeliten*, v. 6, bk. 9, 232.

65. Jost, *Geschichte der Israeliten* (Berlin 1827), v. 7, 207–208.

66. Jost, *Geschichte der Israeliten*, v. 7, 208.

67. Jost, *Geschichte der Israeliten*, v. 6, 244.

68. Jost, *Geschichte der Israeliten*, v. 6, 245.

69. Jost, *Geschichte der Israeliten*, v. 6, 246.

70. Jost, *Geschichte der Israeliten*, v. 6, 247.

71. Jost, *Geschichte der Israeliten*, v. 7, 208–209.

72. Jost, *Geschichte der Israeliten*, v. 7, 221–222.

73. Jost, *Geschichte der Israeliten*, v. 7, 239.

74. See also Ismar Schorsch, "From Wolfenbüttel to Wissenschaft: The Divergent Paths of Isaak Markus Jost and Leopold Zunz," in his *From Text to Context: The Turn to History in Modern Judaism* (Hanover and London 1994), 241–242; and Ismar Schorsch, "Scholarship in the Service of Reform," in his *From Text to Context*, 307.

75. Schorsch, "From Wolfenbüttel to Wissenschaft," 241–242; Schorsch, "Scholarship in the Service of Reform," 307.

76. Ismar Schorsch, "The Myth of Sephardic Supremacy," *Leo Baeck Institute Yearbook* 34 (1989), 58.

77. Heinrich Heine, *The Rabbi of Bacherach: A Fragment*, trans. E. B. Ashton (New York 1947), 4–5.

78. Heine, *Rabbi of Bacherach*, 7–8.

79. The apostasy of Heine's Abarbanel has obvious implications for Heine's own decision to convert, but this is not our concern.

80. Heine, *Rabbi of Bacherach*, 63.

81. Siegbert Salomon Prawer, *Heine's Jewish Comedy* (Oxford 1983), 567.

82. Prawer, *Heine's Jewish Comedy*, 569.

83. Prawer, *Heine's Jewish Comedy*, 580–584.

84. Schorsch, "From Wolfenbüttel to Wissenschaft," 244. See also Michael, *Jewish Historiography*, 207.

85. This was not the view of Solomon Maimon, who writes, "I discovered that in Holland there was nothing for me to do, inasmuch as the main desire of the Dutch Jews is to make money, and they manifest no particular taste for the sciences" (*Autobiography*, 88).

86. Ismar Schorsch, "Breakthrough into the Past: The *Verein für Cultur und Wissenschaft der Juden*," *Leo Baeck Institute Yearbook* 33 (1988), 26.

87. Leopold Zunz, "Salomon ben Isaac, genannt Raschi," *Zeitschrift für die Wissenschaft des Judentums* 2 (1823), 278; cited in Michael, *Jewish Historiography*, 208.

88. Zunz, "Salomon ben Isaac," 285.

89. Zunz, "Salomon ben Isaac," 286.

90. Schorsch, "From Wolfenbüttel to Wissenschaft," 245.

91. Schorsch, "From Wolfenbüttel to Wissenschaft," 246, 248.

92. See Leopold Zunz, "On Rabbinic Literature," in *The Jew in the Modern World: A Documentary History*, 2nd ed., ed. Paul Mendes-Flohr and Jehuda Reinharz, trans. Arthur Schwartz (New York and Oxford 1995), 222. See also Fritz Bamberger, "Zunz's Conception of History," *Proceedings of the American Academy for Jewish Research* 11 (1941), 4; Schorsch, "Emergence of

Historical Consciousness," 433; Ismar Schorsch, "Ideology and History in the Age of Emancipation," in *The Structure of Jewish History and Other Essays*, ed. H. Graetz (New York 1975), 26–31.

93. Wolf Heidenheim's edition of the German prayer book (Rödelheim 1800–1805) was an exception to the disdain and lack of interest in the liturgical poetry of medieval Germany; see Schorsch, "Myth of Sephardic Supremacy," 54.

94. Leopold Zunz, *Gottesdienstliche Vorträge der Juden* (Frankfurt am Main 1892), 432.

95. Zunz, *Gottesdienstliche Vorträge der Juden*, 433.

96. Zunz, *Gottesdienstliche Vorträge der Juden*, 26.

97. Leopold Zunz, *The Sufferings of the Jews in the Middle Ages*, trans. A. Löwy, rev. and ed. George Alexander Kohut (New York 1907), 91.

98. Michael A. Meyer, *Response to Modernity: A History of the Reform Movement in Judaism* (New York and Oxford 1988), passim.

99. Leopold Dukes, *Zur Kentniss der neuhebraischen religiösen Poesie* (Frankfurt am Main 1842), 16–29; Schorsch, "Myth of Sephardic Supremacy," 56.

100. Samuel David Luzzatto, *S. D. Luzzatto's hebräische Briefe* [*Igrot Shadal*], ed. Eisig Gräber (Przemysl 1882), v. 1, 336–337; Schorsch, "Myth of Sephardic Supremacy," 61.

101. Michael Sachs, *Die religiose Poesie der Juden in Spanien* (Berlin 1845); this was also the year in which Zunz's *Zur Geschichte und Literatur* was published.

102. Luzzatto, *Igrot Shadal*, 766.

103. Luzzatto, *Igrot Shadal*, 779. See Schorsch, "Emergence of Historical Consciousness," 426.

104. Luzzatto criticizes Maimonides for petrifying Judaism through codification; see Luzzatto's essay in *Kerem Hemed* 3 (1838), 61–76; Morris B. Margolis, *Samuel David Luzzatto: Traditionalist Scholar* (New York 1979), 65; Schorsch, "Emergence of Historical Consciousness," 426; and Feiner, *Haskalah and History*, 132.

105. See Shmuel Feiner, "A Critique of Modernity: S. D. Luzzatto and the Anti-Haskalah," in Robert Bonfil et al. (eds.), *Samuel David Luzzatto: The Bi-Centennial of His Birth* (Jerusalem 2004), 145–165 (in Hebrew).

106. Schorsch, "Ideology and History," 19–31.

107. Heinrich Graetz, "Introduction to Volume Five of the *History of the Jews*," in his *Structure of Jewish History and Other Essays*, trans. Ismar Schorsch (New York 1975), 135–136.

108. Heinrich Graetz, "The Structure of Jewish History," in his *Structure of Jewish History and Other Essays*, 94. Similarly, Graetz writes that Mendelssohn's philosophy of Judaism was so long in coming because "Judaism had first to recover from the state of exhaustion produced by the chase to which it had been subjected for seventeen hundred years" ("Structure of Jewish History," 122).

109. Graetz, "Introduction to Volume Five," 137. Similarly, Graetz writes that medieval Judaism "gives the most striking evidence of infinite vitality and flexible energy" ("Structure of Jewish History," 94).

110. Graetz, "Structure of Jewish History," 95–96.

111. Graetz sees the Maimonidean controversy as a dialogical element in the march to greater self-consciousness and thus as a positive development rather than a hindrance. See Graetz, "Structure of Jewish History," 107–124; and Michael, *Jewish Historiography*, 313.

112. For example, Graetz sees the attempt by Jacob Berab of sixteenth-century Safed to revive *semikhah* (rabbinic ordination) as an opportunity to recreate a Jewish state. See Graetz, *Geschichte der Juden*, 3rd ed., v. 9, 293.

113. Graetz, *Geschichte der Juden*, 3rd ed. (Leipzig 1895), v. 5, 332–335.

114. Graetz, *Geschichte der Juden*, 3rd ed. (Leipzig 1894), v. 6, 68. For this generalization, Graetz cites a source about the import of a French rabbi to Spain; see Isaac Alfasi, *Responsa*, no. 223.

115. Graetz, *Geschichte der Juden*, v. 6, 96.

116. Graetz, *Geschichte der Juden*, v. 6, 143.

117. Graetz, *Geschichte der Juden*, v. 6, 144.

118. Graetz, *Geschichte der Juden*, v. 6, 154.

119. Graetz, *Geschichte der Juden*, v. 6, 154. In fact, Graetz writes that the decline continued until the modern era, so the precise significance of the Spanish Expulsion remains unclear.

120. Graetz, *Geschichte der Juden*, 4th ed. (Leipzig 1907), v. 7, ix.

121. Graetz, *Geschichte der Juden*, v. 7, ix–x.

122. Abraham Berliner, *Aus dem inneren Leben der deutschen Juden im Mittelalter* (Berlin 1861). Shortly thereafter, Berliner further demonstrated his fidelity to Zunz's call for the scientific study of medieval Ashkenaz by preparing a critical edition of Rashi's commentary on the Pentateuch. For a bibliography of Berliner's writings, see A. Freimann and M. Hildesheimer (eds.), *Festschrift zum siebzigsten Geburstage A. Berliners* (Frankfurt am Main 1903), vii–xxxi. For a collection of Hebrew translations of selected writings, see Abraham Berliner, *Ketavim Nivharim* (Jerusalem 1945–1949).

123. Meir Wiener, *Regesten zur Geschichte der Juden im Deutschland während des Mittelalters* (Hanover 1862). Wiener also published Ibn Verga's *Shevet Yehudah*. On Wiener, see "Weiner, Meir," *Jewish Encyclopedia* (New York 1906), v. 12, 516.

124. Otto Stobbe, *Die Juden in Deutschland während des Mittelalters in politischer, sozialer und rechtlicher Beziehung* (Braunschweig 1886). The works by Berliner and Stobbe were undoubtedly influenced by the *Monumenta Germaniae Historica* project, the first volume of which appeared in 1826. The apogee of this phase of Ashkenazic scholarship was Julius Aronius's *Regesten zur Geschichte der Juden im Fränkischen und Deutschen Reiche biz zum Jahre 1273* (Berlin 1902).

125. In addition to monographs, Jewish periodicals from this period contain numerous articles on the history of individual German-Jewish communities. These works await thorough analysis.

126. Moritz Güdemann, *Geschichte des Erziehungswesens und der Cultur der Abendländischen Juden während des Mittelalters und der Neuren Zeit* (Vienna 1880–1888). Volume 1 focuses on Franco-German Jewry in the tenth to fourteenth centuries; the second volume on the Jews of Italy, and the third on Ashkenazic Jewry in the fourteenth and fifteenth centuries.

127. On Güdemann, see N. M. Yerushalmi, "Dr. Moshe Güdemann," in *The Science of Judaism in Western Europe*, ed. Simon Federbusch (Jerusalem and Tel Aviv 1958), 187–193 (in Hebrew); and Ismar Schorsch, "Moritz Güdemann: Rabbi, Historian, Apologist," *Leo Baeck Institute Yearbook* 11 (1966), 53–61.

128. This is ironic when we consider that Graetz critiqued Jost for writing a history of "suffering and scholars" (*Leidens- und Gelehrentesgeschichte*).

129. Schorsch, "Emergence of Historical Consciousness," 434.

130. See the introduction to Güdemann's *Geschichte des Erziehungswesens*. Schorsch presents this argument as an apologetical response to the antisemitic argument that German society was now being "judaized." See Schorsch, "Moritz Güdemann," 54–55.

131. Schorsch, "Moritz Güdemann," 57.

132. Schorsch, "Moritz Güdemann," 56–57. Israel Abrahams's *Jewish Life in the Middle Ages* (London 1896) was clearly inspired by Güdemann and probably also S. D. Goitein's *A Mediterranean Society* (Berkeley 1967–1993), notwithstanding the time lag.

133. Schorsch, "Moritz Güdemann," 60. Schorsch notes (p. 61) an element of cognitive dissonance in Güdemann's perception of his own achievement. Güdemann saw himself as faithful to the *Wissenschaft* view of the Middle Ages and never admitted his radical methodological innovation (comparative method, social history) and substantive revision (mutual influence, harmonious relations). Furthermore, Güdemann declared that Jewish history was religious history, but his own research unearthed other factors, including family life, communal organization, and political and economic freedom.

134. Güdemann, *Geschichte des Erziehungswesens*, v. 1, 9–61, 107–126.

135. Güdemann, *Geschichte des Erziehungswesens*, v. 1, 62–91.

136. Güdemann, *Geschichte des Erziehungswesens*, v. 1, 128.

137. Michael, *Jewish Historiography*, 429.

138. Ze'ev Ya'avetz, *Toledot Yisra'el*, v. 11 (Tel Aviv 1934), 36.

139. Ya'avetz, *Toledot Yisra'el*, v. 11, 188.

140. Ya'avetz, *Toledot Yisra'el*, v. 11, 9–10. Elsewhere, too, Ya'avetz emphasizes the joie de vivre of Ashkenazic Jewry, which appears to be a response to Graetz's portrayal of their gloomy and ascetic spirit. See Ya'avetz, *Toledot Yisra'el*, v. 11, 7–8.

141. Ya'avetz, *Toledot Yisra'el*, v. 12 (Tel Aviv 1935), 42.

142. Michael, *Jewish Historiography*, 455.

143. Ya'avetz, *Toledot Yisra'el*, v. 12, 178.

144. Ya'avetz, *Toledot Yisra'el*, v. 12, 101–103.

145. On Baer, see David Nathan Myers, *Re-Inventing the Jewish Past* (New York and Oxford 1995), 109–128; Raz-Krakotzkin, *National Narration of Exile*, 144–218; and Israel Jacob Yuval, "Yitzhak Baer and the Search for Authentic Judaism," in *The Jewish Past Revisited: Reflections on Modern Jewish Historians*, eds. David N. Myers and David B. Ruderman (New Haven 1998), 77–87.

146. Yitzhak Baer, *Die Juden im christlichen Spanien*, 2 vols. (Berlin 1929, 1936).

147. Baer explicitly rejects the separation of historical inquiry into discrete disciplines and insists that historians indicate the linkages between social-political history and spiritual-religious history. See his "Towards a Clarification of the State of Our Historical Study," in *Magnes Anniversary Book*, ed. F. I. Baer et al. (Jerusalem 1938), 37 (in Hebrew).

148. Yitzhak Baer, *Toledot ha-Yehudim bi-Sefarad ha-Notzrit*, 2 vols. (Tel Aviv 1945). Baer had completed the German edition in 1938, but it appeared in print in Hebrew. See also Joshua Prawer, "In Memory of Yitzhak Baer," in *In Memory of Yizhak Baer* (Jerusalem 1984), 35–36 (in Hebrew).

149. Yitzhak Baer, "Basic Themes in the Historical Development of Judaism in the Middle Ages" *Moznayim* 23 (1947), 306 (in Hebrew).

150. For some of Baer's most outspoken Zionist rhetoric, see his "Towards a Clarification," 36, 38.

151. Yitzhak Baer, *A History of the Jews in Christian Spain*, trans. Louis Schoffman (Philadelphia 1966), v. 1, 1. Elsewhere, Baer writes that historians need to note "the permanent organic connection (*qesher*) that remains in the soul of Judaism" (Baer, "Towards a Clarification," 37). See also Raz-Krakotzkin, *National Narration of Exile*, 145.

152. See Yitzhak Baer, "Review of Salo Baron, *Social and Religious History of the Jews*,"

Zion 3 (1938), 280; and Baer, "The Educational Value of Jewish History," *Gilyonot* 12 (1940/41–1941/42), 130 (in Hebrew). Similarly, Baer and Benzion Dinaburg, Baer's colleague at the Hebrew University and co-editor of the quarterly *Zion*, stress that different periods and centers are tied by common cultural-historical threads, which the historian must identify (Baer and Dinaburg, "Our Direction," *Zion* 1 [1936], 1–5 [in Hebrew]).

153. Yitzhak Baer, "The Religious-Social Tendency of 'Sepher Hassidim,'" *Zion* 3 (1938), 1–50 (in Hebrew); Yitzhak Baer, "On the Origins of the Organization of the Jewish Community of the Middle Ages," *Zion* 15 (1950), 1–41 (in Hebrew).

154. Baer, "Towards a Clarification," 37.

155. Wilhelm von Humboldt, "Über die Aufgabe des Geschichtschreibers," in *Die sprachphilosophischen Werke W. v. Humboldts*, ed. H. Steinthal (Berlin 1884), 138; cited in Friedrich Engel-Janosi, *The Growth of German Historicism* (Baltimore 1944), 26.

156. Engel-Janosi, *Growth of German Historicism*, 40–41.

157. Baer, "Educational Value," 131. See Prawer, "In Memory," 38. Thus, whatever his personal lifestyle, Baer rejects the secularism or atheism of the modern age. To illustrate, Baer's *Galut* ends as follows: "Every Jew, throughout the Diaspora, must recognize that there is a force that raises the Jewish people above all historical-causal connectivity" (*Galut*, Hebrew ed., trans. from German by Israel Eldad [Jerusalem 1980], 103). Elsewhere Baer asserts that modern secularism represents the non-Jews' rejection of the Jewish component in European culture, although belief in the transcendent and eternal is immanently Jewish, whatever expression this belief ought currently to assume (Baer, "Educational Value," 134–135).

158. In this Baer resembles Marx, but he is not particularly interested in economic issues, such as control over the means of production.

159. Shmuel Ettinger, "Yitzhak Baer (1888–1980)," *Zion* 44 (1980–81), 13–15 (in Hebrew).

160. Baer, *Christian Spain*, v. 1, 4–5; Baer, "Educational Value," 131. Thus Baer sees socialism as rooted in the egalitarian and fraternal spirit of Judaism, "the basic goal of which was to establish a society based on the laws of the pietists" ("Educational Value," 134–135).

161. Baer, "Origins of the Organization."

162. Baer, "Review of Salo Baron," 299.

163. Baer, "Basic Themes," 204. To these elements of German pietism he devoted two articles: "Theory of Natural Equality of Early Man According to Ashkenazi Hasidim," *Zion* 32 (1967), 129–136 (in Hebrew); and "On the Doctrine of Providence in *Sefer Hasidim*," in *Studies in Mysticism and Religion Presented to Gershom G. Scholem on his Seventieth Birthday by Pupils, Colleagues, and Friends*, ed. Ephraim E. Urbach, R. J. Zwi Werblowsky, and Chaim Wirszubski (Jerusalem 1967), 47–62 (in Hebrew).

164. This is, however, clearly not the case for pacifism, another value in Baer's image of the authentic Jewish ethos. Like agriculture, he writes, military might was the prerogative of the Christian majority, rather than of medieval Jewry, which he characterizes as "ascetic-martyrological and pacifistic" (Baer, "Basic Themes," 304–305). See also Baer, "Review of Salo Baron," 293. This ideal was clearly not drawn from the Zionist ethos.

165. Baer, *Galut*, trans. from German by Robert Warshow (New York 1947), 48–49.

166. Baer, *Toledot ha-Yehudim*.

167. Thus it was Baer who highlighted Todros Abulafia's critique of the social-religious ill of sexual relations with "the daughters of alien gods"; see note 32.

168. Baer, "Basic Themes," 308.

169. Baer, "Review of Salo Baron," 294.

170. Baer, "Basic Themes," 307.

171. A student of Baer's explains this paradox by saying, "Baer was too great not to see occasional points of contact" (Prawer, "In Memory," 39).

172. Baer, "Religious-Social Tendency of 'Sepher Hassidim,'" 1–2. Later, however, Baer reverses his position and insists that its emergence is to be regarded as an immanent development. See Baer, "Origins of the Organization," esp. 28; and also Myers, *Re-Inventing the Jewish Past*, 124; Yuval, "Yitzhak Baer," 79–80; and Raz-Krakotzkin, *National Narration of Exile*, 155–157.

173. These parallels are discussed more fully in Chapter 7.

174. Nevertheless, Baer cites Christian—Joachite—influence in his analysis of the social ethos expressed in the *Raya Mehemna*, a kabbalistic work written in Spain, not Ashkenaz. See Baer, "The Historical Background of the 'Raya Mehemna,'" *Zion* 5 (1940), 1–44 (in Hebrew); and Raz-Krakotzkin, *National Narration of Exile*, 157.

175. Baer, "Basic Themes," 307–308.

176. Baer, "Basic Themes," 307.

177. Baer, *Galut* (English), 47; Myers, *Re-Inventing the Jewish Past*, 120–121.

178. Yitzhak Baer, "Ahadut ha-historia ha-yisra'elit u-ve'ayot hitpathutah ha-irgunit" [The unity of Jewish history and the problems of its organizational development], *Gilyonot* 24 (1950–1951), 215–216.

179. Isaiah Sonne, "On Baer and His Philosophy of Jewish History," *Jewish Social Studies* 9 (1947), 66–72, 77–80.

180. Sonne, "On Baer," 67.

181. Sonne, "On Baer," 72.

182. Ephraim Shmueli, "Yitzhak Baer's Philosophical-Historical Doctrine," *Kivunim* 4 (1979), 96–97 (in Hebrew).

183. Shmueli, "Yitzhak Baer's Philosophical-Historical Doctrine," 104, 106. Baron's critique of the prevailing "lachrymose conception of Jewish history" is well known, with obvious implications for his attitude toward the persecution of Ashkenazic Jewry in the Middle Ages; see Myers, *Re-Inventing the Jewish Past*, 52–53; and Schorsch, "The Lachrymose Conception of Jewish History," in his *From Text to Context* (Hanover 1994), 376–388.

184. Shmueli, "Yitzhak Baer's Philosophical-Historical Doctrine."

185. Shmueli also rejects the claim that pneumatic and ascetic tendencies were characteristic of the Tana'im ("Yitzhak Baer's Philosophical-Historical Doctrine," 105).

Chapter Two

For an earlier version of this chapter, see David Malkiel, "Jewish-Christian Relations in Europe, 840–1096: A Historiographical Review," *Journal of Medieval History* 29 (2003), 55–83.

1. Whether, indeed, the First Crusade was as apocalyptically destructive for German Jewry as it is described in medieval sources has been increasingly questioned by historians and is discussed in later chapters. Even if this revision stands, its impact on treatments of the First Crusade—scholarly as well as popular—is barely perceptible, and its implications for other aspects of medieval Jewish history have only begun to be explored.

2. Salo Wittmayer Baron, *A Social and Religious History of the Jews* (New York 1937), v. 2, 40.

3. James Parkes, *The Jew in the Medieval Community* (London 1938), 57.

4. Heinrich Graetz, *Geschichte der Juden* (Leipzig 1895), v. 5, 226.

5. Salo Wittmayer Baron, *A Social and Religious History of the Jews* (Philadelphia 1957), v. 4, 91.

6. Léon Poliakov, *The History of Anti-Semitism* (London 1965), v. 1, 36.

7. Monumenta Germaniae Historica [MGH], Concilia, v. 2, 119–124 (canons 73–76). See Bernhard Blumenkranz, "Germany, 843–1096," in *The Dark Ages: Jews in Christian Europe 711–1096*, ed. Cecil Roth (Tel Aviv 1966), 167; Bernard S. Bachrach, *Early Medieval Jewish Policy in Western Europe* (Minneapolis 1977), 107–108; and Amnon Linder, *The Jews in the Legal Sources of the Early Middle Ages* (Detroit and Jerusalem 1997), 539–548. On Jewish slave ownership, see Michael Toch, "The European Jews of the High Middle Ages: Slave-Traders?" *Zion* 64 (1999), 39–63, esp. 46 (in Hebrew). Toch notes that canon 76 of the Meaux-Paris statutes, which deals with slave ownership, was based on earlier canons of the councils of Clichy, Rheims, and Chalon.

8. J. D. Mansi, *Sacrorum conciliorum amplissima collectio* (Paris 1901), v. 10, col. 596; MGH, Concilia, v. 1, 204; Julius Aronius, *Regesten zur Geschichte der Juden im Fränkischen und Deutschen Reiche biz zum Jahre 1273* (Berlin 1902), no. 60. Linder (*Jews in the Legal Sources*, 480–481) doubts the existence of this council.

9. Aronius, *Regesten*, no. 26; Mansi, *Sacrorum conciliorum*, v. 9, col. 19; Linder, *Jews in the Legal Sources*, 471, 474. See James A. Brundage, *Medieval Canon Law* (London and New York 1995), 15–16.

10. MGH, Capitularia Regum Francorum, v. 2, 419. See Bernhard Blumenkranz, "Deux compilations canoniques de Florus de Lyon et l'action antijuive d'Agobard," *Revue historique de droit français et étranger* 35 (1955), 568–569; Bachrach, *Early Medieval Jewish Policy*, 111.

11. Linder, *Jews in the Legal Sources*, 488.

12. MGH, Epistolae, v. 5, 239. The writer of the letter is uncertain; various archbishops of Lyon have been suggested. See Bachrach, *Early Medieval Jewish Policy*, 121, 185n66.

13. "Dani Burdegalam Aquitaniae, Iudaeis prodentibus, captam depopulatamque incendunt." See *Annales Bertiniani*, MGH, Scriptores [SS], v. 1, 443; *Gallia Christiana*, 2, 796. Cf. J. P. Migne, *Patrologia Latina* [PL], v. 115, 1401; Heinrich Gross, *Gallia Judaica* (Paris 1897), 111.

14. See, for example, Simon Schwarzfuchs, "France Under the Early Capets," in *The Dark Ages: Jews in Christian Europe 711–1096*, ed. Cecil Roth (Tel Aviv 1966), 146.

15. "Mauri Barcinonam, Iudaeis prodentibus, capiunt, interfectisque pene omnibus christianis et urbe vastata, impune redeunt" (MGH, SS, v. 1, 447).

16. MGH, SS, v. 1, 504.

17. For literary sources, see Harry Friedenwald, *The Jews and Medicine* (Baltimore 1944), v. 1, 69–83. On the suspicion of Jewish doctors in the later Middle Ages, see Joseph Shatzmiller, *Jews, Medicine, and Medieval Society* (Berkeley 1994), 78–99.

18. "Est aut fama, quod a quodam Iudaeo, qui vocabatur Sedechias, poculum mortis ei propinatum sit, qui ei familiarius adhaerebat, eo quod in medendis corporum passionibus singularem experientiam habere diceretur; porro hic sycophanta erat, et magicis praestigiis incantationibusque mentes hominum deludebat. Obiit vero pridie Nonas Octobris" (MGH, SS, v. 1, 589).

19. Indeed, Jewish communities did occasionally aid an approaching army, when they judged that the new regime might be more hospitable than the current one. Examples are the support granted to the Persians and Muslims during their contest with Byzantine forces over

the Holy Land in 614 and in the 630s, to the Muslims during their invasion of Spain in 711, and to the Franks in Narbonne in 759. Moreover, on the theological plane, the issue of Jewish loyalty was foreshadowed in the biblical Pharaoh's suspicion that the Israelites would prove treacherous in wartime (Ex. 1:10).

20. Bachrach, *Early Medieval Jewish Policy*, 114. See the introduction by Léon Levillain to the edition prepared by F. Grat, Jeanne Vieillard, and Suzanne Clémencet and published in 1964 by the Société de l'histoire de France.

21. Ben-Zion Dinur, *Israel in the Diaspora*, 2nd ed. (Tel Aviv 1958), v. 1, pt. 1, 161 (in Hebrew).

22. Bernhard Blumenkranz, *Les auteurs chrétiens latins du moyen age sur les juifs et le juda-isme* (Paris 1963), 209; Ferdinand Lot and Louis Haphen, *Le régne de Charles de Chauve* (Paris 1909), 141–148.

23. It is, again, the annals of St. Bertin, written in this period by Richer of Rheims, that attribute Hugues Capet's death, in 996, to Jews: "Hugo rex papulis toto corpore confectus, in oppido Hugonis Iudeis extinctus est." The editor notes the similarity to the record of Charles the Bald's death: "i.e. a Iudeis, medicis fortasse, ut de Karolo Calvo Hincmarus scribit." See MGH, SS, v. 3, 657 and n92. See also Israel Levi, "Les Juifs de France du milieu du IX\ :sup:`e` siècle aux croisades," *Revue des Etudes Juives* 52 (1906), 164.

24. Bachrach, *Early Medieval Jewish Policy*, 115–116.

25. "Anno DCCCLXXXIII [883]. Obiit Ansegisus venerabilis Senonum Archiepiscopus . . . [237] Praetere' domnus Ansegisus, postquam Primatum totius Galliae obtinuit, et superna moderatione secundus Papa appellari meruit, Judaeos certa de cause et Moniales ab urbe Senonica expulit, et ne ulterius in ea habitaculum manendi haberent, sub anathematis jugulo interdixit . . . Anno DCCCLXXXVI [887]." See M. Bouquet (ed.), *Recueil des historiens des Gaules et de la France* (Paris 1871), v. 8, 236–237; PL, v. 142, col. 771; and *Gallia christiana*, v. 12, 27. See also Blumenkranz, *Les auteurs chrétiens*, 253; and Jassuda Bédarride, *Les Juifs en France, en Italie et en Espagne* (Paris 1867), 463.

26. Baron, *Social and Religious History*, 2nd ed. (New York 1957), v. 4 56.

27. Schwarzfuchs, "France Under the Early Capets," 146.

28. Henri Gross, "Étude sur Simson ben Abraham de Sens," *Revue des Etudes Juives* 6 (1883), 170. The source is *Gallia christiana*, v. 12, 126: "Meminisse juvat moniales ab Ansegiso Normannorum metu anno 876 ex urbe ablegatas fuisse." Note that the (unsuccessful) Norman siege of Sens did not come until November 886, after Ansegisus's death.

29. Blumenkranz, *Les auteurs chrétiens*, 253.

30. The manuscript dates to 1045, but Blumenkranz dates the text to sometime after 1032, without explanation (*Les auteurs chrétiens*, 253).

31. Irving Agus (ed.), *Responsa of the Tosaphists* (New York 1954), 40, no. 1 (in Hebrew); Irving Agus, *Urban Civilization in Pre-Crusade Europe* (New York 1965), v. 1, 174.

32. Jean Richard, *Les ducs de Bourgogne et la formation du Duché du XI\ :sup:`e` au XIV\ :sup:`e` Siècle* (Dijon 1954), 8; J. Dhondt, "Une crise du pouvoir capétien 1032–1034," in *Miscellanea mediaevalia in Memoriam J. F. Niermeyer* (Groningen 1967), 141–148; Yves Sassier, *Recherches sur le pouvoir comtal en Auxerrois du X\ :sup:`e` au debut du XIII\ :sup:`e` siècle* (Auxerre 1980), 30–44.

33. Baron, *Social and Religious History*, 2nd ed., v. 4, 91–92.

34. Aronius, *Regesten*, 51–52, no. 119.

35. For the list of councils, see Dinur, *Israel in the Diaspora*, v. 1, pt. 1, 183n56. For the Elvira canons, see Linder, *Jews in the Legal Sources*, 483. Stow asserts that canons of this sort

stem from a fear of Judaizing, which he traces back beyond the IV Toledan Council to Paul (1 Cor. 10:16). Indeed he terms the fear of Judaizing "the central theme of ecclesiastical legislation . . . through the 10th and into the 11th centuries." See Kenneth R. Stow, "Amnon Linder, *The Jews in the Legal Sources of the Early Middle Ages*," *Jewish Quarterly Review* 89 (1999), 463–464.

36. MGH, Concilia, v. 1, 94; Mansi, *Sacrorum conciliorum*, v. 9, col. 118. See Dinur, *Israel in the Diaspora*, v. 1, pt. 1, 183n61.

37. MGH, Constitutiones et Acta Publica, v. 1, 6–7; MGH, Concilia, v. 6, pt. 1, 110–111, 113–114; Aronius, *Regesten*, no. 123; Blumenkranz, "Germany, 843–1096," 167; K. J. Leyser, *Medieval Germany and Its Neighbours, 900–1250* (London 1982), 104; Linder, *Jews in the Legal Sources*, 553–557; Friedrich Lotter, "Zu den Anfängen deutsch-jüdischer Symbiose in frühottonischer Zeit," *Archiv für Kulturgeschichte* 55 (1973), 6–13.

38. Nor was the issue of forced baptism restricted to Latin Europe. The edict of forced conversion issued by Emperor Romanus Lepicanus was only the latest in a series of such decrees in the Byzantine realm between the seventh and tenth centuries.

39. Aronius, *Regesten*, no. 125; Shlomo Simonsohn, *The Apostolic See and the Jews* (Toronto 1988), v. 1, 32–33.

40. Kenneth R. Stow, *Alienated Minority: The Jews of Medieval Latin Europe* (Cambridge, Mass., 1992), 96; Stow, "Ammon Linder," 462.

41. Blumenkranz, *Les auteurs chrétiens*, 219–220, esp. 220n3.

42. Levi, "Les Juifs de France," 163, based on Jean Joseph Vaissette, *Histoire Generale de Languedoc* (Toulouse 1872), v. 3, 813. Vaissette cites the chronicle of Geoffrey, prior of Vigeois. See also Cecil Roth, "The Eastertide Stoning of the Jews and Its Liturgical Echoes," *Jewish Quarterly Review* 35 (1944–1945), 361–362.

43. Graetz, *Geschichte der Juden*, 226.

44. Parkes, *The Jew in the Medieval Community*, 58. The allusion to the outrages of the mid-eleventh century refers to the anti-Jewish violence that took place during the Crusade of 1063.

45. Baron, *Social and Religious History*, v. 4, 53.

46. Poliakov, *History of Anti-Semitism*, v. 1, 33–34. Traditional Church fears of Jewish proselytization mesh here with the powerful impression that the popularity of the Jews at the Carolingian court appears to have made upon Christians. The popularity is exemplified by the famous conversion of Bodo and is made explicit in the fifth chapter of Agobard's *De Insolentia Iudaeorum*. On Church fears of Jewish proselytization, see Solomon Katz, *The Jews in the Visigothic and Frankish Kingdoms of Spain and Gaul* (Cambridge, Mass., 1937), 42–46.

47. Cecil Roth, "European Jewry in the Dark Ages: A Revised Picture," *Hebrew Union College Annual* 23 (1950), 168–169.

48. The name appears to be a perversion of Isaac, in keeping with the apparently common practice, reported by Rabbi Jacob ben Meir Tam, of distorting the names of apostates. See his *Sefer ha-Yashar (ha-She'elot veha-teshuvot)*, ed. S. P. Rosenthal (Berlin 1898), 43, no. 25.

49. Literally, "to putting a goad inside it."

50. There is, however, a vague foreshadowing of the outcome. The narrator reports that Sehok refused to heed his assassins' demand for payment and writes that this stubborn reaction was orchestrated by God, "to harden his heart" (Abraham Meir Habermann, *The Book of the Persecutions of Ashkenaz and France* [Jerusalem 1945], 12 [in Hebrew]). This expression alludes to Pharaoh, whose heart God allegedly hardened in order to precipitate his demise,

and hints that the assassins may have played a role in Sehok's ultimate downfall, possibly assassinating him or engaging him in the duel on the Jews' behalf.

51. Robert Chazan, *Medieval Jewry in Northern France: A Political and Social History* (Baltimore and London 1973), 12. The other incident to which Chazan referred was that of 1007, discussed later.

52. Robert Chazan, "The Persecution of 992," *Revue des Etudes Juives* 129 (1970), 218–219. Chazan identifies the lord as Count Hugh III of Maine.

53. Baron, *Social and Religious History*, 2nd ed., v. 4, 91–92; Schwarzfuchs, "France Under the Early Capets," 148; Avraham Grossman, *The Early Sages of France: Their Lives, Leadership, and Works*, 2nd ed. (Jerusalem 1996), 19 (in Hebrew). See also Shmuel Shepkaru, *Jewish Martyrs in the Pagan and Christian Worlds* (Cambridge 2006), 143–145.

54. Abraham Berliner and David Hoffmann, *Ozar Tov* (Berlin 1877–78), 49–52. The text was later republished (Habermann, *Book of the Persecutions*, 11–15).

55. Ms. Parma 1542/23 (2342; De Rossi 541), fols. 286v–287v. See Benjamin Richler (ed.), *Hebrew Manuscripts in the Biblioteca Palatina in Parma* (Jerusalem 2001), 461.

56. Stow considers the story a parody (*Alienated Minority*, 96).

57. The narrator records that the protagonist placed the wax image "in a wooden box (*tevat 'etz*) in the synagogue, next to the scrolls (*gelilim*) containing the Law of God (*Torat Elohim*)" (Habermann, *Book of the Persecutions*, 13). The wooden box described is clearly the ark, a piece of synagogue furniture so familiar to any Jew that he would not be likely to describe its physical appearance. The same is true for the reference to the scrolls, which a Jewish narrator would describe as "Torah books" (*sifrei Torah*). However, for a non-Jew to provide descriptive rather than technical terms makes perfect sense, for he would not be likely to know an ark or a Torah by name, or at least to feel confident that his audience would identify them as such. Thus, although our text is in Hebrew, and therefore written by a Jew for a Jewish readership, one of the influences that contributed to the fashioning of this text seems to have been Christian.

58. Habermann, *Book of the Persecutions*, 14.

59. These, however, were not particular to the circumstances of 1096 but were the traditional Jewish response to an impending catastrophe. See Ivan G. Marcus, "From Politics to Martyrdom: Shifting Paradigms in the Hebrew Narratives of the 1096 Crusade Riots," *Prooftexts* 2 (1982), 40–52.

60. Marcus, "From Politics to Martyrdom."

61. Elliott Horowitz, "'And It Was Reversed': Jews and Their Enemies in the Festivities of Purim," *Zion* 59 (1994), 129–168 (in Hebrew). Horowitz (p. 144) cites the accusation (mentioned later) leveled at Rome's Jews in the early eleventh century, of abusing an image of the crucified Jesus, and the similar charge, in 1062, hurled at the Jews of Aterno. These incidents did not focus on Purim but demonstrate the notion that the Jews symbolically reenacted the Crucifixion. See also Elliott Horowitz, *Reckless Rites: Purim and the Legacy of Jewish Violence* (Princeton 2006), 160–161.

62. Chazan, *Medieval Jewry*, 12. On p. 15, Chazan notes that in this affair "governmental oppression was accompanied by outbursts of popular antipathy." This would forge a proper link between the events of 992 and 1096, yet popular antipathy does not appear to have materialized in Le Mans, notwithstanding the hopes and rhetoric imputed to the villainous apostate.

63. Blumenkranz, "Germany, 843–1096," 172–173. See also Baron, *Social and Religious History*, 2nd ed., v. 4, 91–92.

64. Robert Chazan, "1007–1012: Initial Crisis for Northern European Jewry," *Proceedings of the American Academy for Jewish Research* 38–39 (1972), 101, 117. Chazan also sees an adumbration of 1096 in the fact that Jews exhibited the readiness for martyrdom that was to receive powerful expression in the First Crusade (Chazan, *Medieval Jewry*, 12). Allan Harris Cutler and Helen Elmquist Cutler write, simply, that the persecution of 1010 "was a prelude to the persecutions at the time of the First Crusade." See Cutler and Cutler, *The Jew as Ally of the Muslim: Medieval Roots of Anti-Semitism* (Notre Dame 1986), 87.

65. Here Landes (see note 66) cites Chazan's, *European Jewry and the First Crusade* (Berkeley 1987), 192–222.

66. Richard Landes, *Relics, Apocalypse, and the Deceits of History: Ademar of Chabannes, 989–1034* (Cambridge, Mass., 1995), 42n106. Landes sees the incidents as "the opening chapter of a peculiarly Western European form of anti-Judaism," but not, he insists, as "a faint foreshadowing of future tragedy." See Landes, "The Massacres of 1010: On the Origins of Popular Anti-Jewish Violence in Western Europe," in *From Witness to Witchcraft*, ed. Jeremy Cohen (Wiesbaden 1996), 83. This is contradicted by his statement, a page earlier, that the forced conversion campaign of Alduin of Limoges was "a harbinger, the distant rumblings of far more terrible things to come." The harbinger approach appears again on pp. 110–111, where Landes refers to the events of 1010 as "a first 'seizure' of apocalyptically-inspired violence against Jews."

67. H. H. Ben-Sasson, *A History of the Jewish People* (Cambridge, Mass., 1976), 411–413. The other sources for Ben-Sasson's conclusion are discussed later.

68. Stow, *Alienated Minority*, 95. This characterization rests, however, on weak foundations, specifically Meshullam ben Qalonymos's characterization of Christianity in a liturgical poem as a violent force that "consumes, destroys and tramples all with its feet."

69. Shepkaru, *Jewish Martyrs*, 160.

70. The First Crusade narrative attributed to Solomon ben Samson records similar stories of women drowning themselves in Trier and Cologne; see Habermann, *Book of the Persecutions*, 56. The association of women with this form of suicide is clearly based on the talmudic legend (*Gittin* 57b) of girls martyring themselves by drowning, for the narrative quotes the biblical prooftext (Ps. 68:23) that served as justification for the suicide reported in the talmudic tale.

71. Habermann, *Book of the Persecutions*, 19.

72. Habermann, *Book of the Persecutions*, 95.

73. That is, Richard II, Count of Normandy. He is an Ahasuerus figure, powerful and potentially lethal yet ultimately the instrument of salvation.

74. Habermann, *Book of the Persecutions*, 19–21. Scholars assume that Arras is the location alluded to here; see Chazan, "1007–1012," 105. The Hebrew refers to the river of "Aryys," and Norman Golb suggests that the spelling reflects local pronunciation. See Golb, *The Jews in Medieval Normandy: A Social and Intellectual History* (Cambridge 1998), 11. It is also possible that the two vowels were originally a superscript indication that the word is a transliteration, to distinguish it from the Hebrew word *ar[e]s*, meaning land.

75. Ms. Parma 1541/27 (2295; De Rossi 563), fols. 127v–129v. This manuscript is the continuation of Ms. Parma 1542/23. See Richler, *Hebrew Manuscripts*, 460.

76. Kenneth R. Stow, *The "1007 Anonymous" and Papal Sovereignty: Jewish Perceptions of the Papacy and Papal Policy in the High Middle Ages* (Cincinnati 1984) (Hebrew Union College Annual Supplement 4), 30–33. The Flanders argument is an argument from silence and hence unconvincing.

77. Stow notes that this papacy was also used as a universal arbiter in the Maimonidean controversy of 1288. Following Moses Shulvass, Chazan infers from the reference in the third section to Jacob's subsequent career that the true purpose of the narrative was to eulogize Jacob ben Yequtiel. See Chazan, "1007–1012," 105. Later, Chazan adduces sources to argue that the 1007 text accurately reflects the level of papal influence in France at this time ("1007–1012," 116).

78. For example, Chazan attacks the argument about currency with the claim that the coin referred to in the story is the Le Mans pound, which was in circulation in eleventh- and twelfth-century Normandy. Chazan also doubts Stow's argument that fear of the ruler's wrath caused the writer of the 1007 tale to couch his political message in esoteric form. I agree, for the text is in Hebrew and would not have been likely to come to the sovereign's attention. Finally, Chazan notes that a crucial quote in Stow's presentation is a conflation of two separate statements, made in different contexts, and hence articulates a position that cannot be attributed to the protagonist. The conflation is a fact, but I fail to see why it disproves the thesis that Jacob ben Yequtiel was propagating a policy of papal sovereignty over the Jews of Christendom, as Stow argues. Moreover, Chazan seems to concede Stow's point, for he writes that the story aims to give the Jews "some simple and simplistic advice with regard to Jewish political affairs." See Chazan, "Review of K. Stow, The '1007 Anonymous,'" Speculum 62 (1987), 728–731. Stow responds to Chazan's critique with a reaffirmation of his claim that the coins of Anjou, Le Mans, and Limoges were replaced with royal coins after 1204. See Stow, "The Avignonese Papacy or, After the Expulsions," in Cohen, From Witness to Witchcraft, 276n5. This, if anything, seems to buttress Chazan's argument for an eleventh- or twelfth-century dating. Stow argues that the thirteenth-century writer planted the historically correct coin in the tale to grant it greater authenticity, but this posits an unrealistically high level of historical awareness among the tale's medieval audience. Elsewhere, Stow notes that the 1007 text contains language from the papal bull Sicut Iudaeis, which did not appear before 1119, thus supplying a terminus a quo for the 1007 document (Stow, The Jews in Rome [Leiden 1995], v. 1, xxii–xxiii).

79. Grossman, Early Sages, 19–20n15. Simonsohn expressed his confidence in the historicity of the 1007 tale by reserving a slot for the missing papal document in his Apostolic See, v. 1 34.

80. Even Chazan concedes that the text was written after the First Crusade, because the guarantees that the pope grants the Jews in the 1007 tale closely resemble those articulated in the papal bull Sicut Iudaeis, first issued in 1119. See Chazan, "1007–1012," 116. The similarity was first noted by Yitzhak Baer, in "The Religious-Social Tendency of 'Sepher Hassidim,'" Zion 3 (1938), 4n7 (in Hebrew). Chazan dates the 1007 tale after 1031, the year of the death of Robert the Pious, because the text states that the events took place "in the days of Robert," supposedly after his reign. This argument is also advanced by Golb (Jews in Medieval Normandy, 6). It is, however, perfectly conceivable that a writer might use this expression with reference to a contemporary ruler. In his review of Stow's 1007 Anonymous Chazan writes that the text was composed in the late eleventh century ("Review of K. Stow," 731).

81. MGH, SS, v. 4, 136–137; PL, 141; Bouquet, Recueil des historiens, v. 10, 152; P. Bourgain (ed.), Ademari Cabannensis Chronicon (Turnhout 1999) (Corpus Christianorum Continuatio Mediaevalis, v. 129), p. 166. See also Bédarride, Les Juifs en France, 468. On Ademar, generally, see Landes, Relics.

82. Blumenkranz, Les auteurs chrétiens, 251n3; Landes, "Massacres of 1010," 84. Note that whereas Blumenkranz implies that the added sentence was interpolated by someone else (pos-

sibly after 1096), Landes claims that Ademar himself made the addition, when he no longer felt constrained to tone down the violence of the incident.

83. MGH, SS, v. 4, 136–137; PL, 141; Bouquet, *Recueil des historiens*, v. 10, 152; Bourgain, *Ademari Cabannensis Chronicon*, 166–167. See also Bédarride, *Les Juifs en France*, 468. Ademar also notes the destruction at this time of the Church of St. George in Ramleh (also noted by Glaber), as well as "many other" churches in Palestine. Elsewhere, Ademar repeats the story of the destruction of the Church of the Holy Sepulchre by al-Hakim, the Fatimid Caliph, but implicates both Saracens and Jews, for which they were punished by God: 900,000 Jews and Saracens died of famine and plague in the span of three years. See H. Duplés-Agier (ed.), *Chronique de Saint-Martial de Limoges* (Paris 1874), 6–7. The destruction of the Church of the Holy Sepulchre actually occurred in September 1009, leading Landes to conclude (Bourgain, *Ademari Cabannensis Chronicon*, 299) that Ademar placed it after Alduin's campaign in order to portray the Jews' overture to the Fatimid Caliph as an act of revenge, rather than as the result of a messianic impulse.

84. MGH, SS, v. 4, 139; Bourgain, *Ademari Cabannensis Chronicon*, 171.

85. On Glaber, see John France (ed., trans.), *Rodulfi Glabri, Historiarum libri quinque* (Oxford and New York 1989), xlii. For the following tale, see France, *Rodulfi Glabri*, bk. 3, pt. 7, sec. 24–25, 132–137. On this particular incident in the chronicles of Glaber and Ademar, see John France, "The Destruction of Jerusalem and the First Crusade," *Journal of Ecclesiastical History* 47 (1996), 1–17.

86. "Erat igitur huius generis apud Aurelianensem Galliarum regiam urbem non modica multitudo, qui ceteris sue gentis tumidiores et inuidi atque audatiores sunt reperti." See France, *Rodulfi Glabri*, 134 (Latin), 135 (English).

87. France notes that Glaber had resided in this abbey, implying that this may have been his source of information (*Rodulfi Glabri*, 134n1).

88. Blumenkranz (*Les auteurs chrétiens*, 257n5) reads into this formulation the assumption that some sort of council was held to decide the Jews' fate.

89. Note that the 1007 text tells of women who drown themselves.

90. "Vtque diuulgatum est, per orbem uniuersum communi omnium Christianorum consensu decretum est ut omnes Iudei ab illorum terris uel ciuitatibus funditus pellerentur. Sicque uniuersi odio habiti, expulsi de ciuitatibus, alii gladiis trucidati, alii fluminibus necati, diuersisque mortium generibus interempti, nonnulli etiam sese diuersa cede interemerunt." See France, *Rodulfi Glabri*, 134 (Latin), 135 (English).

91. By the middle of the eleventh century France had a thriving Jewish community, and Limoges was home to the renowned rabbinic scholar Joseph Bonfils.

92. France writes that Ademar could not have drawn from Glaber's work and doubts that Glaber drew from that of Ademar (*Rodulfi Glabri*, xlvii).

93. Ademar's fabrication of the story of Martial is the focus of Richard Landes's monograph, *Relics*. Note, however, that Dinur accepts Glaber's story as true, if exaggerated (Dinur, *Israel in the Diaspora*, v. 1, pt. 1, 186n90).

94. France, *Rodulfi Glabri*, bk. 3, pt. 6, sec. 19–23, 126–133. See also the account in Hugh of Flavigny, *Chronicon*, MGH, SS, v. 8, 399; Hugh gives the date 1028.

95. Stow (*1007 Anonymous*, 28) posits a literary link between the 1007 source and Glaber's tale of the campaign waged by Robert the Pious against the heretics of Orléans in 1022 because of the similarity between "heresy" and "judaizing." This is supported by the appearance, in Glaber's chronicle, of the story about the heretics of Orléans immediately after the Holy

Sepulchre incident. In the same vein, Stow (*1007 Anonymous*, 29) proposes that the year 1007 should read 1017, the year Glaber gives for the Orléans heresy. Landes ("Massacres of 1010") claims that the three texts (*1007 Anonymous*, Ademar, and Glaber) refer to a single wave of persecution. This view ignores various discrepancies, including those noted by Stow, "Avignonese Papacy," 276–277n6.

96. Chazan, "1007–1012," 107. Later, Chazan rejects Glaber's linkage of the events of 1010 with the Holy Sepulchre incident ("1007–1012," 110).

97. MGH, SS, v. 3, 81. The expulsion is also recorded in the *Annalista Saxo: Die Reichschronik des Annalista Saxo*, ed. Klaus Nass (Hanover 2006) [MGH, SS, v. 37], 327. See also Aronius, *Regesten*, 61, no. 144. Baron (*Social and Religious History*, 2nd ed., v. 4, 66) writes that the expulsion took place in November or December. This assessment fits the appearance of the notice at the end of the record for 1012, as well as Henry's presence in Mainz sometime after November 11, as documented in the Quedlinburg annals (MGH, SS, v. 3, 81).

98. Habermann, *Book of the Persecutions*, 16. Most scholars have at least wondered whether these might have been the circumstances under which Gershom's own son allegedly apostatized. The oft-cited poem by Rabbi Simon ben Isaac of Mainz (Habermann, *Book of the Persecutions*, 22–23), although doubtless rooted in a context of religious conflict, is too stylized to yield any conclusions.

99. "Expulsio Iudaeorum facta est a rege in Moguntia." See Baron, *Social and Religious History*, 2nd ed., v. 4, 271–272n85. Graetz also claims that the expulsion applied to other communities, besides Mainz, based on a poetic lamentation by Rabbi Simon ben Isaac (*Geschichte der Juden*, 338).

100. Poliakov, *History of Anti-Semitism*, v. 1, 36; Bernhard Blumenkranz, *Juifs et chrétiens dans le monde occidental: 430–1096* (Paris 1960), 381; Blumenkranz, "Germany, 843–1096," 172–173.

101. Graetz, *Geschichte der Juden*, 337; Blumenkranz, *Juifs et chrétiens*, 168. For an English translation of the texts of both Wecelin and Henry, see Anna Sapir Abulafia, "An Eleventh-Century Exchange of Letters Between a Christian and a Jew," *Journal of Medieval History* 7 (1981), 165–171. Dinur claims that the Wecelin context fits the comment—which immediately follows in the Quedlinburg annals—about the "refutation of the insanity of some heretics" (*quorundam haereticorum refutata est insania*) (Dinur, *Israel in the Diaspora*, v. 1, pt. 1, 185n85).

102. Baron, *Social and Religious History*, 2nd ed., v. 4, 66, 271–272n85, based on H. Tykocinski, "Die Verfolgungen der Juden in Mainz im Jahr 1012," in *Beiträge zur Geschichte der deutschen Juden: Festschrift zum siebzigsten Geburstage Martin Philippsons* (Leipzig 1916), 4. Friedrich Lotter notes that the investiture, in July 1011, of Archbishop Erchinbald of Mainz as the chief chancellor and chaplain of the empire may have been a factor in the decision to expel the Jews. This, he suggests, dovetails with Baron's suggestion (*Social and Religious History*, 2nd ed., v. 4, 272n85) that at the end of 1012 the expulsion was revoked rather than promulgated. See Lotter, "Die Vertreibung der Juden aus Mainz um 1012 und der antijüdische Traktat des Hofgieslichen Heinrich," in *Judenvetreibungen in Mittelalter und früher Neuzeit*, ed. Friedhelm Burgard et al. (Hanover 1999), 39–40, 65–66.

103. Baron, *Social and Religious History*, 2nd ed., v. 4, 271–272n85; Blumenkranz, "Germany, 843–1096," 172–173.

104. Baron, *Social and Religious History*, 2nd ed., v. 4, 66. The proposed link to the al-Hakim story was suggested by S. Hirsch, *Jahrbuch des deutschen Reichs unter Heinrich II* (Berlin 1864), v. 2, 343 ff., cited in Blumenkranz, *Les auteurs chrétiens*, 250n2.

105. Richard Landes classifies historians as either "lumpers" or "splitters" and, regarding the incidents of 1007–1012, is more a lumper than a splitter himself. See his "Massacres of 1010," 79–112.

106. One may even speculate that the loss of the contract, a woman's most valuable document, was related to the expulsion. For the text of the contract, see *Kerem Hemed* 8 (1854), 106; for an English translation, see Agus, *Urban Civilization*, v. 2, 646–648. The significance of this document was first noted by Graetz, *Geschichte der Juden*, 387, 545.

107. Blumenkranz, *Les auteurs chrétiens*, 250n2. This interpretation allows for the integration into the general scheme of the story of the apostasy of Rabbi Gershom's son. See Baron, *Social and Religious History*, 2nd ed., v. 4, 66.

108. Baer, "Religious-Social Tendency," 4.

109. Baron, *Social and Religious History*, 2nd ed., v. 4, 67. Similarly, Stow writes that between the tenth and the thirteenth centuries "constitutional erosion was also accompanied by growing physical insecurity" (*Alienated Minority*, 101).

110. Ben-Sasson, *History of the Jewish People*, 411–412.

111. Chazan, "1007–1012," 101–118.

112. Stow, *Alienated Minority*, 94–95. Nevertheless, Stow concludes (p. 95) that the tales "do reflect the mood of the late tenth and early eleventh century," citing the characterization of Christianity by Meshullam ben Qalonymos as a violent force that "consumes, destroys and tramples all with its feet." Yet Meshullam was working within the genre of liturgical poetry, which is notoriously difficult to assess because it is so stylized.

113. MGH, SS, v. 8, 182; Aronius, *Regesten*, 67, no. 160.

114. Clerics acted out of concern that the Jews not exceed the bounds of the state of humiliation in which Augustinian doctrine mandated their toleration. There were further instances of this later, such as in 1074, when the Council of Rouen condemned the Jewish employment of servants and wet nurses. Naturally, such episodes reflect a reality of Jewish prosperity, which hardly foreshadows their destruction.

115. Blumenkranz, "Germany, 843–1096," 172.

116. Baron, *Social and Religious History*, 2nd ed., v. 4, 284n2.

117. Schwarzfuchs ("France Under the Early Capets," 148) links this event with the persecution, which according to Maimonides' *Epistle to Yemen* occurred in "Linon," in the land of the Franks, following the appearance of a messianic pretender. However, R. Joseph Kafih dismisses the tale as fiction and a forgery (Kafih, *Igerot* [Jerusalem 1972], 60).

118. See the discussion of apostasy in Chapter 5 and of Jewish-Christian relations in Chapter 7.

119. Baron, *Social and Religious History*, 2nd ed., v. 4, 91–92.

120. Baron, *Social and Religious History*, 2nd ed., v. 4, 91.

121. David Nirenberg, *Communities of Violence: Persecutions of Minorities in the Middle Ages* (Princeton 1996), 3–10.

122. Parkes, *Jew in the Medieval Community*, 57.

123. Similarly, Michael Toch has attributed to the trauma of the Holocaust the emergence of an approach to medieval Jewish history that emphasizes Jewish-Christian conflict, in contrast to the competing school, which stresses coexistence. See Toch, *Die Juden im Mittelalterlichen Reich* (Munich 1998), 120–121. For Croce's generalization, see Edward Hallett Carr, *What Is History?* (New York 1962), 3–35, esp. 22.

Chapter Three

Earlier versions of this chapter include David Malkiel, "Destruction or Conversion: Intention and Reaction, Crusaders and Jews, in 1096," *Jewish History* 15 (2001), 257–280; and David Malkiel, "The Price of Faith in 1096," in *Be'erot Yitzhak: Studies in Memory of Isadore Twersky*, ed. Jay M. Harris (Cambridge, Mass., 2005), *31–*59.

1. Yitzhak Baer, "Basic Themes in the Historical Development of Judaism in the Middle Ages," *Moznayim* 23 (1947), 202 (in Hebrew).

2. H. H. Ben-Sasson, *On Jewish History in the Middle Ages* (Tel Aviv 1958), 175 (in Hebrew). The translation and italics are mine.

3. Shmuel Shepkaru, *Jewish Martyrs in the Pagan and Christian Worlds* (Cambridge 2006), 9–10.

4. Jacob Katz, *Exclusiveness and Tolerance* (Oxford 1961), 88; Salo W. Baron, *A Social and Religious History of the Jews*, 2nd ed. (New York 1957), v. 4, 104.

5. Norman Cohn, *The Pursuit of the Millennium*, 2nd ed. (New York 1970), 70, and similarly on p. 69.

6. Avraham Grossman, "The Roots of Martyrdom in Early Ashkenaz," in *Sanctity of Life and Martyrdom*, ed. Isaiah M. Gafni and Aviezer Ravitzky (Jerusalem 1992), 99 (in Hebrew). See also Avraham Grossman, "Martyrdom in the Eleventh and Twelfth Centuries," *Pe'amim* 75 (1998), 27 (in Hebrew). I am most grateful to Professor Grossman for encouraging me to pursue the present line of inquiry.

7. Haym Soloveitchik, "Religious Law and Change: The Medieval Ashkenazic Example," *AJS Review* 12 (1987), 208.

8. Robert Chazan, "Medieval Antisemitism," in *Harvest of Hate*, ed. David Berger (Philadelphia 1986), 55. See also Robert Chazan, *European Jewry and the First Crusade* (Berkeley 1987), 66: "There was a commitment in principle to eliminate the Jews"; and see also Robert Chazan, "The Hebrew First-Crusade Chronicles," *Revue des Études Juives* 133 (1974), 249; and Robert Chazan, *In the Year 1096: The First Crusade and the Jews* (Philadelphia 1996), 54.

9. Jeremy Cohen, "The Hebrew Crusade Chronicles in Their Christian Cultural Context," in *Juden und Christen zur Zeit der Kreuzzüge*, ed. Alfred Haverkamp (Sigmaringen 1999), 17. Cohen also states, "When all else failed, there remained the options offered by the crusaders: Christianity or death" (p. 20). See also Jeremy Cohen, "Between Martyrdom and Apostasy: Doubt and Self-Definition in Twelfth-Century Ashkenaz," *Journal of Medieval and Early Modern Studies* 29 (1999), 434; and Jeremy Cohen, *Sanctifying the Name of God: Jewish Martyrs and Jewish Memories of the First Crusade* (Philadelphia 2004), 1, 4.

10. Anna Sapir Abulafia, "Invectives Against Christianity in the Hebrew Chronicles of the First Crusade," in *Crusade and Settlement*, ed. Peter W. Edbury (Cardiff 1985), 66.

11. Jonathan Riley-Smith, "The First Crusade and the Persecution of the Jews," in *Persecution and Toleration*, ed. W. J. Shiels (Oxford 1984), 58. See also Jonathan Riley-Smith, *The First Crusade and the Idea of Crusading* (London 1986), 53.

12. Gavin I. Langmuir, "The Transformation of Anti-Judaism," in his *Toward a Definition of Antisemitism* (Berkeley 1990), 97. Langmuir (pp. 64–65) surveys different interpretations of the 1096 events vis-à-vis the motives of the marauders, particularly avarice and millennial fervor, and points out that both interpretations serve to exculpate Christianity. Kenneth Stow states that Emicho and his band of followers embarked on systematic raids that were designed to locate Jews and destroy them, but he does not explore whether eventual converts were

forced or chose conversion; see Kenneth Stow, *Alienated Minority: The Jews of Medieval Europe* (Cambridge, Mass., 1992), 110.

13. Ben-Zion Netanyahu, *The Origins of the Inquisition in Fifteenth-Century Spain* (New York 1995), 163. But Netanyahu strikes a different tone when he adds that in 1096 the crusaders "fell upon the Jews like packs of hungry wolves, and were to give up their desired prey only when warned by lay or Church authorities against killing Christians (which the converts would become)."

14. Jean Flori, *La première croisade: L'Occident Chrétien contre l'Islam (Aux origines des idéologies occidentale)* (Brussels 1992), 53; Jean Flori, "Une ou plusieurs 'premiere croisade'? Le message d'Urbain II et les plus anciens pogroms d'Occident," *Revue historique* 285 (1991), 7–10; Jean Flori, *Pierre l'Ermite et la Première Croisade* (Paris 1999), 261–271. For other proponents of the conventional view, see Steven T. Katz, *The Holocaust in Historical Context* (New York 1994), 327; Amnon Raz-Krakozkin and Ora Limor, *Jews and Christians in Western Europe*, v. 2, *Majority and Minority* (Tel Aviv 1993), 51 (in Hebrew); and Gerd Mentgen, "Die Juden des Mittelrhein-Mosel-Gebietes im Hochmittelalter unter besonderer Berucksichtigung der Kreuzzugsverfolgungen," in *Der Erste Kreuzzug 1096 und sein Folgen* (Düsseldorf 1996), 37–75. Popular treatments of 1096 include Michael Foss, *People of the First Crusade* (New York 1997), 61–62; and Leonard B. Glick, *Abraham's Heirs* (Syracuse 1999), 91–110. These works do not stake out a position.

15. Aryeh Grabois, "Riots Against the Jews as Reflected in Christian Writings: The Persecutions of 1096 as Reflected in the Christian Chronography of the First Half of the Twelfth Century," *'Et ha-Da'at* 1 (1997), 12 (in Hebrew).

16. Benjamin Z. Kedar, "The Forcible Baptisms of 1096: History and Historiography," in *Forschungen zur Reichs-, Papst-, und Landesgeschichte: Peter Herde zum 65. Geburstag con Freunden, Schülern und Kollegen dargebracht* ed. Karl Borchardt and Enno Bünz (Stuttgart 1998), v. 1, 187–200. Kedar marvels that many historiographical accounts of the First Crusade—those not particularly concerned with Jewish history—gloss over this crucial element, and he muses that perhaps it is because Albert of Aachen and later William of Tyre do not depict it as such.

17. In some cases the Jews fell victim not only to crusaders but also to townspeople, who, although they may have shared the crusaders' religious zeal, presumably had other motives as well for attacking their Jewish neighbors. On the possible roles and motives of various segments of the Christian population, such as townspeople, villagers, and clergy, in the events of 1096, see Sara Schiffmann, "Heinrichs IV: Verhalten zu den deutschen Juden zur Zeit des ersten Kreuzzuges," *Zeitschrift für die Geschichte der Juden in Deutschland* 3 (1931), 39–58; Sara Schiffmann, "Die deutsche Bischöfe und die Juden zur Zeit des ersten Kreuzzüges," *Zeitschrift für die Geschichte der Juden in Deutschland* 3 (1931), 233–250; and Sara Schiffmann, *Heinrich IV und die Bischöfe in ihrem Verhalten zu den deutschen Juden zur Zeit des ersten Kreuzzüges* (Berlin 1931). "Crusader" is hence used as a generic term for the Jews' assailants, without intending to obscure the variety of Christian populations and their motivations and behaviors.

18. Israel Jacob Yuval, "The Vengeance and the Curse, the Blood and the Libel: From Tales of Heroes to Blood Libels," *Zion* 58 (1993), 41 (in Hebrew). Riley-Smith also highlights the motif of vengeance, although from the point of view of the crusaders. See Riley-Smith, "The First Crusade," 63, based on a comment in the *Annalista Saxo*, discussed later; and Riley-Smith, *First Crusade*, 54–55. On vengeance in the thought and writings of the First Crusade, see H. E. J. Cowdrey, "Martyrdom and the First Crusade," in *Crusade and Settlement*, ed. Peter W. Edbury (Cardiff 1985), 46–56.

19. See Riley-Smith, "The First Crusade," 69; and Riley-Smith, *First Crusade*, 55–56. The vengeance motif finds eloquent expression in the words of Friar Paul, the apostate who disputed the rabbis in Paris in approximately 1272: "They deserve to be killed, as they killed Him." See Joseph Shatzmiller, *La deuxième controverse de Paris: Un chapitre dans la polémique Chrétiens et Juifs au Moyen Age* (Paris 1994), 56.

20. Vengeance has been linked to the possibly millennial significance of the First Crusade. See Flori, "Une ou plusieurs 'première croisade'?" 20–24; Flori, *La première croisade*, 53–54; Richard Landes, "The Massacres of 1010: On the Origins of Popular Violence in Western Europe," in *From Witness to Witchcraft*, ed. Jeremy Cohen (Wiesbaden 1996), 79–112; Sylvia Schein, "The Crusades as a Messianic Movement," in *Messianism and Eschatology*, ed. Zvi Baras (Jerusalem 1984), 177–189 (in Hebrew); and Cohn, *Pursuit of the Millennium*.

21. For Regensburg, see Abraham Meir Habermann, *The Book of the Persecutions of Ashkenaz and France* (Jerusalem 1945), 56 (in Hebrew). Note that there is also an indication that the Jews of Regensburg were martyred in Habermann, *Book of the Persecutions*, 287. Also for Regensburg, see Joseph Hacker, "On the Persecutions of 1096," *Zion* 31 (1966), 229–231 (in Hebrew). In Kerpen one source reports that the Jews were spared (Habermann, *Book of the Persecutions*, 52), whereas the chronicle of Eliezer ben Nathan reports that they were forcibly converted (Habermann, *Book of the Persecutions*, 80). Similarly, the narrative of Solomon ben Samson states that most of the Jews of Metz were forcibly baptized (p. 56) but also states that they were martyred (p. 52). For Trier, see Habermann, *Book of the Persecutions*, 52–56; and see also Robert Chazan, *God, Humanity, and History: The Hebrew First Crusade Narratives* (Berkeley 2000), 83–93; Robert Chazan, "Christian and Jewish Perceptions of 1096: A Case Study of Trier," *Jewish History* 13 (1999), 9–22.

22. Baron, *A Social and Religious History of the Jews*, 2nd ed., v. 4, 105. Note that Baron emphasizes the texts' literary function and suggests that Eliezer ben Nathan wrote his narrative as "mere explanatory introductions to his elegies describing the downfall of the four communities of Spires, Worms, Mayence, and Cologne (Baron, *Social and Religious History*, 2nd ed., v. 4, 288n9). Baron's thesis is presented more elaborately in Gerson D. Cohen, "The Hebrew Crusade Chronicles and the Ashkenazic Tradition," in *Minhah le-Nahum*, ed. Marc Brettler and Michael Fishbane (Sheffield 1993), 36–53. Baer, in his 1945 introduction to Habermann's *Book of the Persecutions*, surmises that the Hebrew narratives were read in the synagogue, but he does not go so far as to claim that they were written as explications of the poetic dirges (p. 3).

23. Grossman, "Roots of Martyrdom," 121–127; Jeremy Cohen, "The 'Persecutions of 1096': From Martyrdom to Martyrology," *Zion* 59 (1994), 206–207 (in Hebrew); Cohen, "Between Martyrdom and Apostasy," 435–436. On apostasy in medieval Ashkenaz, see Chapter 5. In the same vein, Soloveitchik writes that the chronicles "describe martyrdom so as to induce emulation" ("Religious Law and Change," 215).

24. Ivan G. Marcus, "Hierarchies, Religious Boundaries, and Jewish Spirituality in Medieval Germany," *Jewish History* 1 (1986), 13. Strengthening Jewish morale was also the ostensible purpose of the vituperative, deprecatory references to Christianity strewn throughout the Hebrew chronicles. See Katz, *Exclusiveness*, 89; Jacob Katz, "Martyrdom in the Middle Ages and in 1648–1649," in *Yitzhak F. Baer Jubilee Volume*, ed. Salo W. Baron et al. (Jerusalem 1961), 318–320 (in Hebrew); and Sapir Abulafia, "Invectives," 66–72.

25. See Ivan G. Marcus, "From Politics to Martyrdom: Shifting Paradigms in the Hebrew Narratives of the 1096 Crusade Riots," *Prooftexts* 2 (1982), 42–43; and Ivan G. Marcus, "The Representation of Reality in the Narratives of 1096," *Jewish History* 13 (1999), 37–48.

26. Cohen, *Sanctifying the Name of God*, 106.

27. Robert Chazan, "The Facticity of Medieval Narrative: A Case Study of the Hebrew First Crusade Narratives," *AJS Review* 16 (1991), 46–48; Chazan, "Christian and Jewish Perceptions of 1096."

28. Like Marcus, Eli Yassif debates the historiographical utility of the 1096 narratives; see Eli Yassif, "Legends and History: Historians Read Hebrew Legends of the Middle Ages," *Zion* 64 (1999), 187–200 (in Hebrew). See also Eli Yassif, *The Hebrew Folktale: History, Genre, Meaning*, trans. Jacqueline S. Teitelbaum (Bloomington 1999), 297–321. Yassif's skeptical approach is challenged by Moshe Rosman, who, focusing on Beshtian hagiography, argues that even mythical and legendary material preserves a kernel of historical truth; see Moshe Rosman, "The Art of Historiography and the Methods of Folklore," *Zion* 65 (2000), 209–218 (in Hebrew).

29. Cohen, *Sanctifying the Name of God*, 106.

30. On points of similarity between the Hebrew and Latin sources, see Yitzhak Baer, "Introduction," in Habermann, *Book of the Persecutions*, 3 (in Hebrew); and Yitzhak Baer, "The Persecutions of 1096," in *Sefer Assaf*, ed. Umberto Cassuto, Joseph Klausner, and Joshua Gutmann (Jerusalem 1953), 127–130 (in Hebrew).

31. For the critical evaluation of these texts, see Isaiah Sonne, "Nouvel examen des trois relations hébraïques sur les persecutions de 1096: Suivi de'un fragment de version judéo-allemande inédite de la première relation," *Revue des Études Juives* 96 (1933), 113–156; Isaiah Sonne, "Which Is the Early Version of the First Crusade Massacres?" *Zion* 12 (1947), 74–81 (in Hebrew); Isaiah Sonne, "Critical Annotations to Solomon ben Simon's Record of the Edicts of 1094, including a Fragment of This Text in Judaeo-German," in *The Abraham Weiss Jubilee Volume* (New York 1964), 385–405; Baer, "Introduction," 3; Baer, "Persecutions of 1096," 127–130; Baron, *Social and Religious History*, v. 4, 285–287; Moses A. Shulvas, "Knowledge of History and of Historical Literature in the Cultural Realm of Ashkenazic Jewry in the Middle Ages," in *Hanokh Albeck Jubilee Volume* (Jerusalem 1963), 483–486 (in Hebrew); Chazan, "Hebrew First-Crusade Chronicles," 235–254; Chazan, "The Hebrew First Crusade Chronicles: Further Reflections," *AJS Review* 3 (1978), 79–98; Sapir Abulafia, "The Interrelationship Between the Hebrew Chronicles of the First Crusade," *Journal of Semitic Studies* 27 (1982), 221–239; Chazan, *European Jewry*, 40–49; Chazan, "The Mainz Anonymous: Historiographic Perspectives," in *Jewish History and Jewish Memory*, ed. Elisheva Carlebach, John M. Efron, and David N. Myers (Hanover 1998), 54–69; and Chazan, *God, Humanity, and History*.

32. Massacres were recorded in Speyer, Cologne, Neuss, Wevelinghofen, Xanten, Moers, Kerpen, Trier, and Metz. There were allegedly three other communities in which the Jews of Cologne found refuge, as well as the unidentified "S(h)ela."

33. See, for example, Norman Golb, "New Light on the Persecution of French Jews at the Time of the First Crusade," *Proceedings of the American Academy of Jewish Research* 34 (1966), 1–45; Robert Chazan, *Medieval Jewry in Northern France* (Baltimore 1973), 24–28; and Edna Engel, "The Wandering of a Provencal Proselyte," *Sefunot* 7(22) (1999), 13–21 (in Hebrew).

34. Throughout the chronicles, the binding of Isaac and the legend of the mother and her seven sons underlie stories of slaughtered children; see Habermann, *Book of the Persecutions*, 32, 34, 102. On this scholarly avenue, see, apart from the work of Ivan Marcus cited earlier, Alan Mintz, *Hurban: Responses to Catastrophe in Hebrew Literature* (New York 1984), 84–102; Cohen, "Persecutions of 1096," 176–208; Cohen, *Sanctifying the Name of God*, 73–158; and Elisheva Baumgarten and Rella Kushelevsky, "From 'The Mother and Her Sons' to 'The Mother of the Sons' in Medieval Ashkenaz," *Zion* 71 (2006), 273–300 (in Hebrew).

35. Cohen, "Between Martyrdom and Apostasy," 436; Cohen, *Sanctifying the Name of God*, 158.

36. Chazan, "Facticity of Medieval Narrative," 46–48. Chazan goes on to argue that "what is surely warranted . . . is the uncovering of a series of patterns—patterns of Christian behavior, of Christian thinking, of Jewish behavior, of Jewish thinking" (p. 48). This is strikingly similar to Marcus's approach, notwithstanding their debate over the chronicles' historicity.

37. For a list of the Latin sources, see Julius Aronius, *Regesten zur Geschichte der Juden* (Berlin 1902), 78–93; and Riley-Smith, "The First Crusade," 52. I would like to thank Dov Gera of Ben-Gurion University of the Negev for reading the Latin sources with me.

38. "Iudei in pertinacia sua tumultuarie occiduntur" (Monumenta Germaniae Historica [MGH], Scriptores [SS], v. 5, 27).

39. "Iudei Moguntiae et variis locis occisi" (MGH, SS, v. 3, 7).

40. "Strages Iudaeorum Coloniae et Moguntiae a peregrinis facta est" (MGH, SS, v. 1, 100; MGH, SS, v. 16, 726). Identifying the assailants as pilgrims exculpates other, local participants in the violence. This approach is not shared by all the Latin sources; cf. the narrative of Albert of Aachen, discussed later. Also note the juxtaposition of Cologne and Mainz. This suggests that the Jewish communities of these two cities had similar experiences, which is not the impression granted by the Hebrew sources. See Robert Chazan, "The Story of the Deeds of the Cologne Jewish Community," *'Alei Sefer* 11 (1984), 63–71 (in Hebrew); and Robert Chazan, "The Deeds of the Jewish Community of Cologne," *Journal of Jewish Studies* 35 (1984), 185–195.

41. "Ab his, quia multitudini confidebant, in plerisque urbibus Iudaei coacti baptizabantur, aut interimebantur, aut se ipsos interficiebant" (MGH, SS, v. 3, 134).

42. "Hoc anno [1096] populus innumerabilis ex diversarum gentium partibus armatus Hierosolimam tendens, Iudeos baptizari compulit, rennuentes immensa cede profligavit. Apud Mogontiam Iudei numero virorum ac mulierum et infantum mille et 14 interfecti sunt, et iterum a christianitate recesserunt" (MGH, SS, v. 2, 246). See the marginal note in *Chronica Minor Auctore Minorita Erphordiensi*, MGH, SS, v. 24, 191: "Aput Magunciam Iudei utriusque sexus numero mille et 14 occisi sunt." This would suggest that the near entirety of Mainz Jewry died, and hence baptism would have been a minor part of the entire episode. See Kenneth Stow, "The Jewish Family in the Rhineland: Form and Function," *American Historical Review* 92 (1987), 1085–1110.

43. "Populus innumerabilis ex diversarum gentium partibus armatus Hierosolimam tendens, Iudeos baptizari compulit, rennuentes immensa cede profligavit. Apud Mogontiam Iudei numero virorum ac mulierum et infantum mille et quatordecim interfecti sunt, et maxima pars civitatis exusta est. Iudei per diversas provincias christiani facti sunt, et iterum a christianitate recesserunt" (MGH, SS, v. 3, 106).

44. "Firmissima pace interim ubique composita, et primo Iudeos in urbibus in quibus erant, aggressi, eos ad credendum Christo compellunt; credere nolentes bonis privant, trucidant, aut urbibus eliminant. Aliqui post ad Iudaismum revolvuntur" (*Chronographia*, in MGH, SS, v. 6, 367).

45. Ekkehard thus extends the geographic range of the attacks far beyond Mainz and Cologne.

46. "Per civitates Rheni, Moeni quoque atque Danubii deducti, execrabilem Judaeorum quacumque repertam plebem, zelo Christianitatis etiam in hoc deservientes, aut omnino delere, aut etiam inter ecclesiae satagebant compellere sinum" (*Hierosolymita*, in *Recueil des*

historiens des Croisade, Occidentaux [RHC Occ.], v. 5, pt. 1, 20). The translation is from August Charles Krey (ed.), *The First Crusade: The Accounts of Eye Witnesses and Participants* (Princeton 1921), 53. Ekkehard repeats this account almost verbatim in two other sources: *Chronicum universale* and MGH, SS, v. 6, 208, 215. See also F.-J. Schmale and I. Schmale-Ott (eds.), *Frutolfi et Ekkehardi Chronica* (Darmstadt 1972), 108.

47. "Fuere tamen quidam ex eis, qui falsa specie religionis eandem miliciam aggrederentur, inter quos Emicho quidam comes de partibus Rheni, usurpans sibi ducatum fere 12 milium, Iudaeos ubicunque repperit, vel delere vel ecclesiae incorporare satagebat" (*Chronica sive historia de duabus civitatibus*, 7, 2, in MGH, SS, v. 20, 249). The scholarly edition is A. Hofmeister and W. Lammers (eds.), *Chronica sive historia de duabus civitatibus* (Darmstadt 1961), 502. This source is cited in Sapir Abulafia, "Invectives," 71n2. Otto's report was written after that of Ekkehard and may have been based on it.

48. Kenneth Stow asserts that the Latin sources condemn Emicho for having created a situation of large numbers of insincere Jewish converts, especially because those forcibly baptized quickly reverted; see Kenneth Stow, "Conversion, Apostasy, and Apprehensiveness: Emicho of Flonheim and the Fear of Jews in the Twelfth Century," *Speculum* 76 (2001), 911–933.

49. See Mary Minty, "*Kiddush Hashem* in German Christian Eyes in the Middle Ages," *Zion* 59 (1994), 214 (in Hebrew).

50. On the diabolical stubbornness of the Jews, see Cecil Roth, "The Medieval Conception of the Jew," in *Essays and Studies in Memory of Linda R. Miller*, ed. Israel Davidson (New York 1938), 171–190; and Joshua Trachtenberg, *The Devil and the Jews* (Philadelphia 1943), 11–31 and passim.

51. "Hoc anno in quibusdam civitatibus Iudei magna cede trucidati sunt ab his qui Hierosolimam petierunt; ita dico, ut apud Spiram fugientes in palacium regis et episcopi, etiam repugnando vix se defenderent, eodem episcopo Iohanne illis auxiliante. Qui etiam postea ob hoc ira commotus, et pecunia Iudeorum conductus, quosdam fecit obtruncari christianos. Item apud Wormaciam Iudei persequentes fugiendo christianos, ad episcopum properabant. Qui cum non aliter illis salutem, nisi baptizarentur, promitteret inducias colloquii rogaverunt. Et eadem hora episcopi cubiculum intrantes, nostris foras expectantibus quid responsuri essent; diabolo et propria duricia persuadente, se ipsos interfecerunt" (*Chronicon*, in MGH, SS, v. 5, 464–465). This text is actually a marginal note rather than part of the *Chronicon*.

52. Similarly, the Hebrew narratives report that the burgrave of Moers and the bishop of Trier offered the Jews survival if they would abandon their faith. In these cases, too, the assumption seems to have been that the crusaders would not offer baptism.

53. "Aliqui Iudeorum zelo tenende patrie legis ducti se mutuo trucidant" (MGH, SS, v. 6, 394). On the dating of this text, see Minty, "*Kiddush Hashem* in German Christian Eyes," 214.

54. On Jewish treasure, see Albert of Aachen, discussed later.

55. "Habebant in professione, ut vellent ulcisci Christum in gentilibus vel Iudeis. Unde etiam in civitate Mogontia interfecerunt circiter DCCCC de Iudeis, non parcentes omnino vel mulieribus vel parvulis. Erat tunc episcopus civitatis Rothardus, ad cuius auxilium et defensionem cum tesauris suis confugerant Iudei; quos nec episcopus nec milites eius, quorum tunc ibi multitudo aderat, vel defendere vel eripere poterant ab Hierosolimitis, quia fortasse christiani contra christianos pugnare nolebant pro Iudeis, verum expugnato atrio episcopi, in quo erant ad firmamentum sui, vel etiam expugnatis ipsis penetrabilibus archiepiscopi, omnes interfecti sunt, quotquot ibi inventi sunt, Iudei. Fuerat hec cedes Iudeorum ante dominicam pentecostes, feria III^a, eratque miseria spectare multos et magnos occisorum acervos efferri in

plaustris de civitate Mogontia. Similiter Colonie, Uuormatie, aliisque civitatibus Gallie vel Germanie interfecti sunt Iudei, preter paucos qui ad babtismum confugerunt coacti, cum illi minime debeant ad fidem inviti" (*Die Reichschronik des Annalista Saxo*, ed. Klaus Nass [Hanover 2006] [MGH, SS, v. 37], 490–491).

56. The detail of the loaded wagons also appears in Hebrew sources. See the poem by R. Abraham: "The modest and important daughters of kings are dragged in wagons and hauled nude" (Habermann, *Book of the Persecutions*, 62). For a prose version, see Jehuda Wistinetzki and Jakob Freimann (eds.), *Sefer Hasidim* (Frankfurt am Main 1924), 375, no. 1530: "During the night they [the survivors] brought the dead on the wagons to the cemetery, for it was far from the place where they were killed, and a woman fell off of the wagon without their realizing it."

57. Riley-Smith cites this Latin source as the only one explicitly to mention vengeance; see Riley-Smith, "The First Crusade," 63. Cf. Frutolf and Ekkehard's reference to the religious zeal of the crusaders and Albert of Aachen's closing comment on the ideal of crusading, both discussed later.

58. The casual note about baptism refers to cities other than Mainz, but not in Mainz. This suggests that the chronicler was unfamiliar with the events in other communities, especially because the note is brief and vague.

59. Albert's chronicle is generally thought to have influenced other Latin accounts; see Minty, "*Kiddush Hashem* in German Christian Eyes," 214. On Albert, see also Susan B. Edgington, "Albert of Aachen Reappraised," in *From Clermont to Jerusalem*, ed. Alan V. Murray (Turnholt 1998), 55–67; and Albert of Aachen, *Historia Ierosolimitana: History of the Journey to Jerusalem*, ed. and trans. Susan B. Edgington (Oxford 2007), xxv, xxvi.

60. The view that Jewish suffering represents divine judgment has roots in both Christian and Jewish theology and appears in Hebrew as well as Latin texts.

61. "Aliquo animi errore." William of Tyre and the *Gesta Treverorum* also refer to madness or insanity. On Albert's vacillation, see Benjamin Z. Kedar, "Crusade Historians and the Massacres of 1096," *Jewish History* 12 (1998), 20.

62. "Vnde nescio si uel Dei iudicio aut aliquo animi errore spiritu crudelitatis adversus Iudeorum surrexerunt populum, per quascumque ciuitates dispersos, et crudelissimam in eos exercuerunt necem, et precipue in regno Lotharingie, asserentes id esse principium expeditionis sue, et obsequii contra hostes fidei Christiane" (Albert of Aachen, *Historia Ierosolimitana*, 50 [Latin], 51 [English]). The translation of *expeditionis* as "crusade" is somewhat loose.

63. See the account of the *Annales Brunwilarenses*, discussed earlier.

64. "Thesauros infinitos." Albert reports that the bishop "put away carefully" (*caute reposuit*) the money, but here and in the Hebrew accounts, it is not clear whether he saw himself as safeguarding the Jews' money or taking it from them. Chazan claims that the bishop of Worms and the archbishop of Mainz were as eager as the bishop of Speyer to save the Jews; see Chazan, "Mainz Anonymous," 57.

65. "Habito consilio." The expression "consulted together" appears also in the *Annales S. Disibodi*, suggesting that the two sources may be related. See also the Mainz Anonymous: "held a council" (p. 94), referring to Speyer. The expression also implies that the attacks were perpetrated in cold blood rather than spontaneously, a thesis put forward by Riley-Smith in *First Crusade*, 51–52.

66. See other figures for the number massacred: 1,014 (*Annales S. Albani Moguntini*) and 900 (*Annalista Saxo*). For the view that these figures are inflated, see Simon Schwarzfuchs,

"The Place of the Crusades in Jewish History," in *Culture and Society in Medieval Jewry*, ed. Menahem Ben-Sasson et al. (Jerusalem 1989), 257–259 (in Hebrew).

67. "Iudaei uero uidentes Christianos hostes in se suosque paruulos insurgere, et nulli etati parcere, ipsi quoque in se suosque confratres, natosque, mulieres, matres et sorores irruerunt, et mutua cede se peremerunt. Matres pueris lactentibus, quod dictu nefas est, guttura ferro secabant, alios transforabant, uolentes pocius sic propriis manibus perire, quam incircumcisorum armis extingui" (Albert of Aachen, *Historia Ierosolimitana*, 52 [Latin]; 53 [English]).

68. "Paucisque elapsis, et paucis timore pocius mortis quam amore Christiane professionis baptizatis" (Albert of Aachen, *Historia Ierosolimitana*, 52 [Latin]; 53 [English]).

69. "Pecunie auaricia magis quam pro iusticia Dei graui cede mactauerant, cum iustus iudex Deus sit, et neminem inuitum aut coactum ad iugum fidei Catholice iubeat uenire" (Albert of Aachen, *Historia Ierosolimitana*, 58 [Latin]; 59 [English]).

70. "Pueros teneros cuiusque etatis et sexus in ore gladii percusserunt" (Albert of Aachen, *Historia Ierosolimitana*, 52 [Latin]; 53 [English]). Albert is critical of the behavior of those forces that operated in his home country, but, as we have seen, he writes that those crusaders who persecuted the Jews "in the kingdom of Lotharingia" acted out of religious zeal, not moral corruption. On avarice as a motive for the slaughter of the Jews in 1096, see also Wistinetzki and Freimann, *Sefer Hasidim*, 449, no. 1862. On the fate of the children, see later discussion.

71. The idea that the crusaders sought to baptize brings their conduct into line with Church policy, as formulated by Anselm of Lucca, that fighting should "correct," not punish, and should stem from love, not hate or vengeance. See Tomaz Mastnak, *Crusading Peace: Christendom, the Muslim World, and Western Political Order* (Berkeley 2002), 33. From this perspective the 1096 massacres are a classic example of how Christians should *not* fight, which is Albert of Aachen's explanation of their ignominious failure.

72. For the origins of this text, see Minty, "*Kiddush Hashem* in German Christian Eyes," 214, 215.

73. This is the only source to limit the Jewish victims to those who were already wounded.

74. "Plures tamen occidebantur, quorum substantiae a christianis diripiebantur. Huius itaque doloris immanitate conpulsi Iudei in se ipsos irruerunt, et cultris se invicem vulneratos interemerunt. Viri uxoribus et cognatis non pepercerunt, matres filios cum filiabus mortificaverunt" (MGH, SS, v. 17, 16).

75. That is, Thomas de la Fere, Clarebold de Vendeuil, William Carpenter (viscount of Melun), and possibly Count Hartman of Dyllingen and Kyburg.

76. The reference to madness appears also in the account of Albert of Aachen.

77. Guillaume de Tyr, *Chronique*, ed. R. B. C. Huygens (Turnholt 1986), 156, lines 12–15: "Iudeorum populum in civitatibus et opidis, per que erat eis transitus, nil tale sibi verentem et se habentem incautius crudeliter obtruncabant." Ben-Zion Dinur suggests that *incautius* (folly) refers not only to the lack of precautions but also to the imprecations hurled by Jews at their enemies; see Ben-Zion Dinur, *Israel and the Diaspora* (Tel Aviv and Jerusalem 1965), v. 2, pt. 1, 54n51 (in Hebrew).

78. The juxtaposition of Mainz and Cologne and the exclusion of other communities links this text to the *Annales Brunwilarenses* and to the chronicle of Albert of Aachen.

79. The text condemns Emicho's ignoble conduct before the reference to the Hungarian route. See *Historia rerum in partibus transmarinis gestarum*, bk. 1, ch. 29, in RHC Occ., v. 1, 66–67; Guillaume de Tyr, *Chronique*, 156; and Guillaume de Tyr, *A History of Deeds Done*

Beyond the Sea, ed. and trans. Emily Atwater Babcock and August Charles Krey (New York 1943), v. 1, 112–113, 115.

80. The source of the first quote is Habermann, *Book of the Persecutions*, 24; the second, p. 27.

81. For a similar formulation, see the text of Obadiah the proselyte: A. Scheiber, "Ein aus arabischer Gefangenschaft befreiter christlicher Proselyt in Jerusalem," *Hebrew Union College Annual* 39 (1968), 170. The Mainz Anonymous is similar but lacks the emphasis on vengeance (p. 93). Similarly, Guibert de Nogent attributes to those townsmen of Rouen who decided to embark on the crusade the declaration, "After traversing great distances we desire to attack the enemies of God, although the Jews, of all races the worst foes of God, are before our eyes. That's doing our work backward." See John F. Benton, *Self and Society in Medieval France: The Memoirs of Abbot Guibert of Nogent (1064?–c.1125)*, rev. ed., trans. C. C. Swinton Bland (New York 1970), 134–135. Likewise, Peter the Venerable responds to Louis VII's invitation to join the Second Crusade by asking why one should fight Christianity's enemies in distant lands when the Jews, who are worse than the Muslims, "trample on Christ and the Christian sacraments so freely" at home. See his Letter 130 in Giles Constable (ed.), *The Letters of Peter the Venerable* (Cambridge, Mass., 1967), v. 1, 327–330. See also Jeremy Cohen, "Christian Theology and Anti-Jewish Violence in the Middle Ages: Connections and Disjunctions," in *Religious Violence Between Christians and Jews: Medieval Roots, Modern Perspectives*, ed. Anna Sapir Abulafia (Basingstoke 2002), 49; and Dominique Iogna-Prat, *Order and Exclusion: Cluny and Christendom Face Heresy, Judaism, and Islam (1000–1150)*, trans. Graham Robert Edwards (Ithaca and London 2002), 278, 281.

82. Thus also, "You are the descendants of those who killed our deity and crucified him. Indeed he said: 'A day will surely arrive when my children will come and avenge my blood.' We are his children and it is our responsibility to avenge him upon you" (Habermann, *Book of the Persecutions*, 27). Medieval notions of vendetta and honor form a broader context for the vengeance motif of the First Crusade persecutions. This perspective awaits thorough investigation, including the question of whether vengeance can be obtained by means other than blood, such as baptism or money.

83. Habermann, *Book of the Persecutions*, 26. Godfrey's image in the Jewish historical memory was probably determined by the recollection of his having collected a large bribe from the communities of Cologne and Mainz; see Chazan, *European Jewry*, 53; and on his historiographical image, see Kedar, "Crusade Historians," 16–18. Similarly, Amanieu of Loubens (in Gascony) was reportedly inspired to "fight and kill those opposed to the Christian religion." See C. Grellet-Balguerie, "Cartulaire du prieuré de St.-Pierre de la Réole," *Archives historiques du département de la Gironde* 5 (1863), 140, cited in Riley-Smith, *First Crusade*, 62. Converting the Jews does not appear to have been Amanieu's plan, and he is unlikely to have offered them baptism. To this observation the usual caveats must be added: This source may not accurately reflect Amanieu's mind-set, and in any case other crusaders may have thought differently.

84. Habermann, *Book of the Persecutions*, 94.

85. Habermann, *Book of the Persecutions*, 94.

86. Habermann, *Book of the Persecutions*, 95. It is not reasonable to posit that, when the sources describe the Jews' expectation of destruction, the narrators omit mention of the expectation that an offer of baptism would be made and declined. No such mental process appears, even obliquely, in any text.

87. Flori, who holds that baptism was the assailants' primary goal, claims that the Jews

were slaughtered without a proposal of baptism because of the rage triggered by the rumor about the murdered Christian. See Flori, *Pierre l'Ermite*, 268. Possibly the accusation was of greater significance for the local Christian population than for the crusaders. On the role of the townspeople in the mass murder of 1096, see Robert Chazan, "The Anti-Jewish Violence of 1096: Perpetrators and Dynamics," in *Religious Violence Between Christians and Jews: Medieval Roots, Modern Perspectives*, ed. Anna Sapir Abulafia (Basingstoke 2002), 21–43.

88. Habermann, *Book of the Persecutions*, 95.

89. The chronicle of Solomon ben Samson gives a less detailed account of the destruction of the Worms community, but it also mentions only murder.

90. Habermann, *Book of the Persecutions*, 26, 98.

91. That is, the promise of divine providence and the Jews' status as the chosen people.

92. Habermann, *Book of the Persecutions*, 98. This alludes to the episode of the wondrous goose, mentioned also by Albert and by Solomon ben Samson (Habermann, *Book of the Persecutions*, 28). Samson adds: "in order to take vengeance from his enemies."

93. Habermann, *Book of the Persecutions*, 28, 98.

94. Habermann, *Book of the Persecutions*, 29, 99.

95. The promise appears only in the narrative of Solomon ben Samson (Habermann, *Book of the Persecutions*, 29); and again later, in the story of Qalonymos and his warriors (p. 40). The Mainz Anonymous attributes it to the townspeople of Mainz rather than to the bishop and burgrave (p. 95).

96. Habermann, *Book of the Persecutions*, 29, 99.

97. Habermann, *Book of the Persecutions*, 99.

98. Habermann, *Book of the Persecutions*, 30.

99. Habermann, *Book of the Persecutions*, 31, 100.

100. Habermann, *Book of the Persecutions*, 30, 100.

101. "Verum expugnato atrio episcope, in quo erant ad firmamentum sui . . . omnes interfecti sunt" (*Annalista Saxo*, 490).

102. Habermann, *Book of the Persecutions*, 31, 100.

103. Habermann, *Book of the Persecutions*, 101. In the account of Solomon ben Samson, "they left no remnant, like a date, like two or three seeds" (p. 33). Chazan suggests an emendation: "two or three berries," citing Isaiah 17:6.

104. Ephraim of Bonn, in his commentary on a liturgical poem about 1096, says the enemy "killed all the Jews that there were." See Abraham ben Azriel, *Sefer Arugat ha-Bosem*, ed. Ephraim E. Urbach (Jerusalem 1963), v. 4, 46–47, citing a thirteenth- or fourteenth-century Hebrew manuscript: Parma-Palatina Ms. 655 [3205], fol. 144v. However, another such commentary implies choice when he refers to the plot of a Christian leader (identified by Urbach as Peter the Hermit) "to kill and annihilate the enemies of Israel [i.e., Christianity], whoever would refuse to convert to their faith" [literally, their error] (Azriel, *Sefer Arugat ha-Bosem*, 183). On Peter the Hermit, see Flori, *Pierre l'Ermite*.

105. Habermann, *Book of the Persecutions*, 24, 93. The problematic formulation is basically a reversal of the formula quoted earlier, in which the crusaders call to annihilate the Jews, extending the option of conversion as a secondary option: "Alternatively, let them be like us and acknowledge the son born of promiscuity" (Habermann, *Book of the Persecutions*, 24). Admittedly, this sentence admits the possibility of baptism, leaving the Jews with the element of choice and therefore also of heroic martyrdom, but slaughter, not conversion, is presented as the assailants' principal purpose.

106. Habermann, *Book of the Persecutions*, 31, 101. Solomon ben Samson repeats this sentiment immediately: "'They did not wish to deny the awe of our King or to exchange it for [that of] 'a loathsome offshoot'" (Habermann, *Book of the Persecutions*, 32).

107. Habermann, *Book of the Persecutions*, 48–49.

108. This dynamic has already been noted. See James Parkes, *The Jew in the Medieval Community* (London 1938), 67; and Friedrich Lotter, "'Tod oder Taufe': Das Problem der Zwangstaufen während des Ersten Kreuzzugs," in *Juden und Christen zur Zeit der Kreuzzüge*, ed. Alfred Haverkamp (Sigmaringen 1999), 130, 132.

109. When the murderers offer a few survivors the option of baptism, their offer is refused. This implies that they could not, or would not, baptize the Jews forcibly, and yet the chronicles report that they did so in Regensburg. More likely, the attackers made the baptism offer halfheartedly, after and because they had already achieved their objective, which was mass murder. Thus baptism was not terribly important to them.

110. Habermann, *Book of the Persecutions*, 25.

111. Habermann, *Book of the Persecutions*, 95. The Hebrew sources stress the stripping of the slain and the demoralizing effect this had on the survivors. But it is also a literary motif, rooted in the story of Saul's suicide on Mt. Gilboa and is therefore fertile ground for exploration of the relationship between the social and cultural history of the First Crusade. Jeremy Cohen has suggested a connection to the Crucifixion; see Cohen, "The Hebrew Crusade Chronicles," 27. On the sexual aspect of the description of naked female bodies, see Susan Einbinder, "Jewish Women Martyrs: Changing Models of Representation," *Exemplaria* 12 (2000), 117–119.

112. Habermann, *Book of the Persecutions*, 96.

113. Habermann, *Book of the Persecutions*, 97.

114. Habermann, *Book of the Persecutions*, 97.

115. Habermann, *Book of the Persecutions*, 102; see also p. 39. Defenestration appears several more times in the Hebrew chronicles (pp. 36, 102, 104) and therefore seems to have demoralized the survivors, as the sight of the naked bodies did.

116. Habermann, *Book of the Persecutions*, 35–36, 103.

117. Habermann, *Book of the Persecutions*, 36, 104.

118. Habermann, *Book of the Persecutions*, 40–41. On Qalonymos's fate, see especially Cohen, "Between Martyrdom and Apostasy," 436–441; and Cohen, *Sanctifying the Name of God*, 130–141. Cf. Israel Jacob Yuval, "'The Lord Will Take Vengeance,' Vengeance for His Temple: Historia sine ira et studio," *Zion* 59 (1994), 409–411 (in Hebrew).

119. Habermann, *Book of the Persecutions*, 42.

120. Habermann, *Book of the Persecutions*, 36.

121. Habermann, *Book of the Persecutions*, 37.

122. On cultural motifs here, see Cohen, "Persecutions of 1096," 185–195; and Cohen, *Sanctifying the Name of God*, 91–105.

123. Habermann, *Book of the Persecutions*, 35–36, 103.

124. Habermann, *Book of the Persecutions*, 36, 104.

125. Habermann, *Book of the Persecutions*, 38–39. The narrative of Solomon ben Samson mentions other "saintly" women who were offered baptism at the height of the carnage, which obviously contradicts the paradigms of choice presented here.

126. Habermann, *Book of the Persecutions*, 39.

127. Habermann, *Book of the Persecutions*, 42.

128. Habermann, *Book of the Persecutions*, 97.

129. The indiscriminate slaughter of women and children was uncommon during warfare between Christians, but it was part and parcel of the concept of holy warfare, in the First Crusade (as in the conquest of Ma'arrat and Jerusalem) and at the capture of Béziers in 1209, during the Albigensian crusade. Possibly the crusaders were inspired by the biblical injunction to annihilate the idolatrous nations of Canaan. See Yvonne Friedman, *Encounter Between Enemies: Captivity and Ransom in the Latin Kingdom of Jerusalem* (Leiden 2002), 18–21. Friedman correlates the crusaders' indiscriminate slaughter of Muslims with their initial failure to consider the possibility that their own combatants might be taken prisoner and need to be ransomed (pp. 18–32).

130. Similarly, the *Gesta Treverorum* reports that the Jews of Trier kill their young for fear that they would be "taken" by the crusaders, perhaps for baptism rather than violence: "The Jews, to prevent them from taking their young, planted their knives in their bellies, saying that in order not to become the sport of the great lunacy of the Christians [ne forte christianorum vesaniae ludibrio fierent], it was preferable to hand them over to the bosom of Abraham." See MGH, SS, v. 8, 190. "Sport" (*ludibrio*), in the sense of "object of derision," is ambiguous; it could refer to a fear of baptism, humiliation, or torture. The phrase "bosom of Abraham," which has a New Testament source (Luke 16:22), appears to link this source to the Mainz Anonymous, in which Meshullam ben Isaac of Mainz, speaking to his wife, justifies his decision to kill their son by saying, "He [God] will place him in the bosom of Abraham our ancestor" (Habermann, *Book of the Persecutions*, 96). *Midrash Ekhah* has Miriam bat Tanhum, the legendary mother whose seven sons were martyred by the Romans, console her sixth son with the knowledge that after death he will join his brothers in the bosom of Abraham; see Solomon Buber (ed.), *Midrash Ekhah* (Vilna 1899), 84. On this phrase, see also Jerome Baschet, *Le sein du père: Abraham et la paternité dans l'Occident medieval* (Paris 2000); Ben-Sasson, *Jewish History*, 179; Simon Schwarzfuchs, "Le sein d'Abraham," *Révue des Études Juives* 163 (2004), 283–288; and Shepkaru, *Jewish Martyrs*, 199. On the events in Trier, see Eva Haverkamp, "'Persecutio' und 'Gezerah' in Trier während des Ersten Kreuzzugs," in *Juden und Christen zur Zeit der Kreuzzüge*, ed. Alfred Haverkamp (Sigmaringen 1999), 35–71; and Chazan, "Christian and Jewish Perceptions of 1096."

131. These tales testify that the Jews' motive for slaughtering each other is religious, "out of zeal to preserve their ancestral law," in the words of Sigebert Auctarium Aquicinense. This is altogether different from the story of Masada, in which the victims elect to commit suicide rather than suffer torture and death at the hand of the enemy, which is also the rationale offered by Albert of Aachen. Haym Soloveitchik maintains that the desire to prevent the children's baptism was the overarching reason for the mass martyrdom of Ashkenazic Jewry. See Haym Soloveitchik, "Halakhah, Hermeneutics, and Martyrdom in Medieval Ashkenaz," *Jewish Quarterly Review* 94 (2004), 98–108. For a different interpretation of the "special case," see Simhah Goldin, "The Socialisation for *Kiddush ha-Shem* among Medieval Jews," *Journal of Medieval History* 23 (1997), 134–136.

132. Habermann, *Book of the Persecutions*, 34, 101. For a cultural reading of this story, see Cohen, "Persecutions of 1096," 195–205. The tale has been used as a benchmark of the chronicles' historicity; see Marcus, "Representation of Reality."

133. Habermann, *Book of the Persecutions*, 35, 102.

134. Habermann, *Book of the Persecutions*, 37.

135. Habermann, *Book of the Persecutions*, 95. See Jacob Gellis (ed.), *The Complete Tosaphot: Commentary on the Bible* (Jerusalem 1982), v. 1, 262 (in Hebrew), for the case of "a certain

rabbi that slaughtered many young children during a persecution, because he feared that they would be forced to convert." Similarly, "And from here one learns [that it is permissible] to slaughter the children [*ha-ne'arim*] during persecutions [*bi-gezeroth*] on account of conversion [*ha'avarath hadath*]" (Yomtov Ishbili, *Novellae on Avodah Zarah*, ed. Moshe Goldstein [Jerusalem 1978], 81 [in Hebrew]). Moses of Zurich explains, "And from here one learns [that it is permissible] to slaughter the children [*ha-yeladim*] at the time of persecution, [those] who do not know [the difference] between good and evil, for we are afraid that they will settle [*yishthake'u*] among the gentiles alone when they grow up; it is better that they die in a state of merit [*zaka'im*] than that they die in a state of culpability [*hayyavim*]" (Isaac J. Har-Shoshanim-Rosenberg [ed.], *SeMaQ Zurich* [Jerusalem 1973], v. 1, 58). See also Soloveitchik, "Religious Law and Change," 210–211n8.

136. Minty, "*Kiddush Hashem* in German Christian Eyes," 226–233. On the horror of the Christians at the Jewish slaughter of the children, see Yuval, "Vengeance and the Curse," 75–79.

137. On whether the crusaders set out for the Holy Land with the intention of killing the Saracens or converting them, see Benjamin Z. Kedar, *Crusade and Mission: European Approaches Toward the Muslims* (Princeton 1984), 57–85. Kedar claims that mission was initially absent from crusader ideology but was gradually integrated into it. See also the findings of Yvonne Friedman. My thanks to Elisheva Carlebach for pointing out this perspective. Tomaz Mastnak maintains that the crusader psychology of total war stemmed from the peace movement of the tenth and eleventh centuries, which directed violence away from Christian society and toward the enemies of Christianity. Thus killing took priority over conversion not only in 1096 but also in the Reconquista, as Christian love "turned into the annihilation of those outside the family." See Mastnak, *Crusading Peace*, 125–126.

Chapter Four

This chapter was published earlier in a slightly different form: David Malkiel, "Vestiges of Conflict in the Hebrew Crusade Chronicles," *Journal of Jewish Studies* 52 (2001), 323–340.

1. Jeremy Cohen, *Sanctifying the Name of God: Jewish Martyrs and Jewish Memories of the First Crusade* (Philadelphia 2004), 139.

2. Robert Chazan, *European Jewry and the First Crusade* (Berkeley 1987), 113–114.

3. See, particularly, Cohen, *Sanctifying the Name of God*.

4. The evidence is slim for Jeremy Cohen's assertion that "the common means of survival was conversion to Christianity." See Cohen, *Sanctifying the Name of God*, 57.

5. Jeremy Cohen, "The Hebrew Crusade Chronicles in Their Christian Cultural Context," in *Juden und Christen zur Zeit der Kreuzzüge*, ed. Alfred Haverkamp (Sigmaringen 1999), 22.

6. Chazan, *European Jewry*, 116.

7. See Deuteronomy 12:15, in which the gazelle and deer exemplify animals that may be eaten but are not among those that can be offered as a sacrifice in the Temple. Nonetheless, the following verse (Deut. 12:16) mandates that the blood of animals slaughtered for food, outside the Temple, be spilled on the ground; here lies the analogy to the victims of 1096, who were slaughtered outside the Land of Israel and whose blood was spilled on the ground.

8. Abraham Meir Habermann, *The Book of the Persecutions of Ashkenaz and France* (Jerusalem 1945), 43 (in Hebrew). Similarly, in the narrative of the martyrdom in Xantes, the

chronicle of Solomon ben Samson places the following words in the mouth of the community leader: "Let no one have mercy—neither on himself or on his companion" (p. 48). The assertion about those not designated by name also appears repeatedly in the Mainz Anonymous (Habermann, *Book of the Persecutions*, 97, 102, 104).

9. See Haym Soloveitchik, "Religious Law and Change: The Medieval Ashkenazic Example," *AJS Review* 12 (1987), 208–211. On the nonhalakhic nature of the 1096 martyrdom, see also Chapter 6.

10. Cohen, *Sanctifying the Name of God*, 66–68 and passim. Cohen's interpretations of particular tales are evaluated case by case at various junctures in the present work.

11. For what follows, see Habermann, *Book of the Persecutions*, 30–33, 99–102.

12. Habermann, *Book of the Persecutions*, 31, 100. The extension of the neck is a fairly common act in the chronicles. Its significance is that it is both an active and a passive form of martyrdom. The protagonist expresses his or her willingness to be martyred, and in that sense martyrdom is active; yet he or she is also passive, for death comes at the hand of another agent. On the distinction between active and passive martyrdom, see Abraham Gross, "Historical and Halakhic Aspects of the Mass Martyrdom in Mainz: An Integrative Approach," in *Facing the Cross: The Persecutions of 1096 in History and Historiography*, ed. Yom Tov Assis, Michael Toch, Jeremy Cohen, Ora Limor, and Aharon Kedar (Jerusalem 2000), 171–192 (in Hebrew); Abraham Gross, *Struggling with Tradition: Reservations About Active Martyrdom in the Middle Ages* (Leiden 2004), 14–18; and Abraham Gross, "Reflections on Halakhic and Nonhalakhic Aspects of the Martyrdom in 1096," in *Be'erot Yitzhak: Studies in Memory of Isadore Twersky*, ed. Jay M. Harris (Cambridge, Mass., 2005), *1–*30 (in Hebrew).

13. Habermann, *Book of the Persecutions*, 31.

14. Rachel is the daughter of Rabbi Isaac ben Asher, a well-known scholar (Habermann, *Book of the Persecutions*, 101). See Avraham Grossman, *The Early Sages of Ashkenaz: Their Lives, Leadership, and Works (900–1096)*, 2nd ed. (Jerusalem 1988), 302n26, 404. Yet Rachel also represents the biblical Rachel, who wept over her lost offspring and was disconsolate (Jer. 31:14). Cf. Jeremy Cohen's interpretation of Rachel, in Chapter 7.

15. Habermann, *Book of the Persecutions*, 34, 101–102. The two chronicles, the Mainz Anonymous and the narrative attributed to Solomon ben Samson, are unclear about whether one or more than one woman friend was involved. For a careful comparison of the different versions of this story, see Ivan G. Marcus, "The Representation of Reality in the Narratives of 1096," *Jewish History* 13 (1999), 37–48. Note that this tale appears to contradict Peggy McCracken's generalization that in medieval tales paternal infanticide is portrayed as noble, whereas maternal infanticide is always depicted as murder; see Peggy McCracken, "Engendering Sacrifice: Blood, Lineage, and Infanticide in Old French Literature," *Speculum* 77 (2002), 56. Rachel's story, however, may be the exception that proves the rule, for scholars have seen the 1096 tales as representing an inversion of the natural order. On the significance of the role of women in 1096, see also Chapter 6.

16. Cf. the groundless assumption that Judah is mentioned only after his children have already been slain because "he appears to have been elsewhere fighting the crusaders" (Shmuel Shepkaru, *Jewish Martyrs in the Pagan and Christian Worlds* [Cambridge 2006], 182).

17. Habermann, *Book of the Persecutions*, 51.

18. Habermann, *Book of the Persecutions*, 51.

19. This echoes the binding of Isaac, a central motif in the Crusade narratives. Meshullam invokes the biblical scenario explicitly as the model for his own behavior. Zipporah does

too, wording her request to delay the slaughter of her son in the words of the angel who tells Abraham to stay his hand (Gen. 22:12). We then read—in the language of Genesis—that Meshullam binds Isaac and takes the knife to slaughter him, although the chronicle then adds that Meshullam recites the blessing over slaughter and Isaac says amen in response.

20. This also is a typological motif, modeled after the story of Hagar and Ishmael in Genesis 21:16. Thus this tale is heavily typological, and its historical basis is unclear.

21. Habermann, *Book of the Persecutions*, 96. It is unclear whether Meshullam's final action is a form of suicide, that is, of martyrdom, or an attempt to flee.

22. Habermann, *Book of the Persecutions*, 35, 103. See Shepkaru, *Jewish Martyrs*, 188–189.

23. Habermann, *Book of the Persecutions*, 49–50. Ironically, although the leader provides the "right" answer, he actually tells the convert that he will never achieve total social integration; rather than state that in the world to come the convert will dwell with the other members of the community, he tells the convert that he will keep company with other "true" converts, including Abraham, the first convert.

24. Habermann, *Book of the Persecutions*, 49. See also Cohen, *Sanctifying the Name of God*, 76.

25. For example, in the story of the assault on the Mainz community, the Mainz Anonymous announces, twice, that all the Jews fell but later admits that a few accepted baptism; see Habermann, *Book of the Persecutions*, 101–103.

26. This principle is encapsulated in the term *gezerah*, meaning decree, that is, divine decree.

27. Habermann, *Book of the Persecutions*, 55. It is ironic that the only individual to suffer demoralization is killed rather than converted.

28. On the demography of Ashkenazic Jewry, see Bernhard Blumenkranz, "Germany, 843–1096," in *The Dark Ages: Jews in Christian Europe 711–1096*, ed. C. Roth (World History of the Jewish People, ser. 2, v. 2) (Tel Aviv 1966), 164–165; Simon Schwarzfuchs, "The Place of the Crusades in Jewish History," in *Culture and Society in Medieval Jewry*, ed. Menahem Ben-Sasson et al. (Jerusalem 1989), 257–259 (in Hebrew); and Kenneth Stow, "The Jewish Family in the Rhineland in the High Middle Ages: Form and Function," *American Historical Review* 92 (1987), 1085–1110. Cf. the demography of Spanish-Jewish society, discussed in Chapter 8.

29. An offer of apostasy was not anticipated; see Chapter 3.

30. Note the following description of the enormous power exerted by the group to guarantee conformity in the face of imminent, severe danger: "At times when members of the group believe that the other groups have negative intentions toward them, they prepare themselves for the worst possible coming actions. At these times, cohesiveness and unity are important conditions to withstand the possible threat. In order to achieve these objectives, members who most strongly hold the belief exert pressure on others toward conformity and unity. This pressure can take various forms, among them calls for unity and calls for concealment of disagreement within the group, as well as exerting negative sanctions against those who disagree within the group." See Daniel Bar-Tal, "The Masada Syndrome: A Case of Central Belief," in *Stress and Coping in Time of War*, ed. Norman A. Milgram (New York 1986), 48.

31. Habermann, *Book of the Persecutions*, 33.

32. Only the Mainz Anonymous fails to differentiate between the roles of women and men in the Mainz slaughter; see Habermann, *Book of the Persecutions*, 100–101. However, the Mainz Anonymous adds two details about the glorious behavior of the women in the chambers: They threw money and rocks outside to delay the enemy and allow those inside time to

complete their task, and they also strangled their children and placed their corpses facing the enemy (p. 101).

33. Habermann, *Book of the Persecutions*, 75.

34. The image of women in the martyrdom of 1096 is strikingly at odds with their image in Yosifon, where at Masada they play only the role of victim; see David Flusser (ed.), *The Josippon* (Jerusalem 1981), v. 1, 430 (in Hebrew). Women are equated with self-sacrifice in the story of Jotapata, but the portrait is hardly complimentary: Joseph tells the fighters who seek to convince him to die by his own hand rather than surrender to the Romans that to do so would be unmanly, noting that men confront death without flinching but women die of fear or commit suicide (p. 316). The influence of Yosifon on Ashkenazic Jewry would appear to merit reexamination. Note also that in Jotapata the martyrs are portrayed as dupes, for Joseph escapes death at their hands by convincing them to kill each other and themselves, leaving him alive and free. Cf. Shepkaru, *Jewish Martyrs*, 163.

35. Habermann, *Book of the Persecutions*, 25. The alternative is found in the narrative of Eliezer ben Nathan (p. 73).

36. Habermann, *Book of the Persecutions*, 74; this quotation is from line 13 of Eliezer ben Nathan's poem *Akonen ve-espidah*. On the public nature of martyrdom in the 1096 narratives, see also Gross, "Reflections," *28–*30.

37. *Sanhedrin* 74a.

38. Habermann, *Book of the Persecutions*, 96.

39. Habermann, *Book of the Persecutions*, 25.

40. Habermann, *Book of the Persecutions*, 48–49. The chronicle includes the highly unusual comment that the narrator heard about Rabbi Moses's words from eyewitnesses (p. 49). Naturally one wonders how there could have been eyewitnesses or whether these survivors were an exception to the unanimous decision to the murder and suicide pact. On the cultural connection between this "last supper" and the Christian one, see Jeremy Cohen, "The 'Persecutions of 1096': From Martyrdom to Martyrology," *Zion* 59 (1994), 182–184 (in Hebrew); and Cohen, *Sanctifying the Name of God*, 73–90. This is a relatively convincing example of the narrator's general—paradoxical—tendency, detected by Cohen, to embed Christian ideas, images, and symbols in the Hebrew narratives of the First Crusade.

41. Habermann, *Book of the Persecutions*, 50–51.

42. In Trier, too, the authorities act to prevent the Jews from killing each other and themselves: They seal the well, so the Jews cannot drown their young; they prevent the Jews from ascending the wall of the palace, lest they jump from its height; and they keep a close watch on them during the night. See Habermann, *Book of the Persecutions*, 56.

43. Medieval thinkers, as well as latter-day historians, were aware that social context can even cause people to risk death; see, for example, Jehuda Wistinetski and Jakob Freimann (eds.), *Sefer Hasidim* (Frankfurt am Main 1924), 17, no. 15; and 109, no. 359; and Simone Luzzatto, *Ma'amar al Yehudei Venezia*, trans. D. Lattes (Jerusalem 1950), 104.

44. Habermann, *Book of the Persecutions*, 56.

45. Habermann, *Book of the Persecutions*, 62. Eliezer ben Nathan makes no mention of the particular feelings of the young men and women.

46. Habermann, *Book of the Persecutions*, 35, 102.

47. The description of Helbo and Simeon's extending of the neck is intended to place them in the category of active participants in their own martyrdom, although their cooperation falls short of Bella and Madrona's sharpening of the knife. This incident is also less

impressive, and perhaps even less credible, than that of Bella and Madrona, because Moses and his boys are slaughtered by the enemy rather than by themselves.

48. This dynamic is evident in other pairs of protagonists and not only in siblings. In the tale of the members of Qalonymos's band of fighters in the forest, we learn that Samuel ben Tamar dies together with Abraham ben Asher, whose story was narrated earlier. In the chronicles Samuel expresses solidarity with Abraham, be it for life—that is, apostasy—or death. Like the pairs of siblings, Samuel, who appears to have had nothing to lose but his own life, seems to draw inspiration and courage from the fortitude and resolution of another; see Habermann, *Book of the Persecutions*, 42.

49. Habermann, *Book of the Persecutions*, 45; the identity of this city is disclosed in the narrative of Eliezer ben Nathan (p. 77). Wevelinghofen, like other towns in the region, was a haven for Jews who fled Cologne. Wevelinghofen's river is the Erft, a tributary of the Rhine; see Chazan, *European Jewry*, 347n237.

50. "See seed go forth from us" can be interpreted as the desire either to procreate or to experience the sexual act. The convergence of the motifs of seed and longevity appears to be based on Isaiah 53:10; see *Yoma* 58a.

51. Eliezer ben Nathan writes that the son of Samuel ben Yehiel (whom the chronicle of Solomon ben Samson calls Yehiel) "fled with his father into the water" and extended his neck for slaughter by his father (Habermann, *Book of the Persecutions*, 77). The latter part of the story in Eliezer ben Nathan's version agrees with that of the chronicle of Solomon ben Samson, but the first part omits the story of Yehiel's relationship with his friend Samuel, including the fact that the two youths fled town together and were only later discovered by Yehiel's father by the waters. Thus Eliezer ben Nathan's version effaces crucial signs of discord between father and son.

52. This motif also occurs in the case of the two boys, Aaron and Isaac, in the root story and therefore seems to have been particularly associated with children or youths, even though it also appears in the case of Zipporah of Worms, recounted earlier. Note that Eliezer ben Nathan refers to Menahem as an adolescent (*bahur*) (Habermann, *Book of the Persecutions*, 77).

53. Habermann, *Book of the Persecutions*, 45. Neither Samuel (Yehiel's father) nor Menahem the sexton are among the tower's climbers. The chronicle concedes that Menahem was not anxious to participate in an act of martyrdom. Samuel, the engine in this series of martyrdoms, exhorts Menahem to slaughter him, urging him, "Conquer your will, like a warrior." Menahem's reluctance is perfectly understandable if we assume that he arrived in Wevelinghofen after escaping from Cologne. Indeed, like Isaac ben David, the *parnas* of Mainz, survivors' guilt may explain Menahem's ultimate participation in martyrdom—homicide and suicide alike—at Wevelinghofen.

54. Habermann, *Book of the Persecutions*, 45.

55. Habermann, *Book of the Persecutions*, 46. Eliezer ben Nathan precedes his praise for the father's strength of will with a declaration about the courage of the son: "Behold, all inhabitants of the world, how great was the son's strength, for he was slaughtered without being bound" (p. 77). For the motif of slaughter without binding, see also Eliezer ben Nathan's poem (Habermann, *Book of the Persecutions*, 86). The chronicle of Solomon ben Samson omits the clause in praise of the son, presumably because his narrative says more than enough about the son's reluctance for martyrdom. Also note that similar praise is lavished on the pious ones of Ilna: "Know how they sanctified the holy Name and had no mercy on their children" (p. 47).

56. Scholars are divided as to the identity of the community called Ilna—Altenahr, Eller, and Ellen have been suggested; see Chazan, *European Jewry*, 347–348n250.

57. Eliezer ben Nathan names five Jews, including Judah ben Abraham, who volunteer to slaughter the 300 Jews in the room at Ilna. In his version the five volunteers shut the doors before proceeding; this implies that those in the room are denied the opportunity to escape; see Habermann, *Book of the Persecutions*, 78–79.

58. Habermann, *Book of the Persecutions*, 47. The chronicle depicts Sarit as the betrothed of Judah's son Abraham and even as Judah's daughter-in-law, although Sarit and Abraham had not yet married. It does not seem likely that Sarit's connection to Judah was as strong and intimate as the narrator would have us believe.

59. By having Judah place Sarit in the bosom of his son Abraham just after he exhorts her to "lie in the bosom of Abraham our ancestor" (Habermann, *Book of the Persecutions*, 47), the chronicler has life mimic art. Perhaps Judah choreographs Sarit's and Abraham's execution so as to give her death symbolic, theological content, but it is also possible, if not likely, that events occurred in a more prosaic fashion. One even wonders whether Judah's son was actually named Abraham. On the motif of the bosom of Abraham, see Chapter 3, n130, and see Shepkaru, *Jewish Martyrs*, 201–202.

60. It is unclear whether this was a window looking on the outdoors or perhaps onto the men's section of the synagogue, if that was the scene of the slaughter.

61. Habermann, *Book of the Persecutions*, 31.

62. The chronicle of Solomon ben Samson states that Judah seizes Sarit and kisses her on the mouth, and although the chronicler intimates that the kiss represents the bond and affection shared by relations, it still smacks of lust. Judah's admiration for Sarit is also implied in his homicidal declaration that because she shall not marry his son, she shall marry no one. Judah's last words to Sarit seem to underlie the chronicler's decision to create a familial nexus between Judah and Sarit, which would enable the reader to identify with Judah for foiling Sarit's escape and slaughtering her. It would also neutralize the impression that Judah was in any way motivated by carnal feelings for Sarit. Because of the sexual overtones of this story, Jeremy Cohen writes that this episode "smacks more of rape than of sanctifying the name of God" (*Sanctifying the Name of God*, 144). He later affirms that Sarit's attempted escape, which Judah foils, "renders her violation an act of rape" (p. 147) and quickly moves from suggesting that Judah figuratively raped or violated Sarit to referring to her rape without qualification, as when he refers to Judah as "raping the newlywed wife" (p. 153). It should be stressed that, although Sarit was physically assaulted and her body manhandled, the sources do not report her sexual violation.

63. Habermann, *Book of the Persecutions*, 41–42. Note, however, that the text is inconsistent; immediately thereafter, Seigneur is referred to as "Rabbi." Also puzzling is the appearance of Helbo ben Moses on the list of the members of the second group of Qalonymos's fighters, because the chronicler had already recounted the story of his martyrdom.

64. Habermann, *Book of the Persecutions*, 97.

65. Wistinetski and Freimann, *Sefer Hasidim*, 449, no. 1862. On the concept of "the wicked" in *Sefer Hasidim*, see Chapter 6.

66. *Avodah Zarah* 22a.

67. Wistinetski and Freimann, *Sefer Hasidim*, 83, no. 251.

68. Habermann, *Book of the Persecutions*, 25.

69. Habermann, *Book of the Persecutions*, 41.

70. Habermann, *Book of the Persecutions*, 39. This is among the least heroic stories of martyrdom recorded in the chronicles. The enemy catches Samuel ben Isaac as he attempts to escape to Speyer, after hiding in someone's house. He is asked whether he would accept baptism but does not respond, extends his neck, and is killed. Although the chronicler describes his experience in exalted terms, what stands out is his silence. He seems paralyzed, reluctant to apostatize but also not so resolute as to taunt and curse his adversaries, after the manner of David ben Nathaniel the Gabbai (pp. 36, 104). Coupled with Isaac's participation in Qalonymos's band, martyrdom appears to have been the least preferred choice among the members of this family.

71. Habermann, *Book of the Persecutions*, 39. Chazan writes (*European Jewry*, 266) that the enemy forced the townsman, rather than the women, out of his house, but the printed text indicates clearly that the women were pushed out of the house.

72. The fact that the two Isaacs suffer radically different fates from each other is insignificant for our purposes.

73. Although the chronicle refers to them as the enemy, in this case the enemy consists of local people rather than crusaders from afar. This emerges from the explanation of why Abraham is offered life: "for he was a well-known and comely man." Indeed, the text immediately adds, "There gathered about him some of his acquaintances." The relative friendliness, or benignity, of the Christians who crowd around Abraham is implied by their response to his question about the fate of his children and family members; they do not seek to demoralize him, by lying to him and telling him that all had died, as is often reported in the chronicles, usually with the statement that all lie dead and that there is therefore no hope except through baptism. Abraham's is not the only case in which Jews are entreated by their gentile acquaintances to accept baptism; the same is reported of Natronai ben Isaac of Xanten (Habermann, *Book of the Persecutions*, 49). As in Abraham's case, so too in Natronai's: The chronicle "explains" the gentiles' zeal to convert and save their Jewish friend by describing the latter as "a pleasant and comely young man" (p. 49).

74. Habermann, *Book of the Persecutions*, 42.

75. Habermann, *Book of the Persecutions*, 44.

76. Habermann, *Book of the Persecutions*, 44.

77. A *Sefer Hasidim* passage discusses the dilemma of women who survive the carnage by converting to Christianity even though their husbands are killed; they are now pressed to find security by either entering a convent or marrying a Christian. The historicity of this anecdote cannot be determined, but it reflects awareness of the separation of families in 1096. See Wistinetski and Freimann, *Sefer Hasidim*, 85, no. 262.

78. She dies together with Guta (Habermann, *Book of the Persecutions*, 38–39). The account in the chronicle of Solomon ben Samson includes a reference to Isaac's concern for his money, which apparently underlies his willingness to suffer baptism, although at the climax of the story he spurns earthly treasure (p. 37). In terms of the concern for money, his story resembles that of Rebecca of Cologne.

79. Habermann, *Book of the Persecutions*, 37.

80. According to Eliezer ben Nathan, Isaac slaughters daughters, not sons (Habermann, *Book of the Persecutions*, 75). His account does not mention the children's feelings at all but merely states that Isaac slays them.

81. Cohen, *Sanctifying the Name of God*, 91–105.

Chapter Five

For a slightly different version of this chapter, see David Malkiel, "Jews and Apostates in Medieval Europe: Boundaries Real and Imagined," *Past and Present* 194 (2007), 3–34. Reprinted with kind permission (World Copyright: The Past and Present Society, 175 Banbury Road, Oxford, England).

1. Avraham Grossman, "Offenders and Violent Men in Jewish Society in Early Ashkenaz and Their Influence upon Legal Procedure," *Shenaton ha-Mishpat ha-Ivri* 8 (1981), 135 (in Hebrew). Unlike Grossman, I use the term *Ashkenaz* to refer to France as well as Germany and sometimes also to England, which was a French satellite, culturally if not economically or politically.

2. See Yitzhak Baer, "Introduction," in Abraham Meir Habermann's, *The Book of the Persecutions of Ashkenaz and France* (Jerusalem 1945), 1 (in Hebrew); and Yitzhak Baer, "The Religious-Social Tendency of 'Sepher Hassidim,'" *Zion* 3 (1938), 1, 5 (in Hebrew). See also Israel Jacob Yuval, "Yitzhak Baer and the Search for Authentic Judaism," in *The Jewish Past Revisited*, ed. David N. Meyers and David B. Ruderman (New Haven 1998), 77–87.

3. Jacob Katz, *Exclusiveness and Tolerance: Studies in Jewish-Gentile Relations in Medieval and Modern Times* (Oxford 1961), 85.

4. Simon Schwarzfuchs, "The Place of the Crusades in Jewish History," in *Culture and Society in Medieval Jewry*, ed. Menahem Ben-Sasson, Robert Bonfil, and Joseph Hacker (Jerusalem 1989), 257–259 (in Hebrew).

5. Ivan G. Marcus, "From Politics to Martyrdom: Shifting Paradigms in the Hebrew Narratives of the 1096 Crusade Riots," *Prooftexts* 2 (1982), 42–43. See Chapter 3.

6. Kenneth Stow, "Conversion, Apostasy, and Apprehensiveness: Emicho of Flonheim and the Fear of Jews in the Twelfth Century," *Speculum* 76 (2001), 933. Yet Stow's claims that "all of the chronicles . . . stress the frequency of conversion" and that "the Hebrew chronicles are concerned as much with conversion to Christianity and return to Judaism as they are with Kiddush HaShem" (pp. 923, 925) are exaggerations. The Hebrew narratives stress the acts of mass martyrdom and downplay the forced conversions. Albert of Aachen also dismisses the number of apostates as trivial, and his account is by far the most detailed of the Latin sources. In fact, the martyrological tendency is so pronounced that scholars often overlook the significance of the fact that the narrators bother to mention the apostasies at all.

7. Grossman, "Offenders," 135. See also Shmuel Shepkaru, "Death Twice Over: Dualism of Metaphor and Realia in 12th-Century Hebrew Crusading Accounts," *Jewish Quarterly Review* 93 (2002), 238–247.

8. Jeremy Cohen, *Sanctifying the Name of God: Jewish Martyrs and Jewish Memories of the First Crusade* (Philadelphia 2004), 4, 58. Note, however, that Cohen emphasizes the significance of apostasy in shaping the memory of the First Crusade, not the actual number of forced converts.

9. Julius Aronius, *Regesten zur Geschichte der Juden im Fränkischen und Deutschen Reiche bis zum Jahre 1273* (Berlin 1902), 94, no. 204; Shlomo Simonsohn, *The Apostolic See and the Jews: Documents, 492–1404* (Toronto 1988), 42, doc. 42. The Mainz Anonymous credits a communal leader named Moses ben Yequtiel with obtaining imperial permission for the reversion; see Abraham Meir Habermann, *The Book of the Persecutions of Ashkenaz and France* (Jerusalem 1945), 94. Similarly, Eadmer the monk reports that William Rufus, ruler of Normandy, allowed the Jews of Rouen to revert to Judaism in approximately 1099; see Norman Golb,

The Jews in Medieval Normandy: A Social and Intellectual History (Cambridge 1998), 134–135, 559–560.

10. Habermann, *Book of the Persecutions*, 56. Other communities with large numbers of coerced apostates in 1096 include Metz, Kerpen, Moers, and Trier.

11. Jehuda Wistinetzki and Jakob Freimann (eds.), *Sefer Hasidim* (Frankfurt am Main 1924), 465, no. 1922; see also pp. 74–75, no. 198, and p. 449, no. 1862. See also Joseph Hacker, "About the Persecutions During the First Crusade," *Zion* 31 (1966), 229–231 (in Hebrew).

12. Habermann, *Book of the Persecutions*, 6.

13. Gedalya ibn Yahya, *The Chain of Tradition* (Venice 1587), 2–3 (in Hebrew).

14. Habermann, *Book of the Persecutions*, 56.

15. Kenneth Stow, "Amnon Linder, *The Jews in the Legal Sources of the Early Middle Ages*," *Jewish Quarterly Review* 89 (1999), 464.

16. Avraham Grossman, *The Early Sages of France: Their Lives, Leadership, and Works* (Jerusalem 1995), 151 (in Hebrew). It emerges, then, that the twelfth-century speaker tells the tale of 1096 with an eye on his contemporary audience and that his hagiographical presentation is tendentious rather than naïve. This contradicts Haym Soloveitchik's contention that "it never occurred to the chroniclers that what had transpired was a result of anything other than overwhelming duress"; see Haym Soloveitchik, "Religious Law and Change: The Medieval Ashkenazic Example," *AJS Review* 12 (1987), 215.

17. Jeremy Cohen, "The Hebrew Crusade Chronicles in Their Christian Cultural Context," in *Juden und Christen zur Zeit der Kreuzzüge*, ed. Alfred Haverkamp (Sigmaringen 1999), 22. See also Cohen's more sweeping interpretation of the Hebrew narratives, with the same methodological approach, in Cohen, *Sanctifying the Name of God*. Similarly, comparing the persecution of 1096 with that of the Chmielnicki massacres of the 1640s, Jacob Katz wrote that the 1640s differed from 1096 in that "in this period [the 1640s] the environment's Christianity did not constitute a temptation for the Jew." See Jacob Katz, "Martyrdom in the Middle Ages and in 1648–49," in *Yitzhak F. Baer Jubilee Volume on the Occasion of His Seventieth Birthday*, ed. Salo W. Baron, Ben-Zion Dinur, Samuel Ettinger, and Israel Halpern (Jerusalem 1960), 320 (in Hebrew).

18. Bernhard Blumenkranz, *Juifs et Chrétiens dans le Monde Occidental 430–1096* (Paris 1960), 138.

19. John F. Benton (ed.), *Self and Society in Medieval France: The Memoirs of Abbot Guibert of Nogent (1064?–c.1125)*, trans. C. C. Swinton Bland (New York 1970), 137.

20. Katz, *Exclusiveness and Tolerance*, 67.

21. Katz, *Exclusiveness and Tolerance*, 68.

22. Jeremy Cohen, "The Mentality of the Medieval Jewish Apostate: Peter Alfonsi, Hermann of Cologne, and Pablo Christiani," in *Jewish Apostasy in the Modern World*, ed. Todd Endelman (New York 1987), 23. See also Ronald Dworkin's discussion of the hard case in his *Law's Empire* (Cambridge, Mass., 1986), 254–288 and passim.

23. Salo W. Baron, *A Social and Religious History of the Jews*, 2nd ed., v. 9 (New York 1965), 22–23.

24. Salo W. Baron, *A Social and Religious History of the Jews*, 2nd ed., v. 5 (New York 1957), 113.

25. Soloveitchik, "Religious Law," 214. Similarly, see Simhah Goldin, *Uniqueness and Togetherness: The Enigma of the Survival of the Jews in the Middle Ages* (Tel Aviv 1997), 89 (in Hebrew).

26. Grossman, *Early Sages of France*, 267.

27. Grossman, *Early Sages of France*, 151. See also Avraham Grossman, *The Early Sages of Ashkenaz: Their Lives, Leadership, and Works (900–1096)*, 3rd ed. (Jerusalem 2001), 122n69 (in Hebrew).

28. Avraham Grossman, "The Roots of *Kiddush Hashem* in Early Ashkenaz," in *Sanctity of Life and Martyrdom*, ed. Isaiah M. Gafni and Aviezer Ravitzky (Jerusalem 1992), 125 (in Hebrew).

29. Shraga Rosental (ed.), *Sefer ha-Yashar: Responsa* (Berlin 1898), 45, no. 25.

30. Katz, *Exclusiveness and Tolerance*, 67.

31. Grossman, "Roots," 125; Grossman, *Early Sages of France*, 503. This view is also echoed by Goldin, *Uniqueness and Togetherness*, 87.

32. Aronius, *Regesten*, 73, no. 170; Baron, *Social and Religious History*, v. 9, 20; Robert Chazan, *Church, State, and Jew in the Middle Ages* (New York 1980), 61. The rule regarding inheritance was retained in subsequent imperial legislation, although it continued to provoke ecclesiastical condemnation; see Friedrich Lotter, "Imperial Versus Ecclesiastical Jewry Law in the High Middle Ages: Contradictions and Controversies Concerning the Conversion of Jews and Their Serfs," in *Proceedings of the Tenth World Congress of Jewish Studies*, ed. David Assaf (Jerusalem, 1990), v. B/2, 59–60; and Friedrich Lotter, "The Scope and Effectiveness of Imperial Jewry Law in the High Middle Ages," *Jewish History* 4 (1989), 40–41.

33. Solomon Grayzel, *The Church and the Jews in the XIIIth Century*, 2nd ed. (New York 1966), 296; Baron, *Social and Religious History*, v. 9, 19; Salo W. Baron, *The Jewish Community: Its History and Structure to the American Revolution* (Philadelphia 1942), v. 1, 247–248. It has been suggested that this development regarding inheritance led rabbinic deciders to permit apostates to inherit their parents' estate, contrary to the traditional view; see Goldin, *Uniqueness and Togetherness*, 93.

34. Baron, *Social and Religious History*, v. 9, 23.

35. Ephraim Kanarfogel, "Rabbinic Attitudes Toward Nonobservance in the Medieval Period," in *Jewish Tradition and the Nontraditional Jew*, ed. Jacob J. Schacter (Northvale, N.J., 1992), 3.

36. Solomon Zeitlin, "Mummar and Meshumad," *Jewish Quarterly Review* 54 (1963), 84–86. Similarly, see Saul Lieberman, *Tosefta Ki-fshutah*, 2nd ed. (Jerusalem 1992), pt. 3, 402n45. Cf. John M. G. Barclay, "Who Was Considered an Apostate in the Jewish Diaspora?" in *Tolerance and Intolerance in Early Judaism and Christianity*, ed. Graham N. Stanton and Guy G. Stroumsa (Cambridge 1998), 80–98. On the origins of the term *meshumad*, see also Moshe ben Ya'akov ibn Ezra, *Kitab al-Muhadara wal-Mudhakara*, ed. and Hebrew trans. A. S. Halkin (Jerusalem 1975), 48–49 (in Judeo-Arabic). My thanks to Daniel Frank of Ohio State University for this reference.

37. Goldin, *Uniqueness and Togetherness*, 89–90.

38. See Katz, *Exclusiveness and Tolerance*, 68n6. More to the point, in late antiquity the term *mumar* refers to one who transgresses one or more commandments (for various reasons), whereas in the Middle Ages it becomes one of the terms for apostasy, a phenomenon unknown in the Greco-Roman era.

39. Shlomo Eidelberg rejects the possibility that Gershom's son apostatized during the 1012 persecution on the grounds that he could not possibly have preferred apostasy to banishment, which was the available alternative. See Gershom ben Judah, *Responsa*, ed. Shlomo Eidelberg (New York 1955), 11. For another critique of Graetz's reconstruction, see H. Tykocinski, "Die Verfolgung der Juden in Mainz im Jahre 1012," in *Beiträge zur Geschichte der deutschen Juden: Festschrift zum siebzigsten Geburstage Martin Philippsons* (Leipzig 1916), 2–3.

40. Heinrich Graetz, *History of the Jews* (Philadelphia 1956), v. 3, 246.

41. "Tarah 'avur qehillot u-vitel gezerot." See Heinrich Graetz, *Geschichte der Juden*, 3rd ed. (Leipzig 1895), v. 5, 339, 474. Note that the reference to the annulment of decrees does not appear in the notice about Simon in the Worms *memorbuch* (*Kovez al Yad* 3 [1887], 1).

42. Victor [Avigdor] Aptowitzer, *Introduction to Sefer Rabiah* (Jerusalem 1938), 331 (in Hebrew).

43. James Parkes, *The Jew in the Medieval Community: A Study of His Political and Economic Situation* (London 1938), 38.

44. Grossman, *Early Sages of Ashkenaz*, 90. Cf. the critical remarks of David Berger, "The Study of the Ancient Rabbinate of Ashkenaz," *Tarbiz* 53 (1984), 480 (in Hebrew).

45. Grossman, "Roots," 125; Grossman, *Early Sages of France*, 502. See also Grossman, *Early Sages of Ashkenaz*, 112.

46. That is, *shemad*, which can refer to physical or spiritual destruction, namely, apostasy.

47. Isaac ben Moses, *Or Zaru'a* (Zhitomir 1862), pt. 2, fol. 88c, no. 428.

48. Meir ben Barukh, *The Complete Laws of Mourning*, ed. Akiva Dov Landau and Jacob Aaron Landau (Jerusalem 1976), 58, no. 37 (in Hebrew). See also Meir ben Barukh, *Responsa* (Prague 1608), no. 544; and Mordecai ben Hillel on *Mo'ed Qattan*, no. 937.

49. Meir ben Barukh's signature does not appear at the conclusion of this text, and thus its attribution to him is not absolutely certain. Yet the decision supports the attribution, for the respondent refuses to grant Gershom's behavior authoritative status and rules that one does not mourn the death of apostates. This fits the historical context of Meir ben Barukh of Rothenburg, in whose time relations with non-Jews were considerably worse than in earlier centuries.

50. Mordecai ben Hillel on *Mo'ed Qattan*, no. 886. To recapitulate the chain of tradition, Samson of Coucy was the source for Isaac ben Moses of Vienna, who reported it to Meir ben Barukh of Rothenburg, from whom Mordecai ben Hillel received his information.

51. Isaac ben Moses, *Or Zaru'a*, pt. 2, no. 428.

52. Ben-Zion Dinur, *Israel and the Diaspora* (Tel Aviv 1961), v. 1, pt. 3, 329n65 (in Hebrew).

53. Louis Finkelstein, *Jewish Self-Government in the Middle Ages*, 2nd ed. (New York 1964), 30–31. Finkelstein notes the absence of a distinction between voluntary and coerced apostates.

54. Finkelstein, *Jewish Self-Government*, 126. Finkelstein infers from the existence of such a rabbinical decree that apostasy was rampant in the early eleventh century. Grossman concludes, more conservatively, that reminding penitent apostates of their mistake was a common practice, which created severe tensions within the Jewish community (*Early Sages of France*, 152). Neither of these claims can be accepted without further evidence.

55. See Shepkaru, "Death Twice Over," 253; cf. Jeremy Cohen, "Between Martyrdom and Apostasy: Doubt and Self-Definition in Twelfth-Century Ashkenaz," *Journal of Medieval and Early Modern Studies* 29 (1999), 436–441.

56. Rashi, *Responsa*, ed. Israel Elfenbein (New York 1943), 82, no. 70.

57. Gershom ben Judah, *Responsa*, 57–60, no. 4; S. Horowitz (ed.), *Mahzor Vitry* (Nurenberg 1923), 97, no. 125, and later sources.

58. Gershom ben Judah, *Responsa*, 60–61, no. 5; Ephraim Kupfer (ed.), *Responsa and Rulings by French and German Rabbis* (Jerusalem 1973), 292 (in Hebrew).

59. Grossman, *Early Sages of Ashkenaz*, 125–126. Ironically, whereas Shlomo Eidelberg sug-

gests that Gershom ruled stringently only when the apostate had become a leader or officiant in the service of idolatry, Grossman rejects this solution, because Gershom's two decisions present an identical set of circumstances. Incidentally, Grossman's interpretation suggests that he subscribes to the view that Gershom's son was the victim of forced baptism rather than voluntary apostasy, although he makes no explicit statement to this effect.

60. *Menahot* 109r–v.

61. *Mishneh Torah, Nesi'at Kappayim* 15:3. See Moses Hyamson (ed., trans.), *Mishneh Torah: The Book of Adoration* (Jerusalem 1962), fol. 118r.

62. Gershom ben Judah, *Responsa*, 57–60, no. 4; Rashi, *Responsa*, 190–191, no. 170.

63. Grossman, *Early Sages of Ashkenaz*, 124–125; Grossman, *Early Sages of France*, 152–153.

64. Rabbi Eliezer "the Great," a student of Gershom, did distinguish clearly between voluntary and coerced apostates, allowing only coerced apostates to perform the priestly blessing, but his responsum was unknown in the Middle Ages. See Irving A. Agus (ed.), *Responsa of the Tosaphists* (New York 1954), 45–46 (in Hebrew); and Grossman, *Early Sages of Ashkenaz*, 224–225. The ruling of Joseph Bonfils resembles that of Maimonides, in the tradition of the Babylonian gaonim; see Zedekiah ben Abraham, *Shibolei ha-Leqet ha-Shalem*, ed. Samuel K. Mirsky (New York 1966), 231, no. 33. Grossman also cites Judah ha-Kohen, a student of Gershom, but does not provide a specific primary source.

65. The tosafists cite Rashi's stance on the priest-apostate (which was also Gershom's lenient position), but only after they offer the traditional, more stringent view, signifying that their stance on this issue was anything but slavish; see Tosafot on *Menahot* 109r, s.v. *lo yeshamshu*; Tosafot on *Sotah* 39r, s.v. *ve-khi mehader*. But cf. Tosafot on *Ta'anit* 27r, s.v. *iy mah*, which offers only the lenient ruling. Note that Meir ben Barukh of Rothenburg refuses to follow Rashi's lead; he rules that one does not instruct the penitent priest to perform the priestly blessing but that if he does so of his own accord, he may be allowed to proceed. See Jacob ben Asher, *Arba'ah Turim*, pt. 1, no. 128. This, however, extends beyond the chronological framework of the present study.

66. *Bet Yosef* on *Arba'ah Turim*, pt. 1, no. 128; *Shulhan Arukh*, pt. 1, §128, no. 37. Karo's innovation can be attributed, at least in part, to the loss of tens of thousands of souls to Catholicism in Spain between 1391 and 1492, a catastrophe that generated a wealth of rabbinic discourse on the subject of apostasy, with an abundance of new insights. See Simhah Assaf, "The Conversos of Spain and Portugal in the Responsa Literature," in *In the Tent of Jacob* (Jerusalem 1943), 145–180 (in Hebrew); and B. Netanyahu, *The Marranos of Spain from the Late 14th to the Early 16th Century According to Contemporary Hebrew Sources*, 3rd ed. (Ithaca 1999).

67. "Nuzzelu le-gehinom" (Habermann, *Book of the Persecutions*, 36). The translation, in a slightly modified form, is from Robert Chazan, *European Jewry and the First Crusade* (Berkeley 1987), 263.

68. "Et factus est alienus a communi sepultura Judaeorum, similiter et Christianorum, tum quia factus fuerat Christianus, tum quia ipse, sicut canis reversus ad vomitum, rediit ad Judaicam pravitatem." See William Stubbs (ed.), *Chronica magistri Rogeri de Houedene* (Rerum Brittanicarum Medii Aevi Scriptores [Rolls Series], v. 51) (Wiesbaden 1964 [1868–1871]), v. 3, 13. The translation is from G. G. Coulton, *Life in the Middle Ages*, 2nd ed. (Cambridge 1954), v. 2, 34. See also Cecil Roth, *A History of the Jews in England* (Oxford 1941), 19–20, 22; and Salo W. Baron, *The Social and Religious History of the Jews*, v. 4 (New York 1957), 125, 146.

69. Wistinetzki and Freimann, *Sefer Hasidim*, 465, no. 1922. These dicta do not support Soloveitchik's claim that the Jews of Ashkenaz *never* wondered "to what extent the individual

was simply a victim of circumstances and to what extent his conduct was a consequence of his inner ambiguities" ("Religious Law," 215).

70. Alfred Haverkamp, "Baptised Jews in German Lands During the Twelfth Century," in *Jews and Christians in Twelfth-Century Europe*, ed. Michael A. Signer and John Van Engen (Notre Dame 2001), 262. Haverkamp maintains that "the percentage of children and young women among those who, having been forcibly baptised, remained part of Christianity must have been much higher that that of men," because they were socially dependent. This statement is to be doubted with regard to young women. See also Baron, *Social and Religious History*, v. 4, 146.

71. "Numquam consentit sed penitus contradicit nec rem nec characterem suscipit sacramenti." See Shlomo Simonsohn, *The Apostolic See and the Jews: History* (Toronto 1991), 243–244; Grayzel, *The Church and the Jews*, 101–103; Baron, *Social and Religious History*, v. 9, 13; and Walter Pakter, *Medieval Canon Law and the Jews* (Ebelsbach 1988), 82.

72. This tale is told by Ephraim ben Jacob of Bonn (b. 1132), who stresses that the reversion occurred "in that same year," namely 1147, and he rather triumphantly contrasts the fate of these apostates with that of the crusaders, who left their homes never to be seen again. Oddly, however, Ephraim's account does not include any incidents of forced baptism that correspond to the story of mass reversion; see Habermann, *Book of the Persecutions*, 122.

73. That the Blois incident forced some Jews to accept baptism is confirmed in the version of Robert of Torigni (Robertus de Monte) in *Chronicle of Robert of Torigni, Abbot of the Monastery of St. Michael-in-Peril-of-the-Sea* (London 1890) [*Chronicles of Stephen, Henry II, and Richard I*, ed. Richard Howlett, v. 4; *Rerum Britannicarum Medii Aevi, Scriptores*, Rolls Series, v. 82], 251; Léopold Delisle (ed.), *Recueil des historiens des Gaules et de la France*, 2nd ed. (Paris 1869), v. 13, 315. Whether William actually sanctioned reversion, however, is unclear. The Hebrew letter to this effect, as it has traditionally been interpreted, reads "and he asked for them to return to God" ("ve-sha'al lahem lashuv el YY"). However, a change in the vocalization of a single letter (in what is, in any case, a nonvocalized text) would dramatically alter the meaning. If we read not *ve-sha'al* (meaning "and he asked") but rather *ve-she'al* (i.e., "and that they may not [return to God]"), then the text is saying that, although the bishop facilitated their release from custody, he explicitly forbade their reversion. See Habermann, *Book of the Persecutions*, 145–146. On the Blois incident, see Shalom Spiegel, "*In Monte Dominus Videbitur*: The Martyrs of Blois and the Early Accusations of Ritual Murder," in *The Mordecai Kaplan Jubilee Volume*, ed. Moshe Davis (New York 1953), 267–287 (in Hebrew); Robert Chazan, "The Blois Incident of 1171: A Study in Jewish Intercommunal Organization," *Proceedings of the American Academy of Jewish Research* 36 (1968), 13–31; Susan L. Einbinder, "Pucellina of Blois: Romantic Myths and Narrative Conventions," *Jewish History* 12 (1998), 29–46; and Susan L. Einbinder, *Beautiful Death: Jewish Poetry and Medieval Martyrdom in Medieval France* (Princeton 2002), 45–69.

74. John Gilchrist, "The Perception of Jews in the Canon Law in the Period of the First Two Crusades," *Jewish History* 3 (1988), 13. See also Blumenkranz, *Juifs et Chrétiens*, 104–134.

75. Grayzel, *The Church and the Jews*, 310; Baron, *Social and Religious History*, v. 9, 14. Haverkamp explains that Christians suspected Jewish converts of preserving traces of their Jewish origins even after generations ("Baptised Jews," 265–267).

76. Cf. the similar issue of the speed with which a woman taken captive by gentiles returns to her community. Talmudic law assumes that such a woman has had sexual relations with one or more of her captors, but she may return to her husband if she rejoins her commu-

nity and family at the earliest possible opportunity, because one could then assume that her sexual act had not been consensual. For the earliest discussion of this issue, from late twelfth-century France, see Mordecai ben Hillel on *Qiddushin*, no. 568, and Ephraim E. Urbach, *The Tosaphists: Their History, Writings, and Methods*, 4th ed. (Jerusalem 1980), v. 1, 133 (in Hebrew). See also Gerald I. Blidstein, "The Personal Status of Apostate and Ransomed Women in Medieval Jewish Law," *Shenaton Ha-Mishpat Ha-Ivri* 3–4 (1976–1977), 53 (in Hebrew).

77. See Adolf Jellinek, *Bet ha-Midrasch* (Jerusalem 1938), v. 5, 148–152; Abraham David, "Inquiries Concerning the Legend of the Jewish Pope," in *The A. M. Habermannn Memorial Volume*, ed. Zvi Malachi (Lod 1983), 17–25 (in Hebrew); Abraham David, "Bemerkungen zur Legende vom jüdischen Papst," *Freiburger Rundbrief: Beiträge zur christlich-jüdisch Begegnung* 37/38 (1985–1986), 150–153; and David Levine Lerner, "The Enduring Legend of the Jewish Pope," *Judaism* 40 (1981), 148–170.

78. Urbach, *The Tosaphists*, v. 1, 82.

79. Katz, *Exclusiveness and Tolerance*, 68, citing Heinrich Graetz, *Geschichte der Juden*, 4th ed. (Leipzig 1907), v. 6, 92–93.

80. Habermann, *Book of the Persecutions*, 56.

81. Habermann, *Book of the Persecutions*, 57.

82. See Kanarfogel, "Rabbinic Attitudes," 3; and Netanyahu, *Marranos of Spain*, 8–13. Cf. Soloveitchik's claim that "the fidelity of the converts was unquestioned" ("Religious Law," 215).

83. Agus, *Responsa of the Tosaphists*, 51–52, no. 9.

84. See, similarly, Agus, *Responsa of the Tosaphists*, 238, no. 128, from a later period.

85. Simonsohn, *Apostolic See*, 42, doc. 42.

86. Habermann, *Book of the Persecutions*, 57.

87. Habermann, *Book of the Persecutions*, 96.

88. Habermann, *Book of the Persecutions*, 56.

89. Habermann, *Book of the Persecutions*, 56.

90. "Ivhat herev," as in Ezekiel 21:20. The same phrase appears in the *Sefer Hasidim* passage about a community in which "during a time of persecution some were killed and some apostatized with the intention of returning to Judaism when they could," but they apostatized "on account of fear of the sword" (Wistinetzki and Freimann, *Sefer Hasidim*, 85, no. 262).

91. Rashi, *Responsa*, 188–189, no. 168. The identity of these apostates and the circumstances of their apostasy are unclear. Ben-Zion Dinur assumes that this text refers to those Jews who apostatized under threat of death at the hands of the First Crusaders (*Israel and the Diaspora*, v. 2, pt. 1, 43. Simhah Goldin (*Uniqueness and Togetherness*, 200n43) attributes it to Isaac Dampierre (d. 1185?), based on Urbach, *The Tosaphists*, v. 1, 244–245, who offers no proof for this attribution. Following Urbach, Goldin cites Zedekiah ben Abraham, *Shibolei ha-Leqet: Part 2*, ed. Simhah Hassida (Jerusalem 1988), no. 5 (in Hebrew), but that text contains no clear indication of its authorship. If true, the attribution to Isaac of Dampierre would fit in with Goldin's theory that the attitude toward apostates stiffened or hardened after 1096.

92. Cf., from a later period, Agus, *Responsa of the Tosaphists*, 231–232, no. 125.

93. For the phrase "the end testifies to the beginning," see Eliezer ben Nathan, *Even ha-ʿEzer*, ed. Shalom Albeck (Warsaw 1904), pt. 3, fol. 56d; and Judah ben Asher, *Zikhron Yehudah*, ed. Judah Rosenberg (Berlin 1846), fol. 52b.

94. Cf. Grossman's view that Rashi's statement that the heart of the forced converts is directed heavenward is to be taken at face value (*Early Sages of France*, 154).

95. Rashi, on *Avodah Zarah* 17b. The continuation reads, "and if they do return, they quickly die, because of sorrow and the compulsion of the [Evil] Inclination, and this is the decree of the King [i.e., God], that they die." Cf. Rashi on Proverbs 2:19.

96. Zedekiah ben Abraham, *Shibolei ha-Leqet: Part 2*, 21–22, no. 5. The text was also published in Rashi, *Responsa*, no. 169.

97. Baron, *Social and Religious History*, v. 9, 247n13; Simonsohn, *Apostolic See*, 262–263, doc. 255. Edward Fram attributes the practice of moving after reversion to the fact that political power in medieval Germany was decentralized, and thus this option was unavailable to the new Christians of the increasingly unified and centralized government of fifteenth-century Spain; see Edward Fram, "Perception and Reception of Repentant Apostates in Medieval Ashkenaz and Pre-Modern Poland," *AJS Review* 21 (1996), 313.

98. Rashi, *Responsa*, no. 169. In the late thirteenth century an apostate named Andreas from the south of Italy writes that it is well-known that poor apostates escape "to places where they are not known and revert to their origin." See Joseph Shatzmiller, "Jewish Converts to Christianity in Medieval Europe 1200–1500," in *Cross-Cultural Convergences in the Crusader Period: Essays Presented to Aryeh Grabois on His Sixty-Fifth Birthday*, ed. Michael Goodich, Sophia Menache, and Sylvia Schein (New York 1995), 315.

99. Habermann, *Book of the Persecutions*, 122.

100. It is also possible that relocation was a form of exile, a penance for the act of apostasy; see Maimonides, *Mishneh Torah, Teshuvah* 2:4.

101. Zeitlin, "Mummar and Meshumad," 86.

102. Yosef Hayim Yerushalmi, "The Inquisition and the Jews of France in the Time of Bernard Gui," *Harvard Theological Review* 63 (1970), 365. See also p. 366: "Great hostility toward the apostate, and the sober realization that in most cases his conversion to Christianity was final, combined to make the masses regard him as really no longer a Jew."

103. Gerald Blidstein, "Who Is Not a Jew? The Medieval Discussion," *Israel Law Review* 11 (1976), 376.

104. Louis Rabinowitz, *The Social Life of the Jews of Northern France in the XII–XIV Centuries*, 2nd ed. (New York 1972), 104.

105. Isaac ben Moses, *Or Zaru'a*, pt. 2, no. 428.

106. Wistinetzki and Freimann, *Sefer Hasidim*, 73–74, no. 192, cited by Katz, *Exclusiveness and Tolerance*, 74.

107. Wistinetzki and Freimann, *Sefer Hasidim*, 385, no. 1572. See also Israel Isserlein, *Terumat ha-Deshen*, pt. 1, no. 21.

108. *Sanhedrin* 60r (on cursing God), and N. Z. Y. Berlin on *She'iltot*, no. 110, for the suggestion that apostasy is tantamount to death. The link was noted by Reuven Margaliyot, in his commentary to his own edition of *Sefer Hasidim* (Jerusalem 1957), 187, no. 190.

109. Habermann, *Book of the Persecutions*, 11–15; see also Chapter 2. Sehok, meaning joke, seems to be a perversion of the name Isaac, in keeping with the tradition of giving apostates names of opprobrium; see Margaliyot, *Sefer Hasidim*, 187, no. 191. For a talmudic source for this custom, see *Avodah Zarah* 46r. Alternatively, Sehok may mean pilgrim, the sense in which the word appears in Wistinetzki and Freimann, *Sefer Hasidim*, 75, no. 201; this would fit the detail that Sehok ben Esther wandered from place to place. One even wonders whether his wandering was a pilgrimage, rather than aimless.

110. Mordecai ben Hillel on *Ketubot*, no. 306; *Maimonidean Responsa* (in Hebrew), *Nashim*, no. 10. Similarly, Ephraim of Bonn tells the tale of the encounter, in 1146 just outside

the city of Cologne, between "worthless people" who had been baptized, that is, (voluntary) apostates, and Simon "the Pious" of Trier, and of their efforts to entice him to apostatize. See Habermann, *Book of the Persecutions*, 116. On "worthless people," see Chapter 6.

111. Solomon ibn Adret, *Responsa*, pt. 7, no. 179. On this source and the previous one (Mordecai ben Hillel on *Ketubot*, no. 306), see Urbach, *The Tosaphists*, v. 1, 245; and Soloveitchik, "Religious Law," 214n15. There is evidence, including the Mordecai ben Hillel text, that apostates wishing to revert were forced to undergo ritual immersion before their reintegration into the Jewish community. See Yerushalmi, "Inquisition and the Jews," 372; Joseph Shatzmiller, "Converts and Judaizers in the Early Fourteenth Century," *Harvard Theological Review* 74 (1981), 63–77; Blidstein, "Who Is Not a Jew?" 376n23; Ephraim Kanarfogel, "Returning to the Jewish Community in Medieval Ashkenaz: History and Halakhah," in *Turim: Studies in Jewish History and Literature Presented to Dr. Bernard Lander*, ed. Michael A. Shmidman (New York 2007), 69–97, and, regarding serial apostasy, esp. 90; and Jacob Elbaum, *Repentance and Self-Flagellation in the Writings of the Sages of Germany and Poland 1348–1648* (Jerusalem 1992), 225–227 (in Hebrew). Placing obstacles in the path of reversion seems to be a phenomenon of the later Middle Ages, dating from the thirteenth century.

112. Robert Chazan, *Medieval Jewry in Northern France: A Political and Social History* (Baltimore 1973), 147. Note the Catholic ritual of a second baptism for penitent lapsed converts.

113. Katz, *Exclusiveness and Tolerance*, 75.

114. Katz, *Exclusiveness and Tolerance*, 71; Jacob Katz, "Although He Has Sinned, He Is Still Israel," *Tarbiz* 27 (1958), 203–217 (in Hebrew). See also Yitzhak Baer, "Rashi and the Historical Reality of His Time," *Tarbiz* 20 (1950), 324–332 (in Hebrew). For earlier scholars, see Eliezer of Metz, *Sefer Yere'im Ha-Shalem* (Vilna 1902), fol. 74a, no. 156. See also Abraham ben David, *Temim De'im* (Lemberg 1812), no. 45; and Meir ben Barukh, *Responsa*, no. 799.

115. Simcha Emanuel, *Fragments of the Tablets: Lost Books of the Tosaphists* (Jerusalem 2006), 108 (in Hebrew).

116. Rosental, *Sefer ha-Yashar*, 43–45, no. 25.

117. Rosental, *Sefer ha-Yashar*, 46, no. 26. See also S. Schlesinger (ed.), *Sefer ha-Yashar: Novellae* (Jerusalem 1959), no. 766, 448; and Horowitz, *Mahzor Vitry*, 779–780, no. 134.

118. Wistinetzki and Freimann, *Sefer Hasidim*, 408, no. 1701.

119. Wistinetzki and Freimann, *Sefer Hasidim*, 408, no. 1702.

120. Wistinetzki and Freimann, *Sefer Hasidim*, 385, no. 1571.

121. Wistinetzki and Freimann, *Sefer Hasidim*, 73, no. 190; and 178, no. 679. See also p. 357, no. 1476.

122. Wistinetzki and Freimann, *Sefer Hasidim*, 164, no. 604.

123. Wistinetzki and Freimann, *Sefer Hasidim*, 198, no. 790; 357, no. 1476.

124. Habermann, *Book of the Persecutions*, 146.

125. There exists an analogous story from the Christian side, that of Jacob ben Isaac of Regensburg, who hoards his father's money before his own conversion to Christianity; see Aronius, *Regesten*, 105, no. 226. The source is "Annales Egmundenses," in *Fontes Egmundenses*, ed. Otto Oppermann (Utrecht 1933), 149–150 (cited by Haverkamp, "Baptised Jews," 279–281).

126. Wistinetzki and Freimann, *Sefer Hasidim*, 75, no. 200. See also no. 201; and Fram, "Perception and Reception," 306.

127. Isaac ben Moses of Vienna tells of an apostate who touched wine, which would render it nonkosher, but subsequently claimed to have reverted; see Isaac ben Moses, *Or Zaru'a*, pt. 1, 64d, no. 448.

128. Grossman, *Early Sages of Ashkenaz*, 124.

129. Isaac Arama, of fifteenth-century Spain, cites the practice of Karaite Jews, who view apostates as having died and hence allow the wife of an apostate to remarry without her having received a bill of divorce. See H. H. Ben-Sasson, "The Generation of the Spanish Exiles on Its Fate," *Zion* 26 (1961), 39 (in Hebrew). Clearly Arama did not see Rabbanite Judaism as according an apostate the status of one deceased.

130. Cohen, "Between Martyrdom and Apostasy," 431–471; the quote appears on p. 463. See also Gavin Langmuir, *Toward a Definition of Antisemitism* (Berkeley 1990), 100–133.

131. Grossman, "Roots," 119. Baer, in his 1945 introduction to Habermann's edition of the chronicles, wrote that they were written "to encourage the hearts and strengthen weak knees" (Baer, "Introduction," 3).

132. Grossman, *Early Sages of France*, 267, 502.

133. Grossman, *Early Sages of France*, 125.

134. Grossman, "Roots," 121.

135. Katz, *Exclusiveness and Tolerance*, 75–76.

136. Soloveitchik, "Religious Law," 214. Cf. the typology presented for the later Middle Ages by Shatzmiller in "Jewish Converts."

137. David Berger, *The Jewish-Christian Debate in the High Middle Ages: A Critical Edition of the Nizzahon Vetus* (Philadelphia 1979), 206, no. 211, cited in Cohen, "Between Martyrdom and Apostasy," 462–463. See also Berger, *Jewish-Christian Debate*, 228, no. 242.

138. The philological data presented here are anything but exhaustive and merely provide a point of departure for a thorough philological study.

139. Berger, *Jewish-Christian Debate*, 226, no. 242. Berger's translation requires correction. The Hebrew original includes a third category of offender, namely, "the wicked" (*resha'im*) (Berger, *Jewish-Christian Debate*, 160 [Hebrew pagination]).

140. We also find the pair of terms together in a *Sefer Hasidim* passage about the prayer for the destruction of apostates (*meshumadim*), which is part of the weekday prayer service (Wistinetzki and Freimann, *Sefer Hasidim*, 146, no. 511). The passage explains that the prayer refers to "all the enemies of your people" rather than to "all our enemies," because "there are places in which apostates (*meshumadim*) and heretics (*minim*) are among them, while in others they are not." The reference is to the prayer that in modern liturgical texts is about the eradication of informers or informing, rather than apostates. Cf. Yom Tov Lipman Mülhausen, *Sefer ha-Nizzahon* (Königsberg 1848), 425, no. 349; and Yom Tov Lipman Mülhausen, *Sefer ha-Nizzahon* (Altdorf 1644), 193, no. 348. More equivocal is the terminology in *Sefer Nizzahon Yashan* (Berger, *Jewish-Christian Debate*, 94, no. 78): "These are the apostates (*meshumadim*) who accept their defiling baptism, rebelling against God and denying him. 'For in my holy mountain . . . there shall all the house of Israel serve me' [Ezek. 20:40], i.e., those who believe in me with all their heart and soul."

141. For examples of the use of this phrase, see the commentary of Samuel ben Meir on Exodus 3:22 and 20:12 and Leviticus 19:19. See also Eliezer Touito, "The Exegetical Method of R. Samuel b. Meir in Light of the Historical Reality of His Time," in *Studies in Rabbinic Literature, Bible, and Jewish History Presented to Professor E. Z. Melammed*, ed. Yizhak D. Gilat, Howard I. Levine, and Zvi Meir Rabinowitz (Ramat-Gan 1982), 66 (in Hebrew); Grossman, *Early Sages of France*, 480; and Ora Limor and Amnon Raz-Krakotzkin, *Jews and Christians in Western Europe: Encounter Between Cultures in the Middle Ages and the Renaissance* (Tel Aviv 1993), v. 4, 51–54 (in Hebrew).

142. See Netanyahu, *Marranos of Spain*, 89–90n15.

143. Wistinetzki and Freimann, *Sefer Hasidim*, 215, no. 857.

144. Wistinetzki and Freimann, *Sefer Hasidim*, 336, no. 1376.

145. Wistinetzki and Freimann, *Sefer Hasidim*, 459, no. 1897.

146. Margaliyot, *Sefer Hasidim*, 326, no. 479. See also p. 416, no. 637: "One should not say: 'If I do such and such a thing, I am not a Jew,' for he thereby makes himself a gentile or an apostate, for one ought not to say something evil, even conditionally."

147. Katz, *Exclusiveness and Tolerance*, 74. See also William Chester Jordan, "Adolescence and Conversion in the Middle Ages: A Research Agenda," in *Jews and Christians in Twelfth-Century Europe*, ed. Michael A. Signer and John Van Engen (Notre Dame 2001), 77–93.

148. Baron, *Social and Religious History*, v. 9, 23–24.

149. Simonsohn, *Apostolic See*, 244–245, and 52, doc. 50. The dog vomit image is based on Proverbs 26:11; it had already been used, in the same context, by Gregory the Great; see Simonsohn, *Apostolic See*, 5, doc. 5.

150. Parkes, *The Jew in the Medieval Community*, 144.

151. Grayzel, *The Church and the Jews*, 94–96, doc. 6. Similarly, see pp. 138–139, doc. 29.

152. Grayzel, *The Church and the Jews*, 96–99, doc. 8. See also Baron, *Social and Religious History*, v. 9, 21.

153. Wistinetzki and Freimann, *Sefer Hasidim*, 455, no. 1876.

154. Joel Müller (ed.), *Responsa of the Scholars of France and Lotharingia* (Vienna 1881), fol. 39a–40b, no. 63 (in Hebrew).

155. Emanuel, *Fragments of the Tablets*, 206–207. It is unclear from the text whether the woman has already received a bill of divorce from her Jewish husband. A famous case of romantic conversion is that of an English deacon who was circumcised for love of a Jewish woman and in 1222 was degraded by Stephen, archbishop of Canterbury, at an Oxford council and promptly burned at the stake. See Frederic William Maitland, "The Deacon and the Jewess; or Apostasy at Common Law," in *The Collected Papers of Frederic William Maitland*, ed. H. A. L. Fisher (Cambridge 1911), 385–406; and Langmuir, *Toward a Definition of Antisemitism*, 32–35.

156. Rashi discusses such a case and admits that some [scholars] "make noise"—that is, express doubt—about this rule, but he dismisses their reservations; see Mordecai ben Hillel on *Ketubot*, no. 286. See Blidstein, "Personal Status," 56–59. Blidstein infers from this noise-making that popular practice did not always require reverting apostates to separate from their spouses. He also deduces that reversion was common, but this conclusion, although it may be true, is not warranted by the case at hand. For a similar case from a later period, see Meir ben Barukh, *Responsa*, no. 1020.

157. Solomon ibn Adret, *Responsa*, pt. 7, no. 179, cited in Soloveitchik, "Religious Law," 214n15.

158. This is the approach of Simon Dubnov, *History of the Jews from the Roman Empire to the Early Medieval Period*, trans. Moshe Spiegel (New York 1968), v. 2, 705.

159. Similarly, Jeremy Cohen has argued that Hermann-Judah found it difficult to distinguish between the tenets of Judaism and Christianity ("Between Martyrdom and Apostasy," 446–452).

160. On the low barrier in the late Middle Ages, see Shatzmiller, "Jewish Converts," 301–302. On conversion in the late thirteenth century, see Robert Stacey, "The Conversion of Jews to Christianity in Thirteenth Century England," *Speculum* 67 (1992), 263–283.

161. In the same vein, Peter of Blois concedes that "if one defeats an enemy of the cross in debate, he will in any event not convert in his heart." See Peter of Blois, *Contra perfidiam Judaeorum*, PL 207:825–827, cited in David Berger, "Mission to the Jews and Jewish-Christian Contacts in the Polemical Literature of the High Middle Ages," *American Historical Review* 91 (1986), 580.

162. Qara's remark is conserved in Abraham ben Azriel, *Arugat ha-Bosem*, ed. Efraim E. Urbach (Jerusalem 1947), v. 2, 220, cited by Grossman, *Early Sages of France*, 269.

Chapter Six

1. Israel Isserlein, *Leqet Yosher*, ed. Jacob Freimann (Berlin 1903–1904), pt. 1, 119. The original Hebrew term for "upheld" is *mequyemet*.

2. Yitzhak Baer, *Galut*, trans. Robert Warshow (Lanham 1988), 48–49. I have deviated a little from Warshow's English translation; see the Hebrew edition: Yitzhak Baer, *Galut* (Jerusalem 1980), 44. In the same vein, Baer writes elsewhere that in the thirteenth and fourteenth centuries one can discern in the Ashkenazic communities a tendency to distance the Torah scholars from the communal leadership; clearly Baer was of the view that rabbinic leadership held sway up to that point. See Yitzhak Baer, "An Outline of the Historical Development of Medieval Judaism," *Moznayim* 23 (1947), 306 (in Hebrew).

3. Heinrich Heine, *The Rabbi of Bacherach: A Fragment*, trans. E. B. Ashton (New York 1947), 7–8.

4. *Kol Bo*, no. 142. See Irving Agus, *Urban Civilization in Pre-Crusade Europe* (New York 1965), v. 2, 461–462.

5. Irving Agus, *The Heroic Age of Franco-German Jewry* (New York 1969), 310–313. Agus's interpretation of the *Kol Bo* text, and thus also his overall assessment of the unique nature of Ashkenazic Jewry, is challenged by Avraham Grossman; see Avraham Grossman, *The Early Sages of Ashkenaz: Their Lives, Leadership, and Works (900–1096)*, 3rd ed. (Jerusalem 2001), 22–23.

6. Agus, *Heroic Age*, 313. Agus's level of enthusiasm is even greater than that of Louis Rabinowitz, who wrote that in medieval France "the authority of the Rabbi was supreme and unquestioned." See Louis Rabinowitz, *The Social Life of the Jews in Northern France in the XII–XIV Centuries*, 2nd ed. (New York 1972), 189. In Jacob Katz's formulation, "The Ashkenazic Middle Ages were characterized by strict and spontaneous subordination of the community at large to the bearers of halakhic authority." See Jacob Katz, *The "Shabbes Goy": A Study in Halakhic Flexibility* (Philadelphia 1989), 237.

7. See Avraham Grossman, "Offenders and Violent Men in Jewish Society in Early Ashkenaz and Their Influence upon Legal Procedure," *Shenaton ha-Mishpat ha-Ivri* 8 (1981), 135–152 (in Hebrew).

8. Grossman, "Offenders," 138, citing MS London-Montefiore 98, fol. 82v.

9. Meir ben Barukh, *Responsa* (Lvov 1860), no. 423.

10. On the roughly analogous predicament of the Church regarding the difficulty of enforcing discipline by means of excommunication, see R. W. Southern, *Western Society and the Church in the Middle Ages* (Harmondsworth 1970), 20–21.

11. Deviance is not an objective, ontological entity but rather a label attached to behavior by observers, an audience with its own point (or points) of view. See Erich Goode and Nachman

Ben-Yehuda, *Moral Panics: The Social Construction of Deviance* (Oxford 1994), 71; and Jon Oplinger, *The Politics of Demonology: The European Witchcraze and the Mass Production of Deviance* (London 1990), 25–31. Heresy also is largely a political issue, for it is the church (any church) that delineates the boundary between legitimate and illegitimate doctrine and conduct.

12. Joel Müller (ed.), *Teshuvot Ge'onei Mizrah u-Ma'arav* (Berlin 1888), no. 217, 60b.

13. Grossman, "Offenders," 152.

14. For the comparison of Ashkenaz with Christian Spain, see Chapter 8.

15. This also has implications for our understanding of the problem of modernization. Just as communal controls were the key to observance in medieval Ashkenaz, their loss in the modern period offers an explanation for the disintegration of the traditional observant way of life. See Jacob Katz, *Tradition and Crisis: Jewish Society at the End of the Middle Ages* (New York 1961), 213–274.

16. *Sanhedrin* 74a.

17. Haym Soloveitchik, "Religious Law and Change: The Medieval Ashkenazic Example," *AJS Review* 12 (1987), 209–210; Robert Chazan, *European Jewry and the First Crusade* (Berkeley 1987), 155–159.

18. Soloveitchik, "Religious Law and Change," 211. Abraham Gross locates in the Hebrew narratives of 1096 a distinction between the act of suffering martyrdom at the hands of others, which was widely held to be legitimate, and committing murder or suicide. See Abraham Gross, *Struggling with Tradition: Reservations About Active Martyrdom in the Middle Ages* (Leiden 2004), 1–44.

19. Katz, *Shabbes Goy*, 231, 236–237. Katz assumes that medieval Jews were more obedient to authority than those of the early modern era were, but he provides no evidence (p. 237). See also David Berger, "Jacob Katz on Jews and Christians in the Middle Ages," in *Pride of Jacob: Essays on Jacob Katz and His Work*, ed. Jay M. Harris (Cambridge, Mass., 2002), 44–45. Haym Soloveitchik highlights the chasm separating this type of religious life from a text-based one with respect to the post–World War II era; see Haym Soloveitchik, "Rupture and Reconstruction: The Transformation of Contemporary Orthodoxy," *Tradition* 28 (1994), 64–130.

20. Soloveitchik, *Principles and Pressures: Jewish Trade in Gentile Wine in the Middle Ages* (Tel Aviv 2003), 118n77.

21. Scholars have expressed doubts about the truth of the 1096 narrative, and Avraham Grossman writes that these doubts are particularly warranted regarding women's role as martyrological leaders, a characterization he suspects is both tendentious and exaggerated; see Avraham Grossman, *Pious and Rebellious: Jewish Women in Europe in the Middle Ages* (Jerusalem 2003), 350 (in Hebrew). On women's role in 1096, see Ivan G. Marcus, "From Politics to Martyrdom: Shifting Paradigms in the Hebrew Narratives of the 1096 Crusade Riots," *Prooftexts* 2 (1982), 45 and passim; and Shmuel Shepkaru, *Jewish Martyrs in the Pagan and Christian Worlds* (Cambridge 2006), 177–184. See also David Malkiel, "The Underclass in the First Crusade: A Historiographical Trend," *Journal of Medieval History* 28 (2002), 169–183.

22. See Ephraim Kanarfogel, *Jewish Education and Society in the High Middle Ages* (Detroit 1992); and Judith R. Baskin, "The Education of Jewish Women in the Lands of Medieval Islam and Christendom," *Pe'amim* 82 (2000), 31–49 (in Hebrew).

23. This portrait is not to be confused with the stereotype of women as intuitive rather than rational beings.

24. Tosafot on *Berakhot* 45b, s.v. *sha'ani*.

25. *Roke'ah ha-Gadol* (Jerusalem 1960), 56–57, no. 100. See *Shabbat* 59b.

26. *Shabbat* 59b and also Tosafot on *Shabbat* 59b, s.v. *Man darka*; Eliezer of Metz, *Yere'im ha-Shalem*, ed. S. Z. H. Halberstamm (Vilna 1891), no. 274, 148b–149a. By applying this principle to all types of jewelry, Rabbi Eliezer was expanding the talmudic rule, which refers only to a particularly opulent ornament known as the "city of gold."

27. Tosafot on *Shabbat* 64b, s.v. *R. 'Anani*.

28. *Sefer Ra'avan*, no. 349. It is implicit that medieval rabbis thought that men were not susceptible to the dangers of arrogance and boasting about jewelry. But Nahmanides, of thirteenth-century Barcelona, rejects the premise that men and women are fundamentally different on this issue. True, the Sabbath ban on jewelry was never applied to men, because men never cared for their jewelry enough to show it to others or to appreciate their friends' trinkets. This, he reasons, is not because men are less vain than women but rather because social convention dictates that only women adorn themselves with jewelry. Thus Nahmanides arrives at the startling conclusion that in a society that approves of male self-adornment, the rules for women would apply to men. He cites earrings as an example of a jewelry item that in some societies might be fit for a man. See Nahmanides' *Commentary on the Torah*, trans. and ed. Charles B. Chavel (Jerusalem 1966–1967), v. 1, 528.

29. *Sefer Ra'avan*, nos. 348–349. *Sefer Ra'avan*, no. 348 is about *batei ha-nefesh*, or soul's houses. This term comes from Isaiah 3:20 and was generally understood to refer to a piece of jewelry worn on the chest or throat. Rashi says this is "opposite the heart," and Kimhi says that "it is a jewel which women hang between their breasts, over their heart." Ibn Ezra also places it on the chest, "which is the house of the soul, for the heart is there." Samuel ben Meir, that is, Rashbam, however, opines that it refers to a throat ornament, although medieval contemporaries roundly reject this view; see Tosafot on *Bava Batra* 156b, s.v. *kevinti*. But Rashbam's definition fits Barukh of Worms's statement that wealthy women make a silver or gold key (for a box containing their other keys), to which they attach a pin for closing the area covering their throat; see Barukh of Worms, *Sefer ha-Terumah* (Warsaw 1897), no. 240. This is vaguely similar to Isaac of Vienna's observation that women make their key into a *bat nefesh* with which they close their robe (Isaac ben Moses of Vienna, *Or Zaru'a*, pt. 2, no. 84), although here perhaps the chest rather than the throat is intended. Likewise, see Moses of Coucy, *Sefer Mitzvot Gadol*, negative precept 65. Note that Rashbam's view has a basis in the rabbinic conception of bovine anatomy; see *Mishneh Torah, Avot ha-Tum'ot* 3:6.

30. Rashi on *Shabbat* 59b, s.v. *nizme ha-af*. Note that nose rings were not considered difficult to remove, perhaps because the nose is uncovered but possibly also because the nose ring was thought to rest on the nose rather than hang from a pierced nostril; see Moses of Coucy, *Sefer Mizvot Gadol*, pt. 1, fol. 100r; and Barukh of Worms, *Sefer ha-Terumah*, no. 239, fol. 89b. This assumption may have been based on the Bible's statement that Abraham's servant placed the nezem "upon" Rebecca's nose (Gen. 24:47). In fact, Ibn Ezra describes the nose ring as suspended by a chain from some type of garment or jewelry worn on the forehead. Likewise, the Palestinian Talmud defines a nose ring as something worn on the nose rather than in or through it (Jerusalem Talmud [JT] *Shabbat* 8b).

31. S. Hurwitz (ed.), *Mahzor Vitry* (Nuremberg 1923), v. 1, 131. From this statement it is unclear whether earrings are difficult to remove because they hook through the earlobe or because they are hidden beneath the head covering. Note that Rashi's approach was first suggested by Sar Shalom, a ninth-century gaon in Baghdad, who excluded from the prohibition items that are difficult to remove as well as those that women could but generally do not remove; see *Ozar ha-Ge'onim* on *Shabbat*, 59; also cited in Tosafot on *Shabbat* 64b, s.v.

R. *'Anani*, and *Hagahot Maimuniyot* on *Shabbat* 19:4. For other gaonic views of this matter, see *Ozar ha-Ge'onim* on *Shabbat*, 55–57.

32. Rashi, *Pardes*, 71. Rashi's explanation is supported by visual sources, such as "Caricature of English Jews," dated 1233, which show medieval Jewish women with their ears covered. See Alfred Rubens, *History of Jewish Costume* (New York 1967), 94. It is also supported by the words of Isaac ben Moses of Vienna (d. ca. 1250), who expresses disapproval of the Jewish women of Slavic lands for exposing their ears and earrings, implying that in his own city earrings remain concealed; see Isaac ben Moses of Vienna, *Or Zaru'a*, no. 84, sec. 8, fol. 20a. He refers to the "Canaanite kingdom," a conventional term for Slavic countries. This evidence casts doubt on Diane Owen Hughes's assumption that earrings were unknown in Latin Europe during the high Middle Ages. See Diane Owen Hughes, "Distinguishing Signs: Ear-rings, Jews, and Franciscan Rhetoric in the Italian Renaissance City," *Past and Present* 112 (1986), 3–59. Note that Hughes cites the survival of earrings in Slavic lands, where, according to Isaac ben Moses, they were visible (p. 11n18).

33. Tosafot on *Shabbat* 64b, s.v. *R. 'Anani*; Ephraim Kupfer, *Responsa and Rulings* (Jerusalem 1973), 110–112, no. 65 (in Hebrew). See also Israel M. Ta-Shma, *Ritual, Custom, and Reality in Franco-Germany, 1000–1350* (Jerusalem 1996), 130–148 (in Hebrew).

34. Tosafot on *Shabbat* 64b, s.v. *R. 'Anani*.

35. *Sefer Ra'avia*, ed. Victor Aptowitzer (Berlin 1913), v. 1, nos. 216 and 391 (end). Menahem ha-Meiri, of thirteenth-century Perpignan, dismisses the public domain argument, calling it "an excuse for permitting transgression." See Ta-Shma, *Ritual*, 139.

36. *Sefer Ra'avia*, v. 1, no. 391 (end).

37. JT *Terumot*, ch. 5, 43d; JT *Hagigah*, ch. 1, 76d; JT *Sotah*, ch. 8, 22b.

38. Isaac ben Moses of Vienna, *Or Zaru'a*, pt. 2, no. 84. I have italicized some words in this passage, for greater emphasis.

39. *Piskei ha-Rosh*, *Shabbat*, no. 13. Asher ben Yehiel goes on to quote Rabbenu Tam's *karmelit* argument in further justification of his lenient ruling.

40. *Bezah* 30a; *Bava Bathra* 60b.

41. Tosafot on *Shabbat* 64b, s.v. *R. 'Anani*; Kupfer, *Responsa and Rulings*, 110–112, no. 65; Mordecai on *Shabbat*, no. 355. See also Shalom Albeck, "Rabbenu Tam's Attitude to the Problems of his Time," *Zion* 19 (1954), 110 (in Hebrew); Ta-Shma, *Ritual*, 130–148.

42. *Yevamot* 65b. Surprisingly, Isaac cites the Jerusalem Talmud as the source of this dictum even though it has a Babylonian source.

43. Isaac ben Moses of Vienna, *Or Zaru'a*, pt. 2, no. 84.

44. Note, once again, the importance of the notion of the "important woman" to "women's law."

45. Eliezer of Metz, *Yere'im ha-Shalem*, no. 274. See also Kupfer, *Responsa and Rulings*, 111: "for they will not desist on our account."

46. Isaac ben Moses of Vienna, *Or Zaru'a*, pt. 2, no. 84. See also Barukh of Worms, *Sefer ha-Terumah*, no. 240.

47. *Berakhot* 45a; *'Eruvin* 14b; *Menahot* 35b. Rashi does not understand the adage "Go see . . ." as a call to conduct field research; he views it as a rhetorical device, by which the speaker points out that one of two disputed positions on the matter at hand has already been decided and is implemented in actual practice. See his commentary on *Berakhot* 45a, s.v. *mai 'ama devar*. Use of the expression cannot be consistently correlated with a tendency toward either stringency or leniency. See Isaac ben Moses of Vienna, *Or Zaru'a*, pt. 2, no. 84.

48. Tosafot on *Megillah* 22b, s.v. *ve-she'en*. The custom is known to have been observed also in thirteenth-century Provence and fourteenth-century Spain. See David Kimhi on 1 Samuel 20:19; Yeruham ben Meshullam, *Toledot Adam ve-Hava*, *Adam*, sec. 11, fol. 64r, col. 1; and Jacob ben Asher, *Arba'ah Turim*, *Orah Hayyim*, no. 417.

49. The passage places certain time constraints on the labor moratorium. For example, on the eve of a festival, women may abstain from labor only after the recitation of the afternoon prayer service. In this respect the Rosh Hodesh holiday is exceptional, for it is in effect for the full day; see JT *Ta'anit* 1:6, 64c. The text also states that women abstain from weaving during the first nine days of the month of Av. The text closes with regulations concerning the right to deviate from accepted customs; this rule may or may not be related to the matter of women's holidays.

50. Rashi on *Megillah* 22b, s.v. *roshei hodashim*. This suggestion alludes to a string of rabbinic legends concerning biblical women and their earrings. See also *Kol Bo*, no. 43.

51. This scholar may be Ephraim ben Isaac of Regensburg, a student of Rabbenu Tam. Similarly, we read later in *Shibolei ha-Leqet* that "the author of *Yere'im* wrote: I heard that R. Ephraim of blessed memory counted weeks [of the Omer] without days" (Zedekiah ben Abraham [Zedekiah Anau], *Shibolei ha-Leqet ha-Shalem*, ed. S. K. Mirsky [New York 1966], no. 234, 109a).

52. Zedekiah ben Abraham, *Shibolei ha-Leqet*, no. 184, 71b.

53. Rashi on *Shabbat* 139a.

54. Zedekiah ben Abraham, *Shibolei ha-Leqet*, no. 235, 109b. The author, Zedekiah ben Abraham (Zedekiah Anau), lived in Rome, and hence it may be that the custom was practiced in Rome rather than Ashkenaz. However, this is not necessarily the case, given the volume of Ashkenazic material in Zedekiah ben Abraham's *Shibolei ha-Leqet* and given what we already know of similar women's customs in Ashkenaz, specifically with regard to the abstention from labor. Yet even if it was Roman, it may have also been practiced in Franco-Germany, given the well-known genetic connection between the Jews of Italy and Germany. At any rate, no clear conclusions or assumptions can be drawn on this question.

55. *Sefer Ra'avan*, no. 354. See *Shabbat* 94b and also Ta-Shma, *Ritual*, 131n1.

56. Rashi, *Responsa*, no. 68; Hurwitz, *Mahzor Vitry*, 413–414, no. 359; *Siddur Rashi*, 127–128, no. 267. See Grossman, *Pious*, 309; and Ta-Shma, *Ritual*, 263–271.

57. *Sefer Ra'avan*, no. 87; Ephraim Urbach, *The Tosaphists: Their History, Writings, and Methods*, 4th ed. (Jerusalem 1980), 177 (in Hebrew); Ta-Shma, *Ritual*, 270; Grossman, *Pious*, 310.

58. *Sefer Ha-Asufot*, no. 378; Ta-Shma, *Ritual*, 270. Ta-Shma observes that this statement appears just after a citation of Ra'avan's comment, from which he concludes that this source was written slightly later.

59. Mordecai ben Hillel on *Shabbat*, no. 286; Tosafot on *Eruvin* 96a, s.v. *dilma*. See Grossman, *Pious*, 310

60. Tosafot on *Hagigah* 16b, s.v. *la'asot nahat ru'ah*; Grossman, *Pious*, 312. There is a twelfth-century source about women actually reciting the blessing over the tabernacle, but it does not refer to Ashkenaz; see Grossman, *Pious*, 272. Grossman attributes the time-bound precept phenomenon among women to the rise in their involvement in the economy and society (p. 311).

61. Mordecai ben Hillel on *Pesahim* 37b, citing "the tosafists"; see Grossman, *Pious*, 328.

62. JT *Pesahim* 10:1, fol. 108a. See Grossman, *Pious*, 327.

63. Grossman, *Pious*, 199, 326–327. As Grossman explains, this concept dovetails with

what is known of the economic and social independence of Ashkenazic women in the high Middle Ages.

64. By the same token, "Mar Judah ben Abraham" is described in Solomon ben Samson's chronicle of the First Crusade as a supremely important (!) communal leader (*parnas*) in Ilna, but he is called Mar rather than Rabbi, indicating that he is clearly not a member of the circle of rabbis. See Abraham Meir Habermann, *The Book of the Persecutions of Ashkenaz and France* (Jerusalem 1945), 47. See Agus, *Heroic Age*, 216–217, 251–252.

65. Tosafot on *Eruvin* 104a, s.v. *hakhi gariss*. See Rabinowitz, *Social Life*, 225–226; and Israel Abrahams, *Jewish Life in the Middle Ages* (New York 1896), 379.

66. Hurwitz, *Mahzor Vitry*, 292, no. 94. See also Moses of Coucy, *Sefer Mizvot Gadol*, MLT (negative precept) 65.

67. JT *Shabbat* 19:17; *Pesahim* 66a.

68. *Sefer Ha-Yashar: Responsa*, no. 48, sec. 7. See Israel M. Ta-Shma, *Early Franco-German Ritual and Custom* (Jerusalem 1992), 136–137 (in Hebrew). See also *Sefer Ra'avia*, pt. 1, no. 199.

69. This contrasts with Rabbenu Tam's blanket condemnation of the practice, apparently of males, to eat and drink between the afternoon and evening prayer services on the Sabbath, in violation of talmudic law; see *Sefer Ha-Yashar: Responsa*, no. 45, sec. 6.

70. S. Buber (ed.), *Ha-Oreh* (Lvov 1904–1905), 230–231, no. 158; Ta-Shma, *Early Franco-German Ritual*, 214–216.

71. *Tashbetz ha-Qattan*, no. 447.

72. Zedekiah ben Abraham, *Shibolei ha-Leqet*, no. 211, 86a. The text quotes Proverbs 10:18, in an allusion to a talmudic anecdote about a nonverbal death announcement; see *Pesahim* 3b.

73. *Kol Bo, H. Tish'ah be-Av*, no. 62.

74. Cf. Grossman, *Pious*, 337.

75. The Rabbenu Tam passage is also exceptional, although it is not clear that Rabbenu Tam asked the women for an explanation of their custom.

76. *Kol Bo, H. Tish'ah be-Av*, no. 62; Grossman, *Pious*, 336–337.

77. Rashi on *Shabbat* 139a.

78. *Humra be'alma*. See Rashi, *Pardes*, 3; Buber, *Ha-Oreh*, pt. 2, no. 1; and Hurwitz, *Mahzor Vitry*, 606, nos. 498–499. The last few words of the passage, which I have omitted, praise women for their stringency, because the synagogue is, after all, a "place of purity." However, this conclusion may be a late interpolation, as it does not appear in all the sources. Moreover, Ta-Shma emphasizes Rashi's lack of support for stringency; see Ta-Shma, *Early Franco-German Ritual*, 83.

79. *Sefer Ra'avan, Niddah*, no. 319.

80. Cf. the later discussion about contact between husband and wife following a death (*aninut*).

81. This word appears in the feminine and thus refers to women.

82. Literally "the women do from their own heart."

83. *Hergel 'averah*; see *Shabbat* 1:3.

84. Rashi, *Pardes*, 4–6; Buber, *Ha-Oreh*, pt. 2, 168–170, no. 1; Ta-Shma, *Ritual*, 282–283; Ta-Shma, *Early Franco-German Ritual*, 50–51.

85. Ta-Shma, *Early Franco-German Ritual*, 56–57.

86. Ironically, Ta-Shma also notes that Rashi is wrong! The custom is rooted in ancient Palestinian practice; see Ta-Shma, *Early Franco-German Ritual*, 51n58.

87. *Sefer Ra'avan, Responsa*, no. 25.

88. Ezekiel 36:25, Leviticus 16:19, Leviticus 16:30.

89. Reuven Margaliyot (ed.), *Sefer Hasidim* (Jerusalem 1957), no. 394.

90. *Sefer ha-Manhig*, no. 122. Citing *Menahot* 10:3, the Provençal writer adds, "Some say that [it is] because all of the scholars' dicta come in threes." The meaning of this suggestion eludes me. On the impact of German pietism on the Jews of southern France, see Marc Saperstein, "Christians and Christianity in the Sermons of Jacob Anatoli," in *The Frank Talmage Memorial Volume*, ed. Barry Walfish (Haifa 1992), v. 2, 233, 241n33; and Ephraim Kanarfogel, *"Peering Through the Lattices": Mystical, Magical, and Pietistic Dimensions in the Tosafist Period* (Detroit 2000), 51–58.

91. JT *Pe'ah*, ch. 7, 2c; JT *Ma'aser Sheni*, ch. 5, 56b; JT *Yevamot*, ch. 7, 8a.

92. Ra'avia, *Responsa*, ed. D. Devlitzki (Bnai Brak 1989), no. 991; Isaac ben Moses of Vienna, *Or Zaru'a*, pt. 1, no. 362.

93. *Mo'ed Qatan* 18a. The tool in question is called a *genostar*. Rashi on *Qatan* 18a, s.v. *ginostri*, writes that this is a scissors. *'Arukh*, s.v. *negostar*, describes a double-bladed instrument.

94. Zedekiah ben Abraham, *Shibolei ha-Leqet*, no. 231, 107b. See also Rabinowitz, *Social Life*, 161.

95. Tosafot on *Avodah Zarah* 23a, s.v. *Vetu*.

96. Grossman, *Pious*, 201–202.

97. Ra'avia, *Responsa*, no. 920; Isaac ben Moses of Vienna, *Or Zaru'a*, pt. 1, no. 615. See also Grossman, *Pious*, 202.

98. Tosafot on *Pesahim* 91b, s.v. *shema*. See Jacob Katz, *Exclusiveness and Tolerance: Studies in Jewish-Gentile Relations in Medieval and Modern Times* (Oxford 1961), 77–81.

99. Tosafot on *Pesahim* 91b, s.v. *shema*.

100. Buber, *Ha-Oreh*, pt. 1, 148, no. 113. The identity of the student is unclear.

101. The term *reqim* appears in 2 Samuel 6:20, but this source does not elucidate it. In all likelihood, the Talmud's fairly common epithet *reqa*, the Aramaic cognate and equivalent, was just as relevant to the medieval writer.

102. Ephraim ben Isaac was a student of Rabbenu Tam who fought customs that he deemed erroneous and was blackballed by the scholars of the Speyer yeshivah, whence he removed himself to Worms and eventually to Regensburg; see Urbach, *The Tosaphists*, 83–84, 199–207.

103. Irving Agus (ed.), *Responsa of the Tosaphists* (New York 1954), no. 34 (in Hebrew).

104. Meir of Rothenburg, who lived slightly after the period under discussion, wrote, "We see that most Jews martyr themselves, even *the worthless* [emphasis added] among us, and not even one in a thousand repudiates [God]." See Agus, *Responsa of the Tosaphists*, no. 128. By contrast, "worthless individuals" (*anashim reqim*) refers to apostates in the twelfth-century chronicle of Ephraim of Bonn; see Habermann, *Book of the Persecutions* 116.

105. Margaliyot, *Sefer Hasidim*, no. 328. We find worthless people and ignoramuses in juxtaposition in *Hullin* 92a. *Sefer Hasidim* uses a variety of epithets to denounce nonpietists, and the terms in which they are stigmatized cannot be taken at face value. See Haym Soloveitchik, "Three Themes in the *Sefer Hasidim*," *AJS Review* 1 (1976), 330–335; and Ivan G. Marcus, *Piety and Society: The Jewish Pietists of Medieval Germany* (Leiden 1981), 59–65.

106. See the statement by Rabbi Ephraim, presented in Zedekiah ben Abraham, *Shibolei ha-Leqet*, cited earlier in the context of the Hanukkah moratorium.

107. Rashi on *Megillah* 21b.

108. Eliezer of Metz, *Sefer Yere'im ha-Shalem* (Jerusalem 1973), no. 268. My thanks to

Ephraim Kanarfogel for bringing this source to my attention. See Ephraim Kanarfogel, "Prayer, Literacy, and Literary Memory in the Jewish Communities of Medieval Europe," in *Tradition, Authority, Diaspora: Critical Terms in Jewish Studies*, ed. R. Boustan et al. (forthcoming).

109. Zedekiah ben Abraham, *Shibolei ha-Leqet*, no. 64.

110. Rashi, *Responsa*, ed. Israel Elfenbein (New York 1943), no. 61. Halevi proceeds to declare that he had ruled thus for substantive reasons and that his ruling should therefore not be considered subject to appeal.

111. Tosafot on *Megillah* 32a, s.v. *gollelo*.

112. *Hagigah* 22a.

113. Tosafot on *Hagigah* 22a, s.v. *ke-man*.

114. Isaac ben Moses of Vienna, *Or Zaru'a*, pt. 2, no. 42, sec. 12. The principle of ignoring the Talmudic hierarchy for the sake of peace is attributed to Natronai Gaon, long before the tosafist era; see Hurwitz, *Mahzor Vitry*, no. 123.

115. Meir of Rothenburg asks an interlocutor (his teacher, Judah ha-Kohen; Urbach, *The Tosaphists*, 526–527) not to use such strong language vis-à-vis Yedidiah (of Nürnberg, Meir's younger colleague; Urbach, *The Tosaphists*, 567–570). He explains that he is making this request "so that simple folk not mock. If only all students of Torah could act as one, and if only we could stand [together] and beat the rebels and transgressors (*poshe'im*)." See Agus, *Responsa of the Tosaphists*, no. 90.

116. This is not the place for a philological study of the antecedent usages of the term in biblical and rabbinic parlance.

117. Literally, *shom'im le-raheq o (lo) le-qarev*.

118. Simon Shlesinger (ed.), *Sefer Ha-Yashar: Novellae* (Jerusalem 1959), no. 140.

119. Margaliyot, *Sefer Hasidim*, no. 702.

120. Margaliyot, *Sefer Hasidim*, no. 61.

121. Margaliyot, *Sefer Hasidim*, no. 644.

122. Margaliyot, *Sefer Hasidim*, no. 251.

123. *'Ovrei averah*, transgressors, is another pejorative label that appears in *Sefer Hasidim* to express disapproval of the behavior of individuals, who are not, however, altogether impious; see Jehuda Wistinetzki and Jakob Freimann (eds.), *Sefer Hasidim* (Frankfurt am Main 1924), 390, no. 1592, and the discussion by Ephraim Kanarfogel in his "R. Judah *he-Hasid* and the Rabbinic Scholars of Regensburg: Interactions, Influences, and Implications," *Jewish Quarterly Review* 96 (2006), 17–37. For *'avaryan*, which likewise means transgressor, the following entries appear in the subject index of Wistinetzki and Freimann, *Sefer Hasidim*: p. 59, no. 118; p. 129, no. 444; and p. 320, no. 1295.

124. Agus, *Responsa of the Tosaphists*, no. 11.

125. Tosafot on *Berakhot* 48a, s.v. *ve-let*. Isaac of Corbeil echoes Rabbenu Tam's position and formulation; see Isaac of Corbeil, *'Amudei ha-Golah*, no. 109.

126. Rashi, *Responsa*, no. 229; Buber, *Ha-Oreh*, pt. 2, 217–218, no. 123. See Haym Soloveitchik, *Pawnbroking: A Study in the Inter-Relationship Between Halakhah, Economic Activity, and Communal Self-Image* (Jerusalem 1985), 28–29 (in Hebrew). For another instance of a dubious money-lending transaction that is granted legitimation, this time by Rabbenu Gershom, see Gershom ben Judah, *Responsa*, ed. Shlomo Eidelberg (New York 1956), no. 25. The writer of this text adds, "And in any case the people [*ha'am*] acted as though it were permitted." This last comment relates directly to deviant behavior, for it means that people would not have heeded the decision to prohibit the financial transaction.

127. Rashi, *Responsa*, no. 128; Rashi, *Pardes*, 253. See also Hurwitz, *Mahzor Vitry*, 210–211, no. 245; and *Siddur Rashi*, no. 345. Rashi's choice of prooftext is modeled after the Jerusalem Talmud, which cites this verse in its definition of the pious fool: "Everyone who seeks to take stringencies upon himself, and to observe the stringencies of both the House of Shammai and Hillel, of him it is said: 'a fool walks in darkness.'" The assumption of unnecessary stringencies is thus the defining characteristic of the pious fool. See JT *Sotah* 3:4, 19a.

128. Margaliyot, *Sefer Hasidim*, no. 155.

129. On the pietist's quest for stringencies, see Soloveitchik, "Three Themes," 311–325.

130. Ta-Shma, *Ritual*, 242. See also Katz, *Exclusiveness and Tolerance*, 27–36.

131. Gershom ben Judah, *Responsa*, no. 1; see Ta-Shma, *Ritual*, 244.

132. Rashi on *Avodah Zarah* 11a. See also Rashi on *Avodah Zarah* 7b; and Rashi, *Responsa*, no. 327.

133. For a number of cases involving this formulation or variations of it, see Albeck, "Rabbenu Tam's Attitude," 105–106.

134. Tosafot on *Avodah Zarah* 2a, s.v. *assur*. See Ta-Shma, *Ritual*, 249.

135. Rashi, *Responsa*, no. 159. See also Buber, *Ha-Oreh*, pt. 2, 214, no. 108; and *Issur ve-heter*, no. 95, 22b–23a. On the Ashkenazic taboo on libation wine, see Soloveitchik, *Principles and Pressures*. For another dietary law violation that was met with rabbinic apathy, see Buber, *Ha-Oreh*, pt. 2, 212, no. 103; *Issur ve-heter*, no. 109, 25a–b; Isaac ben Moses of Vienna, *Or Zaru'a*, pt. 1, no. 776; and *Siddur Rashi*, no. 612.

136. Isaac ben Moses of Vienna, *Or Zaru'a*, pt. 2, 150, no. 358. Katz contrasts Ra'avia's response to the despair expressed by Hayyim, Jacob ben Meir Tam's student, about the popular practice of sending servants to the market on the Sabbath to procure bread and ale, in violation of the Sabbath. Hayyim reacts to the popular disregard for rabbinic authority in an exasperated outburst: "Are there no judges in Israel? Why do our people have the temerity to follow their personal inclination [Dt. 29:18; Jer. 11:8]." See Katz, *Shabbes Goy*, 66. I have altered the translation slightly.

137. Joel Müller (ed.), *Responsa of the Scholars of France and Lotharingia* (Vienna 1881), no. 5, 4b (in Hebrew). See also Rashi, *Pardes*, no. 243; Tosafot on *Avodah Zarah* 67b, s.v. *mi-klal*; and Tosafot on *Pesahim* 44b, s.v. *ve-Rabbanan*.

138. Cf. the later discussion of clapping at weddings.

139. Tosafot on *Shabbat* 55a, s.v. *ve'af 'al gav*; Tosafot on *Bava Bathra* 60b, s.v. *mutav*; Tosafot on *Avodah Zarah* 4a, s.v. *shehaya*.

140. *Bava Mezi'a* 31a.

141. *Sefer Ra'avia*, pt. 3, no. 772.

142. Margaliyot, *Sefer Hasidim*, no. 39.

143. Margaliyot, *Sefer Hasidim*, no. 5.

144. JT *Shabbat* 19:17; *Pesahim* 66a.

145. Rashi, *Responsa*, no. 258.

146. The "prophets" adage appears elsewhere in Rashi's *Pardes*; see p. 265 (by the Makhirites) and p. 302 (by Rashi).

147. *Sefer ha-Terumah*, H. *'Akum*, no. 144. See also Hurwitz, *Mahzor Vitry*, 769–770, no. 90.

148. Isaac ben Moses of Vienna, *Or Zaru'a*, pt. 4, no. 136.

149. Tosafot on *'Avodah Zarah* 21a, s.v. *af*. See also Isaac ben Moses of Vienna, *Or Zaru'a*, pt. 4, no. 137.

150. *Sefer Ra'avan*, H. *Avodah Zarah*, no. 291.

151. *Yere'im*, no. 364.

152. Meir ben Barukh, *Responsa* (Cremona 1537), no. 108; Urbach, *The Tosaphists*, 82; Rabinowitz, *Social Life*, 178. See also Tosafot on *Pesahim* 113b, s.v. *ve-en lo banim*.

153. Tosafot on *Shabbat* 49a, s.v. *ke-Elisha ba'al kenafayim*. There is a talmudic source to this effect (*Shabbat* 130a; JT *Berakhot* 2:3), but this is not to be confused with the contemporary scene depicted in the tosafist text.

154. Hurwitz, *Mahzor Vitry*, 64. See Rabinowitz, *Social Life*, 177.

155. See Joseph Kolon, *Responsa* (Venice 1559), no. 174.

156. Moses of Coucy, *Sefer Mitzvot Gadol*, positive precept 3. Moses of Coucy writes that he preached to the Jews of Spain "and in other lands" on this subject, presumably including his home country as well. For more on the neglect of *tefillin* in the Islamic realm, see N. S. Greenspan, "On the History of the Commandment of *Tefillin* and Its Neglect," *Ozar ha-Hayyim* 4 (1928), 159–164 (in Hebrew).

157. Margaliyot, *Sefer Hasidim*, no. 10.

158. Joseph Bekhor Shor, *Bible Commentary*, ed. Yehoshafat Nevo (Jerusalem 1994), 259–260 (on Num. 12:8) (in Hebrew).

159. See Bekhor Shor's interpretation of Exodus 13:9 in Martin I. Lockshin (ed., trans.), *Rashbam's Commentary on Exodus: An Annotated Translation* (Atlanta 1997), 129, including Lockshin's no. 10. See also Elazar Touitou, *Exegesis in Perpetual Motion: Studies in the Pentateuchal Commentary of Rabbi Samuel Ben Meir* (Ramat-Gan 2003), 248–250 (in Hebrew).

160. Reuben ben Hayyim testifies, in his *Sefer ha-Tamid*, to the existence among "those in error" of the notion that the commandments are nothing but allegories, a view he explicitly rejects. See Jacob Moses Toledano, "*Sefer ha-Tamid* by Reuben b. Hayyim," *Ozar ha-Hayyim* 11 (1935), 10, cited (inaccurately) by Isadore Twersky, *Rabad of Posquières: A Twelfth-Century Talmudist*, 2nd ed. (Philadelphia 1980), 24n19.

161. See Tosafot on *Berakhot* 44v, s.v. *ve-livnei ma'arava*. See Ephraim Kanarfogel, "Rabbinic Attitudes Toward Nonobservance in the Medieval Period," in *Jewish Tradition and the Nontraditional Jew*, ed. Jacob J. Schacter (Northvale 1992), 8. See also Tosafot on *Rosh Hashanah* 17a, s.v. *Karkafta*; Meir ben Barukh of Rothenburg, *Responsa* (Prague 1608), no. 649; and Jacob of Marvege, *Responsa from Heaven*, ed. R. Margaliyot (Jerusalem 1957), no. 26 (in Hebrew).

162. Zedekiah ben Abraham, *Shibolei ha-Leqet*, 89. As noted, a good deal of material from this work stems from Ashkenaz.

163. Wistinetzki and Freimann, *Sefer Hasidim*, 258, no. 1031. For the slogan, see *Yoma* 30a, *Kiddushin* 54a.

164. See Rabinowitz, *Social Life*, 176. On halakhic grounds, one might argue that avoiding a positive precept is preferable to reciting a redundant blessing, which constitutes taking the name of God in vain, but this still seems like an unlikely choice.

165. Tosafot on *Niddah* 61b, s.v. *aval 'oseh otam*. See also Tosafot on *'Avodah Zarah* 65b, s.v. *aval osin oto*; Tosafot on *Berakhot* 18a, s.v. *le-mahar*; Tosafot on *Bava Bathra* 74a, s.v. *piskei*; Isaac ben Moses of Vienna, *Or Zaru'a*, pt. 2, no. 421; and Moses of Coucy, *Sefer Mitzvot Gadol*, negative precept 283.

166. *Sefer Ra'avan*, no. 40. The same point is made in most of the sources cited in the previous note. For additional sources see Kanarfogel, "Rabbinic Attitudes," 13n29.

167. See also Rabinowitz, *Social Life*, 177.

168. *'Al mah samkhu*. See Rashi, *Responsa*, no. 355.

169. Tosafot on *Megillah* 22a, s.v. *sha'ani*.

170. *Sefer Ra'avan*, no. 42. See Israel M. Ta-Shma, *Prayer in Early Ashkenaz* (Jerusalem 2003), 30; and Kanarfogel, "Prayer, Literacy and Literary Memory."

171. Joel ben Isaac Halevi of Bonn is the son-in-law of Eliezer ben Nathan of Mainz (Ra'avan) and a student of Ephraim; see Urbach, *The Tosaphists*, 202–203, 209–212.

172. Isaac ben Moses of Vienna, *Or Zaru'a*, pt. 2, no. 42; *Sefer Ra'avia*, pt. 2, 260.

173. In the case at hand, one wonders what factors could have led the writer to presume that his addressee had powers that he himself lacked. Urbach attributes Ephraim's lack of power to a personality defect, which is eloquent testimony to the dearth of more convincing alternative explanations. Moreover, Urbach's theory implies that rabbis did not normally think that they lacked power, which we have seen is not to be taken for granted. See Urbach, *The Tosaphists*, 201, 204.

174. JT *Bezah*, ch. 5, fol. 63a.

175. *Sefer Ra'avan, Bezah* no. 448.

176. See earlier discussion of Ra'avan's historical explanation of cooking and baking during menstruation.

177. *Sefer Ra'avan, Niddah*, no. 336.

178. That is, during the state known as *aninut*.

179. *Sefer Ra'avia*, pt. 1, no. 173.

180. Tosafot on *Megilah* 5b, s.v. *she'assurim be-hesped*.

181. Rashi, *Responsa*, no. 23.

182. *Yihusei tana'im ve-amora'im*, s.v. *tavla*, 478; see also Ta-Shma, *Early Franco-German Ritual*, 50.

183. This apparently refers to circular lines, not to the shape of the letters.

184. Tosafot on *Mo'ed Qattan* 19a, s.v. *vetoveh*.

185. See earlier discussion regarding the abstention from labor on Hanukkah.

186. Hurwitz, *Mahzor Vitry*, 243–244, no. 275. The tosafists also distinguish between whether or not the public knows that a stringent practice is actually permitted, and they rule that it may be abrogated when it is rooted in ignorance. Isaac of Dampierre refers to such a custom as a foolish custom (*minhag shtut*). See Tosafot on *Pesahim* 51a, s.v. *i ata rashai lehatiran bifneihen*.

187. Rashi, *Responsa*, no. 66. For the talmudic dictum, see *Pesahim* 50b and *Nedarim* 81b.

188. An additional reference: Eliezer of Metz writes, "I have seen and heard of a number of good people that went to Egypt, and I wondered what their basis was [for doing so]." He goes on to suggest a rationale. See Eliezer of Metz, *Sefer Yere'im ha-Shalem*, no. 309. The source for this prohibition is the biblical prohibition against returning to Egypt (Deut. 17:16).

189. See *Bezah* 30a, *Shabbat* 148b.

190. Müller, *Responsa of the Scholars*, no. 17, 10a. See also Agus, *Urban Civilization*, v. 1, 306–308.

191. Agus, *Urban Civilization*, v. 1, 308.

192. Agus, *Heroic Age*, 246.

193. See also Agus, *Urban Civilization*, v. 1, 445: "In a community where tremendous social pressure was exerted on every individual to act in such a way as to appear in the eyes of his brethren as an upright, honest and pious person." On the role of social pressure on Jewish behavior in 1096, see Chapter 4.

194. Rabinowitz, *Social Life*, 178.

195. Urbach, *The Tosaphists*, 82, citing Meir ben Barukh, *Responsa* (Cremona ed.), no. 108. See also Urbach, *The Tosaphists*, 135.

196. Jacob Katz, review of Urbach, *Kirjath Sepher* 31 (1955–1956), 14 (reprinted in Jacob Katz, *Halakhah and Kabbalah* [Jerusalem 1984], 346 [in Hebrew]). Katz makes the same point in his discussion of the recitation of the evening prayer service (Katz, *Halakhah and Kabbalah*, 186).

197. Soloveitchik, "Religious Law and Change," 211–213.

198. Soloveitchik, *Pawnbroking*, 111; Haym Soloveitchik, "Halakhah, Hermeneutics, and Martyrdom in Medieval Ashkenaz (Part I of II)," *Jewish Quarterly Review* 94 (2004), 101; Haym Soloveitchik, "Halakhah, Hermeneutics, and Martyrdom in Medieval Ashkenaz (Part II of II)," *Jewish Quarterly Review* 94 (2004), 228. In an early work, Soloveitchik imputes this attitude to pre-Crusade scholars, including Rabbenu Gershom; see Haym Soloveitchik, "Pawnbroking: A Study in *Ribbit* and of the Halakah in Exile," *Proceedings of the American Academy of Jewish Research* 38–39 (1972), 239. See also Grossman, *Pious*, 304.

199. Soloveitchik, "Religious Law and Change," 213.

200. Soloveitchik, "Religious Law and Change," 214, 216.

201. Wistinetzki and Freimann, *Sefer Hasidim*, 4–5, no. 2; and 43, no. 43. See Marcus, *Piety and Society*, 151.

202. Soloveitchik, "Religious Law and Change," 217.

203. Katz, *Shabbes Goy*, esp. 231, 237–238. See also Malkiel, "Underclass," 181.

204. Soloveitchik, "Religious Law and Change," 220; Soloveitchik, *Principles and Pressures*, 118n77.

205. Soloveitchik, "Religious Law and Change," 221.

206. See Ephraim Kanarfogel, "Halakha and *Meziut* (Realia) in Medieval Ashkenaz: Surveying the Parameters and Defining the Limits," *Jewish Law Annual* 14 (2003), 200.

207. This cultural attribute is obviously related to Germany's highly decentralized and chaotic political structure throughout the Middle Ages and early modern era. Germany and Italy are alike in this respect, both politically and halakhically: decentralized and heterogeneous.

208. This trend parallels the importance of customary law in northern Europe in general during these same centuries, before the recovery of Roman law in twelfth-century Bologna; see Marc Bloch, *Feudal Society*, trans. L. A. Manyon (Chicago 1961), v. 1, 109–116.

209. Gershom ben Judah, *Responsa*, no. 68.

210. Ta-Shma, *Ritual*, 135–137.

211. Ta-Shma, *Ritual*, 283.

212. See the passage quoted earlier in the discussion on menstruation and white days.

213. See also Ta-Shma, *Ritual*, 26–27.

214. With respect to the martyrdom of 1096, Ta-Shma and others have espoused the view that the people's behavior was determined by the dictates of the rabbis, even though the medieval narratives do not support this and in fact impute the leadership role to women. See Malkiel, "Underclass," 182–183.

Chapter Seven

1. Ephraim Urbach, *The Tosaphists: Their History, Writings, and Methods*, 4th ed. (Jerusalem 1980), 240 (in Hebrew).

2. Urbach, *The Tosaphists*, 745.

3. Jacob Katz, *Exclusiveness and Tolerance: Studies in Jewish-Gentile Relations in Medieval and Modern Times* (Oxford 1961), 7.

4. Irving Agus, *The Heroic Age of Franco-German Jewry* (New York 1969), 349.

5. Yitzhak Baer, "Basic Contours of the Historical Development of the Jews in the Middle Ages," *Moznayim* 23 (1947), 206–207 (in Hebrew).

6. For a similar portrayal of Jewish-Christian relations in the Middle Ages, see Jonathan Elukin, *Living Together, Living Apart: Rethinking Jewish-Christian Relations in the Middle Ages* (Princeton 2007).

7. See, for example, Shalom Albeck, "Rabbenu Tam's Attitude to the Problems of His Age," *Zion* 19 (1954), 123 (in Hebrew).

8. See Haym Soloveitchik, *Principles and Pressures: Jewish Trade in Gentile Wine in the Middle Ages* (Tel Aviv 2003) (in Hebrew).

9. This issue is discussed more fully later. See Katz, *Exclusiveness and Tolerance*, 27–36; and Israel M. Ta-Shma, *Ritual, Custom, and Reality in Franco-Germany, 1000–1350* (Jerusalem 1996), 241–261 (in Hebrew).

10. *Hullin* 13b.

11. Gershom ben Judah, *Responsa*, ed. Shlomo Eidelberg (New York 1955), no. 21.

12. Rashi, *Responsa*, ed. Israel Elfenbein (New York 1943), no. 327.

13. *Sanhedrin* 63b.

14. Tosafot on *Sanhedrin* 63b, s.v. *asur la'adam she-ya'aseh shutefut*. See Katz, *Exclusiveness and Tolerance*, 35; and Urbach, *The Tosaphists*, 65.

15. Abraham Meir Habermann, *The Book of the Persecutions of Ashkenaz and France* (Jerusalem 1945), 93 (in Hebrew).

16. Habermann, *Book of the Persecutions*, 101; Robert Chazan, *European Jewry and the First Crusade* (Berkeley 1987), 237. The longer narrative of the 1096 saga, associated with Solomon ben Samson, uses the same sort of rhetoric. The source of much of the colorful anti-Christian imagery is *Toledot Yeshu*, composed in the early centuries CE. See Anna Sapir Abulafia, "Invectives Against Christianity in the Hebrew Chronicles of the First Crusade," in *Crusade and Settlement*, ed. Peter W. Edbury (Cardiff 1985), 66–72.

17. Habermann, *Book of the Persecutions*, 35, 51.

18. Habermann, *Book of the Persecutions*, 39.

19. Habermann, *Book of the Persecutions*, 42.

20. Habermann, *Book of the Persecutions*, 97.

21. See Avraham Grossman, "The Roots of *Kiddush Hashem* in Early Ashkenaz," in *Sanctity of Life and Martyrdom*, ed. Isaiah M. Gafni and Aviezer Ravitzky (Jerusalem 1992), 125 (in Hebrew). This issue is discussed more fully in Chapter 5.

22. Literally *tehom*, meaning abyss. Eliezer ben Nathan (Ra'avan) of twelfth-century Mainz cites the use of euphemism to excuse his contemporaries of violating the prohibition against mentioning false gods, and one of his examples is *tehom*. See Ra'avan, *Sefer Ra'avan*, *Sanhedrin*, s.v. *Tania*.

23. David Berger, *The Jewish-Christian Debate in the High Middle Ages: A Critical Edition of the Nizzahon Vetus with an Introduction, Translation, and Commentary* (Philadelphia 1979), 69. Henry and Qalonymos are probably stock names rather than historical personages.

24. Judah Rosenthal (ed.), *Sepher Joseph Hamekane* (Jerusalem 1970), 14. Cf. the translation by Ivan G. Marcus, "A Jewish-Christian Symbiosis: The Culture of Early Ashkenaz," in *Cultures of the Jews: A New History*, ed. David Biale (New York 2002), 483.

25. Bernhard Blumenkranz, "The Roman Church and the Jews," in *The Dark Ages: Jews in Christian Europe 711–1096* (World History of the Jewish People, 2nd series, v. 2), ed. Cecil Roth (Tel Aviv 1966), 85.

26. Agus, *Heroic Age*, 11–20.

27. On Wecelinus, see Anna Sapir Abulafia, "An Eleventh-Century Exchange of Letters Between a Christian and a Jew," *Journal of Modern History* 7 (1981), 165–171. For the 1096 sources, see Habermann, *Book of the Persecutions*, 35, 103 (Jacob ben Sullam), and 49 (Xanten). See also Ben-Zion Wacholder, "Cases of Proselytizing in the Tosafist Responsa," *Jewish Quarterly Review* 51 (1960–1961), 288–315.

28. Emily Taitz, *The Jews of Medieval France: The Community of Champagne* (Westport 1994), 121, 124.

29. David Berger, "Mission to the Jews and Jewish-Christian Contacts in the Polemical Literature of the High Middle Ages," *American Historical Review* 91 (1986), 579. In the continuation of his essay, Berger assumes that Jews really did utter the aggressive barbs attributed to them in the polemical literature and may even have initiated the bold encounters (pp. 589–590). See also Berger, *Jewish-Christian Debate*, 21–23, esp. n61. Elsewhere Berger notes that it was the powerlessness of medieval Jews that enabled them to adopt a position of unadulterated hostility; see David Berger, "Jacob Katz on Jews and Christians in the Middle Ages," in *The Pride of Jacob: Essays on Jacob Katz and His Work*, ed. Jay M. Harris (Cambridge, Mass., 2002), 62–63.

30. Efraim Urbach, "Études sur la littérature polemique au Moyen-Age," *Revue des Études Juives* 100 (1935), 60. I incline toward the psychological, as opposed to the social, explanation; for a late, eighteenth-century example, see my edition of *Asham Talui* by Joshua Segre of Scandiano: David Malkiel, *The Jewish-Christian Debate on the Eve of Modernity* (Jerusalem 2004) (in Hebrew).

31. See Rashi on Jeremiah 49:32.

32. Isaiah 53:7.

33. Habermann, *Book of the Persecutions*, 22, verses 3 and 4.

34. See Eliav Shohetman, "Jew-Gentile Relations: 'For the Sake of Peace' and 'On Account of Enmity,'" *Mahanayyim* 1 (1992), 52–73 (in Hebrew). Note that enmity is also a consideration in matters concerning relations between Jews. See, for example, Isaac ben Moses of Vienna, *Or Zaru'a*, pt. 2, no. 42.

35. For the 1051 incident, see Julius Aronius, *Regesten zur Geschichte der Juden Im Fränkischen und Deutschen Reiche biz zum Jahre 1273* (Berlin 1902), 65–66, no. 155; for Cologne, see Aronius, *Regesten*, 68–69, no. 165.

36. This is plain from the 1084 charter of the Speyer community, issued by Archbishop Rudiger, as well as from stories of the efforts of bishops and archbishops to save their Jewish constituents from the hands of the crusaders in 1096. See Bernhard Blumenkranz, "Germany, 843–1096," in *The Dark Ages: Jews in Christian Europe 711–1096*, ed. Cecil Roth (Tel Aviv 1966), 168.

37. Avraham Grossman, *The Early Sages of Ashkenaz: Their Lives, Leadership, and Works (900–1096)*, 3rd ed. (Jerusalem 2001), 17 (in Hebrew). See *Tosefta, Gittin* 3:14.

38. Tosafot on *Avodah Zarah* 31b, s.v. *ve-tarvayhu mishum hatenut*.

39. The text actually says "cakes" (*'ugot*), but loaves is preferable, because Rashi later rules on the permissibility of eating the bread.

40. Rashi, *Responsa*, 142, no. 114.

41. On non-Jews giving food gifts to Jews in Mainz, see also Abraham Epstein and Jakob Freimann (eds.), *Ma'aseh ha-Geonim* (Berlin 1909), 27, no. 42.

42. Rashi on *Avodah Zarah* 11a. See also Rashi on *Avodah Zarah* 7b; Rashi, *Responsa*, no. 327. For Rashbam, see Isaac ben Moses of Vienna, *Or Zaru'a, Avodah Zarah*, pt. 4, fol. 15c, no. 96, cited in Ta-Shma, *Ritual*, 245.

43. *Sefer ha-Yashar, Responsa*, 66, no. 37; Tosafot on *Ketubot* 98b, s.v. *amar Rav Papa*; *Bava Qamma* 113b. See also Albeck, "Rabbenu Tam's Attitude," 138–139.

44. *Bava Batra* 45b, which cites Psalms 144:8, as does Rabbenu Tam. The talmudic dictum refers to gentiles as underhanded, rather than as liars, but the difference is insignificant, and in any case the Psalms prooftext mentions lying explicitly.

45. See, for example, *Shevi'it* 5:9, *Gittin* 5:8. Rashi draws the connection between the concepts of "on account of enmity" and "for the sake of peace," but other scholars distinguish between them; see Me'ir Ish-Shalom, "On the Burial of a Noahide in a Jewish Cemetery," *Bet Talmud* 4 (1885), 66–67 (in Hebrew). I am grateful to Moshe Benovitz for this reference.

46. Tosafot on *Shabbat* 19a, s.v. *notnin mezonot*.

47. Tosafot on *Shabbat* 19a, s.v. *notnin mezonot*; Isaac ben Moses of Vienna, *Or Zaru'a*, pt. 2, no. 53.

48. Samson ben Zaddok, *Tashbetz Qattan*, no. 179. See also Rashi, *Responsa*, no. 131. In other sources the objection to this practice is attributed to Rabbi Qalonymos "the Elder"; see Epstein and Freimann, *Ma'aseh ha-Geonim*, 46, no. 56; Zedekiah ben Abraham (Zedekiah Anau), *Shibolei ha-Leqet ha-Shalem*, ed. Salomon Buber (Vilna 1886), no. 202; Irving Agus, *Urban Civilization in Pre-Crusade Europe* (New York 1965), v. 2, 796–797; Avraham Grossman, *The Early Sages of France: Their Lives, Leadership, and Works*, 2nd ed. (Jerusalem 1996), 143n81 (in Hebrew); and Elisheva Baumgarten, *Mothers and Children: Jewish Family Life in Medieval Europe* (Princeton 2004), 132.

49. *Ha-Oreh*, 219; Ta-Shma, *Ritual*, 209.

50. *Ra'avia*, pt. 2, v. 3, 528, no. 841; *'Amudei ha-Golah*, no. 97. See *Mo'ed Qattan* 15a–b.

51. For funerals see *Ra'aviah*, pt. 2, v. 3, 656–657, no. 885; for Tisha b'Av, see *Arba'ah Turim*, *Orah Hayyim*, no. 554.

52. *Mo'ed Qattan* 15a, 24a; Rashi, *Pardes*, 266; *Ha-Oreh*, 224, cited by Hirsch Jakob Zimmels, *Ashkenazim and Sephardim: Their Relations, Differences, and Problems as Reflected in the Rabbinical Responsa* (Oxford 1958), 218–219; Louis Rabinowitz, *The Social Life of the Jews in Northern France in the XII–XIV Centuries*, 2nd ed. (New York 1972), 243.

53. *Sefer Mitzvot Gadol*, positive precept 2. The distinction between "the gentiles" and the three other categories (domestic servants, slaves, and lads) is unclear, for the other categories are also non-Jews (except, perhaps, the lads); it may be a distinction between those outside and inside the home.

54. *Ma'aseh ha-Ge'onim*, 40, no. 51; *ha-Pardes*, no. 179; Zedekiah ben Abraham, *Shibolei ha-Leqet*, no. 319. This is a rare instance in northern Europe of the use of the term "the sanctification of God's name" (*Kiddush ha-Shem*) in a nonmartyrological context. This is also peculiar because Jewish law obligates one to sanctify the name of God only in the presence of Jews.

55. Joel Müller (ed.), *Responsa of the Scholars of France and Lotharingia* (Vienna 1881), no. 40 (in Hebrew).

56. Jehuda Wistinetzki and Jakob Freimann (eds.), *Sefer Hasidim* (Frankfurt am Main 1924), 321, no. 1301. See Urbach, *The Tosaphists*, 744.

57. Wistinetzki and Freimann, *Sefer Hasidim*, 109, no. 359. See also *Avot* 1:3.

58. Wistinetzki and Freimann, *Sefer Hasidim*, 242, no. 985, cited in H. H. Ben-Sasson, *On Jewish History in the Middle Ages* (Tel Aviv 1958), 190 (in Hebrew). The tension between bravery and the avoidance of shame appears also in the Hebrew narratives of the First Crusade; see Chapter 4. See also Shmuel Shepkaru, *Jewish Martyrs in the Pagan and Christian Worlds* (Cambridge 2006), 197.

59. This would explain why the illicit sexual congress typically involves Jewish males and Christian females, and hence Jewish domination, rather than the reverse.

60. "Ne a pecoris turbe insolencia facile turbarentur"; see Aronius, *Regesten*, 70, no. 168. The Hebrew account of the founding of the Speyer community offers almost the identical formulation; see Habermann, *Book of the Persecutions*, 60.

61. The word *goyim*, namely, gentiles, appears in brackets in the Hebrew text.

62. Rashi, *Pardes*, 10.

63. Barukh of Worms, *Sefer ha-Terumah* (Warsaw 1897), *Eretz Yisra'el*, fol. 78d. The Hebrew term for lawless behavior is *me'ansin*.

64. See Israel Abrahams, *Jewish Life in the Middle Ages* (New York 1896), 295–301. The Bird's Head haggadah, from fourteenth-century Germany, depicts Jews as wearing a distinctive hat. See M. Spitzer (ed.), *The Bird's Head Haggadah in the Bezalel National Art Museum in Jerusalem* (Jerusalem 1967), v. 1, 24.

65. Louis Finkelstein, *Jewish Self-Government in the Middle Ages* (New York 1924), 225.

66. The terms cited in the prohibition of certain forms of hair design are of talmudic origin but probably reflect medieval fashion nonetheless. See *Bava Qamma* 83a; *Qiddushin* 76b; *Mishneh Torah, Avodat Kokhavim* 11:1; and *Arba'ah Turim, Yoreh De'ah*, no. 178.

67. Wistinetzki and Freimann, *Sefer Hasidim*, 154–155, no. 554.

68. Thus the fact that ultra-Orthodox Israeli Jews converse in Hebrew does not imply their allegiance to the State of Israel. Their choice to wear quaint eastern European garb is an excellent example to the contrary, for the attire is an explicit rejection of modernity.

69. Habermann, *Book of the Persecutions*, 164–166. El'azar's younger daughter was named Hannah.

70. Haim Schwarzbaum, *The Mishle Shu'alim (Fox Fables) of Rabbi Berechiah Ha-Nakdan: A Study in Comparative Folklore and Fable Lore* (Kiron 1979). On Süsskind of Trimberg, see Heinrich Graetz, *History of the Jews* (Philadelphia 1894), v. 3, 419–420.

71. Tosafot on *Sukkah* 45a, s.v. *mi-yad tinoqot*. This text also appears in the collected rulings of Isaac of Corbeil, no. 43; see Ben-Zion Dinur, *Israel in the Diaspora* (Tel Aviv 1971), v. 2, pt. 5, 59.

72. Tosafot on *Bava Qamma* 58a, s.v. *iy*. See also Urbach, *The Tosaphists*, 240–241.

73. Wistinetzki and Freimann, *Sefer Hasidim*, 106, no. 346. The passage adds that this is also forbidden when no adults are present. This taboo also has metahalakhic concerns, for the continuation of this section applies the prohibition to when the infant is asleep, because the tune might kill him. See also Léon Poliakov, *A History of Anti-Semitism* (London 1974), v. 1, 89; Baumgarten, *Mothers and Children*, 136–137.

74. Wistinetzki and Freimann, *Sefer Hasidim*, 106, no. 347.

75. S. Hurwitz (ed.), *Mahzor Vitry* (Nuremberg 1923), no. 508.

76. Ivan G. Marcus, *Rituals of Childhood: Jewish Acculturation in Medieval Europe* (New Haven 1996), 83–101.

77. For a similar phenomenon from a later period, see David Malkiel, "Infanticide in Passover Iconography," *Journal of the Warburg and Courtauld Institutes* 56 (1993), 85–99.

78. Yitzhak Baer traces the martyrological fervor of Ashkenazic Jewry to the Cluniacensian movement of religious revival and thus earlier than 1096, to the early eleventh century. See Yitzhak Baer, "The Religious-Social Tendency of 'Sepher Hassidim,'" *Zion* 3 (1938), 3–5 (in Hebrew). This has been questioned by later scholars. Jeremy Cohen notes the significance, in the Hebrew narratives, of other contemporary Christian social and religious phenomena, includ-

ing popular piety, atonement for sin, and millennial fervor. See Jeremy Cohen, "From History to Historiography: The Study of the Persecutions and Constructions of Their Meaning," in *Facing the Cross: The Persecutions of 1096 in History and Historiography*, ed. Yom Tov Assis, Michael Toch, Jeremy Cohen, Ora Limor, and Aharon Kedar (Jerusalem 2000), 25 (in Hebrew).

79. Chazan, *European Jewry*, 132.

80. In this respect, the martyrdom of 1096 is seen as outdoing the classic Jewish act of faith, the binding of Isaac. See, for example, *Yalqut Shim'oni*, Deut. 26, no. 938; and more generally, Shalom Spiegel, *The Last Trial*, trans. Judah Goldin (Philadelphia 1967).

81. Habermann, *Book of the Persecutions*, 34. This is the root story presented in Chapter 4.

82. Jeremy Cohen, "The 'Persecutions of 1096': From Martyrdom to Martyrology—The Sociocultural Context of the Hebrew Crusade Chronicles," *Zion* 59 (1994), 199–205 (in Hebrew); Jeremy Cohen, "The Hebrew Crusade Chronicles in Their Christian Cultural Context," in *Juden und Christen zur Zeit der Kreuzzüge*, ed. Alfred Haverkamp (Sigmaringen 1999), 26–27; Jeremy Cohen, *Sanctifying the Name of God: Jewish Martyrs and Jewish Memories of the First Crusade* (Philadelphia 2004), 120–127. Cohen claims that the association between Rachel and Mater Ecclesia was "in the air" and "most likely well known even to the rank and file of the Jewish minority" (p. 121), but he fails to support this last assertion.

83. Cohen posits that the Jews of twelfth-century Germany attained an exceptionally high degree of exposure to Christianity during the year following their forced baptism (Cohen, *Sanctifying the Name of God*, 58–59). That forced converts would familiarize themselves with the tenets of a faith forced on them on pain of death is doubtful; in view of the circumstances of their baptism, they would be more likely to regard Christianity with singular hostility and revulsion and with a lesser measure of curiosity than one might normally suppose.

84. This is apparent from the anti-Christian polemical tracts of the twelfth and thirteenth centuries. See Jacob ben Reuben, *Milhamot Hashem*, ed. Judah Rosenthal (Jerusalem 1963), pt. ii, 141–156; Robert Chazan, *Fashioning Jewish Identity in Medieval Western Christendom* (Cambridge 2004), 282–290; Mordechai Breuer, *Sefer Nizzahon Yashan (Nizzahon Vetus): A Book of Jewish-Christian Polemic, a Critical Edition* (Ramat-Gan 1978), 133–143 (in Hebrew); and Berger, *Jewish-Christian Debate*, 167–198. See also Daniel J. Lasker, *The Refutation of the Christian Principles by Hasdai Crescas* (Albany 1991), passim.

85. Arthur Green, "Shekhinah, the Virgin Mary, and the Song of Songs: Reflections on a Kabbalistic Symbol in Its Historical Context," *AJS Review* 26 (2002), 1–52; Peter Schäfer, *Mirror of His Beauty: Feminine Images of God from the Bible to the Early Kabbalah* (Princeton 2002), 147–243. But see also the critique by Yehuda Liebes, "Indeed the Shekhina a Virgin? On the Book by Arthur Green," *Pe'amim*, 101–102 (2005), 303–313 (in Hebrew).

86. This is how the tale is told by Albert of Aachen, *Historia Ierosoloymitana*, ed. and trans. Susan Edgington (Oxford 2007), 58. See also Guibert de Nogent, *Dei gesta per Francos*, ed. R. B. C. Huygens (Turnhout 1996) (*Corpus Christianorum Continuatio Mediaevalis*, v. 127a), 331. In the somewhat garbled Hebrew version of this story, the goose's female owner merely claims that it also wants to embark on crusade; see Habermann, *Book of the Persecutions*, 28–29, 98–99.

87. Yitzhak Baer, "The Foundations and Beginnings of Jewish Self-Government in the Middle Ages," *Zion* 15 (1950), 28–41 (in Hebrew); Aryeh Grabois, "The Leadership of the *Parnasim* in the Communities of Northern France in the Eleventh and Twelfth Centuries: The '*Boni Viri*' and the 'Elders of the Cities,'" in *Culture and Society in Medieval Jewry*, ed. Menahem Ben-Sasson, Robert Bonfil, and Joseph Hacker (Jerusalem 1989), 303–314 (in Hebrew). See also Avraham Grossman, "The Jewish Community in Ashkenaz in the 10th–11th Centuries," in

Kehal Yisrael: Jewish Self-Rule Through the Ages, v. 2, *The Middle Ages and Early Modern Period*, ed. Avraham Grossman and Yosef Kaplan (Jerusalem 2004), 57–74 (in Hebrew).

88. *Sefer ha-Yashar, Responsa*, 125, no. 56, cited by Albeck ("Rabbenu Tam's Attitude," 112) and Urbach (*The Tosaphists*, 741).

89. Urbach, *The Tosaphists*, 752. How scholars utterly committed to the authority of the ancient sources could cavalierly ignore or modify them for the sake of latter-day exigency is a question Urbach does not consider, and he is criticized for it by Jacob Katz and Isadore Twersky in their reviews of his work: Jacob Katz, "Review of E. E. Urbach, *The Tosaphists*," *Kirjath Sepher* 31 (1955–1956), 13 (reprinted in Jacob Katz, *Halakhah and Kabbalah* [Jerusalem 1984], 345–346); and Isadore Twersky, "Review of E. E. Urbach, *The Tosaphists*," *Tarbiz* 26 (1956), 221–222.

90. Wistinetzki and Freimann, *Sefer Hasidim*, 191, no. 752. On the affinity to the scholastic method, see Albeck, "Rabbenu Tam's Attitude," 112–113; José Faur, "The Legal Thinking of Tosafot: An Historical Approach," *Diné Israel* 6 (1975), xlii–lxxii; and Urbach, *The Tosaphists*, 85, 744–752.

91. Urbach, *The Tosaphists*, 86–87.

92. Urbach, *The Tosaphists*, 747.

93. Urbach, *The Tosaphists*, 748.

94. Urbach, *The Tosaphists*, 748.

95. Urbach, *The Tosaphists*, 744. Jacob Katz questions the comparison between the method of the tosafists and that of the Sages, whose method, he insists, also awaits systematic analysis. See his review of Urbach, *The Tosaphists*, 12 (reprinted in Katz, *Halakhah and Kabbalah*, 344).

96. This point is also made by Katz in "Review of E. E. Urbach," 11 (reprinted in Katz, *Halakhah and Kabbalah*, 343).

97. Twersky, "Review of E. E. Urbach," 218–219. Twersky questions a series of other parallels cited by Urbach as well on pp. 220–221.

98. Urbach, *The Tosaphists*, 87.

99. Urbach, *The Tosaphists*, 745. Likewise, "The two societies lived side by side in a state of unequal struggle. Christianity sought to force Judaism to capitulate, and attempted to impose its faith with all the force at its disposal. Judaism, notwithstanding its political weakness, struggled to maintain its independent existence, without abandoning the possibility of convincing others that it was the true religion" (p. 752).

100. Beryl Smalley, *The Study of the Bible in the Middle Ages* (Oxford 1952), 83–185; Aryeh Grabois, "The *Hebraica Veritas* and Jewish-Christian Intellectual Relations in the Twelfth Century," *Speculum* 50 (1975), 613–634; Michael A. Signer, "*Peshat, Sensus Litteralis*, and Sequential Narrative: Jewish Exegesis and the School of St. Victor in the Twelfth Century," in *Frank Talmage Memorial Volume I*, ed. Barry Walfish (Haifa and Hanover 1993), 203–216.

101. Herman Hailperin, *Rashi and the Christian Scholars* (Pittsburgh 1963), 137–246; Deeanna Copeland Klepper, *The Insight of Unbelievers: Nicholas of Lyra and Christian Reading of Jewish Text in the Later Middle Ages* (Philadelphia 2006).

102. Sarah Kamin, *Rashi's Exegetical Categorization: In Respect to the Distinction Between Peshat and Derash* (Jerusalem 1986) (in Hebrew); Morris B. Berger, *The Torah Commentary of R. Samuel ben Meir*, Ph.D. dissertation (Harvard University 1982); Elazar Touitou, *Exegesis in Perpetual Motion: Studies in the Pentateuchal Commentary of Rabbi Samuel Ben Meir* (Ramat-Gan 2003) (in Hebrew). See also the English translations of the Pentateuch commentary of Rashbam, edited and annotated by Martin I. Lockshin.

103. Yitzhak Baer singles out Rashi's commentaries on Isaiah, Zechariah, and Daniel as well as Psalms; see Yitzhak Baer, "Rashi and the Historical Reality of His Time," *Tarbiz* 20 (1950), 325 (in Hebrew) (reprinted in Yitzhak Baer, *Studies in the History of the Jewish People* [Jerusalem 1985], v. 2, 167 [in Hebrew]).

104. The term *minim* may refer more particularly to apostates; see the discussion in Chapter 5.

105. On anti-Christian polemic in Rashbam's Pentateuchal commentary, see Elazar Touitou, "*Peshat* and Apologetics in Rashbam's Commentary on the Biblical Stories of Moses," *Tarbiz* 51 (1981–1982), 227–238 (in Hebrew) (reprinted in Touitou, *Exegesis in Perpetual Motion*, 164–176). For Rashi, see Judah Rosenthal, "Anti-Christian Polemic in Rashi's Bible Commentary," in Judah Rosenthal, *Studies and Sources* (Jerusalem 1967), v. 1, 101–116 (in Hebrew); and Erwin I. J. Rosenthal, "Anti-Christian Polemic in Medieval Bible Commentaries," *Journal of Jewish Studies* 11 (1960), 115–135. For a synthetic discussion of French-Jewish literalism, including its polemical element, see Grossman, *Early Sages of France*, 457–506.

106. A. Lukyn Williams, *Adversus Judaeos* (Cambridge 1935); Heinz Schreckenberg, *Die christlichen Adversus-Judaeos-Texte und ihr literarisches und historisches Umfeld (1.-11. Jh.)* (Frankfurt am Main 1982).

107. Rosenthal, *Sepher Joseph Hamekane*; Berger, *Jewish-Christian Debate*.

108. Berger, *Jewish-Christian Debate*, 78, 37 (Hebrew pagination) (bracketed Bible verse in the original).

109. The Jewish answer is rather feeble, which is not atypical of this literature, and probably relates to the fact that it is not associated with rabbinic scholars of the first rank.

110. Gilbert Crispin, *Disputatio Iudei et Christiani*, ed. Bernhard Blumenkranz (Utrecht 1956); Peter Abelard, *A Dialogue of a Philosopher with a Jew and a Christian*, trans. Pierre J. Payer (Toronto 1979). See R. J. Z. Werblowsky, "Crispin's Disputation," *Journal of Jewish Studies* 11 (1960), 69–77; Hans Liebeschütz, "The Significance of Judaism in Peter Abelard's *Dialogue*," *Journal of Jewish Studies* 12 (1961), 1–18; and Jeremy Cohen, *Living Letters of the Law: Ideas of the Jew in Medieval Christianity* (Berkeley 1999), 180–185, 275–288. See also the studies by Anna Sapir Abulafia in Anna Sapir Abulafia, *Christians and Jews in Dispute: Disputational Literature and the Rise of Anti-Judaism in the West (c.1000–1050)* (Aldershot 1998).

111. Thus Avrom Saltmann has questioned the historicity of the autobiographical account of Herman of Cologne's conversion; see Avrom Saltmann, "Hermann's *Opusculum de conversione sua*: Truth or Fiction?" *Revue des Études Juives* 147 (1988), 31–56. The literary disputations differ in this respect from *Sefer Yosef ha-Meqanneh*, which records anecdotes of real social exchanges, such as the one quoted.

112. "Idque potius fidei causa et tui amore facio quam studio disputandi" (Crispin, *Disputatio Iudei et Christiani*, 29). Whether or not the disputation took place as described, it is widely thought that Crispin had friendly relations with one or more Jewish acquaintants. See Werblowsky, "Crispin's Disputation," 70–74; Sapir Abulafia, "Christians Disputing Belief: St. Anselm, Gilbert Crispin, and Pseudo-Anselm," in *Religionsgespräche im Mittelalter*, ed. Bernard Lewis and Friedrich Niewöhner (Wiesbaden 1992), 135.

113. Amos Funkenstein, "Changes in Christian Anti-Jewish Polemics in the Twelfth Century," in Amos Funkenstein, *Perceptions of Jewish History* (Berkeley 1993), 172–201. Similarly, David Berger sees the verbal polemical exchanges between Christians and Jews as evidence of lively interaction (Berger, "Mission to the Jews," 589–590).

114. Rashbam on Exodus 8:15.

115. Rashbam on Leviticus 11:3. On the rationalist interpretations of commandments by Joseph Qara, a French literalist who lived two generations before Rashbam, see Grossman, *Early Sages of France*, 302–305; on Qara's rationalist exegesis, generally, see Grossman, *Early Sages of France*, 316–323.

116. Ora Limor, *Jews and Christians in Western Europe: Encounter Between Cultures in the Middle Ages and Renaissance* (Tel Aviv 1993), v. 4, 46–47 (in Hebrew).

117. Baer, "Rashi," 325–328; Elazar Touitou, "Rashbam's Exegetical Method in Light of His Historical Context," in *Studies in Rabbinic Literature, Bible, and Jewish History*, ed. Y. D. Gilat et al. (Ramat-Gan 1982), 62–73 (in Hebrew).

118. Limor, *Jews and Christians*, v. 3, 35.

119. Baer, "Rashi," 325–327.

120. Salo W. Baron, *Social and Religious History of the Jews* (New York 1958), v. 6, 218. In the same vein, see Grossman, "Roots of *Kiddush Hashem*," 119; and Grossman, *Early Sages of France*, 498–504. In addition, see Chapter 5.

121. Gavin Langmuir, *Toward a Definition of Antisemitism* (Berkeley 1990), 115–133.

122. Jeremy Cohen, "Between Martyrdom and Apostasy: Doubt and Self-Definition in Twelfth-Century Ashkenaz," *Journal of Medieval and Early Modern Studies* 29 (1999), 432. See also Ivan G. Marcus, "Hierarchies, Religious Boundaries, and Jewish Spirituality in Medieval Germany," *Jewish History* 1 (1986), 7–26; and Ivan G. Marcus, "Jews and Christians Imagining the Other in Medieval Europe," *Prooftexts* 15 (1995), 209–226.

123. Cohen, "Between Martyrdom and Apostasy," 452–463; Grossman, *Early Sages of France*, 502.

124. Smalley, *Study of the Bible*, 156–157, 164. Similarly, Funkenstein suggests that Nahmanides' typological biblical exegesis failed to win adherents among medieval Jewish exegetes because of its resemblance to Christianity. See Amos Funkenstein, "History and Typology: Nachmanides' Reading of the Biblical Narrative," in Amos Funkenstein, *Perceptions of Jewish History* (Berkeley 1993), 98–120.

125. See n64 with regard to the distinctive clothing worn by Jews. See also the discussion of the etiology of apostasy in Chapter 5.

126. Baer, "Religious-Social Tendency."

127. Joshua Prawer describes this paradox as follows: "Baer was too great not to see occasional points of contact"; see Joshua Prawer, "Remarks in Memory of Yitzhak Baer," in *In Memory of Yitzhak Baer* (Jerusalem 1984), 39 (in Hebrew).

128. Baer, "Religious-Social Tendency," 1–2. As mentioned, Baer later reversed his position and insisted that the emergence of the Jewish community was an immanent development; see Yitzhak Baer, "The Origins of the Organisation of the Jewish Community of the Middle Ages," *Zion* 15 (1950), esp. 28 (in Hebrew) (English translation: "The Origins of Jewish Communal Organization in the Middle Ages," in *Studies in Jewish History*, ed. Joseph Dan [New York 1989]). See also David Nathan Myers, *Re-Inventing the Jewish Past* (New York 1995), 124; Amnon Raz-Krakotzkin, *The National Narration of Exile: Zionist Historiography and Medieval Jewry*, Ph.D. dissertation (Tel Aviv University 1996), 155–157 (in Hebrew); and Israel Jacob Yuval, "Yitzhak Baer and the Search for Authentic Judaism," in *The Jewish Past Revisited: Reflections on Modern Jewish Historians*, ed. David N. Myers and David B. Ruderman (New Haven 1998), 80.

129. Baer, "Religious-Social Tendency," 3–5.

130. Baer also sees the German pietists as espousing a martyrological ethos akin to that of Francis and his disciples, as well as the values of poverty and humility, but subsequent scholar-

ship has largely rejected these parallels. For the martyrological ethos, see Ivan G. Marcus, *Piety and Society: The Jewish Pietists of Medieval Germany* (Leiden 1981), 150–151n57.

131. Cf. Baer's assertion that "exegetes, such as Rashi and others, read the theological compositions of the Christians" (Baer, "Religious-Social Tendency," 5).

132. Yitzhak Baer, "The Theory of the Natural Equality of Early Man According to Ashkenazi Hasidim," *Zion* 32 (1966), 129–136 (in Hebrew). See Yitzhak Baer, "On the Doctrine of Providence in *Sefer Hasidim*," in *Studies in Mysticism and Religion Presented to Gershom G. Scholem on his Seventieth Birthday*, ed. Ephraim E. Urbach, R. J. Zwi Werblowsky, and Chaim Wirszubski (Jerusalem 1968), 47–62 (in Hebrew).

133. On the pietists' penitential program, see Baer, "Religious-Social Tendency," 18–20; Marcus, *Piety and Society*, 37–52; Joseph Dan, *Ashkenazi Hasidism in the History of Jewish Thought* (Tel Aviv 1990), v. 2, 55–97 (in Hebrew); and Talya Fishman, "The Penitential System of Hasidei Ashkenaz and the Problem of Cultural Boundaries," *Journal of Jewish Thought and Philosophy* 8 (1999), 201–229.

134. Wistinetzki and Freimann, *Sefer Hasidim*, 23, no. 19. Equivalent passages appear in the laws of repentance set down by El'azar of Worms, a disciple of Judah ben Samuel, in his halakhic compendium *Roke'ah* and in numerous anonymous manuscript penitentials. See Ivan G. Marcus, "*Hasidei 'Ashkenaz* Private Penitentials: An Introduction and Descriptive Catalogue of Their Manuscripts and Early Editions," in *Studies in Jewish Mysticism*, ed. Joseph Dan and Frank Talmage (Cambridge, Mass., 1982), 57–83. Marcus has questioned the alleged Franciscan influence, but I do not find his arguments compelling; see Marcus, *Piety and Society*, 150n54.

135. Mortification of the flesh, according to *Sefer Hasidim*, is more than a mechanism for atonement; it is the pietist's way of life. Thus we read of a pietist (*hasid*) who would lie on the ground among fleas in the summer and soak his feet in freezing water in the winter (Wistinetzki and Freimann, *Sefer Hasidim*, 381, no. 1556). German pietism may be said to transform atonement from an occasional or periodic incident in a person's life into a routine.

136. Gershom Scholem, *Major Trends in Jewish Mysticism* (New York 1940), 84–118; Peter Schäfer, "The Ideal of Piety of the Ashkenazi Hasidim and Its Roots in Jewish Tradition," *Jewish History* 4 (1990), 9–23.

137. Haym Soloveitchik, "Three Themes in the *Sefer Hasidim*," *AJS Review* 1 (1976), 317.

138. Wistinetzki and Freimann, *Sefer Hasidim*, 321, no. 1301. See Urbach, *The Tosaphists*, 19; and Marcus, "Jewish-Christian Symbiosis," 449.

139. Yitzhak Baer, "The Historical Background of the 'Raya Mehemna' (A Chapter in the History of the Religious-Social Movements in Castile During the 13th Century)," *Zion* 5 (1940), 3 (in Hebrew) (reprinted in Yitzhak Baer, *Studies in the History of the Jewish People* [Jerusalem 1985], v. 2, 307–308).

Chapter Eight

1. See, for example, Yosef Hayim Yerushalmi, "L'antisémitisme racial est-il apparu au XXe siècle? De la *limpieza de sangre* espagnole au nazisme," *Esprit* 190 (1993), 7–8.

2. For a detailed survey of the events, see Yitzhak Baer, *A History of the Jews in Christian Spain* (Philadelphia 1966), v. 2, 95–110. Baer also published a number of important primary sources; see Fritz Baer, *Die Juden im Christlichen Spanien* (Berlin 1936), v. 2, 232–234.

3. Benzion Netanyahu describes the attacks as originating in Seville and spreading to other communities, and he therefore attributes enormous significance to Martinez's antisemitic rhetoric; see Benzion Netanyahu, *The Origins of the Inquisition in Fifteenth-Century Spain* (New York 1995), 127. In contrast, Dan Pagis represents the view that the attacks broke out spontaneously in various cities, with no linear progression; see Dan Pagis, "Dirges on the Persecutions of 1391 in Spain," *Tarbiz* 37 (1968), 357 (in Hebrew).

4. See Crescas's letter to the Jews of Avignon: Solomon ibn Verga, *Shevet Jehuda*, ed. M. Wiener (Hanover 1855), 129. He also states that about 800 fled to the fortress and survived and "the rest" apostatized; the number of apostates cannot be calculated because we do not know the size of Palma's Jewish population before the tragic events.

5. Ibn Verga, *Shevet Jehuda* (Hanover ed.), 129. A contemporary narrative, by Bartolomé Villalor, reports that several hundred Jews were killed in Valencia; see José Amador de los Rios, *Historia de los Judíos en España y Portugal* (Madrid 1876), v. 2, 598. See also Isidore Loeb, "Le sac des Juiveries de Valence et de Madrid en 1391," *Revue des Études Juives* 13 (1886), 243.

6. Ibn Verga, *Shevet Jehuda* (Hanover ed.), 129. Netanyahu (*Origins of the Inquisition*, 159) claims that more than 300 were slaughtered in Barcelona on August 8 but provides no source. Baer states that about 400 were killed in Barcelona (Baer, *History of the Jews*, v. 2, 105). Solomon ibn Verga describes the persecution of Aragonese Jewry in fairly mild terms, writing that "many" sanctified the name of God in Aragon, Valencia, Majorca, Barcelona, and Lérida, whereas only "some" opted for apostasy; see Solomon ibn Verga, *Shevet Yehuda*, ed. Azriel Shohat (Jerusalem 1947), 71, no. 27. His account is much later than the actual events and cannot be accepted in light of contemporary documents. For Lérida, a contemporary account puts the number of victims at seventy-eight; see Amador de los Rios, *Historia de los Judíos*, v. 2, 380n2.

7. Diego Ortiz de Zuñiga, *Annuales eclesiásticos y seculars de Sevilla* (Madrid 1677), 252, cited by Amador de los Ríos, *Historia de los Judíos*, v. 2, 358.

8. Amador de los Ríos, *Historia de los Judíos*, v. 2, 362.

9. See Israel al-Nakawa, "Maratiyah on Castile and Aragon," in *Menorat ha-Maor*, ed. H. G. Enelow (New York 1930), v. 2, 446–447 (in Hebrew). The text was originally published by Adolphe Neubauer in *Israelitische Letterbode* 6 (1880), 33–37. See also Cecil Roth, "A Hebrew Elegy on the Martyrs of Toledo, 1391," *Jewish Quarterly Review*, n.s., 39 (1948), 123–150. The death in 1391 of Judah ben Asher, great-grandson of Asher ben Yehiel, is also recorded in Abraham Zacut, *Sefer Yuhassin ha-Shalem*, ed. Herschell Filipowski (Frankfurt am Main 1925), 51, 222 (in Hebrew). Another source states that Judah was burned alive in Toledo, together with al-Nakawa, while holding a Torah scroll; see Abraham Gabison, *'Omer ha-shikhehah* (Livorno 1748), fol. 137b–138a, cited by Ram Ben-Shalom, "Kiddush ha-Shem and Jewish Martyrdom in Aragon and Castile in 1391," *Tarbiz* 70 (2001), 234 (in Hebrew).

10. The fact that the names of spiritual leaders who martyred themselves along with their families and disciples are recorded does not necessarily mean that they were the Toledo community's only martyrs.

11. Ibn Verga, *Shevet Jehuda* (Hanover ed.), 129. On the martyrdom of Crescas's son in Barcelona, see Marc Saperstein, "A Sermon on the Akedah from the Generation of the Expulsion and Its Implications for 1391," in *Exile and Diaspora*, ed. Aharon Mirsky, Avraham Grossman, and Yosef Kaplan (Jerusalem 1991), 111–113.

12. Ibn Verga, *Shevet Jehuda* (Hanover ed.), 130. Profiat Duran refers to the martyrdom of the three "shepherds" of Gerona, apparently a reference to rabbis; see Profiat Duran, *Ma'aseh Efod* (Vienna 1865), 194. On Gerona, see Baer, *History of the Jews*, v. 2, 107.

13. Pablo de Santa Maria, formerly Solomon Halevi, the rabbi of Burgos, dissents from the standard version of events and describes the mass apostasy as occurring not in the course of the riots but in their wake, as the result of demoralization. See Michael Glatzer, "Pablo de Santa Maria—Solomon Halevi—and His Attitude to the 1391 Riots," in *Antisemitism Through the Ages*, ed. Shmuel Almog (Jerusalem 1980), 151–152 (in Hebrew).

14. Reuben ben Nissim recorded the 1391 events on the back of the first column of his father's Torah scroll. See Abraham M. Hershman, *Rabbi Isaac ben Sheshet Perfet and His Times* (Jerusalem 1955–1956), 124–125 (in Hebrew); and S. Z. Havlin, "The Torah Scroll That Rabbi Nissim Gerondi Wrote for Himself," *Alei Sefer* 12 (1986), 7–8 (in Hebrew). Abraham ben Solomon of Torrutiel and Joseph ibn Zaddiq are those who put the number at more than 200,000; see Adolph Neubauer, *Medieval Jewish Chronicles* (Oxford 1887), 98, 110. On the unreliability of these figures, see Gerson D. Cohen, "Review of Benzion Netanyahu, *The Marranos of Spain from the Late 14th to the Early 16th Century According to Contemporary Hebrew Sources*," *Jewish Social Studies* 29 (1967), 182.

15. This figure is based on the assumption that families averaged 1.5 children per family; see Kenneth R. Stow, "The Jewish Family in the Rhineland in the High Middle Ages: Form and Function," *American Historical Review* 92 (1987), 1085–1110. Netanyahu assumes a family size of five people per family, positing a population of 30,000, but he puts the number of apostates at approximately 25,000; see Benzion Netanyahu, *The Marranos of Spain from the Late 14th to the Early 16th Century According to Contemporary Hebrew Sources*, 3rd ed. (Ithaca 1999), 240–241; elsewhere he writes that they numbered "no less than 20,000" (Netanyahu, *Origins of the Inquisition*, 149). Even the latter figure is inflated; if the number of souls was 30,000–35,000, "most" would still yield a figure of only 15,000–18,000 apostates.

16. Caspar Escolano, *Década Primera de la Historia de Valencia* (Valencia 1610), pt. 1, bk. 5, cap. 10, col. 958, cited by Netanyahu, *Marranos of Spain*, 241.

17. Heinrich Graetz, *Geschichte der Juden*, 3rd ed. (Leipzig 1890), v. 8, 62.

18. Baer, *Die Juden im Christlichen Spanien*, v. 2, p. 236 for Madrid and p. 232 for Córdoba. For Córdoba, see also Pagis, "Dirges," 367, "Issfu li," lines 38–39.

19. Hayyim Schirmann, "Elegies About the Persecution in Palestine, Africa, Spain, Germany, and France," *Kovetz al Yad* 3 (13) (1939), 67 (in Hebrew). For Burgos, see also Ibn Verga, *Shevet Yehuda* (Jerusalem ed.), 119, no. 47.

20. Schirmann, "Elegies," 67. On the difficulty of deriving historical information from dirges of this sort, see Pagis, "Dirges," 290, and Chapter 3.

21. See the maps provided by Baer at the end of the Hebrew edition of his *History of the Jews in Christian Spain*, 2nd ed. (Tel Aviv 1965).

22. On the voluntary nature of the 1391 conversions, see Norman Roth, *Conversos, Inquisition, and the Expulsion of the Jews from Spain* (Madison 1995), 33–47.

23. See Frank Talmage, "Trauma at Tortosa: The Testimony of Abraham Rimoch," *Mediaeval Studies* 47 (1985), 379–415.

24. See Baer, *History of the Jews*, v. 2, 134–138; and Jefim Schirmann, *The History of Hebrew Poetry in Christian Spain and Southern France*, ed., suppl., and annot. Ezra Fleischer (Jerusalem 1997), 588–593 (in Hebrew).

25. Zacut, *Sefer Yuhassin ha-Shalem*, 225. As noted earlier, this figure can be regarded as an exaggeration, intended to convey the dimensions of this particular mass apostasy.

26. Solomon Alami, *Igeret Mussar*, ed. Abraham M. Haberman (Jerusalem 1946), 39–40.

27. See Jeremy Cohen, *Living Letters of the Law: Ideas of the Jew in Medieval Christianity* (Berkeley 1999), 23–65.

28. Bernhard Blumenkranz, "The Roman Church and the Jews," in *The Dark Ages: Jews in Christian Europe 711–1096*, ed. Cecil Roth (Tel Aviv 1966), 70–79; Shlomo Simonsohn, *The Apostolic See and the Jews: History* (Toronto 1991), v. 7, 133–146.

29. See Baer, *History of the Jews*, v. 2, 166–169; and Netanyahu, *Origins of the Inquisition*, 191–202.

30. Netanyahu, *Marranos of Spain*, 95–96.

31. Ha-Lorki himself apostatized at a later date.

32. For the Hebrew text of ha-Lorki's letter, see L. Landau, *Das Apologetsche Schreiben des Josua Lorki* (Antwerp 1906). See also Baer, *History of the Jews*, v. 2, 143–150; H. H. Ben-Sasson, "Assimilation in Jewish History," in *Continuity and Variety*, ed. Joseph Hacker (Jerusalem 1984), 63 (in Hebrew); Michael Glatzer, "Between Joshua ha-Lorki and Solomon Halevi: Towards an Examination of the Causes of Apostasy Among Spanish Jewry in the Fourteenth Century," *Pe'amim* 54 (1993), 103–116 (in Hebrew); and Benjamin Gampel, "A Letter to a Wayward Teacher: The Transformations of Sephardic Culture in Christian Iberia," in *Cultures of the Jews: A New History*, ed. David Biale (New York 2002), 389–426.

33. Joseph Yahalom, "Poetry as an Expression of Spiritual Reality in the Late Sephardi Piyyut," in *Exile and Diaspora*, ed. Aharon Mirsky, Avraham Grossman, and Yosef Kaplan (Jerusalem 1991), 340 (in Hebrew).

34. See also Jacob Katz's assertion that Jews everywhere were willing to submit to martyrdom rather than convert to Christianity "so long as attachment to tradition was not enfeebled through the undermining influence of rationalism or other spiritual or social factors." He thus concludes that "the Ashkenazi Middle Ages outshine all other periods of Jewish history as an epoch of heroic steadfastness"; see Jacob Katz, *Exclusiveness and Tolerance* (Oxford 1961), 85.

35. Nahem Ilan, *"Pursuing the Truth" and "A Way for the Public": Studies in the Teaching of Rabbi Israel Israeli of Toledo*, Ph.D. dissertation (Hebrew University of Jerusalem 1999) (in Hebrew). See also Baer, *History of the Jews*, v. 1, 237.

36. See Raphael Jospe, "Ramban (Nahmanides) and Arabic," *Tarbiz* 57 (1988), 67–93 (in Hebrew). Ibn Adret may have wanted to protect the Jews of Rome from the potentially subversive impact of Maimonidean thought, particularly in the wake of the two explosive affairs that had recently rocked Roman Jewry: Abraham Abulafia's messianic activism in 1280 and the Solomon Petit affair five to ten years later. Indeed, there are grounds for supposing that at least some of the Jews of Barcelona did know Arabic: (1) A reply to the Arabic anti-Jewish polemic of Ibn Hazm is attributed to Ibn Adret himself; and (2) a corpus of documents from the Crown of Aragon from this period includes documents about translation from Arabic in Barcelona by Jews; see Jean Regné, *History of the Jews in Aragon: Regesta and Documents 1213–1327*, ed. Yom Tov Assis (Jerusalem 1978), passim.

37. *Encyclopedia of Islam*, 2nd ed., ed. Bernard Lewis, Victor Louis Ménage, Charles Pellat, and Joseph Schacht (Leiden 1971), v. 3, 913, s.v. Ibn Rushd. This is the upshot of the famous parable of the three precious stones, narrated in Boccaccio's *Decameron*.

38. Baer, *History of the Jews*, v. 2, 137–138, 163–164, 253–259.

39. *Kuzari*, pt. 1, no. 1. This stance undercuts the belief in messianic redemption, which would fit ha-Lorki's "history" explanation.

40. Alami, *Igeret Mussar*, 41–42. This interpretation of the downfall of Sephardic Jewry becomes a common theme in post-Expulsion reflections on the fate of Spanish Jewry. Joseph

Yaʿavetz, a Spaniard who settled in Italy after the Expulsion, expatiates at length on the destructive impact of philosophy on the Jews of Spain. See the introduction to Joseph Yaʿavetz, *Or ha-Hayyim* (Ferrara 1554), and also ch. 3, fol. 6v, cited in H. H. Ben-Sasson, "The Generation of the Spanish Exiles on Its Fate," *Zion* 26 (1961), 48 (in Hebrew). See also Isaac E. Barzilay, *Between Reason and Faith: Anti-Rationalism in Italian Jewish Thought 1250–1650* (Leiden 1967), 133–149; and Gedalia Nigal, "The Opinions of R. Joseph Yawetz on Philosophy and Philosophers, Torah, and Commandments," *Eshel Beer-Sheva* 1 (1976), 258–287 (in Hebrew).

41. Shemtov ibn Shemtov, *Sefer ha-Emunot* (Ferrara 1556), introduction, esp. fol. 4a–b. See also Baer, *History of the Jews*, v. 2, 234–239.

42. H. Z. Hirschberg, *History of the Jews in North Africa* (Leiden 1974), v. 1, 123–139.

43. Abraham Halkin and David Hartman, *Crisis and Leadership: Epistles of Maimonides* (Philadelphia 1985), 31–32, 79–80. See also David Hartman, "Maimonides' Epistle on Martyrdom," *Jerusalem Studies in Jewish Thought* 2 (1982–1983), 362–403 (in Hebrew); and Haym Soloveitchik, "Maimonides' *Iggeret Ha-Shemad*: Law and Rhetoric," in *Joseph Lookstein Memorial Volume*, ed. Leo Landman (New York 1980), 281–319.

44. *Encyclopedia of Islam*, v. 10, 134–136, s.v. *takiyya*; Bernard Lewis, *The Jews of Islam* (Princeton 1984), 82–84; Mark R. Cohen, *Between Crescent and Cross: The Jews in the Middle Ages* (Princeton 1994), 176; Avraham Grossman, "Martyrdom in the Eleventh and Twelfth Centuries: Between Ashkenaz and the Muslim World," *Peʿamim* 75 (1998), 29–30 (in Hebrew). Haym Soloveitchik distinguishes between the Jews of Islam and the Jews of Spain, for the Spanish Jews acted on the notion of *takiyya* but nonetheless berated themselves thereafter; see Haym Soloveitchik, "Ben Hevel ʿArav le-Edom," in *Sanctity of Life and Martyrdom*, ed. Isaiah M. Gafni and Aviezer Ravitzky (Jerusalem 1992), 149–152 (in Hebrew).

45. Ashkenazic Jewry knew nothing of *takiyya* and thus could not have been influenced by it. However, this is largely irrelevant because the number of apostates in 1096 is believed to have been much greater than the Hebrew narratives would lead one to believe; furthermore, in 1096 most of those killed did not enjoy the element of choice (see Chapter 3).

46. Isaiah Sonne, "On Baer and His Philosophy of Jewish History," *Jewish Social Studies* 9 (1947), 61–80.

47. Sonne, "On Baer," 70.

48. Sonne situates Baer's disdain for intellectualism and the elite and his preference for popular (*völkisch*) religion in the context of the intellectual climate of Weimar Germany (Sonne, "On Baer," 72). He sees Baer's enchantment with mysticism as indebted to the thought of Gutmann, Buber, Rosenzweig, and Scholem (p. 68).

49. Sonne also doubts the assumption that martyrdom was the nearly universal Ashkenazic response to the persecution of the First Crusade, and he proposes that greater attention be devoted to the dimensions of apostasy in Ashkenaz and of martyrdom in Spain. Moreover, he maintains, as I have argued, that the 1096 assailants were bent on murdering the Jews, not converting them (Sonne, "On Baer," 78–79).

50. Sonne, "On Baer," 72.

51. Haym Soloveitchik portrays the laxity of Spanish Jewry in terms of the classic combination of Averroism and hedonism; see Haym Soloveitchik, *Pawnbroking: A Study in the Inter-Relationship Between Halakhah, Economic Activity, and Communal Self-Image* (Jerusalem 1985), 118 (in Hebrew). Elsewhere, however, Soloveitchik comments, "Whether philosophy played the major corrosive role in Spain that Y. Baer attributed to it is an open question." See Haym Soloveitchik, "Religious Law and Change: The Medieval Ashkenazic Example," *AJS Review* 12

(1987), 213n12. Similarly, Carmi Horowitz, having assessed the social critique of Hispano-Jewish society in the sermons of Joshua ibn Shu'eib of fourteenth-century Tudela, concludes, "What is not clear in ibn Shu'eib is whether or not philosophic culture is also a source for undermining the religious observance of this [courtier] class." See Carmi Horowitz, *The Jewish Sermon in 14th-Century Spain: The Derashot of R. Joshua ibn Shu'eib* (Cambridge, Mass., 1989), 47n48.

52. Ben-Sasson, "Generation of the Spanish Exiles," 59–61; Roth, *Conversos*, 61–65. Gerson D. Cohen traces the topos of philosophy bashing to *Sefer Yosifon* and Ibn Daud's *Sefer ha-Qabbalah*; see Cohen, "Review," 182.

53. For Jacob ben Makhir, see Solomon ibn Adret, *Responsa*, ed. H. Z. Dimitrovski (Jerusalem 1990), v. 2, ch. 58, 506–513; for Yedaiah ha-Penini, see Solomon ibn Adret, *Responsa*, pt. 1, no. 415, fol. 53r–60r. See also Daniel J. Lasker, "Averroistic Trends in Jewish-Christian Polemics in the Late Middle Ages," *Speculum* 55 (1980), 294–504.

54. Solomon ibn Adret's persecution of Levi ben Hayyim is a case in point; see Abraham S. Halkin, "Why was Levi b. Hayyim Hounded?" *Proceedings of the American Academy of Jewish Research* 34 (1966), 65–76.

55. Shemtov ibn Shemtov, *Sefer ha-Emunot*, introduction. See also Baer, *History of the Jews*, v. 1, 241, and v. 2, 234–239.

56. Ya'aqov ben Sheshet, *Sefer Meshiv Devarim Nekhohim*, ed. Georges Vajda (Jerusalem 1968), 67–70.

57. Meir ibn Gabbai, *Mar'ot Elohim ['Avodat ha-Qodesh]* (Venice 1567), pt. 3, ch. 15–24. See also Baer, *History of the Jews*, v. 2, 232–243; Netanyahu, *Marranos of Spain*, 85–110; Isadore Twersky, "Talmudists, Philosophers, Kabbalists: The Quest for Spirituality in the Sixteenth Century," in *Jewish Thought in the Sixteenth Century*, ed. Bernard D. Cooperman (Cambridge, Mass., 1983), 442; and Jacob Elbaum, *Openness and Insularity: Late Sixteenth Century Jewish Literature in Poland and Ashkenaz* (Jerusalem 1980), 154–222 (in Hebrew).

58. On Abner, see Baer, *History of the Jews*, v. 1, 327–354, esp. 343; and Yitzhak Baer, "The Qabbalistic Doctrine in the Christological Teaching of Abner of Burgos," *Tarbiz* 27 (1958), 278–289 (in Hebrew). See also Sonne, "On Baer," 79–80; and Glatzer, "Between Joshua ha-Lorki and Solomon Halevi," 114–115.

59. Ben-Sasson, "Generation of the Spanish Exiles," 60–63. Ben-Sasson also suggests that, although the mass apostasies of 1391 and 1412–1414 were not the result of the kind of cynicism characteristic of Averroism, the experience of forced conversion may have encouraged such an attitude toward religion (p. 63).

60. See E. Gutwirth, "Conversions to Christianity Amongst Fifteenth-Century Jews: An Alternative Explanation," in *Shlomo Simonsohn Jubilee Volume* (Tel Aviv 1993), 102.

61. Ben-Sasson, "Generation of the Spanish Exiles," 61.

62. Ben-Sasson, "Generation of the Spanish Exiles," 28–34.

63. Isadore Twersky, "Aspects of the Social and Cultural History of Provençal Jewry," in *Jewish Life Through the Ages*, ed. H. H. Ben-Sasson and S. Ettinger (New York 1971), 189. Twersky notes, "On the whole, Prof. Baer's thesis needs modification" (p. 189n15).

64. Menahem ben Zerah, *Zedah la-Derekh* (Warsaw 1880), fol. 63a–b. Note that *Zedah la-Derekh* is dedicated to a courtier, Don Samuel Abravanel. The critique of astrology is also the subject of the last two paragraphs of the introduction to *Zedah la-Derekh*. Cf. Haim Beinart, "The Image of the Jewish Courtier Class in Christian Spain," in *Elites and Leading Groups* (Jerusalem 1966), 70 (in Hebrew). Ben Zerah's critique is an almost verbatim copy of Judah ben Asher's words in *Zikhron Yehudah*, no. 91, fol. 44b–45a. On the popularity of astrology, see also

Dov Schwartz, "The Spiritual-Religious Decline of the Spanish Jewish Community at the End of the Fourteenth Century," *Pe'amim* 46–47 (1991), 101 (in Hebrew); and Dov Schwartz, *The Philosophy of a Fourteenth-Century Jewish Neoplatonic Circle* (Jerusalem 1996), 15–28 (in Hebrew).

65. See Maimonides' letter on astrology: Alexander Marx, "The Correspondence Between the Rabbis of Southern France and Maimonides About Astrology," *Hebrew Union College Annual* 3 (1926), 350. See also Bezalel Safran, "Bahya ibn Paquda's Attitude Toward the Courtier Class," in *Studies in Medieval Jewish History and Literature*, ed. Isadore Twersky (Cambridge, Mass., 1979), 162–165.

66. Jefim Schirmann, *Hebrew Poetry in Spain and Provence* (Jerusalem and Tel Aviv 1956), v. 2, pt. 2, 525–528 (in Hebrew). Of the lines quoted, the first three are the poem's first four lines, the second two are lines 17 and 18, and the last two are its closing couplet.

67. Isaac Polgar, *Ezer ha-Dat* [A Defense of Judaism], ed. Jacob S. Levinger (Tel Aviv 1984), pt. 3, 105–153, esp. 140–153. See Baer, *History of the Jews*, v. 1, 332–333; Yitzhak Baer, "Minhat Qena'ot by Abner of Burgos and Its Impact on Hasdai Crescas," *Tarbiz* 11 (1940), 190–206 (in Hebrew); Julius Guttmann, *The Philosophy of Judaism*, trans. David W. Silverman (Northvale 1988), 203–207; Colette Sirat, *A History of Jewish Philosophy in the Middle Ages* (Cambridge 1985), 308–322; Shlomo Pines, "Scholasticism After Thomas Aquinas and the Teachings of Hasdai Crescas and His Predecessors," *Proceedings of the Israel Academy of Sciences and Humanities* 1 (1963–1967), 6–10; and Charles H. Manekin, "Freedom Within Reason? Gersonides on Human Choice," in *Freedom and Moral Responsibility: General and Jewish Perspectives*, ed. Charles H. Manekin and Menachem M. Kellner (College Park 1997), 165–204. Polgar also sees a threat to Judaism from those who deny life after death and therefore also reward and punishment, but such materialists would not likely prefer Christianity to Judaism. See also the critical remarks by Abraham Rimoch in Talmage, "Trauma at Tortosa," 405–407.

68. Uriel Simon, "Interpreting the Interpreters: Supercommentaries on Ibn Ezra's Commentaries," in *Rabbi Abraham ibn Ezra: Studies in the Writings of a Twelfth-Century Jewish Polymath*, ed. Isadore Twersky and Jay M. Harris (Cambridge, Mass., 1993), 111–121; Eliezer Gutwirth, "Fourteenth Century Supercommentaries on Abraham ibn Ezra," in *Abraham ibn Ezra y Su Tiempo*, ed. Fernando Díaz Esteban (Madrid 1990), 147–154. On Ibn Wakkar, see Georges Vajda, *Recherches sur la philosophie et la Kabbale* (Paris 1962), 249–253.

69. Matti Huss, *Don Vidal Benveniste's* Melitsat Efer ve-Dinah: *Studies and Critical Edition* (Jerusalem 2003) (in Hebrew).

70. Huss, *Benveniste's* Melitsat Efer ve-Dinah, 187–200.

71. Huss, *Benveniste's* Melitsat Efer ve-Dinah, 101–109. See also Matti Huss, "Erotic Tale or Moral Allegory? *Melizat Efer ve-Dina* by Don Vidal Benvenist," *Jerusalem Studies in Hebrew Literature* 14 (1993), 115–153 (in Hebrew). Ezra Fleischer rejects Huss's interpretation, arguing that Benveniste presented the tale as an allegory to defuse criticism of its bawdy nature; see Schirmann, *History of Hebrew Poetry*, 613n42.

72. Soloveitchik, "Religious Law and Change," 221.

73. Yom Tov Assis, "Sexual Behavior in Mediaeval Hispano-Jewish Society," in *Jewish History: Essays in Honour of Chimen Abramsky*, ed. Ada Rapoport-Albeck and Steven T. Zipperstein (London 1988), 27. See also Ephraim Kanarfogel, "Rabbinic Attitudes Toward Nonobservance in the Medieval Period," in *Jewish Tradition and the Nontraditional Jew*, ed. Jacob J. Schacter (Northvale 1992), 23.

74. Assis, "Sexual Behavior," 46, 48. Presumably Assis meant "prevalent" rather than "frequent."

75. Todros ben Judah Halevi, *Gan ha-Meshalim veha-Hidot*, ed. David Yellin (Jerusalem 1934), v. 2, pt. 1, 130; for more erotic poetry, see pp. 124–132. See also Assis, "Sexual Behavior," 28. For Todros Halevi as a historical source, see Yitzhak Baer, "Todros b. Judah Halevi and His Age," *Zion* 2 (1937), 19–55 (in Hebrew); and Baer, *History of the Jews*, v. 1, 237–239.

76. Huss, *Benveniste's* Melitsat Efer ve-Dinah, 151, lines 9–10.

77. Joseph Weiss, "Courtly Culture and Courtly Poetry," in *World Congress of Jewish Studies* (Jerusalem 1952), 403 (in Hebrew); Jefim Schirmann, "The Ephebe in Medieval Hebrew Poetry," *Sefarad* 15 (1955), 55–68; Norman Roth, "Deal Gently with the Young Man: Love of Boys in Medieval Hebrew Poetry of Spain," *Speculum* 57 (1982), 20–51; Ross Brann, *The Compunctious Poet: Cultural Ambiguity and Hebrew Poetry in Muslim Spain* (Baltimore 1991); Raymond P. Scheindlin, *Wine, Women, and Death: Medieval Hebrew Poems on the Good Life* (Philadelphia 1986), 77–78; and cf. Raymond P. Scheindlin, "Merchants and Intellectuals, Rabbis and Poets: Judeo-Arabic Culture in the Golden Age of Islam," in *Cultures of the Jews: A New History*, ed. David Biale (New York 2002), 367.

78. Baer, *History of the Jews*, v. 1, 238–239. See also the other responsa about concubinage discussed by Kanarfogel, "Rabbinic Attitudes," 18–22.

79. Horowitz, *Jewish Sermon*, 46–47.

80. Assis, "Sexual Behavior," 42–44. See also David Nirenberg, "Conversion, Sex, and Segregation: Jews and Christians in Medieval Spain," *American Historical Review* 107 (2002), 1065–1093.

81. Assis, "Sexual Behavior," 36–40; Kanarfogel, "Rabbinic Attitudes," 17–22. For a rabbinic discussion of concubinage in thirteenth-century Spain, see Moses ben Nahman, *Responsa*, ed. Charles B. Chevel (Jerusalem 1975), 160, no. 105. For the fourteenth century, see Isaac ben Sheshet Perfet, *Responsa*, nos. 217, 351, 395. Abraham Zacut linked Spanish concubinage to the tribulations meted out to them by the Christians (Zacut, *Sefer Yuhassin ha-Shalem*, pt. 5, fol. 225a). See also Louis M. Epstein, "The Institution of Concubinage Among the Jews," *Proceedings of the American Academy of Jewish Religion* 6 (1935), 182–188; and Hershman, *Rabbi Isaac ben Sheshet Perfet*, 92–93.

82. *Sefer Mitzvot Gadol*, negative precept 112.

83. Mordechai Akiva Friedman, *Jewish Polygyny in the Middle Ages* (Jerusalem 1986), 291–339 (in Hebrew).

84. Menahem ben Zerah, *Zedah la-Derekh*, fol. 68d. See also Solomon ibn Adret, *Responsa*, pt. 5, no. 242. For more on the licit and illicit sexual mores of the Jews in Christian Spain, see Assis, "Sexual Behavior," 25–59.

85. Menahem ben Zerah, *Zedah la-Derekh*, fol. 4a.

86. Similarly, Haim Beinart's portrait of courtier culture in Christian Spain does not cite Averroism as a significant contributing force in the courtiers' ultimate downfall; see Beinart, "Image of the Jewish Courtier Class," 55–71.

87. Kanarfogel, "Rabbinic Attitudes," 25–26.

88. Proverbs 1:20–22. See Ibn Shu'eib, *Derashot 'al ha-Torah* (Cracow 1573), fol. 38a, cited in Horowitz, *Jewish Sermon*, 49, 52. The Zohar also equates the ignorant with deficient observance; see Zohar, pt. 2, fol. 93a; and Isaiah Tishby, *Mishnat ha-Zohar* (Jerusalem 1961), v. 2, 680–702; these sources are cited in Horowitz, *Jewish Sermon*, 52n79.

89. *Berakhot* 28b; *Bava Qama* 82a; *Sanhedrin* 3a; and Rashi on *Berakhot* 28b, s.v. *mi-yoshevei qeranot*.

90. *Derashot* 53b; Horowitz, *Jewish Sermon*, 53.

91. Judah ben Asher, *Zikhron Yehudah*, no. 91, fol. 44b. Similarly, his brother, Jacob, counseled his son to avoid scoffers and corner sitters as well as traveling merchants; see Solomon Schechter, "The Rebuke of Rabbi Jacob b. Asher to His Sons," *Bet Talmud* 4 (1885), 378–379 (in Hebrew).

92. Israel Abrahams, *Hebrew Ethical Wills* (Philadelphia 1926), 176.

93. Rabbis are perhaps the exception, for their extreme fidelity, but even this is not absolutely certain.

94. Judah ben Asher, *Zikhron Yehudah*, no. 91, fol. 44a; Menahem ben Zerah, *Zedah la-Derekh*, fol. 67b. For an earlier expression of concern with swearing, see Jonah Gerondi, *Sha'arei Teshuvah* (Fano 1505), 4.

95. Judah ben Asher, *Zikhron Yehudah*, no. 91, fol. 44b; Menahem ben Zerah, *Zedah la-Derekh*, fol. 11a, 21d.

96. Menahem ben Zerah, *Zedah la-Derekh*, fol. 137d. Similarly, Profiat Duran attributes the catastrophe of 1391 to the mechanical nature of most people's performance of the commandments rather than to the pernicious impact of philosophy; see Duran, *Ma'aseh Efod*, 192; and Baer, *History of the Jews*, v. 2, 156–157. Note that Duran himself submitted to baptism in 1391; see Richard Emery, "New Light on Profayt Duran 'The Efodi,'" *Jewish Quarterly Review* 58 (1967–1968), 331–333. See also Duran, *Ma'aseh Efod*, 197.

97. Judah ben Asher, *Zikhron Yehudah*, no. 91, fol. 43a–45b.

98. Alami, *Igeret Mussar*, 48–49. The sheer range of Alami's attack militates against focusing on Averroism as the prime cause of the mass apostasy.

99. *Avot* 4:21. See Horowitz, *Jewish Sermon*, 45

100. Barukh Mevorach, "Review of 'Azriel Shohat, *'Im Hilufei Tequfot*,'" *Kiryat Sefer* 37 (1962), 153–154 (in Hebrew). See also Jacob Katz, "On *Halakha* and *Derush* as Historical Sources," *Tarbiz* 30 (1960), 68 (in Hebrew). Jewish sermons are also of limited utility for the study of history for other reasons; see Marc Saperstein, *Jewish Preaching 1200–1800: An Anthology* (New Haven 1989), 80–85.

101. Gerson D. Cohen, *Messianic Postures of Ashkenazim and Sephardim* (New York 1967) (*Leo Baeck Memorial Lecture*, no. 9), 37.

102. Elisheva Carlebach, *Between History and Hope: Jewish Messianism in Ashkenaz and Sepharad* (New York 1998) (Annual Lecture of the Victor J. Selmanowitz Chair of Jewish History, no. 3), 2.

103. Israel Jacob Yuval, "The Vengeance and the Curse, the Blood and the Libel: From Tales of Heroes to Blood Libels," *Zion* 58 (1993), 41, 63–68 (in Hebrew); Israel Jacob Yuval, *"Two Nations in Your Womb": Perceptions of Jews and Christians* (Tel Aviv 2000), 109–124 (in Hebrew). (English edition: *"Two Nations in Your Womb": Perceptions of Jews and Christians in Late Antiquity and the Middle Ages*, trans. Barbara Harshav and Jonathan Chipman [Berkeley 2006], ch. 3, sec. 1.)

104. Yuval, "Vengeance and the Curse," 45–50; Yuval, *Two Nations in Your Womb* (Hebrew ed.), 124–131 (English ed., ch. 3, sec. 2).

105. Ezra Fleischer, "Christian-Jewish Relations in the Middle Ages Distorted," *Zion* 59 (1994), 295–301 (in Hebrew); Mordechai Breuer, "The Historian's Imagination and Historical Truth," *Zion* 59 (1994), 319 (in Hebrew); David Berger, *From Crusades to Blood Libels to Expulsions: Some New Approaches to Medieval Antisemitism* (New York 1997) (Annual Lecture of the Victor J. Selmanowitz Chair of Jewish History, no. 2), 21.

106. Fleischer, "Christian-Jewish Relations," 270–276, 290–292; Avraham Grossman,

"'Redemption by Conversion' in the Teachings of Early Ashkenazi Sages," *Zion* 59 (1994), 325–342 (in Hebrew).

107. Ben-Shalom, "Kiddush ha-Shem," 227–282.

108. Ben-Shalom, "Kiddush ha-Shem," 231–232. See Haim Beinart, "The Great Conversion and the Converso Problem," in *The Sephardi Legacy*, ed. Haim Beinart (Jerusalem 1992), v. 1, 347. "Survival" encompasses those who hid or fled as well as those who were somehow overlooked.

109. See Pagis, "Dirges," 364–365, 368, line 74. On the presence of the martyrological ethos in Sephardic tradition, see also Saperstein, "Sermon on the Akedah," 103–124, esp. 117, lines 30–34; and Joseph Hacker, "'If We Have Forgotten the Name of Our God' (Ps. 44:21): Interpretation in Light of the Realities in Medieval Spain," *Zion* 57 (1992), 253–264 (in Hebrew). Both of these studies refer to texts composed after the mass apostasy of 1391 but that nevertheless extol martyrdom as a normative value, to which Jews everywhere supposedly adhere.

110. Ben-Shalom, "Kiddush ha-Shem," 259–262. On the martyrological ethos among the Jews of Islam, see the words of Joseph ibn Aqnin in Abraham S. Halkin, "On the History of the Persecution in the Time of the Almohades," in *The Joshua Starr Memorial Volume* (New York 1953), 104 (in Hebrew). Whether a martyrological ethos was particular to the Jews of Franco-Germany echoes the debate, mentioned earlier, between Yuval on the one hand and Fleischer and Grossman on the other over the Ashkenazic and Sephardic conceptions of redemption.

111. Ben-Shalom, "Kiddush ha-Shem," 110.

112. See Chapter 4. This dynamic would probably have had a much weaker effect had the Jews of Ashkenaz inclined toward apostasy, because that was certainly considered a less noble option, even if technically it was the correct halakhic one.

113. Similarly, Jacob Katz maintains that the early modern period was one of less scrupulous religious observance than the Middle Ages in part because the Jewish community was much smaller in the Middle Ages than later. See Jacob Katz, *The "Shabbes Goy": A Study in Halakhic Flexibility*, trans. Yoel Lerner (Philadelphia 1989), 237. This generalization merits further investigation.

114. The difficulty of integrating the New Christians because of their numbers was obviously not limited to the courtier class, but the courtiers played a more influential role than mere numbers would justify on account of their of political, economic, and social power.

115. David Nirenberg, *Communities of Violence: Persecution of Minorities in the Middle Ages* (Princeton 1996), 43–68.

116. Salo W. Baron, *A Social and Religious History of the Jews*, 2nd ed. (New York 1967), v. 11, 230.

117. H. H. Ben-Sasson, *A History of the Jewish People* (Cambridge, Mass., 1976), 568–570; Baer, *History of the Jews*, v. 1, 364–367.

118. Baer, *History of the Jews*, v. 2, 102; Robert Chazan, *In the Year 1096: The First Crusade and the Jews* (Philadelphia 1996), 166.

119. Baer, *History of the Jews*, v. 2, 104.

120. Philippe Wolff, "The 1391 Pogrom in Spain: Social Crisis or Not?" *Past and Present* 50 (1971), 12–16; Angus MacKay, "Popular Movements and Pogroms in Fifteenth-Century Castile," *Past and Present* 55 (1972), 39. But cf. Maurice Kriegel, *Les Juifs à la fin du Moyen Age dans l'Europe méditerranéenne* (Paris 1979), 182–196; and Anna Foa, *The Jews of Europe After the Black Death*, trans. Andrea Grover (Berkeley 2000), 85–86.

Index